# Office 365 Essentials

Get up and running with the fundamentals of Office 365

**Nuno Árias Silva**

**BIRMINGHAM - MUMBAI**

# Office 365 Essentials



**Commissioning Editor:** Gebin George
**Acquisition Editor:** Prateek Bharadwaj, Rahul Nair
**Content Development Editor:** Devika Battike
**Technical Editor:** Swathy Mohan
**Copy Editor:** Safis Editing, Dipti Mankame
**Project Coordinator:** Judie Jose
**Proofreader:** Safis Editing
**Indexer:** Rekha Nair
**Graphics:** Tom Scaria
**Production Coordinator:** Nilesh Mohite

First published: May 2018

Production reference: 1230518

Published by Packt Publishing Ltd.
Livery Place
35 Livery Street
Birmingham
B3 2PB, UK.

ISBN 978-1-78862-207-3

www.packtpub.com

# Contributors

## About the author

With a master's degree in IT and more than 20 years of working experience, **Nuno Árias Silva** is a specialist in Office 365, focusing on Exchange, Virtualization, and System Center. Nuno has over 30 certifications—MCT, MCSE, MCITP, MCSA, MCTS, and many more. He has worked in the aerospace, transportation, financial services, government, and health care industries. Currently, he is a manager at Gfi Portugal, and he has assisted Microsoft with various workshops. He also contributes to blogs. He has been a speaker at Microsoft events such as Microsoft Ignite, SPS Events, and TUGA IT.

*There are a number of people who have made this project possible. I would like to thank Devika Battike for her patience and valuable guidance throughout the project, and Prateek Bharadwaj, the acquisition editor. Many thanks to André Vala and Tiago Costa, my colleagues and partners; Microsoft, who helped this book happen; and GFi. Finally, my family, who gave me strength, support, and time to write this book.*

# About the reviewers

**Mark Dunkerley** is a motivated and passionate technology leader residing in Orlando, Florida. He holds a bachelor's degree of science in business administration and a master's in business administration. He has worked in the technology field for over 15 years, and he has experience in multiple technical areas. He has earned certifications from AirWatch, Microsoft, CompTIA, VMware, AXELOS, Cisco, and EMC.
Mark is a speaker at multiple conferences, including Microsoft and VMware events. He has authored *Learning AirWatch*, is an active blogger, and has published multiple case studies.

**Tiago Costa** is an IT consultant for Microsoft technologies. For the past 15 years, he has been architecting and developing solutions for clients using Azure, Office 365, SharePoint, .Net, and SQL Server. He has a lot of real-world experience, and he regularly teaches Azure, Office 365, SharePoint, .Net, and SQL Server. He has several Microsoft Certifications, and he is also a Microsoft Certified Trainer—MCT. In 2013, he was nominated as an MCT Regional Lead by Microsoft Corporation. In 2016, he was awarded with the Microsoft MVP Award in Office Server and Services.

> *It was a great pleasure to review this book because it's a great resource for professionals who need to implement and manage Microsoft Office 365 and are not yet familiar with the service.*

**André Vala** is a Microsoft MVP for Office Servers and Services and a SharePoint solutions architect. He has been working with SharePoint for the past 12 years on projects that range from corporate intranets and extranets to large internet portals. He has been an invited speaker at several Microsoft events, such as TechDays and DevDays in Lisbon, Road To SharePoint 2010, and community and user group events such as the Portuguese SharePoint User Group and the Portuguese Office 365 User Group meeting.

> *Office 365 is large and complex topic, given the huge amount of services and features it has. Nuno was able to break it down into set of easy-to-read introductory chapters that span the most important workloads and focus on the essential pieces of planning, deploying, adopting, and monitoring Office 365. I believe this will be an invaluable resource, covering the first steps with a challenging set of technologies.*

# Packt is searching for authors like you

If you're interested in becoming an author for Packt, please visit `authors.packtpub.com` and apply today. We have worked with thousands of developers and tech professionals, just like you, to help them share their insight with the global tech community. You can make a general application, apply for a specific hot topic that we are recruiting an author for, or submit your own idea.

# Table of Contents

# Preface

Microsoft Office 365 is a suite of productivity tools and services that can be used both online as well as through desktop versions. Some of the productivity programs that are included within Microsoft Office 365 are Word, Excel, PowerPoint, Outlook, SharePoint, and OneNote, but there are many others.

It can either be called Microsoft Office 365, using Microsoft's brand, or, as in this book, just Office 365. There are other books that cover the use of Office 365, but this book covers how to use Office 365 and start using new technologies. This integration is often necessary for organizations that already have, or will need to have, integration with some level of on-premises infrastructure for administration or other purposes.

Most organizations leverage Microsoft Active Directory (AD) as their primary identity system to manage users, groups (distribution or security), and group policies. AD is the identity management solution that is most widely used in enterprises, and the intention is not for it to be replaced by Office 365. Most organizations that are migrating to Office 365 have their on-premises email systems, such as Exchange, and leverage on-premises technologies such as AD for security and authentication purposes.

With Office 365, your organization has the option to utilize some or all of its programs, or simply use and adapt parts of mailboxes to Office 365 or other programs such as SharePoint and OneDrive. These are all examples of conclusions that organizations see using studies to go to cloud, and this book addresses these kinds of everyday operations with planning, distribution, setup, support, and management of Office 365 programs.

By the end of this book, you will have hands-on experience working with Office 365 and its collaboration tools and services.

Office 365 being a dynamic technology, the reference links included in the chapter are subject to timely updates.

# Who this book is for

This book is designed for readers who have a fundamental understanding of Office 365 services, but might not have technical expertise in the administration and configuration of the on-premises technologies equivalent to those services such as Exchange, SharePoint, Office, and Skype for Business. Office 365 has various technologies, and this book assumes that the audience for each of these technologies has the relevant expertise to administer and change some configurations on those workloads. This book includes information that can serve multiple audiences and roles, such as information on how to implement the fundamental workloads in areas such as migration plan, identity plan, network assessments, and security. The audience must have some operational expertise for managing AD, running network assessments, and making configuration changes such as Domain Name System (DNS), proxies, and firewalls. Is not required but is advised in all implementations to have a separate environment to test in lab and to implement the topics covered in this book.

# What this book covers

`Chapter 1`, *Introduction to Office 365*, describes what Office 365 is, gives an introduction to Microsoft cloud productivity  services, what they are where they reside, and what the vision for the future is.

`Chapter 2`, *Fundamentals of Office 365*, explains the fundamentals or deploying technologies in Office 365.

`Chapter 3`, *Office 365 Basic Workloads*, explains the basic workloads of Office 365.

`Chapter 4`, *Identities and Authentication*, explains basic identities and how to integrate Office 365 into your organization.

`Chapter 5`, *Configuring Office 365*, explains how to configure Office 365 and its services.

`Chapter 6`, *Managing Office 365*, understand how to manage Office 365 and who do we manage.

`Chapter 7`, *Exchange Online*, provides an introduction to Exchange Online, planning, migrating, and administering Exchange Online.

`Chapter 8`, *SharePoint Online*, describes what SharePoint Online is and how to implement it.

`Chapter 9`, *Skype for Business*, describes what Skype for Business is and how to implement it.

`Chapter 10`, *Working with Microsoft Teams*, introduces a new way to work as a team, understand what is the future and so on.

`Chapter 11`, *Delve*, describes what Delve is and how to use it to be more productive.

`Chapter 12`, *Managing Workloads*, describes how to manage workloads, from basic to complex tasks.

`Chapter 13`, *Adopting Office 365*, describes how to adopt Office 365.

`Chapter 14`, *Monitoring and Support*, describes how to monitor and how to support Office 365.

# To get the most out of this book

The software required to this book is Office 365 subscription, it could be a trial that are described in this book how to be created and also could be necessary additional software depending on the workloads and scenarios that you need to implement. Those additional necessary are described in each section of the chapter of the book.

## Download the color images

We also provide a PDF file that has color images of the screenshots/diagrams used in this book. You can download it from `https://www.packtpub.com/sites/default/files/downloads/Office365Essentials_ColorImages.pdf`.

## Conventions used

There are a number of text conventions used throughout this book.

`CodeInText`: Indicates code words in text, database table names, folder names, filenames, file extensions, pathnames, dummy URLs, user input, and Twitter handles. Here is an example: "Fill in your domain name, for example, `yourdomainname.com`, and click on the **Next** button."

A block of code is set as follows:

```
Start-ADSyncSyncCycle -PolicyType Delta
```

When we wish to draw your attention to a particular part of a code block, the relevant lines or items are set in bold:

```
$UserCredential = Get-Credential
Connect-MsolService -Credential $UserCredential
```

Any command-line input or output is written as follows:

```
Get-MsolUser -UserPrincipalName user365@o365pt.org | FL
```

**Bold**: Indicates a new term, an important word, or words that you see onscreen. For example, words in menus or dialog boxes appear in the text like this. Here is an example: "Choose the **Sign-in status**, assign licenses, and click **Next.**"

Warnings or important notes appear like this.

Tips and tricks appear like this.

# Get in touch

Feedback from our readers is always welcome.

**General feedback**: Email `feedback@packtpub.com` and mention the book title in the subject of your message. If you have questions about any aspect of this book, please email us at `questions@packtpub.com`.

**Errata**: Although we have taken every care to ensure the accuracy of our content, mistakes do happen. If you have found a mistake in this book, we would be grateful if you would report this to us. Please visit `www.packtpub.com/submit-errata`, selecting your book, clicking on the Errata Submission Form link, and entering the details.

**Piracy**: If you come across any illegal copies of our works in any form on the Internet, we would be grateful if you would provide us with the location address or website name. Please contact us at `copyright@packtpub.com` with a link to the material.

**If you are interested in becoming an author**: If there is a topic that you have expertise in and you are interested in either writing or contributing to a book, please visit `authors.packtpub.com`.

# Reviews

Please leave a review. Once you have read and used this book, why not leave a review on the site that you purchased it from? Potential readers can then see and use your unbiased opinion to make purchase decisions, we at Packt can understand what you think about our products, and our authors can see your feedback on their book. Thank you!

For more information about Packt, please visit `packtpub.com`.

# 1
# Introduction to Office 365

In this chapter, we will introduce you to the foundations of Office 365. This chapter will cover the following topics:

- Office 365 products
- Office 365 plans
- Licensing
- Terminology

With this introduction of the foundations of Office 365, you will have a better understanding of what Office 365 is.

## Products within Office 365

The cloud is the latest innovation in the **information technology** (**IT**) world. Companies are changing the way they use their technologies, migrating their workloads to the cloud to access new technologies, and optimizing their budgets to be more competitive in the market. These kinds of technologies have their own innovations and new features that are only available in the cloud, while others might, eventually, be available on premises at a later time.

Office 365 is a **software as a service** (**SaaS**) product, which means you don't need to worry about energy, data centers, hardware, redundancy, operating systems, security, or features updates. It is an enterprise solution available to organizations of all sizes, and one of its big advantages is that you only pay for what you want to use.

# Office 365 Enterprise versus Office 365 Home

The difference between Office 365 Enterprise and Office 365 Home has to do with the difference between the requirements of enterprises and large organizations versus those of home users. Home users simply want to use the email system and simple editing tools, and be able to share documents and files. Organizations need security auditing and access to other types of information that the home users do not need.

# Office 365 plans

*What are the Office 365 plans?* Plans are predefined mixes of products and features of Office 365 that you can use in your organization based on your needs.

This mix of products will consist of a combination of Exchange, SharePoint, Skype for Business, and other workloads and features, for example:

- **Office 365 ProPlus or Essentials**: Desktop productivity suite
- **Exchange Online**: Enterprise-class email solution
- **SharePoint Online**: Collaboration, repository, and file sharing
- **Skype for Business**: Online communication, including video and voice calls

These productivity tools have their own features and, combined with other products, they will have the integration that the end users need. Organizations need to keep their software and solutions updated to be competitive in the market, and they need to evaluate their IT costs based on what is needed and when. But with Office 365, these features are updated on a weekly or monthly basis to help organizations stay up to date without requiring big upgrade projects, such as those that are needed for on-premises systems.

While this book is based on a technology that is constantly changing, the core products and plans have not changed much since the beginning of Office 365. The Office 365 plans differ with respect to the Enterprise and Business plans according to the size and type of your organization.

At the time of writing this chapter, the plans are divided into six different groups:

- Home
- Small business
- Education
- Nonprofit
- Enterprise
- Firstline Workers

There are also individual services, such as the following:

- Business-class email, for information refer to `https://products.office.com/en/exchange/exchange-online`)
- File storage and sharing, for information refer to `https://products.office.com/en/onedrive-for-business/online-cloud-storage`)
- Online meetings, for information refer to `https://products.office.com/en/skype-for-business/online-meetings`)

You can view the updated version of these plans here at `https://products.office.com/en/business/compare-more-office-365-for-business-plans`. The plan that is most used by organizations is the Enterprise plan.

# Periodic table of Office 365

One of the best ways to understand Office 365 is to start with the periodic table of Office 365, created by Matt Wade and Niels Gregers Johansen. To have access to the full-site experience of the periodic table of Office 365, go to `http://jumpto365.com/`.

This periodic table was created for potential customers and users to easily and quickly understand the products that make up Office 365, and to visualize the features combined in the areas of each workload.

Office 365 encompasses several workloads, and the periodic table of Office 365 shows these as being grouped in several areas:

- **Presentations**: The tools to give and show presentations are as follows:
    - **Sway**: Sway is an app in Office 365 that allows users to easily create dynamic presentations in a web format. It is the next-generation tool to create and share information. You can read more at `https://support.office.com/en-us/article/getting-started-with-sway-2076c468-63f4-4a89-ae5f-424796714a8a?ui=en-US&rs=en-US&ad=US`.
    - **PowerPoint Online**: PowerPoint Online is the web version of PowerPoint, and is the light version of the desktop edition of PowerPoint. It can be installed on a PC or Mac. You can create presentations with images, transitions, and videos, among other features. You can read more at `https://support.office.com/en-us/article/create-a-presentation-in-powerpoint-online-21360025-7eef-4173-9d7c-08281d55f64a`.
- **Office Online**: The tools to be more productive are as follows:
    - **Word Online**: Word Online is the web version of Word, and is the light version of the desktop release of Word. It can be installed on PC or Mac. You can create and edit documents with basic commands. You can read more at `https://support.office.com/en-us/article/video-what-is-word-aee9c7ff-f9c5-415f-80dc-103ad5e344d7?ui=en-USamp;rs=en-USamp;ad=US`.
    - **Excel Online**: Excel online is the web version of Excel, and is the light version of the desktop edition of Excel. It can be installed on PC or Mac. You can create and edit spreadsheets with basic features. You can read more at `https://support.office.com/en-us/article/video-what-is-excel-842fb550-07cb-42d1-9a9f-c55789efed57?ui=en-USamp;rs=en-USamp;ad=US`.
    - **OneNote Online**: OneNote Online is the web version of OneNote, and is the light version of the desktop edition of OneNote. It can be installed on PC or Mac. You can create and edit notes with basic commands. You can read more at `https://support.office.com/en-us/article/get-started-with-the-new-onenote-ab84fcc2-f845-41ac-9c29-89b0720c8eb3`.

    - **PowerPoint Online**: PowerPoint Online is the web version of PowerPoint, and is the light version of the desktop edition of PowerPoint. It can be installed on a PC or Mac. You can create presentations with images, transitions, and videos among other features. You can read more at `https://support.office.com/en-us/article/create-a-presentation-in-powerpoint-online-21360025-7eef-4173-9d7c-08281d55f64a`.

- **File storage and collaboration**: The way that you storage and collaborate are as follows:
    - **SharePoint Online**: SharePoint Online is a web-based collaboration platform that is designed to be the place where teams work together in your organization. It can be used to create intranets and extranets, and can be used to share your work with other people and take your collaboration to the next level. You can read more at `https://products.office.com/en-us/sharepoint/sharepoint-online-collaboration-software`.
    - **OneDrive for Business**: OneDrive for Business is a cloud storage service delivered by Microsoft that is part of Office 365, and is built on the top of SharePoint. With OneDrive for Business, you can store all your files, and share and access them from anywhere. You can read more at `https://support.office.com/en-us/article/what-is-onedrive-for-business-187f90af-056f-47c0-9656-cc0ddca7fdc2`.
    - **Delve**: Delve is a search and discovery experience provided by Office 365 that gives you a view and a central place to discover content and people in your organization, with insights powered by Microsoft Graph. You can read more at `https://support.office.com/en-us/article/what-is-office-delve-1315665a-c6af-4409-a28d-49f8916878ca`.
- **Business application platform**: The applications that you can leverage to the next level of automation are as follows:
    - **PowerApps**: PowerApps is a no-code tool to create next-generation business applications that can connect your Office 365 services to your system's data in a fast and easy way. You can read more at `https://powerapps.microsoft.com/en-us/`.
    - **Flow**: Flow is the new generation of cloud-based workflow engines created to automate business processes and help you with your daily repetitive tasks. You can read more at `https://flow.microsoft.com/en-us/`.

- **Power BI**: Power BI is a powerful data-visualization and exploration tool that can connect to multiple data sources and easily generate dynamic and great-looking dashboards. You can read more at `https://powerbi.microsoft.com/en-us/`.

- **Outlook**: The tool to work on your daily basis are as follows:
    - **Mail**: Mail is the email service of Office 365 that is based on Exchange Server provided as a service by Microsoft. You can read more at `https://support.office.com/en-us/article/mail-in-outlook-web-app-ed7b1cb9-ef40-4fbd-a302-278cc7f4dcf5`.
    - **Calendar**: Calendar is the part of your mailbox in which you manage your schedule. You can read more at `https://support.office.com/en-us/article/calendar-in-outlook-web-app-5219c457-d1fe-4c2f-9032-1a816b88e936`.
    - **People**: People is the part of your mailbox where you manage your contacts. You can read more at `https://support.office.com/en-us/article/people-overview-outlook-web-app-5fe173cf-e620-4f62-9bf6-da5041f651bf?ui=en-USamp;rs=en-USamp;ad=US`.
    - **Tasks**: Tasks is the place within your mailbox where you can create and manage tasks. You can read more at `https://support.office.com/en-us/article/getting-started-in-outlook-web-app-0062c7be-f8e3-486e-8b14-5c1f793ceefd`.
- **Project management**: The way that you have to manage your projects are:
    - **Planner**: Planner is a simple and visually based work-management tool that comes as part of Office 365. It allows you to create plans, assign tasks to your team, and view these tasks in a Kanban board. You can read more at `https://products.office.com/en-us/business/task-management-software`.
    - **Project Online**: Project Online is a central management tool that you can use to manage complex projects and your project portfolio. You can read more at `https://support.office.com/en-us/article/get-started-with-project-online-e3e5f64f-ada5-4f9d-a578-130b2d4e5f11`.
- **Chat and conferencing**: The tools to collaborate more efficiently are as follows:
    - **Skype for Business**: Skype for Business is the enterprise unified communication tool, with support for chat, audio and video calls, conferencing, and online meetings. You can read more at `https://www.skype.com/en/business/`.

    - **Teams**: Teams is the next-generation, team-collaboration tool that takes the place of the Hub to coordinate teamwork. It leverages content from SharePoint, email, chat, and other tools to work seamlessly, according to your daily needs. You can read more at `https://products.office.com/en-us/microsoft-teams/group-chat-software`.
- **Small business applications**: The small business applications are as follows:
    - **Bookings**: Bookings is a simple, self-service scheduling application designed for small and medium businesses, with native integration with your calendar and availability. You can read more at `https://products.office.com/en/business/scheduling-and-booking-app`.
    - **StaffHub**: StaffHub is a simple shift- and schedule-management tool designed for firstline workers. It helps to manage teams that work in shifts and facilitates communication between team members and managers. You can read more at `https://staffhub.office.com/`.
- **Employee profiles**: The way you search the people to collaborate are:
    - **Delve**: Delve is a search and discovery experience provided by Office 365 that gives you a central place to view and discover content and people in your organization, with insights powered by Microsoft Graph. You can read more at `https://support.office.com/en-us/article/what-is-office-delve-1315665a-c6af-4409-a28d-49f8916878ca`.
    - **People**: People is the part of your mailbox where you manage your contacts. You can read more at `https://support.office.com/en-us/article/people-overview-outlook-web-app-5fe173cf-e620-4f62-9bf6-da5041f651bf?ui=en-USamp;rs=en-USamp;ad=US`.
- **Forms**: This is where you can do some forms:
    - **Forms**: Forms is a new tool for creating simple forms and polls, and allows you to collect feedback from your organization's employees or customers. You can read more at `https://forms.office.com/`.
    - **PowerApps**: PowerApps is a no-code tool to create next-generation business applications that can connect your Office 365 services to your systems data in a fast and easy way. You can read more at `https://powerapps.microsoft.com/en-us/`.

- **Task management**: The daily task management tools to collaborate daily are as follows:
    - **Tasks**: Tasks is the place within your mailbox where you can create and manage tasks. You can read more at `https://support.office.com/en-us/article/getting-started-in-outlook-web-app-0062c7be-f8e3-486e-8b14-5c1f793ceefd`.
    - **To-Do**: This is a task-management tool that is focused on the individual. It comes with a mobile companion app and integrates with Outlook. You can read more at `https://products.office.com/en-us/microsoft-to-do-list-app`.
    - **Planner**: Planner is a simple work-management tool that is part of Office 365, and allows you to create plans, assign tasks to your team, and view these tasks in a Kanban board. You can read more at `https://products.office.com/en-us/business/task-management-software`.
- **Social networking**: This is where you can share to the organization using a wide network:
    - **Newsfeed**: Newsfeed is a simplified social experience based on SharePoint that provides light social features to your intranet. You can read more at `https://support.office.com/en-gb/article/what-items-appear-in-your-newsfeed-bd3d9268-0408-4ad4-bc51-2e4ec5406e16`.
    - **Yammer**: Yammer is a secure social network for your organization that provides many powerful collaboration features not only for internal users, but also for collaboration with users external to your organization. You can read more at `https://products.office.com/en/yammer/yammer-overview`.

In summary, this periodic table will help you understand the services and tools that are included in Office 365.

If you are Portuguese like me, you can view the translated version (made by me) at `http://jumpto365.com/#/periodictable/pt`.

# Home

In Office 365 Home, there are four plans:

- Office 365 Home
- Office 365 Personal
- Office Home & Student 2016 for PC
- Office Home & Business 2016

These plans have the following features:

- Office 365 Home:
    - Office installed on PC, Mac, or mobile devices
    - 1 TB of OneDrive for Business
- Office 365 Personal:
    - Office installed on PC, Mac, or mobile devices
    - 1 TB of OneDrive for Business
- Office 365 Home & Student:
    - Office installed on PC, Mac, or mobile devices
- Office 365 Home & Business:
    - Office installed on PC, Mac, or mobile devices

To view all the latest features, go to `https://products.office.com/en/office-365-home`.

# Business

In Office 365 Business, there are three plans:

- Office 365 Business
- Office 365 Business Premium
- Office 365 Business Essentials

The main features of these plans are as follows:

- Office 365 Business:
    - Office installed on PC, Mac, or mobile devices
    - 1 TB of OneDrive for Business
- Office 365 Business Premium:
    - Office installed on PC, Mac, or mobile devices
    - 50 GB of mailbox
    - 1 TB of OneDrive for Business
- Office 365 Business Essentials:
    - 50 GB of mailbox
    - 1 TB of OneDrive for Business

To view the latest features, go to `https://products.office.com/en/business/office-365-business`.

# Education

In Office 365 Education, there are two plans:

- Office 365 for Education (100% free)
- Office 365 Education E5

The main features of these plans are as follows:

- Office 365 for Education (100% free):
    - Office on the web
    - 50 GB of mailbox
    - 1 TB of OneDrive for Business
- Office 365 Education E5:
    - Office installed on PC, Mac, or mobile devices
    - 100 GB of mailbox
    - 1 TB of OneDrive for Business

To view the latest features, go to `https://www.microsoft.com/en-us/education/products/office/default.aspx`.

## Nonprofit

In Office 365 Nonprofit, there are five plans:

- Office 365 Nonprofit Business Essentials
- Office 365 Nonprofit Business Premium
- Office 365 Nonprofit E1
- Office 365 Nonprofit E3
- Office 365 Nonprofit E5

The main features of these plans are as follows:

- Office 365 Nonprofit Business Essentials:
    - Office on the web
    - 50 GB of mailbox
    - 1 TB of OneDrive for Business
- Office 365 Nonprofit Business Premium:
    - Office installed on PC, Mac, or mobile devices
    - 50 GB of mailbox
    - 1 TB of OneDrive for Business
- Office 365 Nonprofit E1:
    - Office on the web
    - 50 GB of mailbox
    - 1 TB of OneDrive for Business
- Office 365 Nonprofit E3:
    - Office installed on PC, Mac, or mobile devices
    - 100 GB of mailbox
    - 1 TB of OneDrive for Business
- Office 365 Nonprofit E5:
    - Office installed on PC, Mac, or mobile devices
    - 100 GB of mailbox
    - 1 TB of OneDrive for Business

To view the latest features, go to `https://products.office.com/en/nonprofit/office-365-nonprofit-plans-and-pricing?tab=1`.

# Enterprise

In Office 365 Enterprise, there are four plans:

- Office 365 ProPlus
- Office 365 Enterprise E1
- Office 365 Enterprise E3
- Office 365 Enterprise E5

The main features of these plans are as follows:

- Office 365 ProPlus:
    - Office installed on PC, Mac, or mobile devices
- Office 365 Enterprise E1:
    - Office on the web
    - 50 GB of mailbox
    - 1 TB of OneDrive for Business
- Office 365 Enterprise E3:
    - Office installed on PC, Mac, or mobile devices
    - 100 GB of mailbox
    - 1 TB of OneDrive for Business
- Office 365 Enterprise E5:
    - Office installed on PC, Mac, or mobile devices
    - 100 GB of mailbox
    - 1 TB of OneDrive for Business
    - Advanced security
    - Analytics (My Analytics)
    - Advanced voice features **Public Switched Telephony Network (PSTN)**

To view the latest features, go to `https://products.office.com/en/business/compare-more-office-365-for-business-plans`.

# Firstline Workers

In Office 365 Firstline there is, currently, only one plan:

- Office 365 F1

In this plan, the main features are:

- Office on the web
- 2 GB of mailbox
- 2 GB of OneDrive for Business

To view the latest features, go to `https://products.office.com/en-us/business/enterprise-firstline-workers`.

# Office 365 plans – summary

This summary is intended to provide you with a better understanding of the fact that the plans that Microsoft has created are always based on the type and size of your organization. It is possible to combine plans in the enterprise that fit your needs based on your experience of these kinds of products. However, it is advised that you contact a gold productivity partner to help you select which plans best fit your organization.
You can also see that the Office 365 service descriptions provide additional details about each plan. For more information you can refer to `https://technet.microsoft.com/en-us/library/office-365-service-descriptions.aspx`.

# Feature availability across Office 365 plans

For specific information about the plans pricing and features regarding specific business types, see the following web pages:

- **Business**: Office 365 Business plans and pricing (`https://products.office.com/en-in/compare-all-microsoft-office-products?tab=2`)
- **Education**: Office 365 Education plans and pricing (`https://products.office.com/en-IN/academic/compare-office-365-education-plans#`)

- **U.S. Government**: Office 365 U.S. Government plans (`https://products.office.com/en-IN/government/compare-office-365-government-plans`)
- **Nonprofit**: Office 365 Nonprofit plans and pricing (`https://products.office.com/en-IN/nonprofit/office-365-nonprofit-plans-and-pricing?tab=1`)
- **Office 365 Germany**: Office 365 Germany plans (`https://products.office.com/en/business/office-365-germany`)

Many of the Office 365 business plans have add-ons that you can buy for your subscription. An add-on offers added functionality to the subscription. For more information, you can see the specific add-ons that are available for different versions of Office 365 for Business at `https://support.office.com/en-us/article/buy-or-edit-an-add-on-for-office-365-for-business-4e7b57d6-b93b-457d-aecd-0ea58bff07a6?ui=en-US&rs=en-US&ad=US`.

To view the latest features, go to `https://technet.microsoft.com/en-us/library/office-365-plan-options.aspx`.

The following table is a summary of features across business subscriptions:

| **Features** | **Office 365 Business Essentials** | **Office 365 Business** | **Office 365 Business Premium** | **Office 365 Education** | **Office 365 Enterprise E1** | **Office 365 Enterprise E3** | **Office 365 Enterprise E5 /Office 365 E5 Education** | **Office 365 Enterprise F1** |
|---|---|---|---|---|---|---|---|---|
| Administers Office 365 by using the Office 365 admin center or Windows PowerShell | Yes | Yes | Yes | Yes | Yes | Yes | Yes | Yes |
| Protects content by using Azure Information Protection | No | No | No | No | No | Yes | Yes | No |

| Features | Office 365 Business Essentials | Office 365 Business | Office 365 Business Premium | Office 365 Education | Office 365 Enterprise E1 | Office 365 Enterprise E3 | Office 365 Enterprise E5 /Office 365 E5 Education | Office 365 Enterprise F1 |
|---|---|---|---|---|---|---|---|---|
| Microsoft Bookings | No | No | Yes | No | No | No | No | No |
| Microsoft Flow | Yes | No | Yes | Yes | Yes | Yes | Yes | Yes |
| Microsoft Forms | Yes | Yes | Yes | Yes | Yes | Yes | Yes | Yes |
| Microsoft Graph API | Yes | Yes | Yes | Yes | Yes | Yes | Yes | Yes |
| Microsoft MyAnalytics | No | No | No | No | No | No | Yes | No |
| Microsoft Planner | Yes | No | Yes | Yes | Yes | Yes | Yes | No |
| Microsoft PowerApps | Yes | No | Yes | Yes | Yes | Yes | Yes | Yes |
| Microsoft StaffHub | No | No | No | Yes | Yes | Yes | Yes | Yes |
| Microsoft Teams10 | Yes | No | Yes | Yes | Yes | Yes | Yes | Yes |
| Office Delve | Yes | Yes | Yes | Yes | Yes | Yes | Yes | Yes |
| Office 365 Groups | Yes | No | Yes | Yes | Yes | Yes | Yes | Yes |
| Office 365 Video | No | No | No | Yes | Yes | Yes | Yes | Yes |
| OneNote Class Notebook | No | No | No | Yes | No | No | Yes | No |
| Sway | Yes | Yes | Yes | Yes | Yes | Yes | Yes | Yes |

To view the entire table, refer to `https://technet.microsoft.com/en-us/library/mt844095.aspx(Saved%20copy)`.

# Licensing

Office 365's licensing is based on the type of organization you have. Office 365 is Microsoft's productivity solution in the cloud. It is sold as suites that are available for every organization, regardless of their size. Depending on the suite, Office 365 can include the full downloadable Office client, also available as a set of web-based applications (Word, Excel, PowerPoint, and so on), business-class email, file sharing, meeting and communications solutions, and an internal collaboration social network—all while helping to keep data private and protected from potential threats. Office 365 provides users with simple management IT solutions, grants them access to the productivity solution from anywhere, and comes with a financially backed service level agreement.

## Subscription model

Office 365 provides the ability for organizations to add and remove licenses, and enterprises are billed on an annual or monthly basis, depending on the type of subscription and the way that you purchased them from our partner.

## Office 365 volume licensing

For companies with enterprise agreements or similar contracts with Microsoft, Office 365 can also be licensed in volume. For more information on this, refer to the licensing guide at: `http://docplayer.net/17893150-Office-365-licensing-brief.html`.

# Office 365 technical dependencies

The previously mentioned Office 365 suites are a collection of online services that, when purchased together, give customers what we call a suite discount. Customers who do not need or want to buy full suites can purchase individual services as separate products. Note that some of these online services have technical dependencies on others. For example, **Exchange Online Protection** (**EOP**) provides an added level of security to the Exchange Online and/or Exchange server services; customers can't use EOP if they don't have either Exchange Online or Exchange server deployed.

For more information on the technical dependencies, refer to `https://technet.microsoft.com/en-us/library/office-365-service-descriptions.aspx`.

# Terminology

As more and more organizations move to the cloud, Office 365 is continuing to grow in popularity. With this growth comes a variety of new terms that users and organizations need to understand. The following is a list of common Office 365 terms that you should familiarize yourself with as you explore this new world:

- **Microsoft Office 365**: Microsoft Office 365 is a suite of productivity tools and services that can be used both online and through desktop versions. Microsoft Office 365 includes many productivity programs, such as Word, Excel, PowerPoint, Outlook, SharePoint, and OneNote among others. It can be used like a brand or just Office 365.
- **Microsoft 365**: Microsoft 365 is a packaged offering of Windows, Office 365, and security products.
- **OneNote**: Microsoft OneNote is an application that helps you to take and share notes, and supports multiple users editing at the same time. Users can use it to take both handwritten and typed notes, audio, drawings, and screenshots.
- **OneDrive for Business**: OneDrive for Business allows users to store, modify, sync, and share files collaboratively in real time. OneDrive is a fully cloud-based service.
- **Sway**: Sway is a digital storytelling tool that helps to create new types of presentation or personal stories.
- **SharePoint**: SharePoint allows organizations to create websites to store, share, and organize information from almost any device. With SharePoint, all of an organization's important data can be accessed from any web browser and with any device.
- **Outlook**: Microsoft Outlook is the business email client that is part of the Office 365 suite. Outlook can also refer to a webmail client, **Outlook Web Access (OWA)**, which can be used to access email through a web browser.
- **Excel**: Microsoft Excel is a spreadsheet tool that offers organizations the ability to access and analyze many types of data.
- **PowerPoint**: Microsoft PowerPoint is a program that helps to create presentations. Users integrate data from other Office programs directly into their presentations for presenting and sharing, and to share knowledge.

- **Skype for Business**: Skype for Business is an enterprise product that is used for messaging, voice calling, and video calling. Skype for Business has tools that help organizations to communicate in an easy way. The following are some of these tools:
    - **Skype Meeting Broadcast**: Skype Meeting Broadcast is a platform that helps organizations to broadcast and host online meetings to large audiences of up to 10,000 attendees
    - **PSTN Conferencing**: PSTN Conferencing is a feature that allows users to dial into a meeting from a physical phone as opposed to a mobile device or PC
    - **Cloud PBX with PSTN Calling**: Cloud PBX with PSTN Calling allows people in your organization the ability to connect to the existing PSTN
- **Microsoft Teams**: Microsoft Teams is a new way of coworking, and is quickly becoming the next generation of digital workplaces. It combines multiple Office 365 products, and exposes them so that they can be accessed in a central place. Some examples of these products are Skype for Business, SharePoint, OneDrive, and Planner, among others.
- **Yammer**: Yammer is a private social network for your organization. Yammer helps your organization to connect and share information, and can be configured to have groups outside of your organization.
- **Office Online**: Office Online is a suite of full, web-based versions of Word, Excel, OneNote, and PowerPoint. It helps the users to work with documents from any device using a browser.
- **Microsoft Stream**: Microsoft Stream is a new cloud-based video service that uses the power of intelligent enterprise video to enable knowledge sharing, easier communication, and connectivity in a secure enterprise environment. Microsoft Stream is the successor to Office 365 Video, built on Azure Media Services. It allows playback at scale across any device.
- **Azure Rights Management Services (Azure RMS)**: Azure RMS is an information-security solution to help organizations protect their data where the content resides.
- **Data Loss Prevention (DLP)**: DLP in Office 365 allows the management and monitoring of and response to sensitive information within your organization through content analysis.

- **Delve**: Office Delve helps the users of your organization to reach and collaborate more in a way that can view what is happening within your organization and across Office 365.
- **Azure AD Connect**: Azure AD Connect helps your organization to synchronize its on-premises identities to Office 365.
- **PowerShell**: PowerShell is another tool that helps organizations to automate and perform several tasks. It allows administrators to write PowerShell scripts to create users, create external contacts, and change user attributes.
- **Admin delegation**: Using admin delegation in Office 365, organizations can assign some or all of Office 365's admin tasks to other users or to a Microsoft Cloud Partner.
- **Hybrid identity**: If our organization includes both cloud and on-premises infrastructure, hybrid identity management provides a method to integrate both environments. With Azure AD Connect, you can synchronize users, groups, contacts, and passwords to Office 365.
- **Exchange Online**: Exchange Online is a hosted email messaging solution of Office 365 cloud-based services.
- **Tenant**: The word *tenant* refers to an Office 365 cloud area specific to your organization.
- **Tenant name**: The tenant name is your domain name, such as `yourdomain.onmicrosoft.com`. It is set up when you subscribe to Office 365 and it cannot be changed. When you create your tenant, the wizard that creates your Office 365 subscription asks for your organization's name. If it is available, it can be used. Now, with Office 365, within many organizations worldwide you may have to choose a different name, such as `yourdomaincorp.onmicrosoft.com` because some other organization in another country may have chosen that name already.

- **Screenshots and examples**: The screenshots, examples, and instructions described in this book are based on Office 365 with the 2016 versions of the software in a tenant that has the first release option active, which might include features that are previews of the final release before this book's publication date. Given the constant evolution of Office 365, your Office 365 may not match some of the instructions or screenshots in this book. This book will have regular updates to address the changes to this new world.

- **Trust Center**: This is a portal in which Microsoft shows, with great transparency, a lot of information about security and privacy. In this portal, you can see which products and services within your location have which certifications. You can access it at `https://www.microsoft.com/en-us/trustcenter/cloudservices/office365`. The Office 365 Trust Center is the portal that aggregates all updated privacy and security issues related to Office 365 in just one location. The Trust Center has three pillars:
    - Privacy
    - Security
    - Compliance

In this portal, you will have access to recommended resources, documents, blogs, white papers, and the service trust platform.

# Summary

In this chapter, you learned about the main Office 365 products that are used in organizations, the Office 365 plans that best fit most companies and which benefits Microsoft has to give your organization, a summary of licensing that Microsoft uses for organizations and how it will cover your support, and finally, terminology to help you in this book to learn or to go over certain points or products that your organization already has or will have in the near future.

You now have more information on what can be used in Office 365, and this chapter has helped you understand the foundations of Office 365.

In the next chapter, you will learn the fundamentals of Office 365 to help you implement Office 365 in your organization successfully.

# 2
# Fundamentals of Office 365

In this chapter, we will cover the fundamentals of Microsoft Office 365, based on the experience and best practices gathered from previous implementations. We will go through the following topics:

- Planning Office 365
- Evaluating Office 365
- Deployment Office 365
- Descriptions Office 365
- Analysis Office 365

With this knowledge, you will have a better understanding of how to implement Office 365 in your organization.

There are business challenges in all implementations of Office 365. The following are some statements from organizations that have gone through the process:

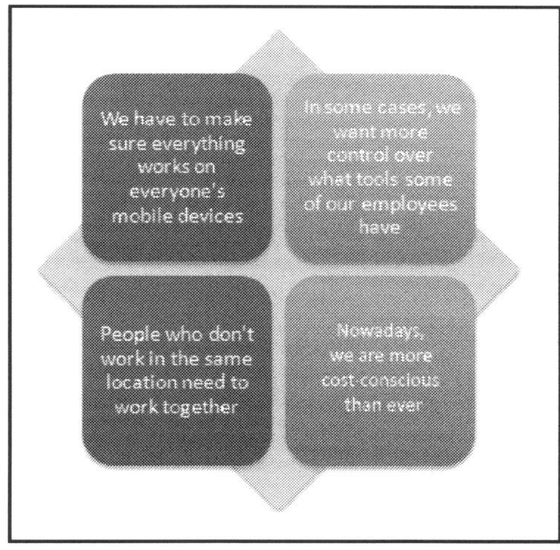

# Planning Office 365

Office 365 is a platform that was created to bring Office to the cloud and make it available not only for large enterprises, but also for small organizations.

All organizations, regardless of size, need careful preparation, even for small migrations. Organizations that have on-premises solutions need to be integrated with Office 365, and may require additional preparation, depending on each workload (as is the case with Exchange, for instance). The requirements and objectives for each type of migration can vary depending on the complexity of the environment, the on-premises version, and other factors.

The planning phase is critical to using the base technologies to leverage and implement Office 365. Office 365 includes several cloud-optimized productivity services, such as Exchange Online, SharePoint Online, Yammer, Skype for Business, and Microsoft Teams hosted by Microsoft, that will take your organization to the next level.

Using Office 365, you will have the following advantages:

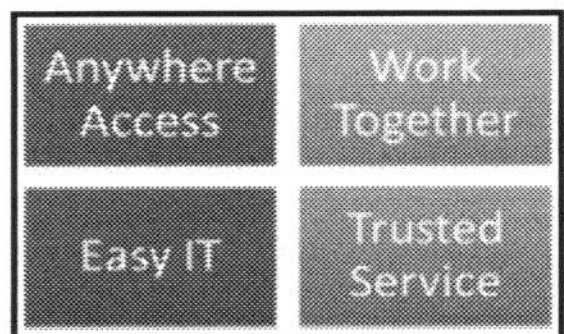


# How to plan for Office 365

It is advised that all organizations do a proof of concept to adopt any new technology. It is the same with Office 365. When you are evaluating a new technology that you are not familiar with, it is always recommended to pilot this new technology in your organization to improve the chances of a successful project.

To plan according to the size of your organization, you will need to perform a set of tasks related to the base service and to each specific workload, such as planning according to your environment.

## Base service

All projects, regardless of the size of the organization, need to have planning. These are initial tasks that are needed for a project to be successful, assuming that all workloads work as expected. We need to remediate some tasks in order to avoid issues during deployment and to have a good experience with collaborators.

One issue that is common in some organizations when moving to a cloud solution is the stability and performance of their internet access. Another issue could be how the organization will manage Office 365 and whether they have the right skills to support, implement, and maintain it as this book describes.

All these kinds of issues must be resolved before we go live with a project on Office 365.

## What is Office 365?

Office 365 is a productivity suite of services hosted in Microsoft's public cloud that also includes the latest version of Office desktop applications.

To know where your data is stored based on your location, please go to `https://products.office.com/en-us/where-is-your-data-located?geo=All` to see all the regions where Microsoft has data centers that host Office 365 services.

If your organization is based in Europe, and the headquarters is in Portugal, for example, the data center locations, by default, are as follows:

- Ireland
- Netherlands
- Austria
- Finland

If your location is in a specific country, such as the UK, Germany, or France, then there are other data centers available in your region.

Continuing with the example of the main services in the Europe region, you can see where each service resides based on its location:

If you need to know more about where your data is, such as how the data is stored and who owns and has access to it, you can access the following sites:

- **Office 365 Trust Center**: For more information refer to `https://products.office.com/en-us/business/office-365-trust-center-welcome`
- **Data location**: For more information refer to `http://o365datacentermap.azurewebsites.net/`

## How is a data center built and what components can it have?

A typical data center can have several components, such as the following:

- Networking
- Computing
- UPS

- Transformers
- Generators
- Power supply
- **Computer room air conditioning** (**CRAC**)
- Chiller
- Condenser
- Cooling towers
- Water supply

The following image is a graphical representation of all the components that a data center can have, along with their connections to the IT load:

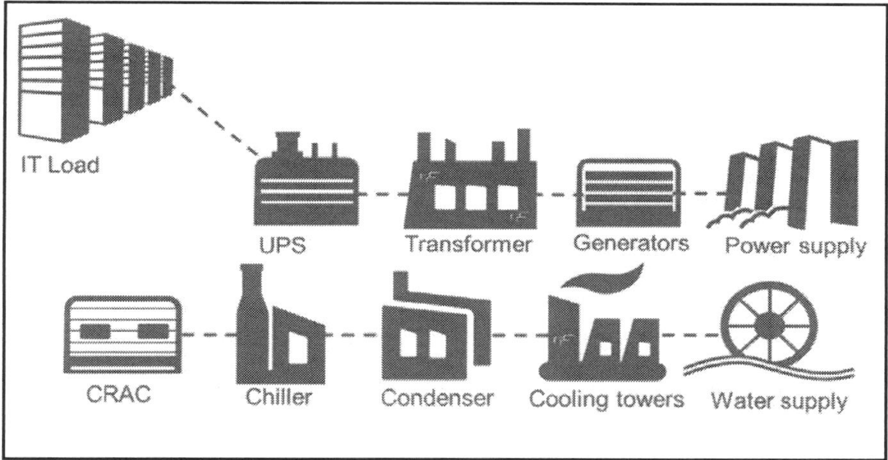


The evolution of data centers has now reached the fifth generation, with optimizations in energy efficiency based on the evolution of engineering, new technologies, and consolidation.

You can see a video called *Discover World Class Security at Microsoft's Datacenters* at `https://www.youtube.com/watch?v=r1cyTL8JqRg`.

If you need to know more about where your data is located, you can go to `https://www.microsoft.com/en-us/TrustCenter/Privacy/where-your-data-is-located` where you'll find all the information that you need.

Microsoft is constantly expanding its Azure datacenter regions. You can refer to the updated datacenter regions at `https://azure.microsoft.com/en-us/global-infrastructure/`.

You can see the regions of Office 365 by visiting at `https://products.office.com/en-us/where-is-your-data-located?geo=All`.

## Specific products

Office 365 is a suite of products and services provided by Microsoft. All these products, such as Exchange, Teams, SharePoint, and Office, have their roles in Microsoft's approach to productivity and the modern workplace. Your organization should know the differences between them before implementation.

If your organization is moving personal files to OneDrive for Business, the implementation of Office 365 ProPlus may require some adjustments to your infrastructure. You should create a plan for deploying each workload required on each phase of your deployment and project. You need to resolve possible issues and perform the remediation tasks required to accomplish your goals.

# Initiating an Office 365 project

To start the implementation plan for Office 365, you need tools that are required for enterprise customers. You can use third-party tools that are available to partners to help you plan your project.

Microsoft has resources that help you to organize projects and, if your organization requires it, you can also use some of the following:

- Deployment guides
- Office 365 readiness checks
- Service descriptions
- Remote connectivity analyzer
- Bandwidth and reliability network analyzer

There are many tools available online that can help you. For example, you can have **Office 365 Admin center**, which is available in your tenant.

It is available using `https://portal.office.com/adminportal/home#/homepage`, if you already have an Office 365 tenant. In the next section of this chapter, we will see how to create one.

You can learn more about it at `https://support.office.com/en-us/article/About-the-Office-365-admin-center-758befc4-0888-4009-9f14-0d147402fd23` or `https://support.office.com/en-us/office365admin`.

There is also the Microsoft Tech Community, which has several communities available at `https://techcommunity.microsoft.com/t5/Communities/ct-p/communities`.

# Evaluating Office 365

In every project or deployment of Office 365, it is advised that you evaluate Office 365 regardless of whether it is for a small, medium, or large organization.

Office 365 is a suite of products that is ready to use. It comes with a basic configuration of the products, but it's necessary to deploy the featured technologies themselves, such as Exchange, SharePoint, Skype for Business, and Office. Some preparation may be required depending on the size of your organization. If it's an enterprise organization, you will probably want to integrate it with on-premises technologies, such as your **Active Directory** (**AD**).

To try out Office 365, follow the instructions to create the Office 365 trial in the following section.

# Installing the Office 365 trial

In every organization, it is advised that you create a separate, nonproduction Office 365 tenant to achieve several objectives, such as the following:

- Experiment with new releases
- Develop new concepts
- Learn more
- Create lab and development initiatives
- Test prior to going into production

To create an Office 365 tenant, go to `https://products.office.com/en/try` and select the desired Office 365 plan. You will see how to create an Office 365 E3 trial by going to `http://go.microsoft.com/fwlink/p/?LinkID=403802`:

1. At the start of the process, the following screen will appear:

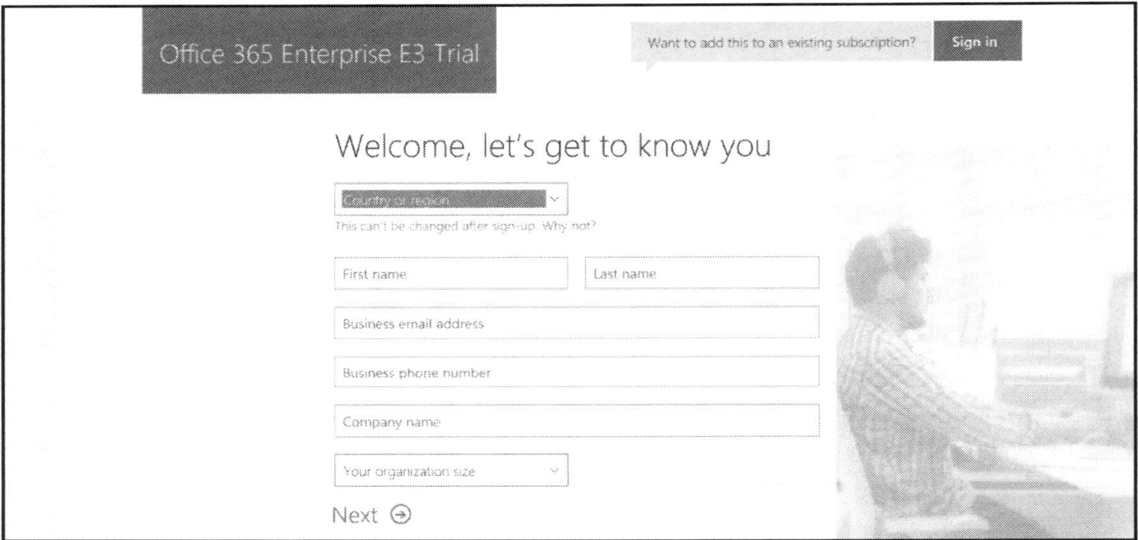


2. At this step you need to fill out all the requested data fields, as shown in the following screenshot. Once you have filled all the data fields, click on **Next**:

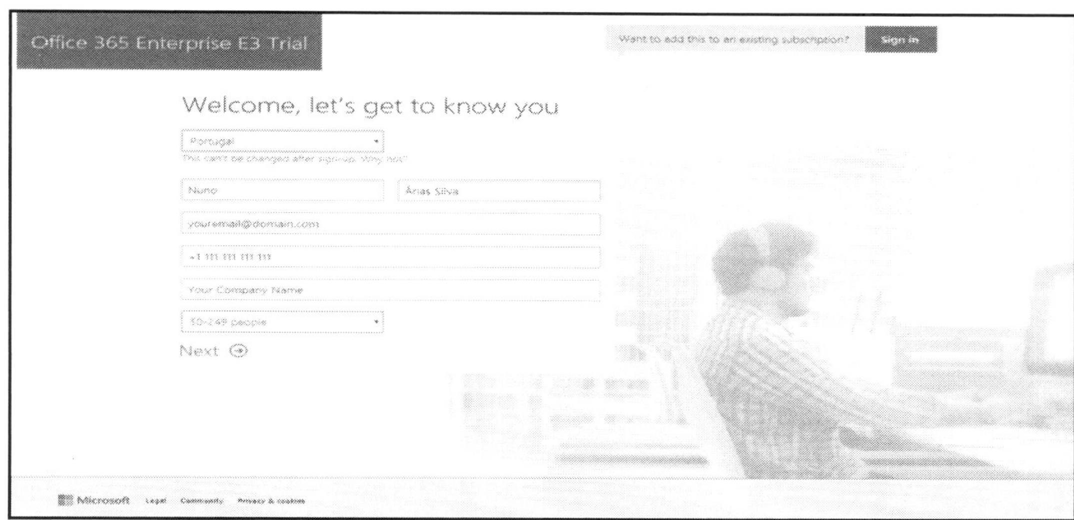

When you select your country, the Office 365 service will create the tenant in the datacenters of your region. At the time of creation, the place where your tenant will reside can't be changed, and if you need to change the region, you will have to perform a migration.

3. Now fill in the required details, as shown in the following screenshot:

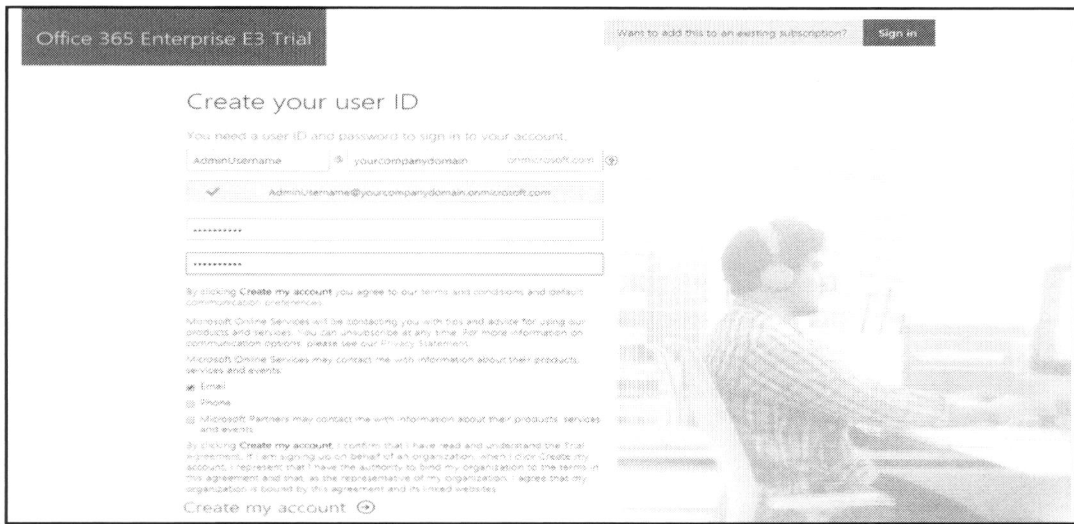

4. It is advised that you create an admin account that is used only for Office 365. Select a username that is different from any other user within your on-premises system or email system within your organization.

After you choose a tenant name, such as `yourcompanydomain.onmicrosoft.com`, you won't be able to change it anymore, because Microsoft uses this name to differentiate tenants from each other. It will remain your tenant's name hereafter, without the possibility of being changed. This tenant name is used, for example, to access SharePoint Online, proxy addresses for Exchange mailboxes, OneDrive, and so on.

5. In the next screen you will be asked to prove that it is not an automated system that is creating the tenant, to avoid the mass creation of tenants:
6. Select either the **Text me** or **Call me** option, and you will receive a confirmation code. I have received the following code to confirm that I'm not a robot:

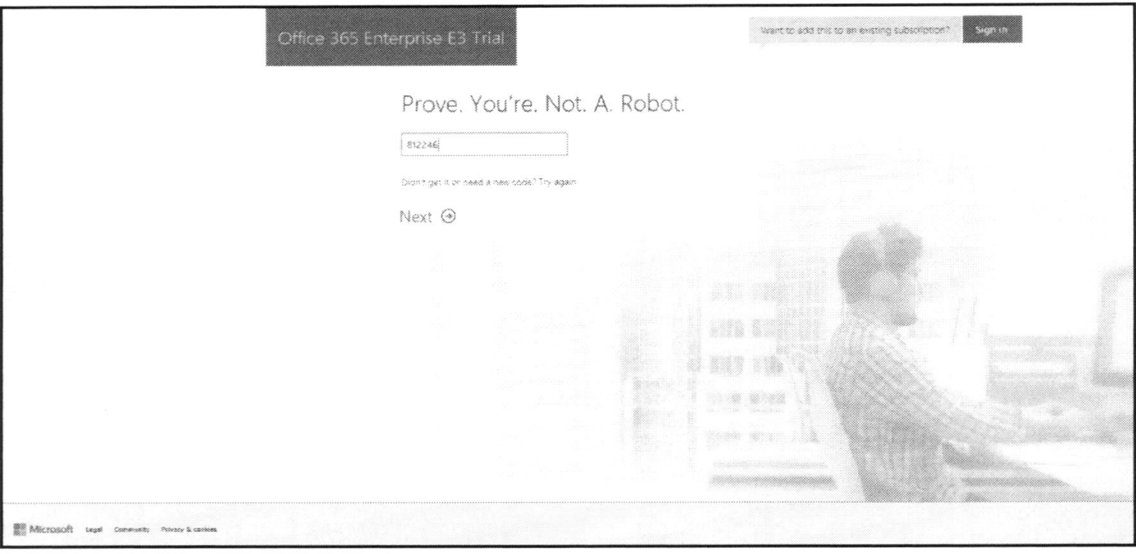


7. After you click **Next**, Office 365 starts creating your tenant, and will request that you wait for a few minutes, as shown in the following screenshot:

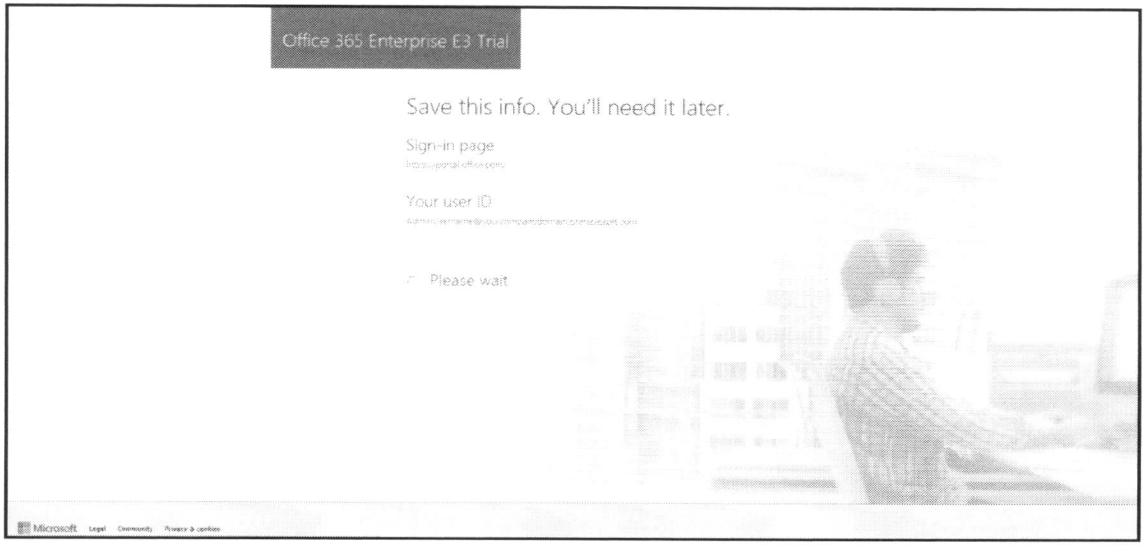


8. After the creation of the Office 365 tenant, it will ask you to save the URL of the Office 365 portal (`http://portal.office.com`) and your user ID.
9. After you click on the **You're ready to go...** option, the Office 365 tenant is created:

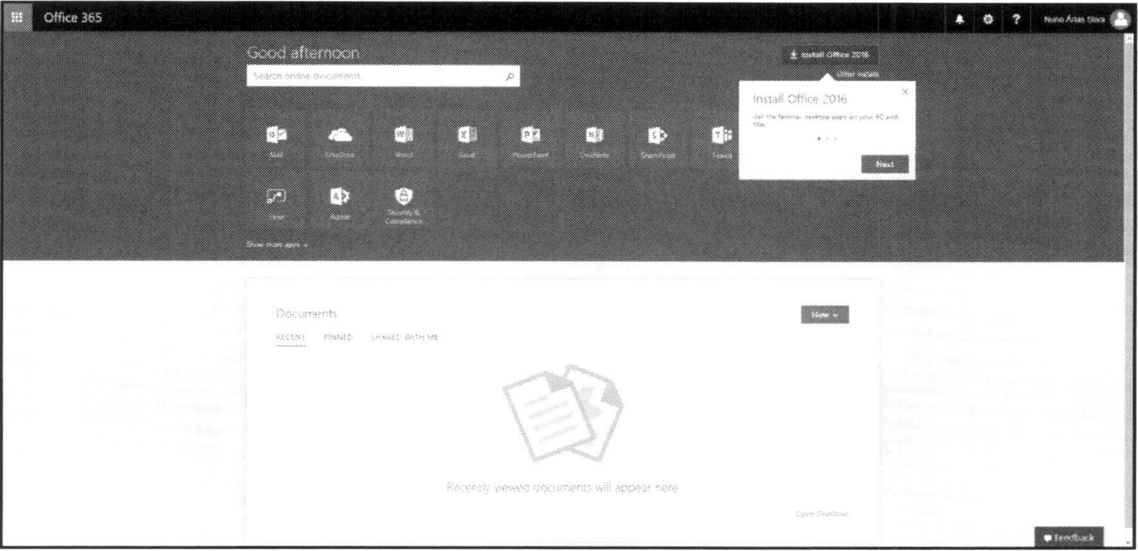

You can now start using Office 365. Since it is a trial version, you will have 25 user licenses available to use during the period of a month.

10. You can now start by going to the **Admin center** and clicking on **Admin** to learn more as shown in the following screenshot:

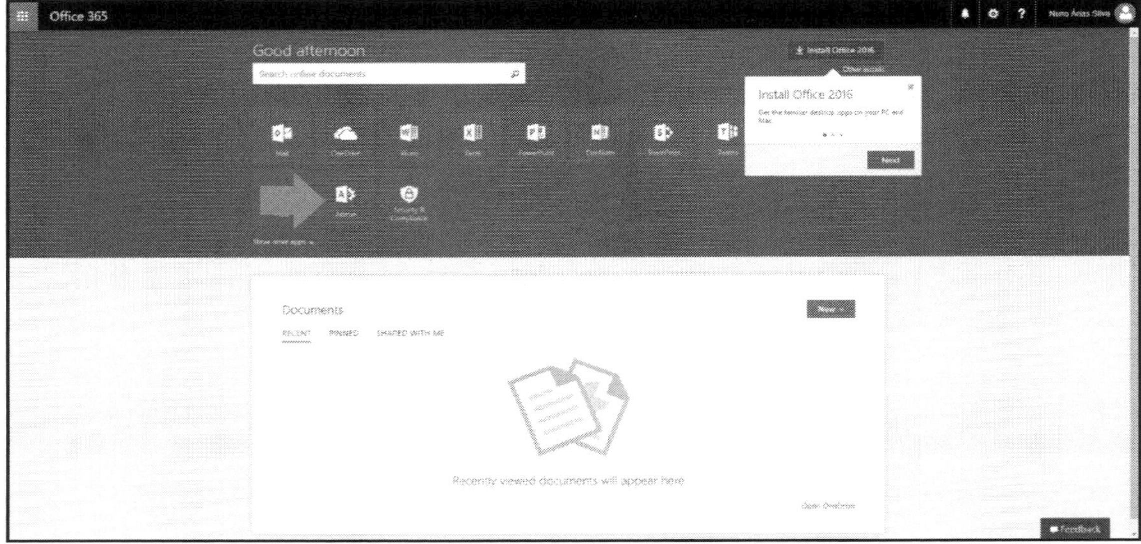


11. The following is the view of the **Office 365 Admin center**, where you have access to the **Admin centers** of all other services:

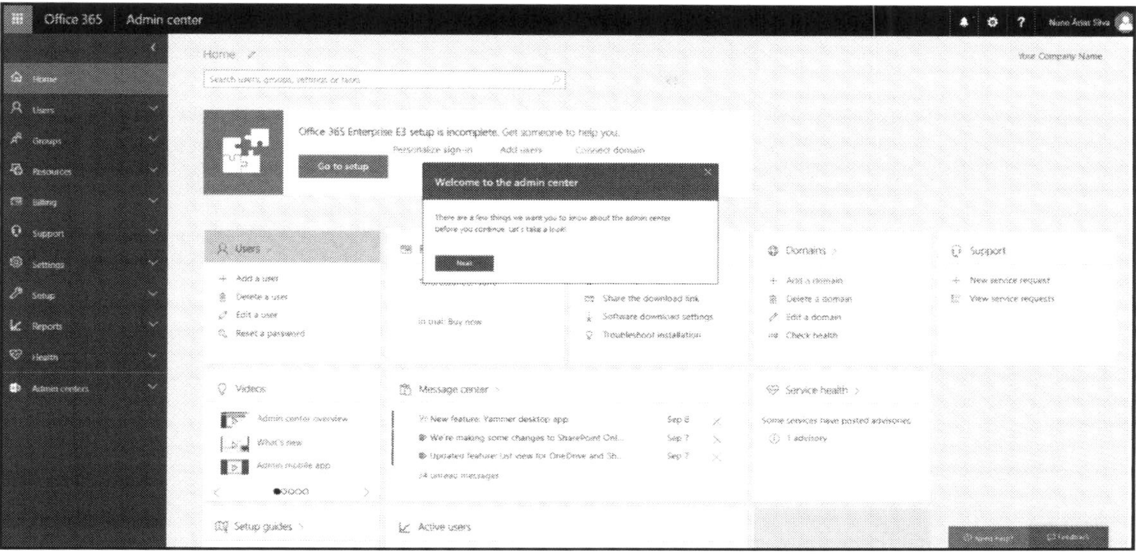


In the Admin center, you can do the following:

- Search for users, groups, settings, or tasks using the search box
- Navigate to the **Admin centers**, using the menu
- Access the homepage of the **Admin centers** to find the most-used and common tasks

This part of the evaluation is the phase in which you, as an administrator, create the Office 365 tenant and prepare for the deployment phase.

# Deployment

The deployment phase is a very important part in implementing Office 365. It is where you set up and start using your products based on the requirements of your organization.

When you start planning your deployment of Office 365, it is advised that you follow the best practices described in the following steps:

1. **Start of the project**: This stage is initiated when the planning phase described earlier in this chapter ends and it is accepted. At this time, the project manager starts coordinating the activities of the team and starts providing feedback to the sponsor of the project.
2. **Assessment**: At this stage, the planning team starts to create an inventory of all areas needed in the on-premises environment that could necessitate updates to the infrastructure. This step is essential in order to avoid problems with the deployment, and requires configuring the relevant features for the integration with Office 365 workloads, such as Exchange Online, desktops, network, firewall, and others. We need to see whether the products that will be integrated with the online services match the currently supported versions. The result of this stage will be that you find the areas that are in need of remediation and which risks are critical to fix before the project goes further. It is advised that you create a checklist based on the workloads that you are going to deploy in order to have sufficient data for the next phase, based on what has been discovered so far.
3. **Remediation**: The issues detected and risks identified in the assessment phase need to be mitigated by the members of the team to safeguard the deployment. At the end of this stage of the project, the project manager can confirm that the enabling phase should start and informs the sponsor of the project.
4. **Enabling**: If your organization needs to have a common identity system between Office 365 (which relies on Azure AD) and the on-premises system, and if you'd like to have the same login as the email address, then you will need to install and configure **AD Connect** to enable synchronization of the objects-users, groups, and so on with your Office 365 tenant. You'll also need to identify the necessary team members to perform these tasks and to set up the initial plan.
5. **Migration**: In this stage, if your main objective of the project is the migration of email, you will need to migrate the mailboxes with all information regarding emails, calendars, and contact data to Office 365. You'll also need to plan what the best migration type is, depending on the requirements, and to plan according to best practices.
6. **End phase**: The project is completed when all the initially planned objectives are completed. At this stage, a subset of users starts actually working on Office 365. The sponsor needs to confirm that the scope of the project is done and all documentation is completed.

7. **User feedback**: It is a best practice in all projects where you implement the latest technologies, such as cloud services, that your end user accepts the project and provides feedback that all people are satisfied. Without this important phase, you will not know how the users are using the products, and what the next projects are, and you will not be able to start using your system with your users satisfied.

The following is a cycle that you can use in all projects:

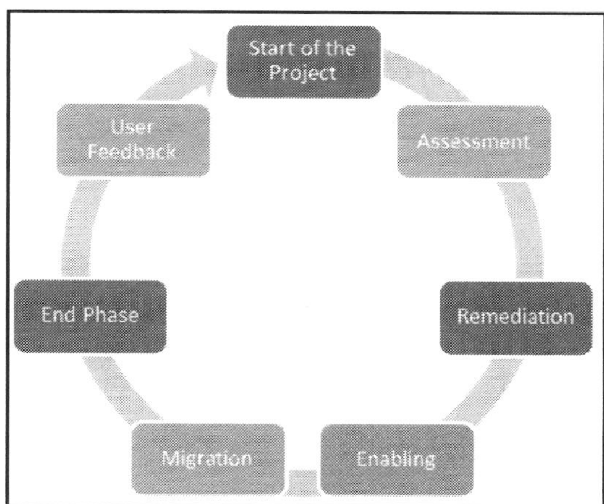


# Office 365 descriptions

The Office 365 descriptions are what I call the Bible of Office 365. This information can help any organization to learn about Office 365 and its services. You find information about many of the services at `https://technet.microsoft.com/en-us/library/office-365-service-descriptions.aspx`.

To learn more about each service, see its description:

- Office 365 Platform Service Description
- Office Applications Service Description
- Office Online Service Description
- Exchange Online Service Description
- Exchange Online Protection Service Description
- Exchange Online Advanced Threat Protection Service Description

- Exchange Online Archiving Service Description
- OneDrive for Business Service Description
- SharePoint Online Service Description
- Skype for Business Online Service Description
- Workplace Analytics Service Description
- Power BI Service Description
- Project Online Service Description
- Yammer Service Description
- Microsoft Dynamics 365 (online) Service Description

In these descriptions, you will find information such as the following:

- The SLA that the services have
- The limitations of your mailboxes
- How much storage space you have in SharePoint Online and OneDrive for Business
- What the limits are when sending emails with Exchange Online
- The difference between Office 365 plans

# Office 365 analysis

To analyze any environment on-premises that might be needed for Office 365 to work, you can use tools such as the following:

- Deployment guide
- Office 365 readiness checks
- Service descriptions
- Remote connectivity analyzer
- Bandwidth and reliability network analyzer

There are references provided by Microsoft that describe the best practices in starting a project. The following is a summary of each tool and guide to help you with each project:

- **Deployment guide**: For more information on deploying Office 365 Enterprise in your organization refer to `https://support.office.com/en-us/article/Deploy-Office-365-Enterprise-for-your-organization-ee73dafb-be54-492e-bcfd-0fbfb5f65e94`
- **Set up Office 365**: To set up Office 365, follow these steps:
    1. Start an Office 365 trial
    2. Assign your domains to Office 365
    3. Install AD Connect to synchronize objects
    4. Configure services and apps on Office 365
    5. Migrate your data to Office 365
    6. Help your employees to adopt and use Office 365
- **Office 365 readiness checks**: For more information on setup with health, readiness, and connectivity checks, refer to `https://technet.microsoft.com/en-us/library/dn771227.aspx`
- **Service descriptions**: For more information on Office 365 service descriptions, refer to `https://technet.microsoft.com/en-us/library/office-365-service-descriptions.aspx`
- **Remote Connectivity Analyzer**: For more information on remote connectivity analyzer refer to `https://testconnectivity.microsoft.com/`
- **Bandwidth and reliability network analyzer**: For more information fast track network analysis refer to `http://em1-fasttrack.cloudapp.net/o365nwtest`

There are many other Microsoft tools that you can use, such as Office 365 Checks, which is the best way to learn if you are ready to work with Office 365.

You can go to `https://configure.office.com/Scenario.aspx?sid=11` and choose the options that you need. I will describe this process as follows:

It is advised that you run this process on a machine that is on your AD domain and that is connected to your network to do the assessment.

Select the option that you need:

**Quick (basic checks that completes in just a few minutes)** is the option that you can choose if you just want to learn the basics:

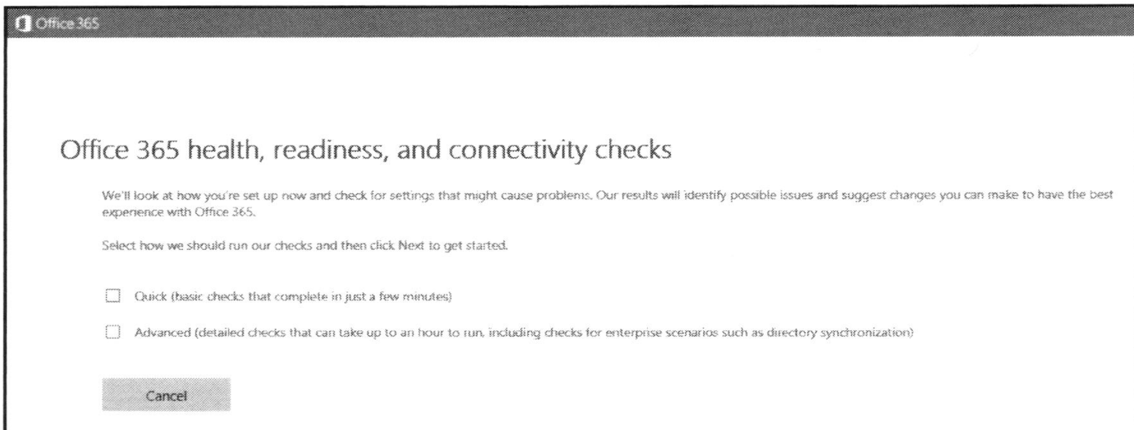


When you select Quick, you will see the following screen:

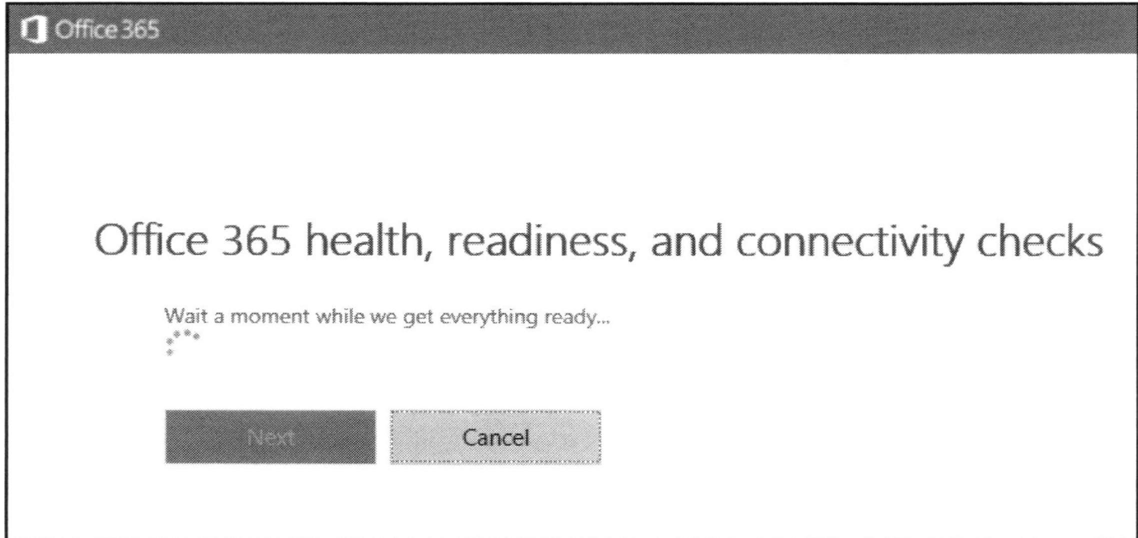

The subsequent steps will be different depending on which option you choose; follow the steps according to what your preferred option is. At the end, it will evaluate possible issues that you need to remediate in your on-premises environment prior to implementation, for example, AD Connect and Exchange hybrid.

Another tool is the *Office 365 Best Practices Analyzer for Exchange Servers*, which you can access using `https://support.office.com/en-us/article/about-the-office-365-best-practices-analyzer-for-exchange-server-c137e46e-c05d-4bdc-b968-67fe5ae68765?ui=en-USrs=en-USad=US`.

You can use the Office 365 Best Practices Analyzer in the following environments:

- On-premises Exchange server only (Exchange 2013 or later)
- Hybrid configuration (with Exchange 2013 or later)

You can also go to `https://portal.office.com/Tools` to have access to several tools like Skype for Business, SharePoint, OneDrive for Business, Yammer and so on.

# Summary

In this chapter, you have learned about the fundamentals of Office 365. Planning is key whenever you need to execute a project, regardless of its size. Evaluation is a continuous process that is advisable for any project and implementation. We went through a summary of a standard deployment process to learn more about successfully deploying Office 365. You have also learned about the various service descriptions within Office 365, and learned which Office 365 service maps to which Office 365 plan and how to map them with each other. You also learned about their service limits and how to analyze their vulnerabilities in order to always keep them updated.

You now have more information that will help you to understand the fundamentals of Office 365.

In the next chapter, you will learn the basic workloads of Office 365. It will cover the three most used workloads of Office 365 to help you get started quickly.

# 3
# Office 365 Basic Workloads

In this chapter, you will learn or understand more about the most used workloads on Office 365. This chapter will cover the following topics:

- Exchange
- SharePoint
- Skype for Business and Microsoft Teams

With this foundation, you will learn more about each service and how to use them in the base system.

## Microsoft Exchange Online

Microsoft Exchange Online is the email service provided by Microsoft. At the time of writing, the most current version is Exchange 2016. This version was designed with Office 365 in mind, specifically to support multiple tenants in each Exchange organization, with the required logical separation and security controls in place.

The main function of Exchange is to provide a robust and secure email platform that can be used to communicate, make appointments, manage tasks, and organize emails in inboxes.

Exchange server is an enterprise class server that was first launched in 1996 and is currently the most widely-used email system in organizations. It provides a rich set of features such as:

- Routing and transport rules
- Encrypted and secure mail
- In-place hold that allows you to retain emails forever
- eDiscovery features to search for specific content throughout the whole organization

Microsoft Exchange Online is divided into three main workloads, depending on where the mail is stored and what the destination is:

- **Exchange Online Protection (EOP)**: It is a Microsoft service that protects the Exchange platform from malware and spam.
- **Exchange Online**: Exchange Online is the main component of the Exchange platform and where the user data resides.
- **Exchange Online Archive**: It is a system that is used for archiving the email that is not needed in an offline device. Some plans have an unlimited storage quota.

The following diagram shows how email messages go through each of the Exchange platform components:

When Office 365 first receives an email, it goes through EOP and the message hygiene is analyzed; a set of algorithms are run to detect whether the message is safe to be delivered to its destination. After the email has passed through EOP, it goes to the Exchange Online mailbox, where you normally work with your inbox and folders. The last service is the archive, which is the part of the platform that handles old emails as a secondary mailbox.

In Exchange Online, you can choose from two separate plans, **Plan 1** and **Plan 2**. The main differences between these plans are as follows:

| Exchange Online plan | Plan 1 | Plan 2 |
|---|---|---|
| Capacity in primary mailbox | 50 GB | 100 GB |
| Capacity in archive | 50 GB | Unlimited |
| Communications | Not available | Instant messaging |
| Retention and preservation | Not available | In-place hold |

It is possible, in the same tenant, to have different subscriptions and combine the products needed for each organization to accommodate its needs at any point in time. However, each user can only be assigned one plan for each workload.

You can switch licenses at any time, but it is advised that the operation of the switch be done simultaneously, and not in two steps, to avoid removing and then adding the license. These simultaneous operations will evict, for example, the deletion of the mailbox and a reconnect to the same user which may cause some issues.

When you remove a license, the data is removed, and you have 30 days to recover it, if it was a mistake. Unless the data is under a legal hold, after 30 days of being deleted, it will no longer be recoverable.

# Exchange Online Protection

Exchange Online Protection configuration is integrated into the **Exchange Admin Center** (**EAC**).

This service was created to protect the Exchange system. It holds the responsibility of protecting, filtering, and maintaining the hygiene of all emails, as a protective layer, before they hit the inbox of the end users.

As a layer that exists outside of the Exchange core, it creates a protective shield that mitigates some security risks. This system was created as a distributed computational platform, across all Microsoft data centers, to have the ability to scan, protect, and deliver legitimate emails in the fastest way possible.

The view of EOP administration is shown in the following screenshot:

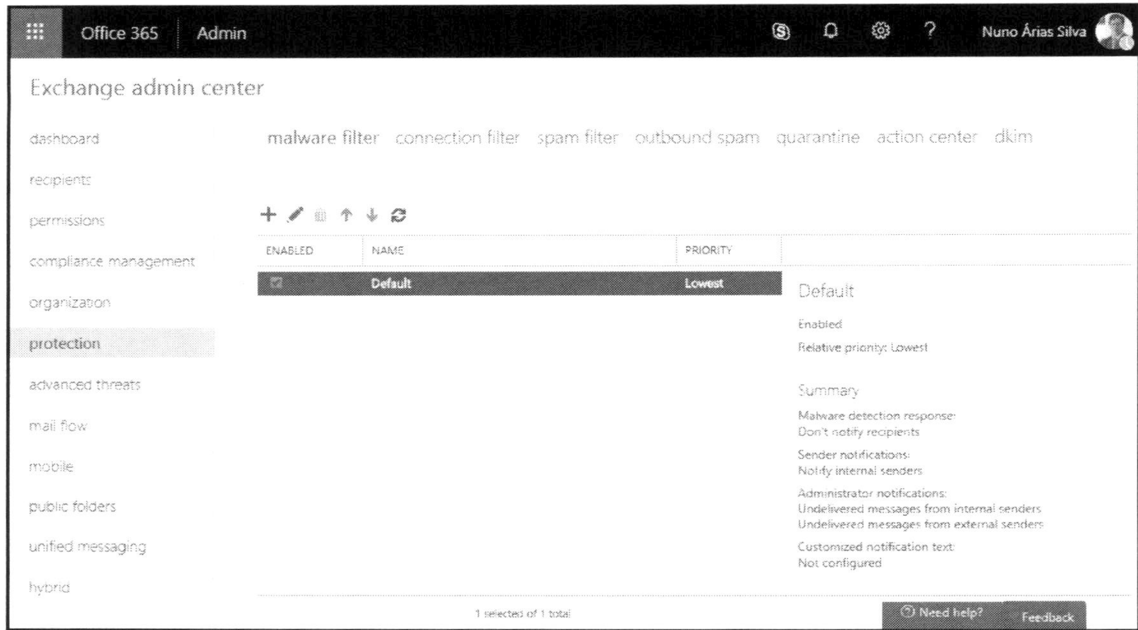


# Exchange Online

Microsoft Exchange Online is the system where all the main actions of the users happen, and that is why it is a core part of the platform. It is where users have their inboxes, calendars, and so on, and where they access the services that they need for their daily tasks, either using a mobile, tablet, or other devices like a PC.

In Exchange Online, there are some limits to avoid behaviors that could damage your reputation. For example, it's only possible to send 30 emails per minute from a user's mailbox. If you need to send emails in bulk, for a marketing campaign, for example, it is advised that you use third-party services or use other systems with different infrastructures.

Here, you can see the view of a mailbox in Office 365, using Outlook Online:

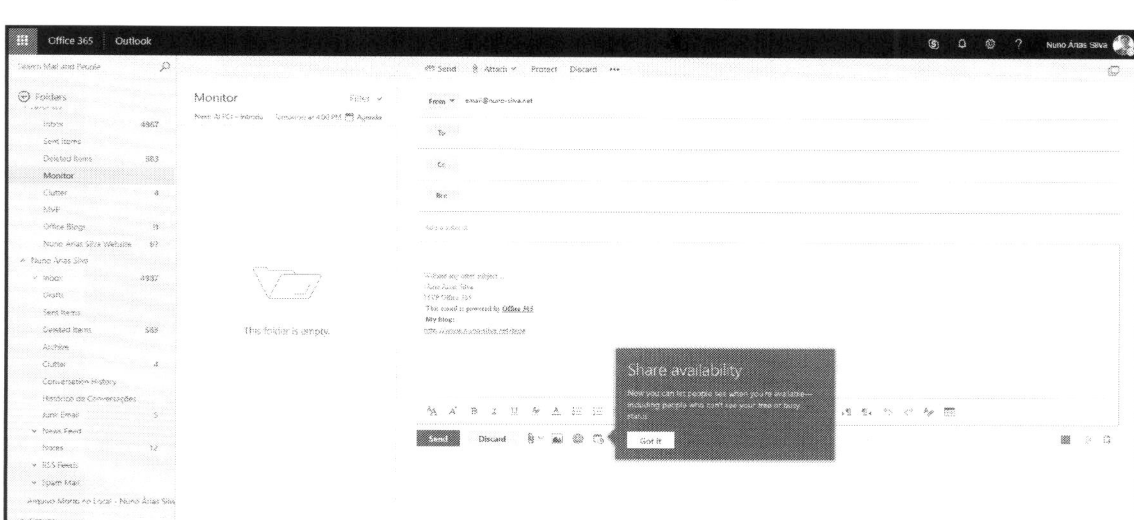


# Exchange Online Archive

The Microsoft Exchange Online Archive is the system that provides the end user with an archive for the emails that are not needed offline. It is a feature that must be enabled by the administrator and will help users with large mailboxes before they hit maximum capacity, by storing older emails in an online archive. As the name says, these emails are only accessible while the user is online, as in, with internet access to Office 365. If, for example, you use Outlook desktop and you have offline cache active to your primary mailbox, you will not have access to the archive if you are working in an offline context, without internet access.

In Exchange Online Plan 2, you have archive with unlimited storage.

The following screenshot shows a view of Exchange Online Archive:

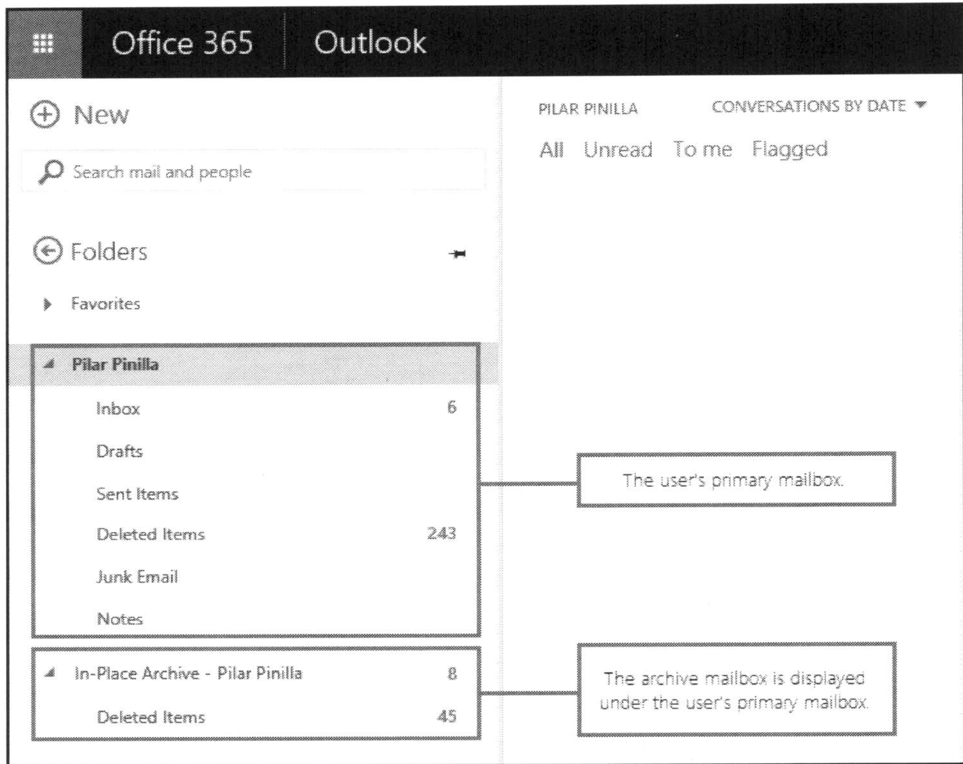


To access EAC, go to `https://portal.office.com`. Select the **Admin** option, as shown in the following screenshot:

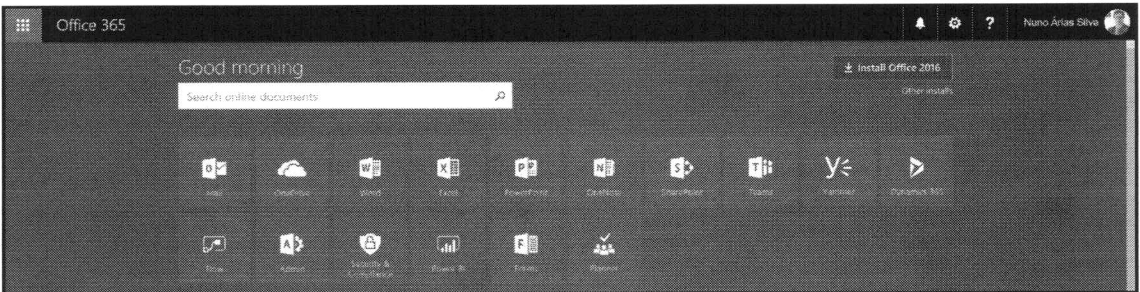

In the Admin center, in the **Admin centers** section, select the **Exchange** option:

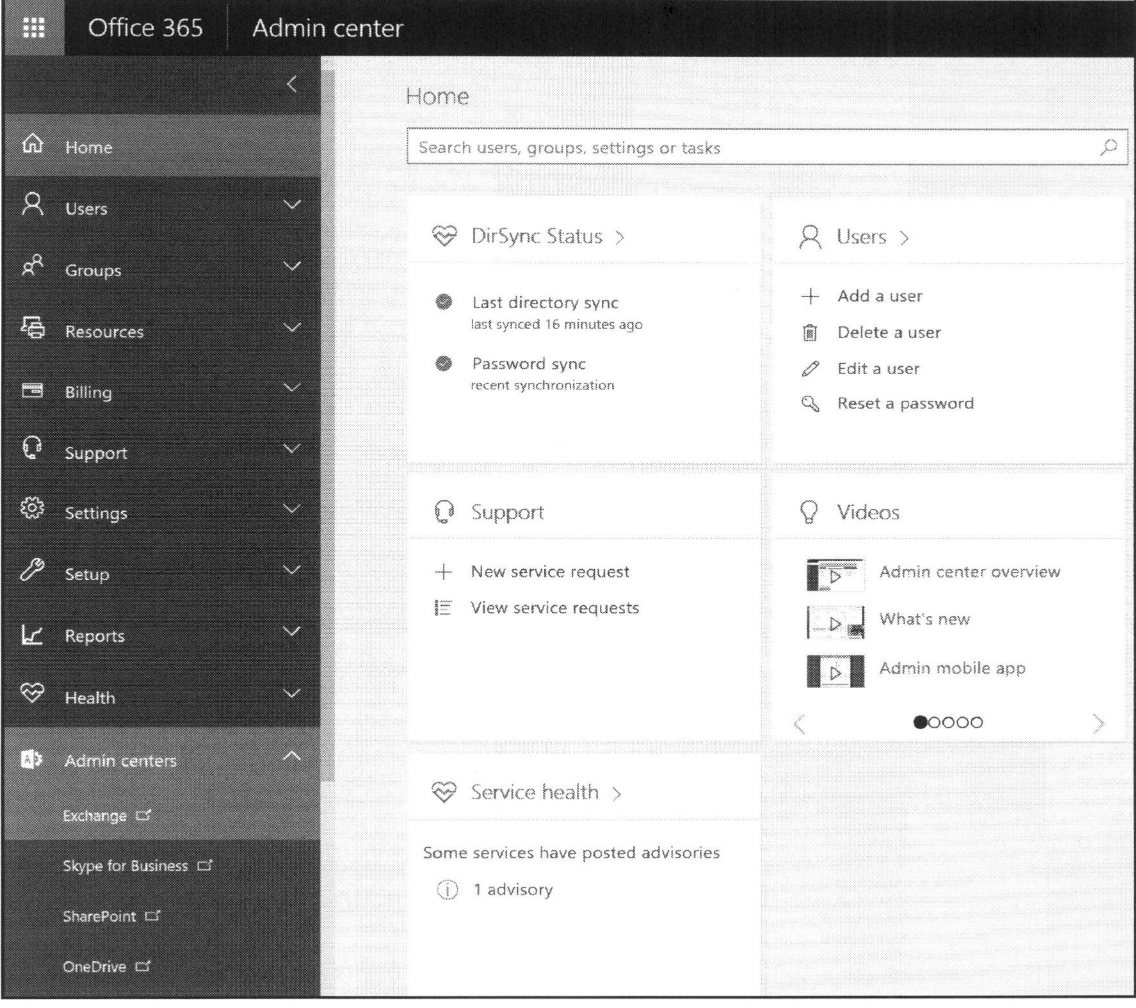

After connecting to Exchange Online administrator, you will have access to a website that allows you to centrally manage everything about Exchange, as shown in the following screenshot:

In `Chapter 7`, *Exchange Online*, we will dive deeper into Exchange Online.

# SharePoint

Microsoft SharePoint is a web-based collaboration platform that allows organizations to manage content in a secure and central place, and is meant for teams to work together. It can be used to create the intranet portal for the organization, as well as different types of sites, such as team sites, Wikis, document repositories, and much more. These sites can store and organize information, which can be shared with others, and accessed from almost any device. Microsoft has launched specific mobile applications for the most used mobile operating systems—Android, iOS, and Windows Mobile.

SharePoint Online is the cloud hosted version of SharePoint server technology that started as SharePoint Portal Server 2001 and whose current version is named SharePoint Server 2016. At the time of writing, Microsoft has already announced the next version, SharePoint Server 2019, to be launched by the end of 2018.

As a productivity service built for collaboration and document management, SharePoint is well suited to serve as the organization's intranet. With a huge set of features and out-of-the-box integration with other Office 365 services such as Microsoft Flow and PowerApps, it can also support business processes and applications.

SharePoint Online has many capabilities that enable scenarios, such as:

- Intranet portals
- Extranet portals (supporting external access to company information)
- Collaboration portals, as a place for teamwork, or for specific projects
- Document center leveraging metadata, workflows, document templates, and information policies
- Enterprise search supporting powerful relevance-based faceted search across multiple content stores
- Workflows either using its internal workflow engine or Microsoft Flow
- Forms both using native forms or more advanced forms based on Microsoft PowerApps

Being a highly extensible platform, you may also develop your own custom applications (called **SharePoint Add-Ins**), or install applications developed by third parties and made available through the SharePoint store, to provide additional capabilities to SharePoint.

For SharePoint Online, there are individual plans—SharePoint Online **Plan 1** and **Plan 2**, which you can buy separately.

The main differences between the plans are as follows:

| **SharePoint Online plan** | **Plan 1** | **Plan 2** |
|---|---|---|
| Capacity of OneDrive | 1 TB | Unlimited * |
| Capacity on archive | 50 GB | Unlimited |
| Retention and preservation | Not available | In-place hold |

* For subscriptions of five or more users, Microsoft will initially provide 5 TB of OneDrive storage per user, but allows customers to request additional storage space by contacting Microsoft support.

The following screenshot shows an example of a team site in SharePoint Online:

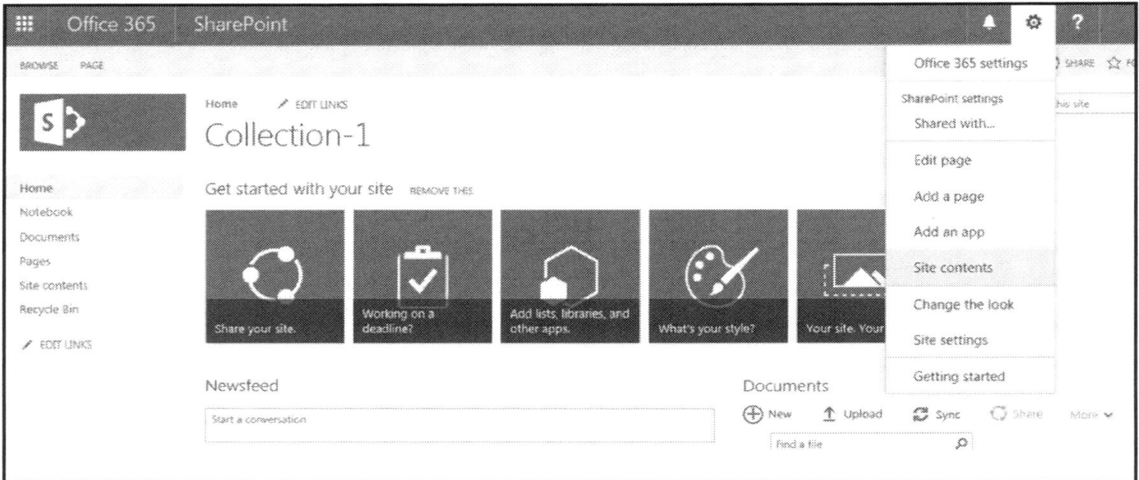


To access the SharePoint Online admin center, go to `https://portal.office.com`. Select the **Admin** option as shown in the following screenshot:

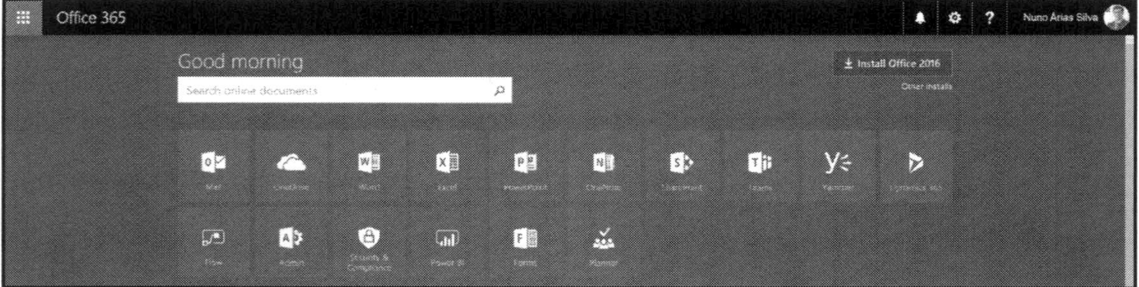


In the Admin center, in the **Admin centers** section, select **SharePoint** option, as shown in the following screenshot:

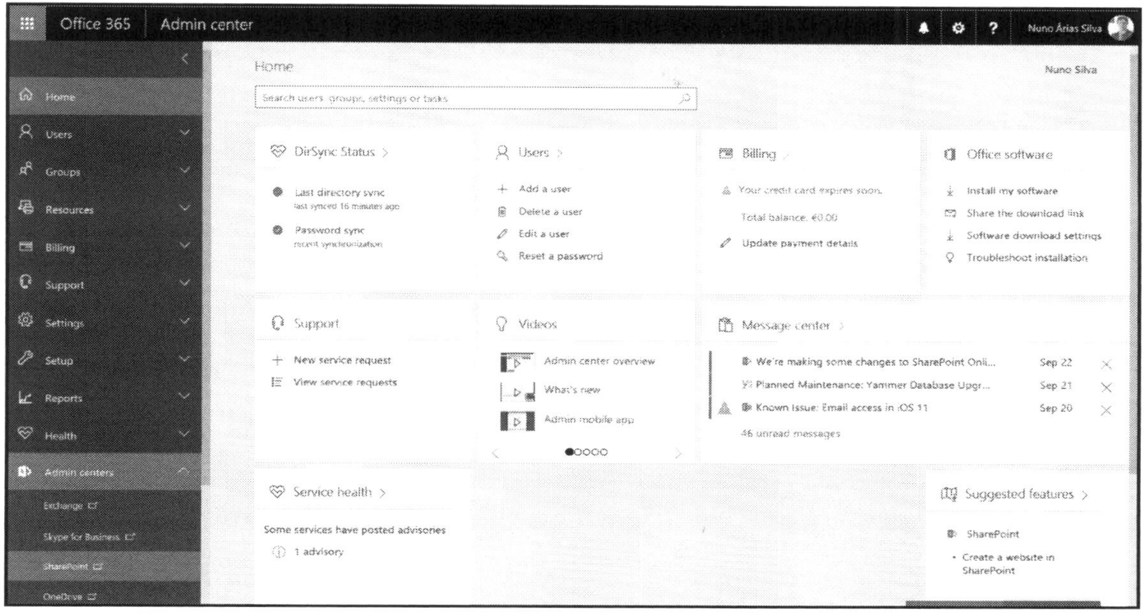


After connecting to SharePoint Online administrator, you will have access to a central place to administer SharePoint, as shown in the following screenshot:

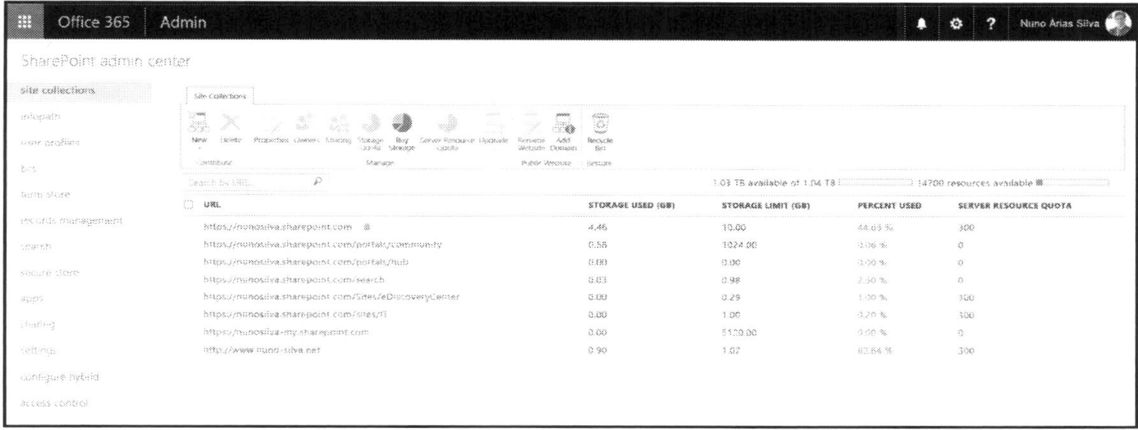


In `Chapter 8`, *SharePoint Online*, we will dive deeper into SharePoint Online.

# Skype for Business and Microsoft Teams

Besides SharePoint, Office 365 includes two other important tools in the collaboration space—Skype for Business and Microsoft Teams.

## Skype for Business

Microsoft Skype for Business is the enterprise unified communications tool that supports chats, audio and video calls, conferencing, and online meetings.

Connect your teams through the applications they use on a daily basis, such as Office. With Skype for Business Online, you can make things easier within your organization, with one platform for calling, conferencing, video, and sharing.

This journey started in 2003 when Microsoft released the Live Communications Server 2003, followed by Microsoft Office Communicator and Lync, which later became Skype for Business in 2014. Skype for Business is available across devices, both mobile and desktop.

To access the Skype for Business Online admin center, go to `https://portal.office.com`. Select the **Admin** option, as shown in the following screenshot:

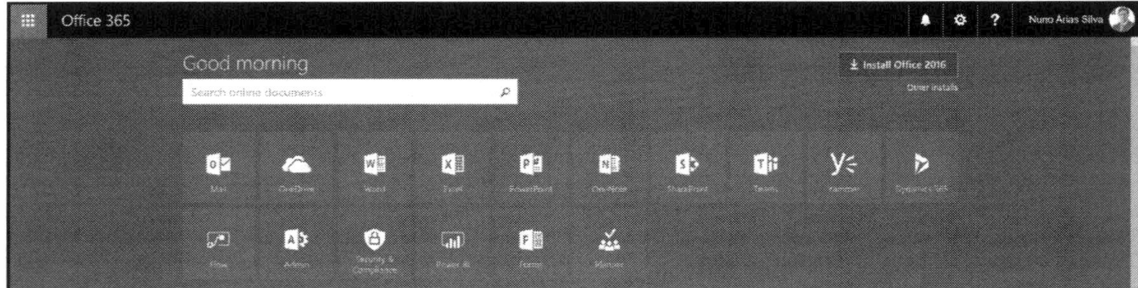

In the **Admin centers** section, select **Skype for Business** option, as shown in the following screenshot:

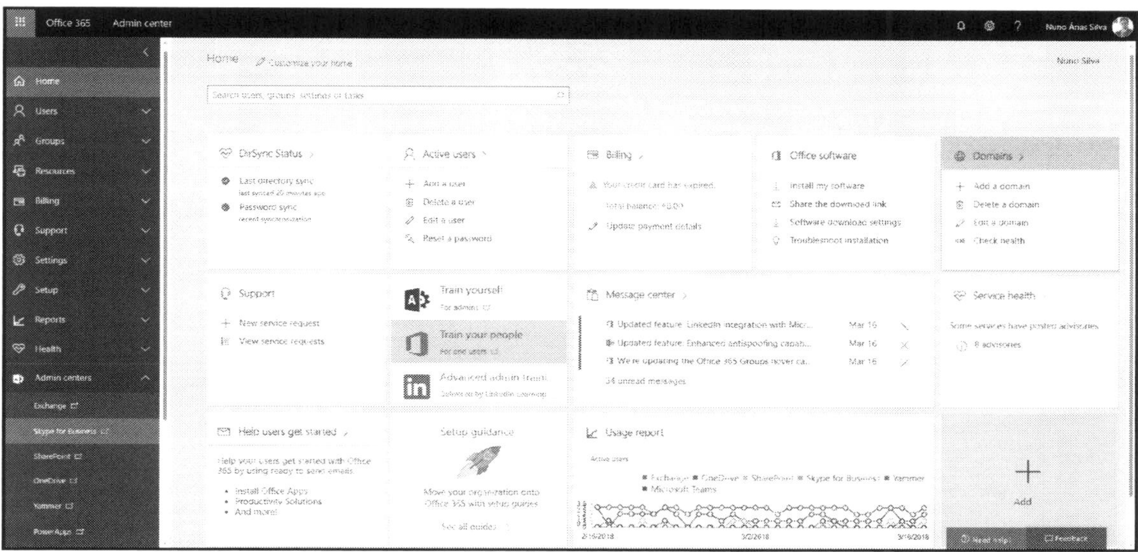


After connecting to the Skype for Business admin center, you will have access to a central place to administer Skype for Business, as shown in the following screenshot:

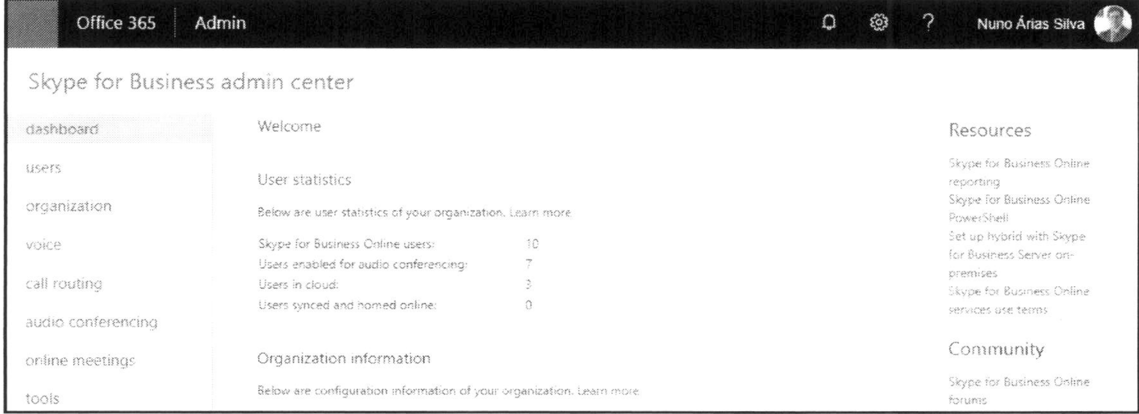

# Microsoft Teams

Microsoft Teams is a new tool in Office 365. It is the next generation of collaboration tool, designed to be the hub for teamwork, with deep integration with SharePoint, email, chat, and other tools.

It became generally available on March 14, 2017 and after just 1 year, thousands of organizations adopted this powerful tool included in the Office 365 suite. It has become the ultimate hub for teamwork, allowing team members to perform all their actions without having to leave the tools interface. Its impressive extensibility enables several integration scenarios, which also contribute to its popularity in organizations.

The following screenshot shows the Microsoft Teams client application:

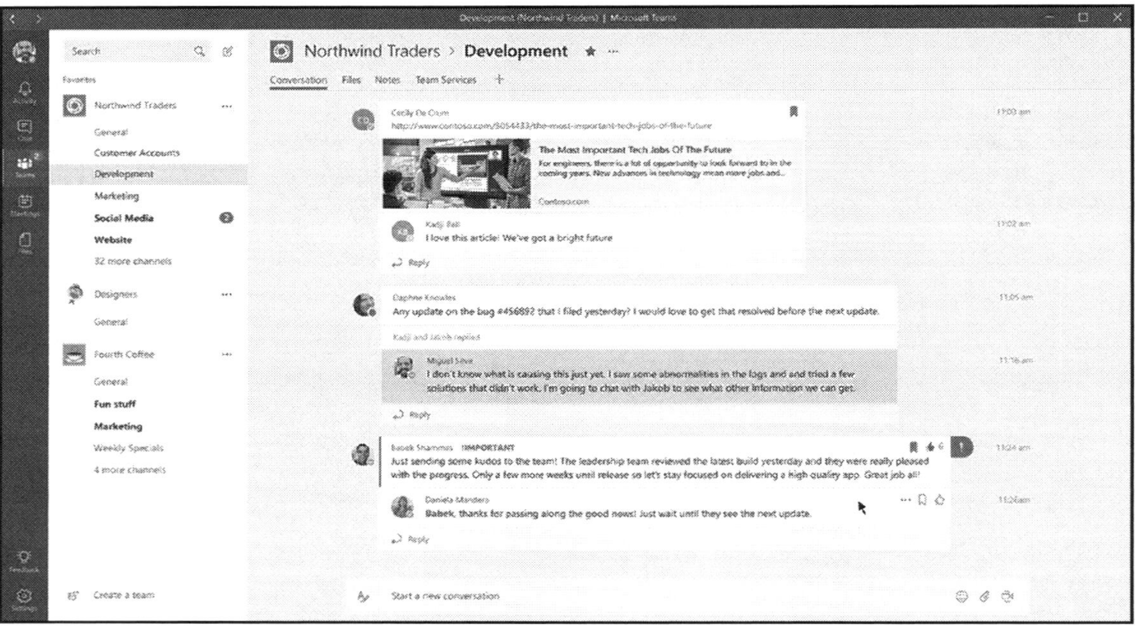


Microsoft is bringing Skype for Business Online capabilities into Microsoft Teams, and you can read more here at `https://blogs.office.com/en-us/2017/09/25/a-new-vision-for-intelligent-communications-in-office-365/`.

To access Microsoft Teams configuration, go to `https://portal.office.com`. Select the **Admin** option, as shown in the following screenshot:

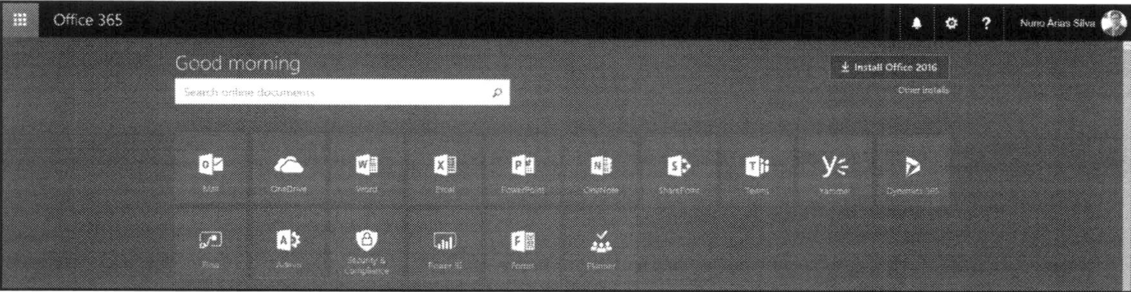


In the Admin center, in the **Settings** section, select **Services & add-ins** option, as shown in the following screenshot:

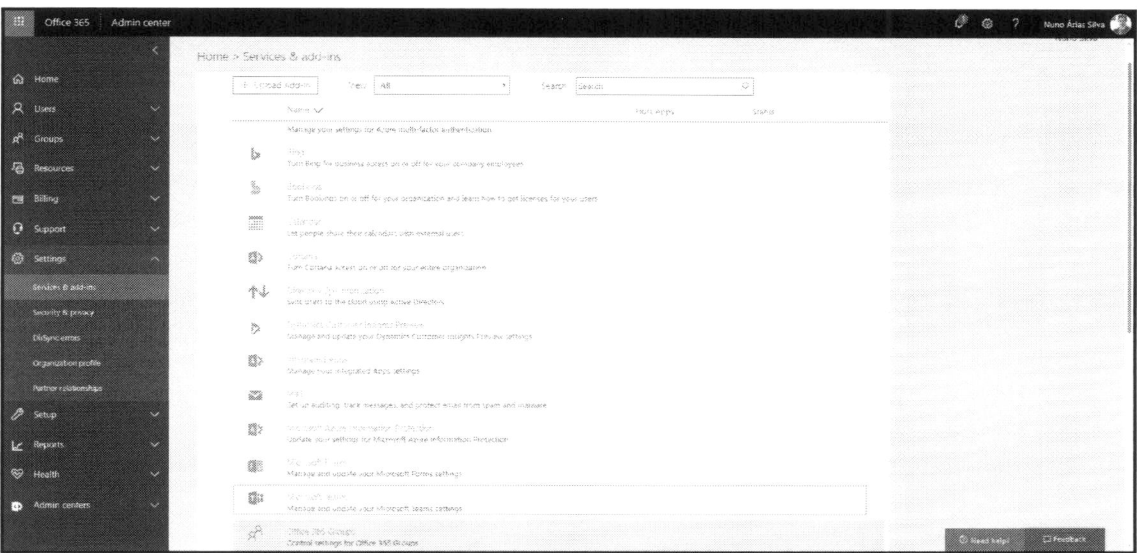

In the **Services & add-ins** section, select **Microsoft Teams** option:

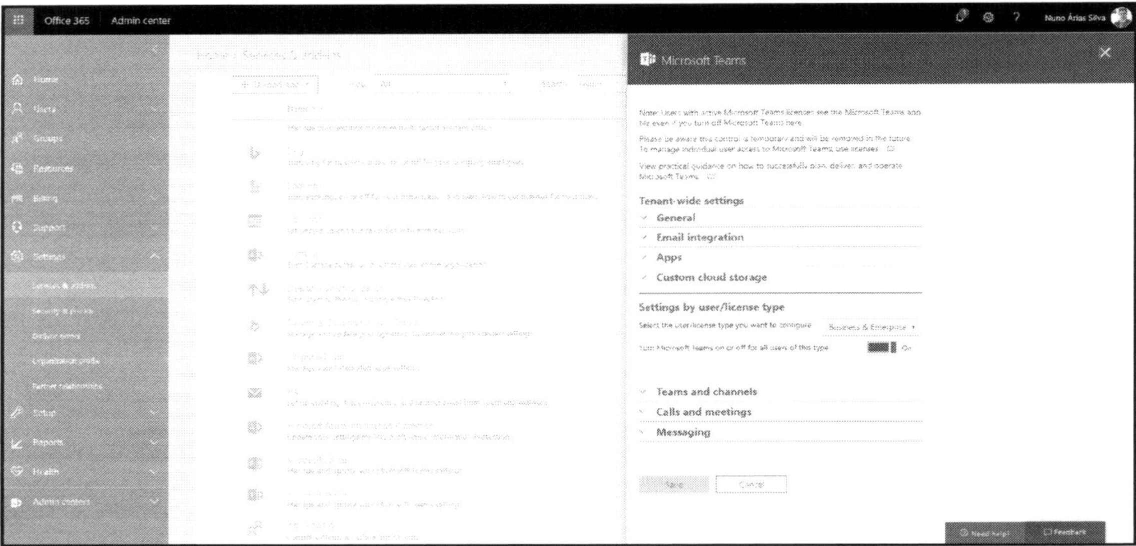


In this panel, you have the general configuration of Microsoft Teams where you can configure several settings. To get access to the client version of Microsoft Teams, download it at `https://teams.microsoft.com/downloads`:

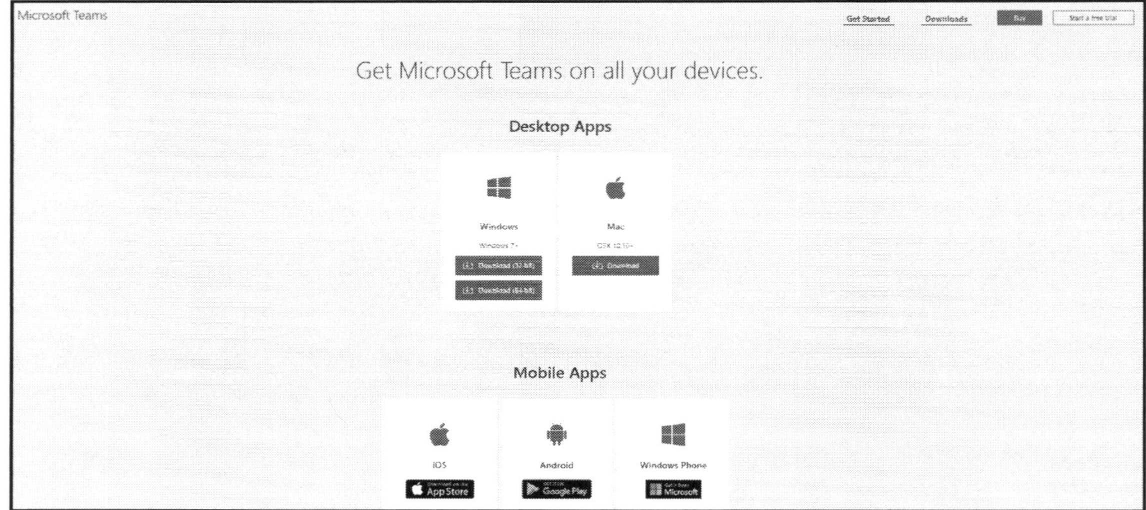

On this page, you have access to the client versions both for desktop and mobile platforms.

To get access to new features and see what is coming, go to the Roadmap page of Office 365 at `https://products.office.com/en-US/business/office-365-roadmap`:

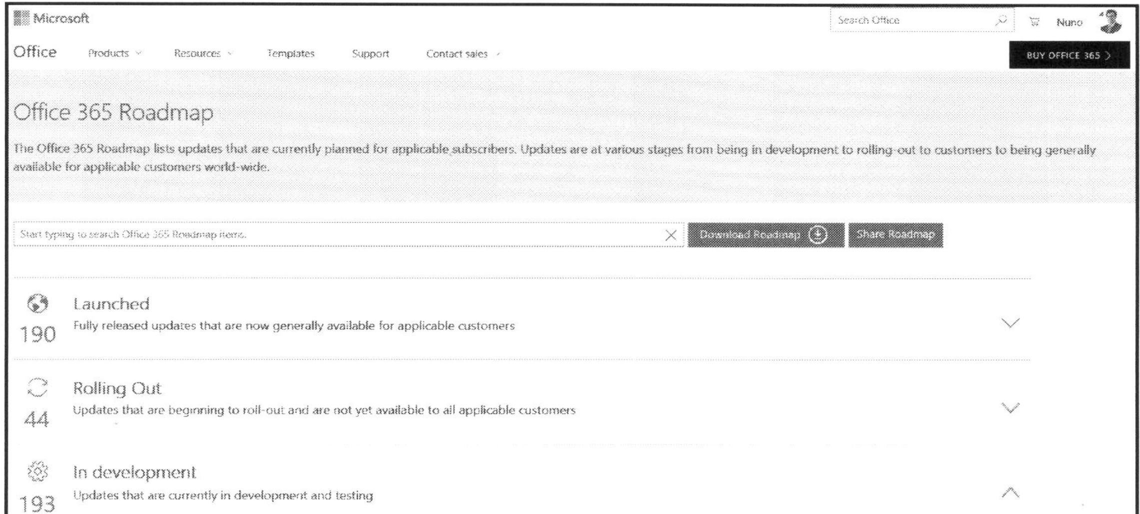


# Summary

In this chapter, you have learned about the most widely used workloads in Office 365. Exchange Online is the platform that is most used to collaborate and communicate, supporting workloads such as emails and calendars. SharePoint Online is the collaboration platform used for intranet portals and business processes. Skype for Business Online is a real-time communication platform.

You now have more information about the most widely used workloads, the contexts they are commonly applied to, as well as how to access their management portals.

In the next chapter, you will learn basic and advanced scenarios of authentication and identities used in Office 365. The chapter will cover the three most widely used architectural scenarios for identity and authentication.

# 4
# Identities and Authentication

In this chapter, you will learn and understand more about identities and the implementation of the different authentication scenarios supported in Office 365. These topics are discussed across the following three sections:

- Azure AD
- Core identity scenarios
- Office 365 management

With this foundation, you will learn more about each scenario and decide which one best fits your organization.

## Azure AD – user management

Azure AD was the first service made available on Azure, and it is the authority service for user management in Microsoft Office 365. It is a core service, built on a global infrastructure, meant to provide a base identity management system to each organization.

*What is identity management?* It is a foundational system for any environment, which maintains the identity of each user object in a central location and controls access to other users, resources, and objects of that environment.

Identity management has two components—authentication and authorization, as shown in the following figure:

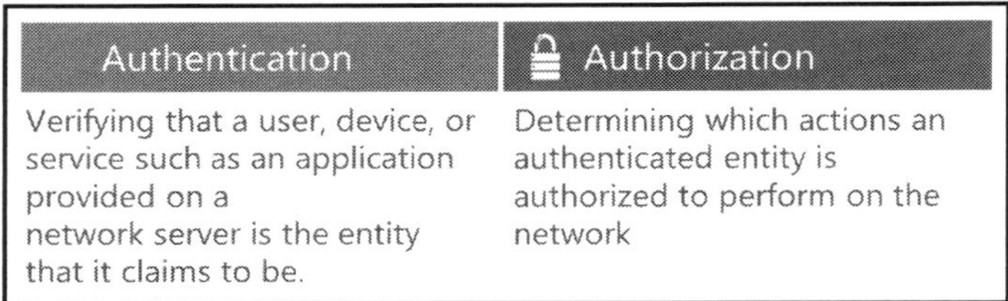


As shown in the following figure, your organization may want to connect its on-premises AD with Office 365:

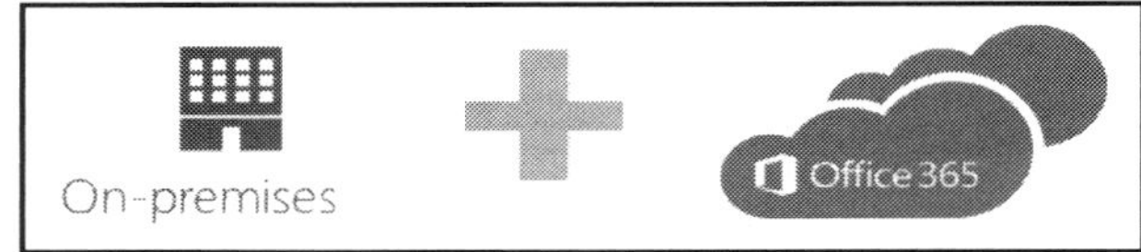


# What is Microsoft Azure AD?

The following points describes the Microsoft Azure AD:

- Core service used as the identity provider for Office 365 and other Azure services
- It has the ability to be integrated as a solution for enterprise identity
- It has the capability to be used as a **single sign-on** (**SSO**) solution for Office 365 as well as other applications and partners

# What is Microsoft Azure AD not?

Microsoft Azure AD is not the same as deploying your on-premises AD domain controllers to Microsoft Azure. However, it is possible to convert an Azure AD into domain controllers running on Azure in a simple step. This is not necessary for Office 365 though.

It is possible to have your AD running on Azure **Virtual Machines** (**VMs**), and it is advised that you deploy the whole environment in a central and high-availability environment.

# Core identity scenarios

In Microsoft Office 365, we have three basic authentication scenarios:

- Cloud identity
- Directory and password synchronization
- Federated identity

Each scenario fits a different type of organization, as explained in the following figure:

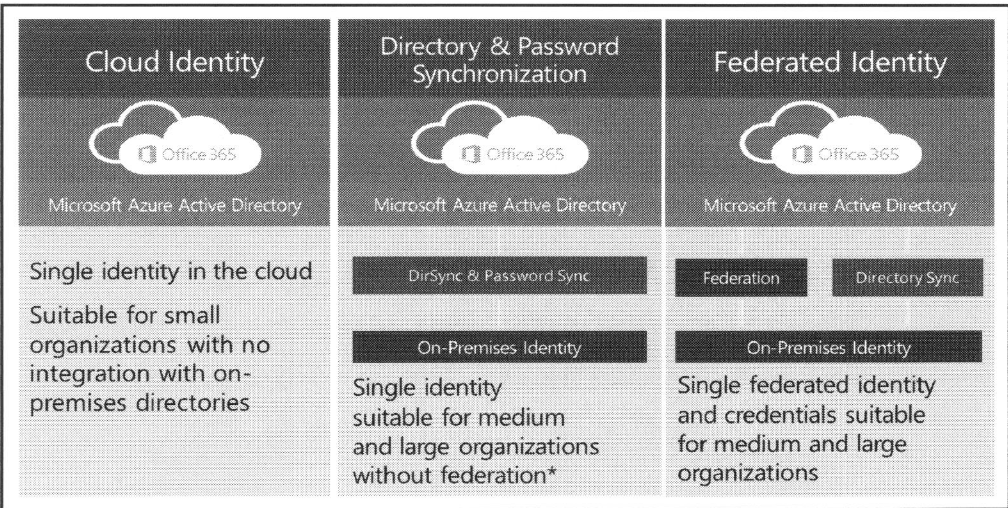


## Cloud identity

The cloud identity scenario is the default option for all Office 365 environments. Every user created in Office 365 is provisioned in Azure AD. It is also possible to create users directly on the Azure portal and through Azure PowerShell.

The information that you fill on an Azure portal is used in your Office 365 environment, but, for example, passwords are only stored in Azure AD. This happens not only for security reasons, but also because Azure AD is the authentication authority for Office 365.

Only Azure PowerShell supports all the available features; that is why, it is used in most organizations, with scripts to automate some processes and to perform bulk operations such as assigning permissions, adding licenses, or changing properties.

# Directory and password synchronization

This is the most used scenario in organizations because many of them have started the identity management journey using AD installed on on-premises servers as their own identity management system.

This authentication scenario leverages your existing identity management architecture by expanding your on-premises AD and synchronizing your users and groups to Azure AD using a tool called **Azure AD Connect**. This tool is responsible for synchronizing the AD objects to the cloud, namely, users, security groups, distribution groups, and contacts.

It is also possible to synchronize the password hash to Azure AD, providing the user with the experience of logging in with his/her **User Principal Name** (**UPN**), which is usually his/her email address, and with the same password used in the on-premises AD.

In AD environments, the key features for this scenario are:

- Best experience in most contexts
- Support for exchange coexistence scenarios
- Coupled with **Active Directory Federation Services** (**AD FS**) provide the best option for federation and synchronization of identities
- Supports password synchronization at no additional cost
- Does not require any additional software licenses

The following figure summarizes the architecture for an environment where the source identity is managed on-premises and then synchronized to Azure AD:

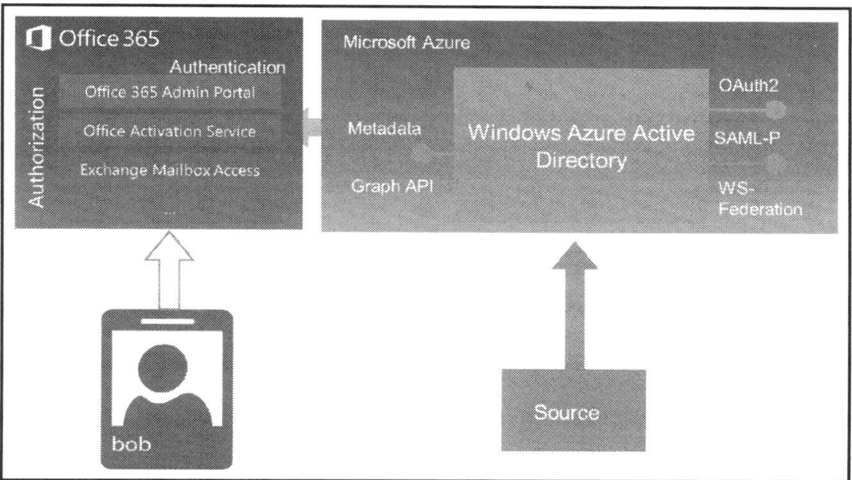


Some facts about synchronization are as follows:

- Any existing user, group, or contact object that is deleted from on-premises is deleted from Office 365.
- Existing user objects that are disabled on-premises are disabled in Office 365.
- However, licenses are not automatically unassigned. It is possible to use a feature named license management using groups, which requires an additional license called **Enterprise Mobility Suite** (**EMS**) E3 or E5. You can read more about this process at `https://docs.microsoft.com/en-us/azure/active-directory/active-directory-licensing-group-assignment-azure-portal`.
- Objects are recoverable within 30 days of deletion.

# How synchronization works

The synchronization happens within the Azure AD Connect tool and follows the steps described here:

- **Sync cycle step 1**: This is the first step where the process import users, groups, and contacts from source AD forest
- **Sync cycle step 2**: The second step is where the users, groups, and contacts are imported from Microsoft Online services through **Autodiscover Web Services** (**AWS**)
- **Sync cycle step 3**: This is the process where the users, groups, and contacts are exported, that do not already exist in Microsoft Online services

The following figure shows these steps for an environment that has on-premises email and a synchronized identity in a hybrid scenario with Exchange:

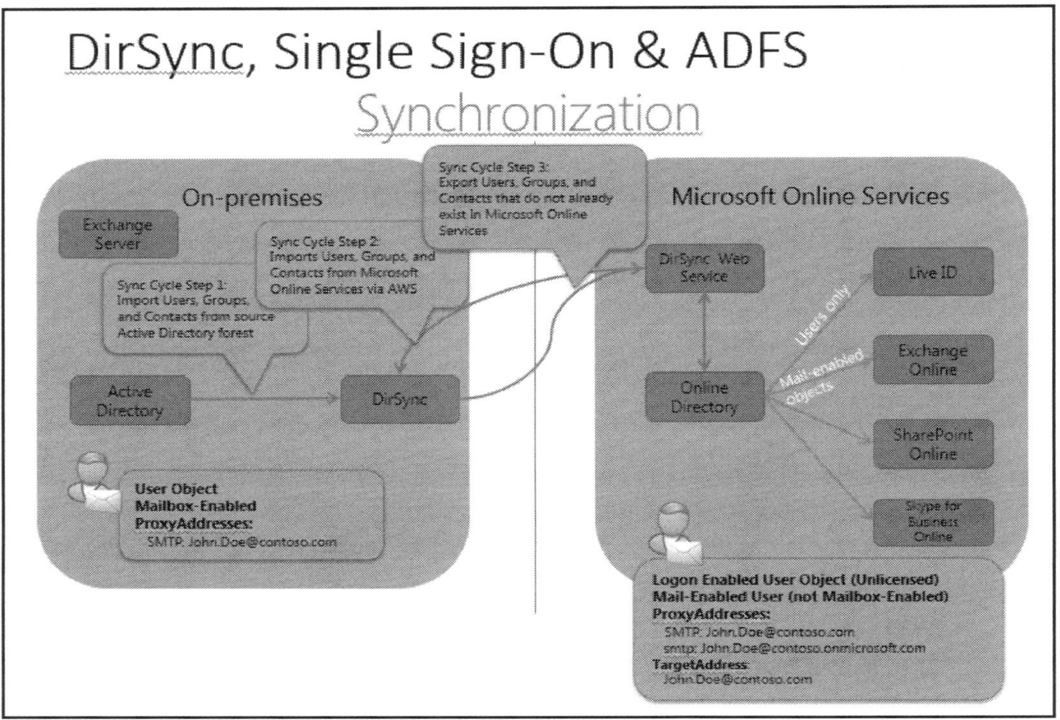


# Federated identity

This scenario uses AD FS to provide the true SSO experience to the end users. With this solution, it is also required to have the synchronization of your on-premises AD with Azure AD using the Microsoft Azure AD Connect.

Most organizations that need an SSO solution use this architecture because besides providing the best possible user experience, it also supports scenarios where companies have security restrictions that, for example, require the authentication to be performed in the on-premises AD infrastructure. With federated identity, a user on a domain-joined computer connected to the company's on-premises infrastructure and logged in to AD will be able to access any of the Office 365 resources and tools transparently, without having to retype a password.

Some features of the federated identity scenario are as follows:

- Single identity and sign-on for on-premises and Office 365 services
- Identities mastered on-premises with a single point of management
- Directory synchronization to synchronize directory objects into Azure AD
- Secure token-based authentication
- Client access control based on IP address with AD FS Proxies
- Strong factor authentication options for additional security with AD FS

The following figure summarizes the architecture for federated identity:

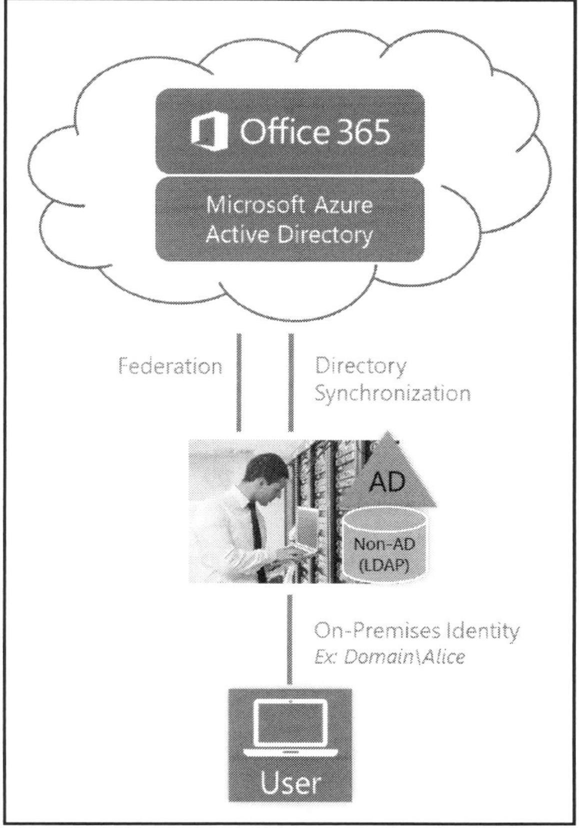

In AD environments, the key features for this scenario are:

- SSO
- Secure token-based authentication
- Support for web and rich clients
- Microsoft supported
- Works with Office 365 hybrid scenarios
- Requires on-premises servers, licenses, and support

The following figure shows a standard design for an AD FS environment. The figure also shows sample scenarios having AD FS infrastructure on premises and AD FS proxies on the DMZ network:

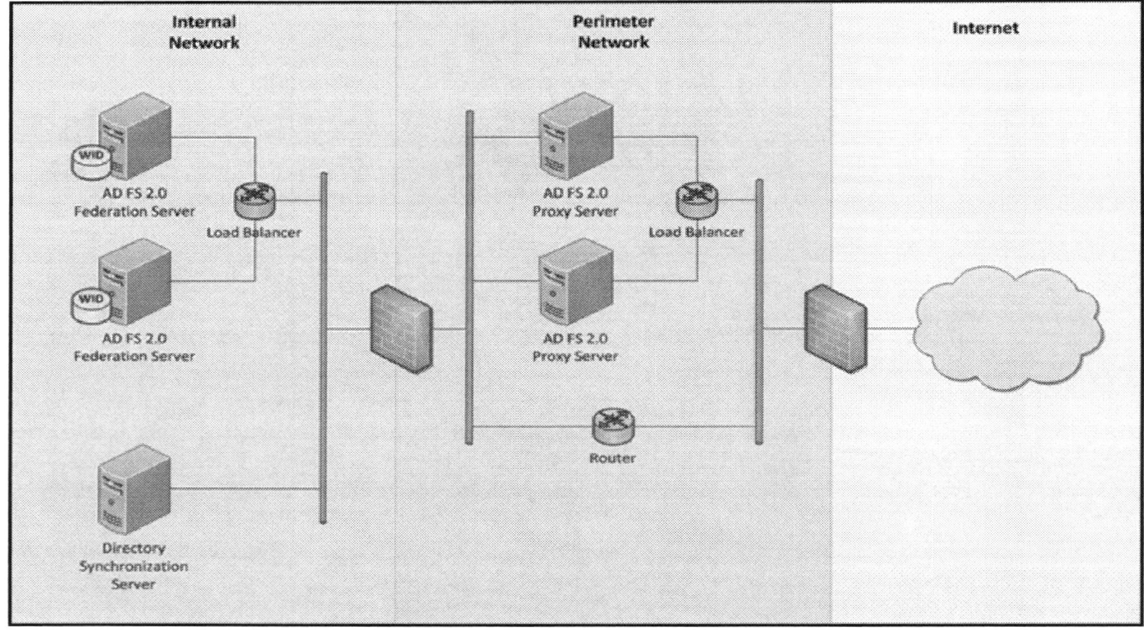

The following figure shows how connections between the on-premises infrastructure and Office 365 are made:

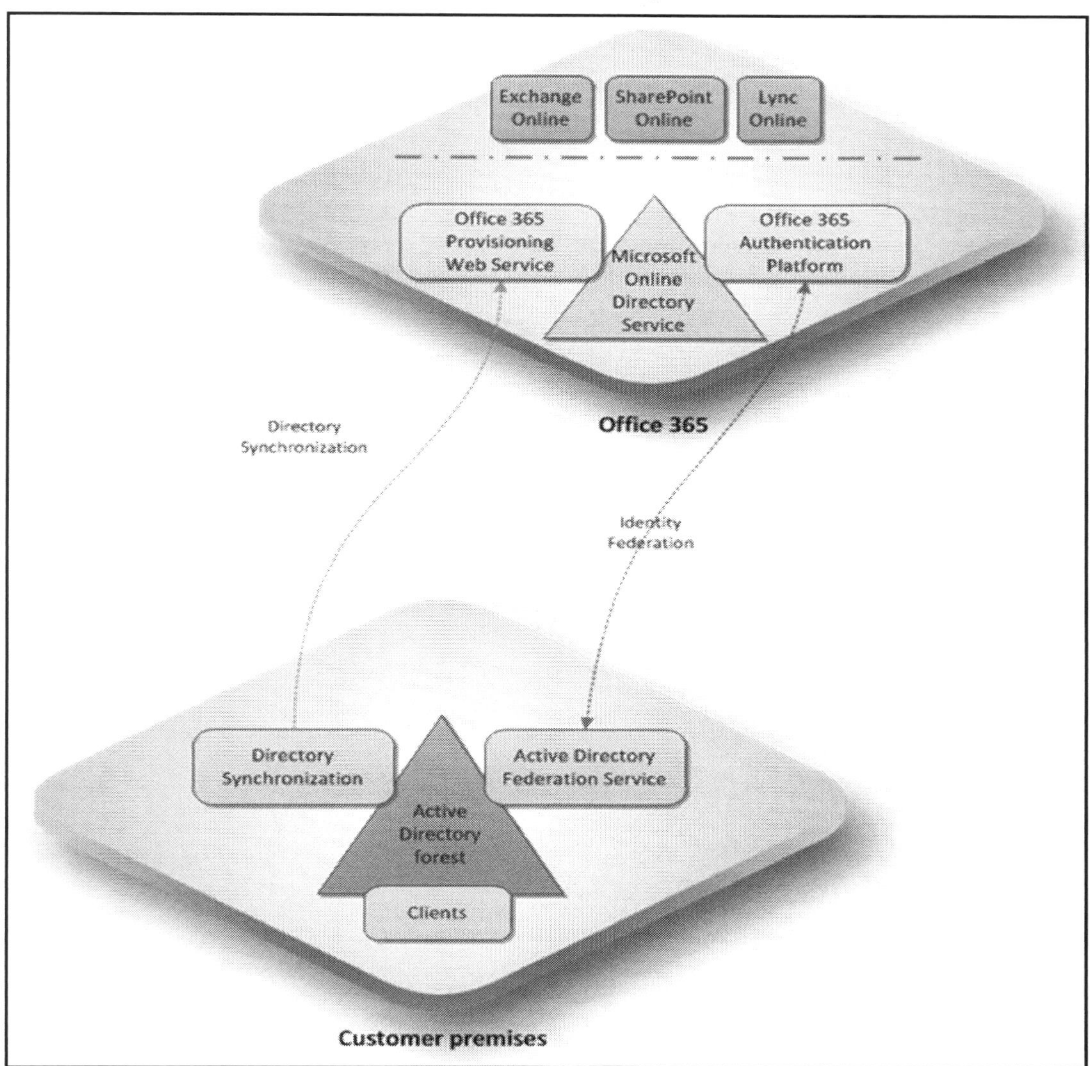

# Other scenarios

You have other scenarios and authentication methods available, namely:

- **Azure Active Directory Seamless Single Sign-On** (**Azure AD Seamless SSO**)
- Password hash synchronization
- Pass-through authentication
- **Multifactor Authentication** (**MFA**)
- Self-service password reset
- Azure AD Basic versus Premium

## Azure AD Seamless SSO

This scenario was created to be used with Pass-through Authentication or password hash synchronization. It is an alternative to the AD FS scenario because it provides the user with the seamless login experience when connected to the on-premises network with a domain joined machine.

The following figure shows how the user interacts with the network to consume Office 365 services:

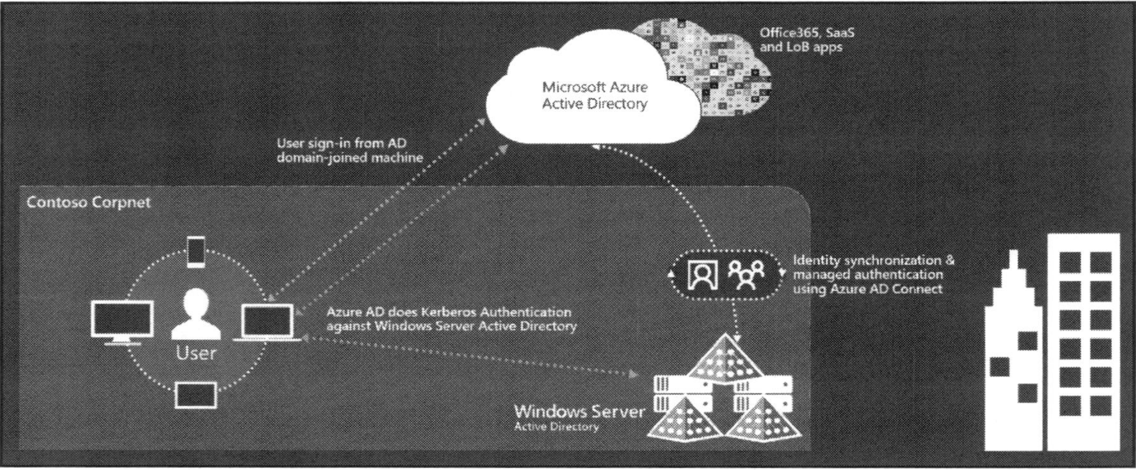

The following figure shows how the request flows when using this scenario to access any application:

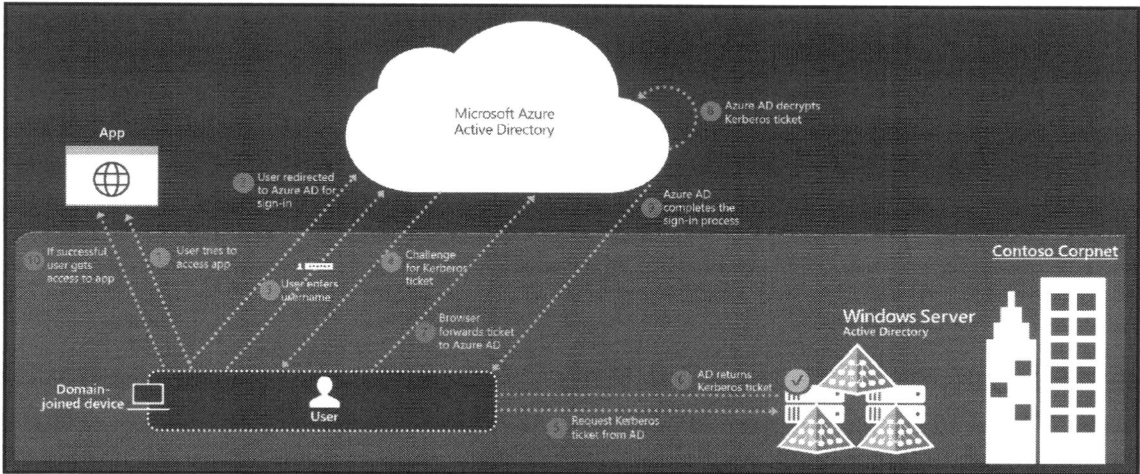


You can read more about this scenario at `https://docs.microsoft.com/en-us/azure/active-directory/connect/active-directory-aadconnect-sso`.

# Password hash synchronization

This is the most common scenario in organizations because it is so easy to set up, and although it does not provide a seamless sign-on experience, users still access Office 365 with a single domain password. It synchronizes the user object from the on-premises AD to Azure AD, including the user's password hash.

The following figure illustrates this scenario, using Azure AD Connect on a sign-on process:

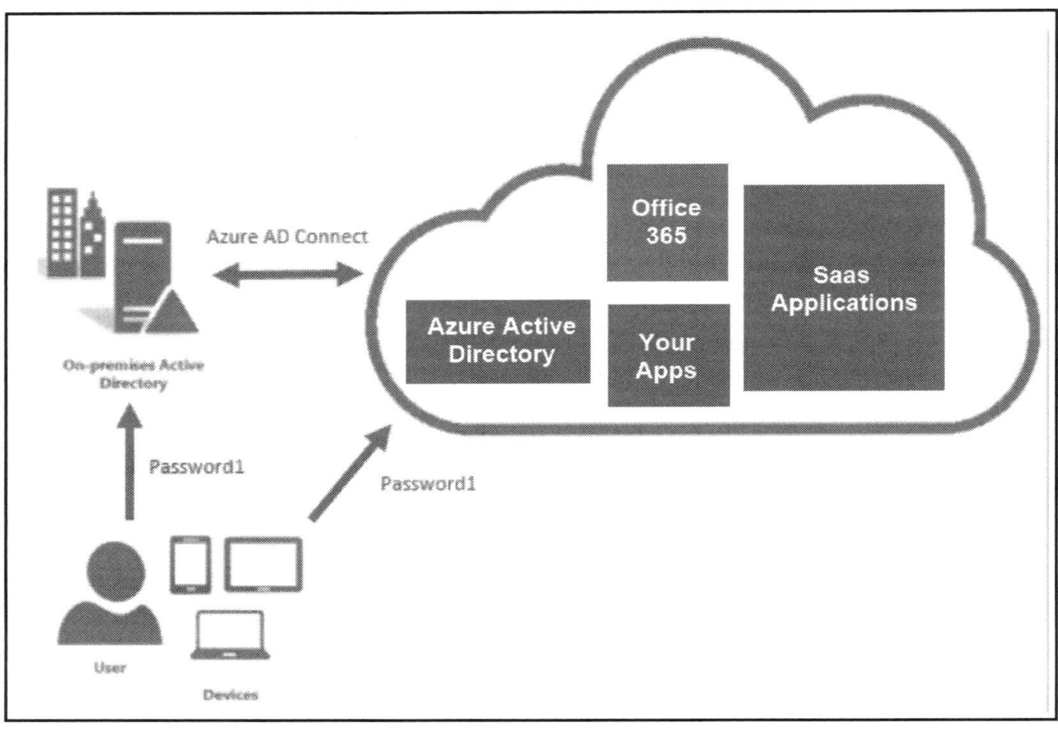


To know more about the synchronization process, check the following figure:

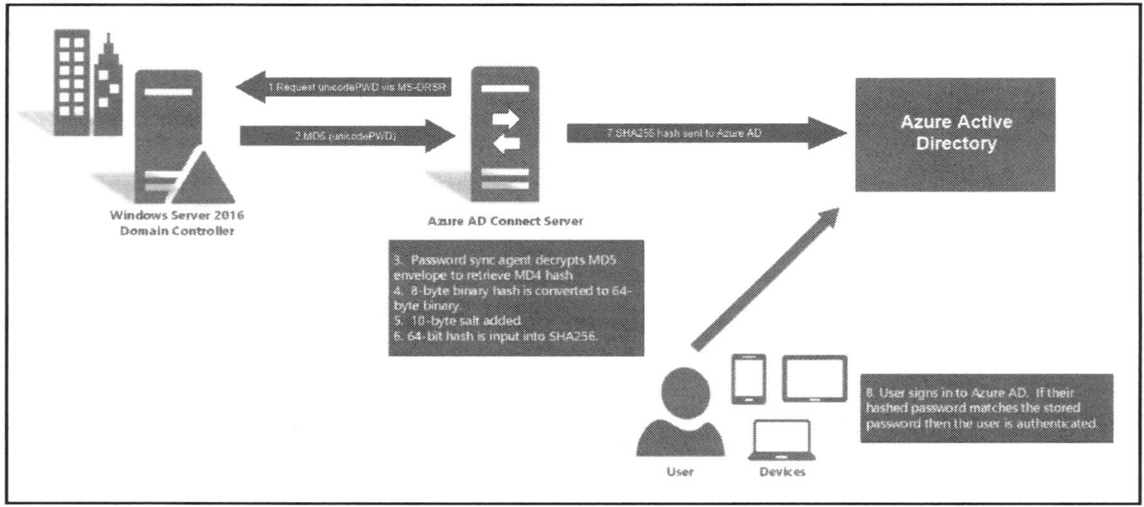

To learn more, continue reading from `https://docs.microsoft.com/en-us/azure/active-directory/connect/active-directory-aadconnectsync-implement-password-synchronization`.

## Pass-through Authentication

This scenario is an alternate scenario to Azure AD Sync with password synchronization, which is usually considered for organizations that have concerns about using user password hashes outside their network. Instead, it uses an agent installed on an on-premises server to connect Azure AD to your domain controllers and perform the authentication process for the user.

The following figure shows this architecture, using an agent that receives the authentication request from Office 365:

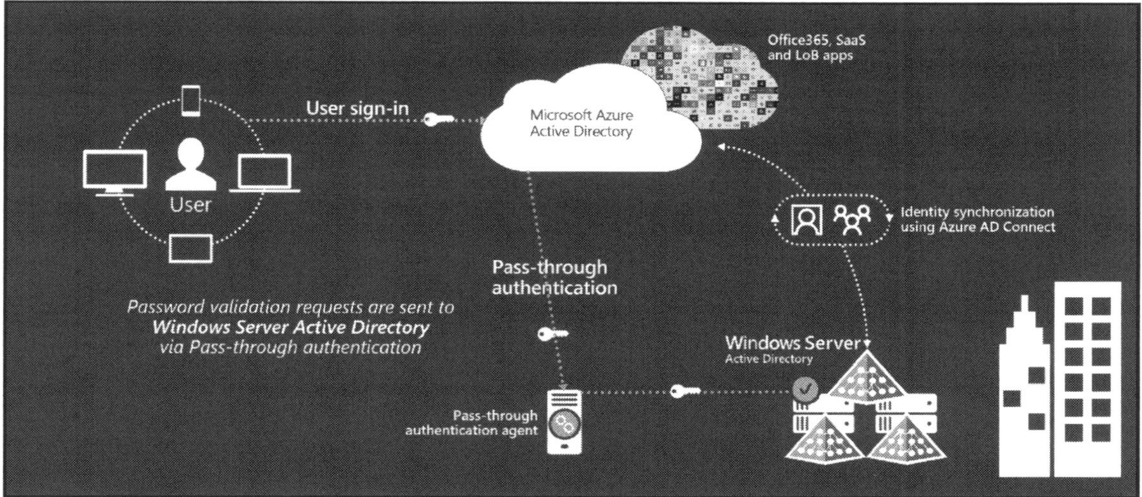

The following figure shows the sign-on process of a user when connecting to Office 365 using Azure AD:

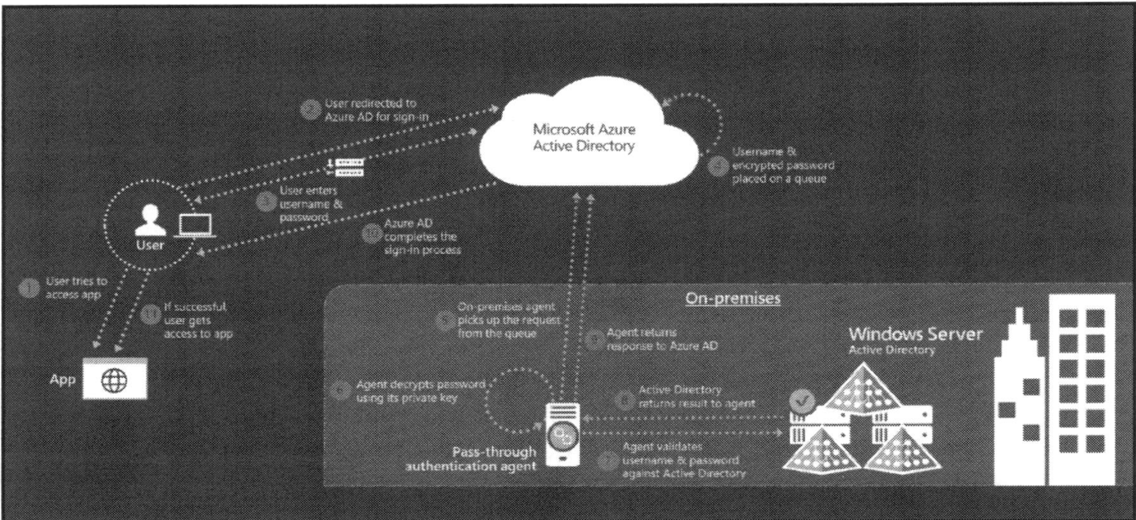


The following figure shows how the agent works in the process of registration:

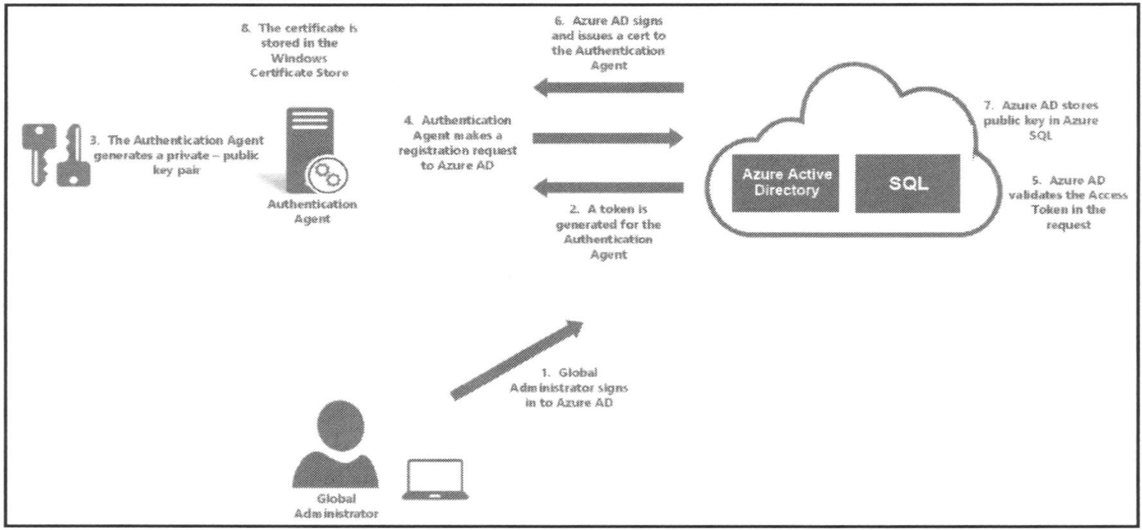

The process of a user when signing on to Office 365 is shown in the following figure:

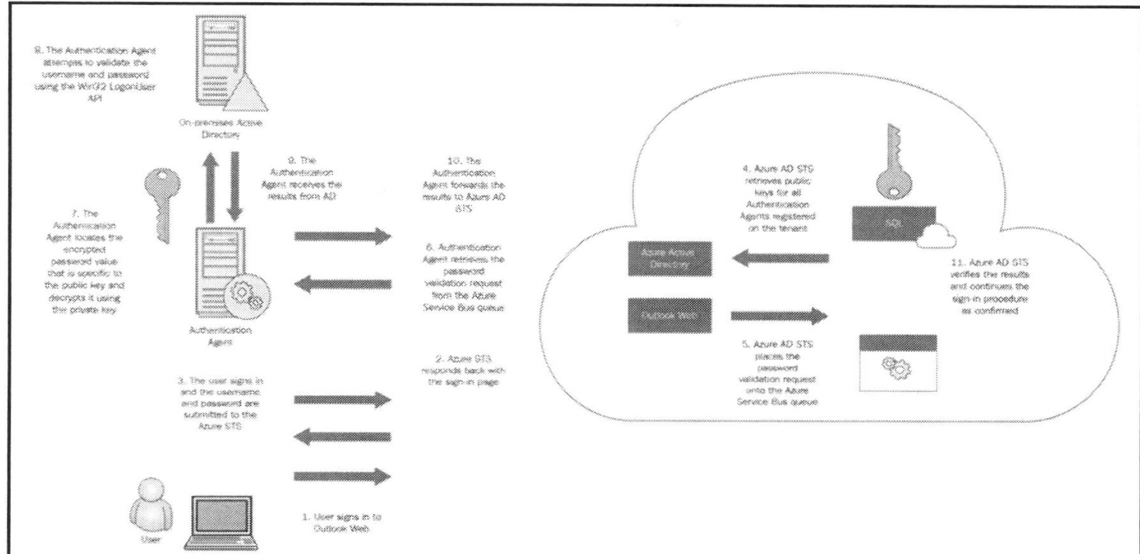


To learn more about Pass-through Authentication, continue reading at `https://docs.microsoft.com/en-us/azure/active-directory/connect/active-directory-aadconnect-pass-through-authentication`.

## MFA

Office 365 with Microsoft Azure AD is an enterprise-level cloud-based identity and access management solution.

You can continue reading *Office 365 Multi-factor Authentication with Microsoft Azure Active Directory* at `https://blogs.msdn.microsoft.com/microsoft_press/2015/03/23/from-the-mvps-office-365-multi-factor-authentication-with-microsoft-azure-active-directory/`.

*What is Azure Multi-Factor Authentication?* at `https://docs.microsoft.com/en-us/azure/multi-factor-authentication/multi-factor-authentication`.

# Self-service password reset

This service was created so that the end users can reset their own passwords to access Office 365. It can also be configured to support writeback to the on-premises AD. It's a simple process to activate.

Go to `http://portal.azure.com` and then to your Azure AD panel, and select the **Password reset** option.

The following screenshot shows the blade on the Azure Portal showing how to configure it:

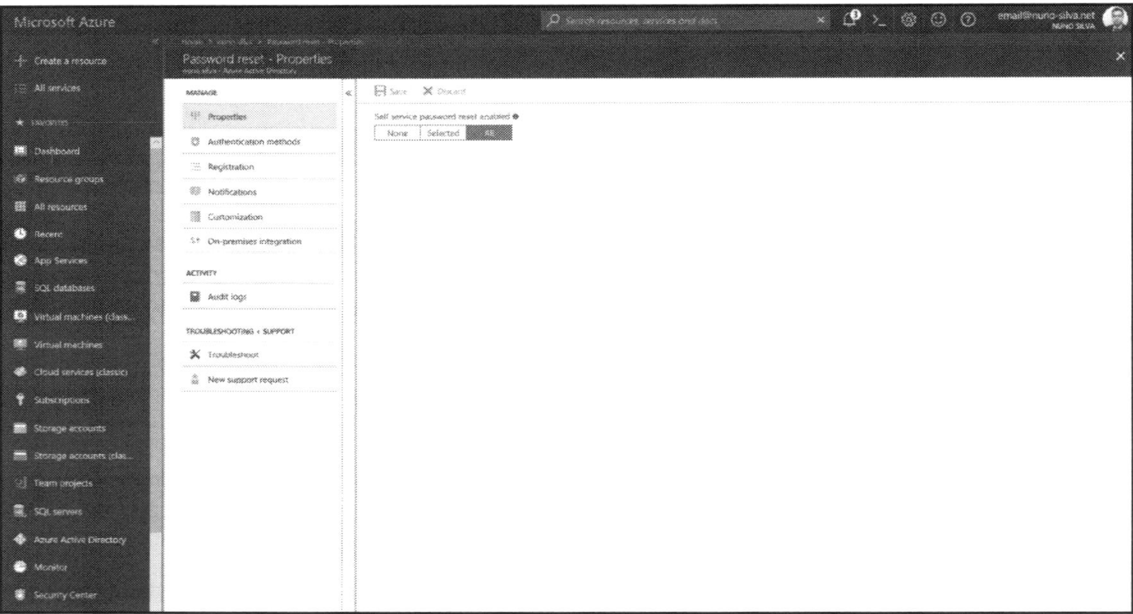


You can also select the **Authentication methods** option as shown in the following screenshot:

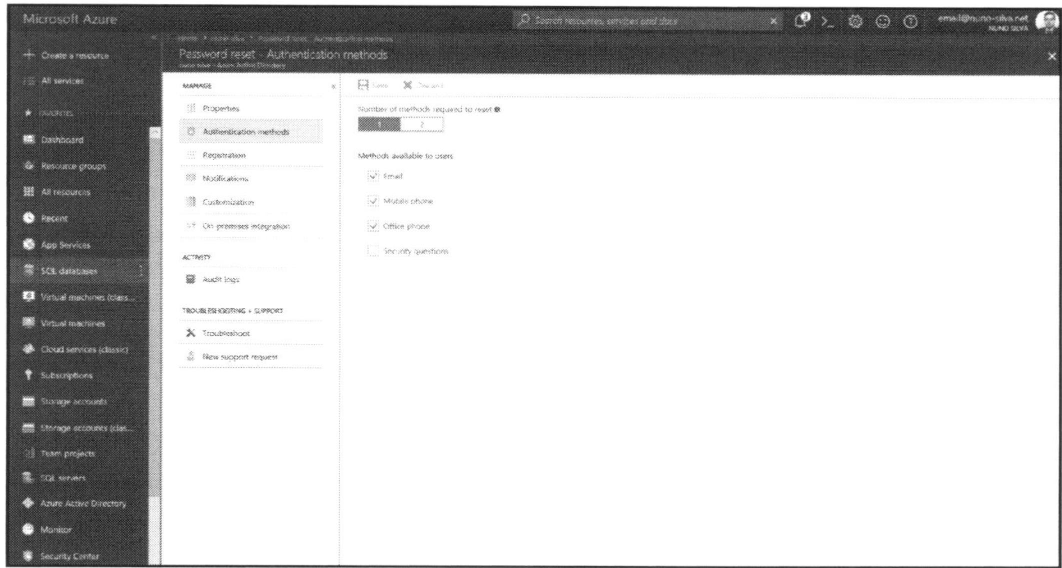


If you have Azure AD Connect installed on-premises, you can also enable the writeback password, as shown in the following screenshot:

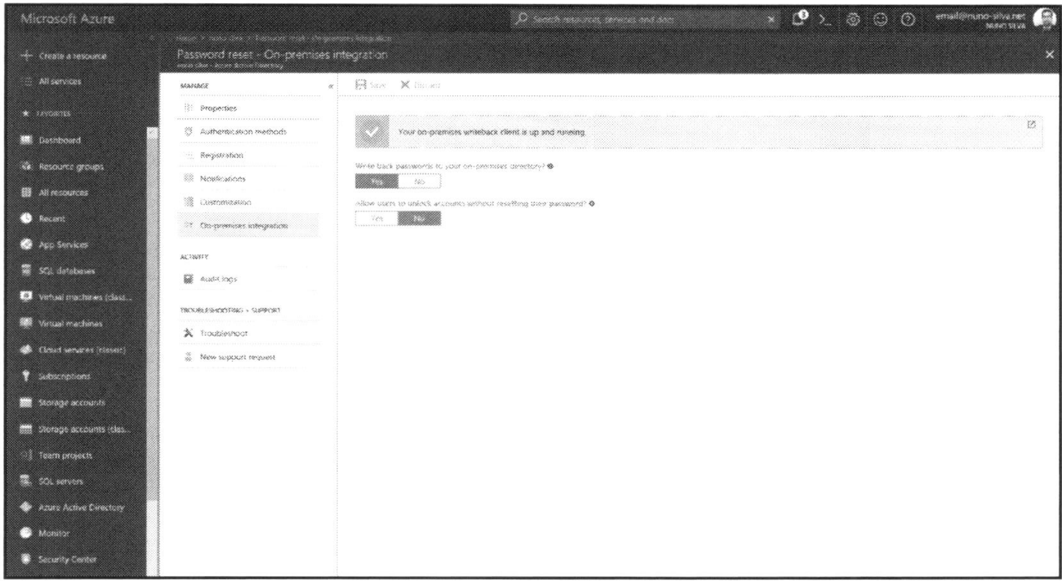

To learn more about self-service password reset, continue reading at `https://docs.microsoft.com/en-us/azure/active-directory/active-directory-passwords-getting-started`.

## Azure AD Basic versus Premium

For some scenarios, you might have to change your edition of Azure AD, depending on the features you need.

The following screenshot shows the common features in the different plans:

| | FREE | BASIC | PREMIUM P1 | PREMIUM P2 | OFFICE 365 APPS |
|---|---|---|---|---|---|
| **Common Features** | | | | | |
| Directory Objects[1] | 500,000 Object Limit | No Object Limit | No Object Limit | No Object Limit | No Object Limit |
| User/Group Management (add/update/delete)/ User-based provisioning, Device registration | ✓ | ✓ | ✓ | ✓ | ✓ |
| Single Sign-On (SSO) | 10 apps per user[2] (pre-integrated SaaS and developer-integrated apps) | 10 apps per user[2] (free tier + Application proxy apps) | No Limit (free, Basic tiers + Self-Service App Integration templates[5]) | No Limit (free, Basic tiers + Self-Service App Integration templates[5]) | 10 apps per user[2] (pre-integrated SaaS and developer-integrated apps) |
| B2B Collaboration[7] | ✓ | ✓ | ✓ | ✓ | ✓ |
| Self-Service Password Change for cloud users | ✓ | ✓ | ✓ | ✓ | ✓ |
| Connect (Sync engine that extends on-premises directories to Azure Active Directory) | ✓ | ✓ | ✓ | ✓ | ✓ |
| Security/Usage Reports | Basic Reports | Basic Reports | Advanced Reports | Advanced Reports | Basic Reports |

You can continue reading more about the editions at `https://azure.microsoft.com/en-us/pricing/details/active-directory/`.

# AD Connect setup and screenshots of console

To install the Azure AD Connect and configure the synchronization process of your AD or other **Lightweight Directory Access Protocol** (**LDAP**) server to Azure AD, follow `https://docs.microsoft.com/en-us/azure/active-directory/connect/active-directory-aadconnect`.

After the installation and configuration, the user login process can be depicted as shown in the following image:

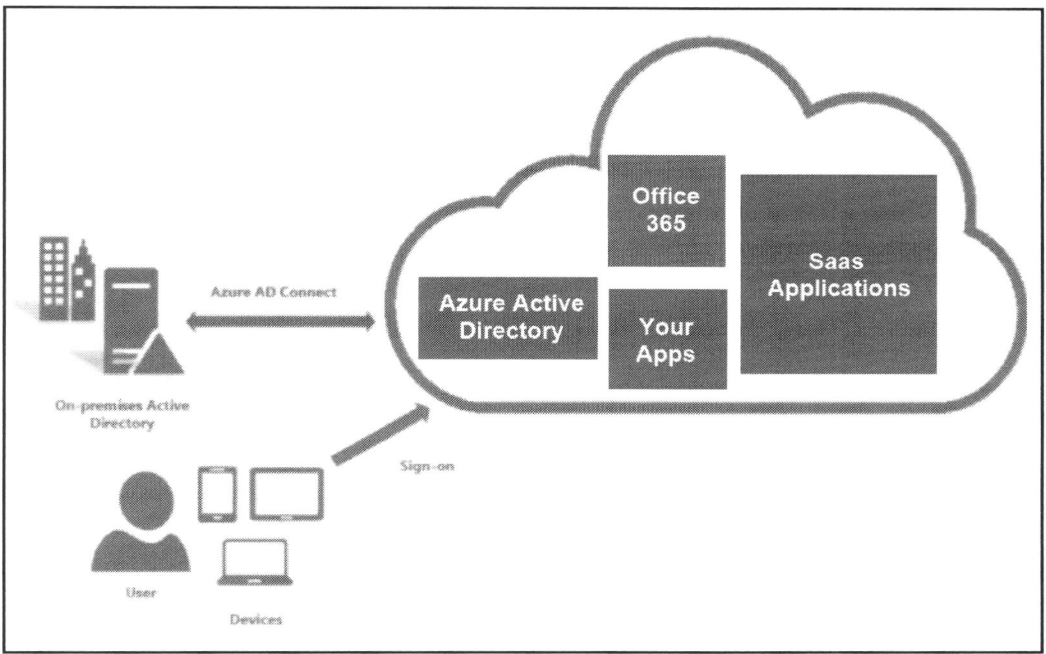


After the installation, I advise you to create a script to perform a delta synchronization whenever you need to force a delta synchronization.

It is a simple script with a single line:

```
Start-ADSyncSyncCycle -PolicyType Delta
```

To use it, just run it using the console, as shown in the following image:

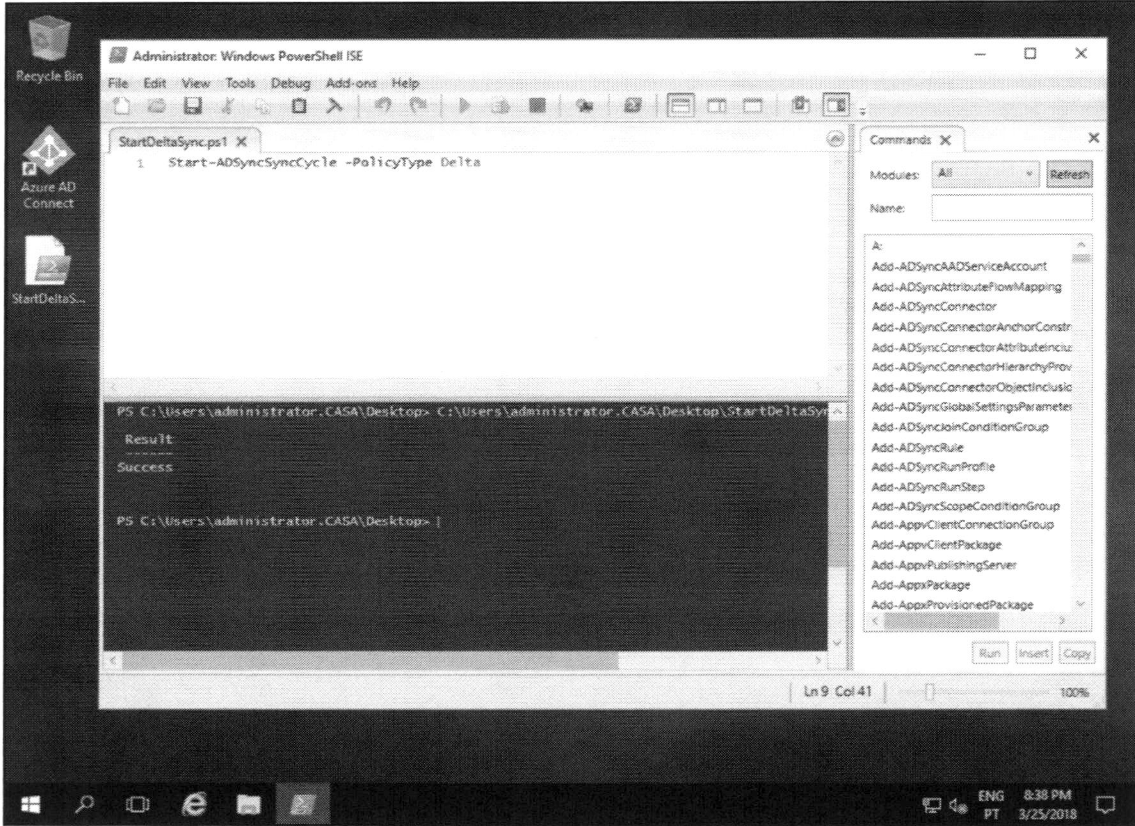

You can see the synchronization progress running the **Synchronization Service** shortcut in your start menu, as shown in the following screenshot:

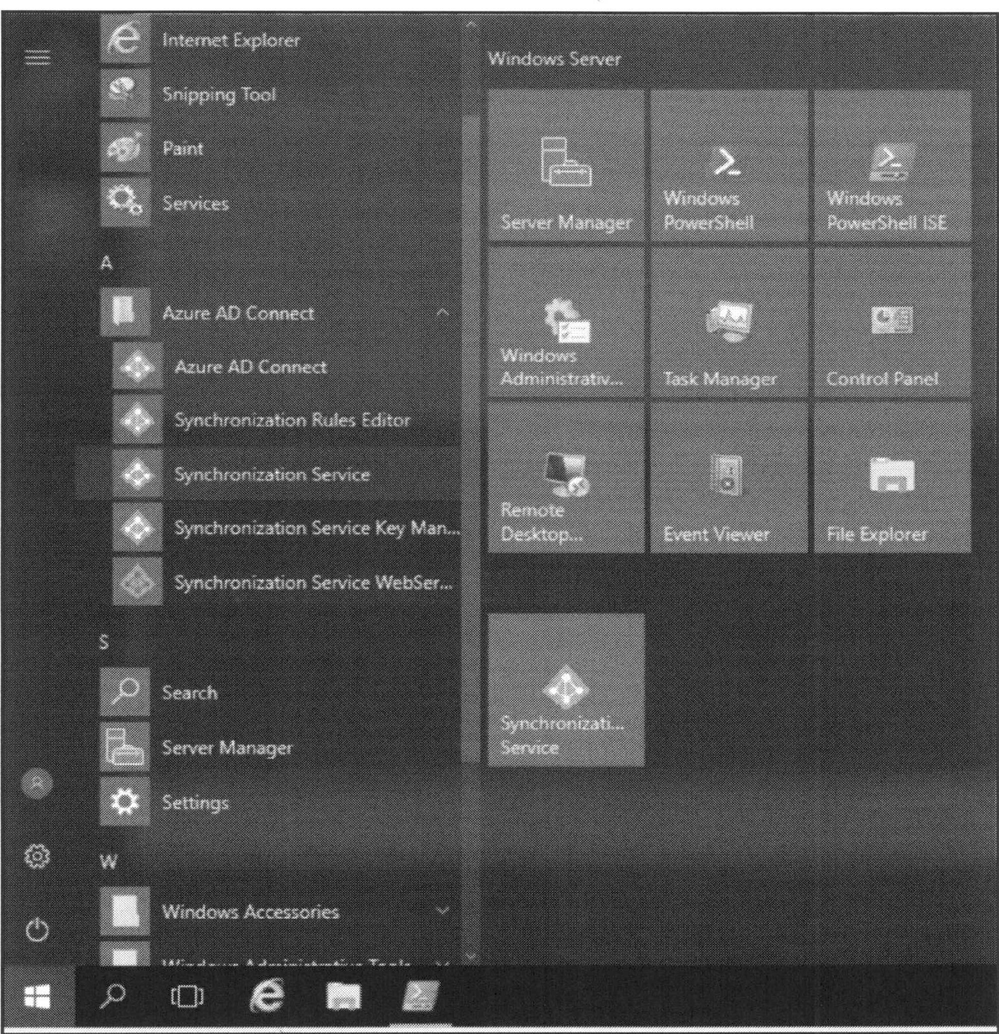

After you run the Delta Synchronization, you can see the various processes and operations running, as shown in the following screenshot:

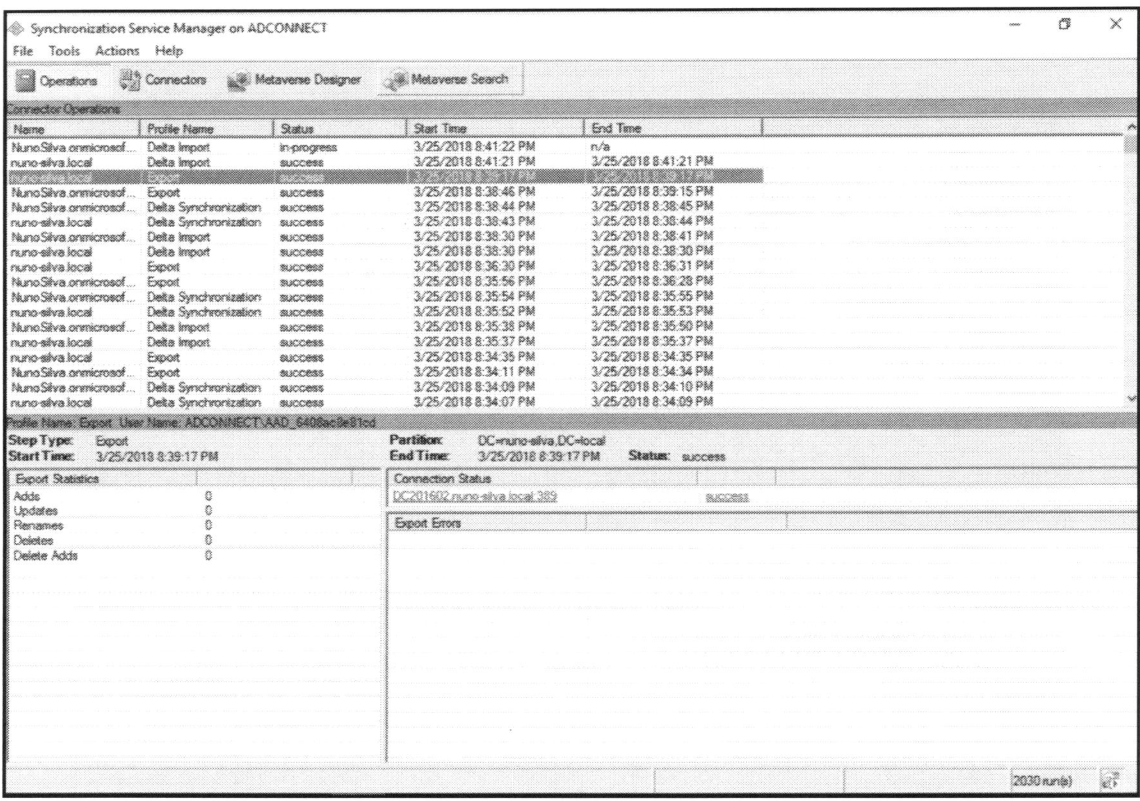

Refer to *Select which installation type to use for Azure AD Connect* to know how to install Azure AD Connect at `https://docs.microsoft.com/en-us/azure/active-directory/connect/active-directory-aadconnect-select-installation`.

# Office 365 management

Let's learn more about Office 365 management using user roles.

## User roles

On the Office 365 administration portal, there are several roles that you can assign to users in your organization. These roles are based on the most common scenarios for Office 365 daily administration tasks.

The summary of the permissions that each role has are as follows:

| Permission | Billing administrator | Global administrator | Password administrator | Service administrator | User management administrator |
|---|---|---|---|---|---|
| View company and user information | Yes | Yes | Yes | Yes | Yes |
| Manage support tickets | Yes | Yes | Yes | Yes | Yes |
| Reset user passwords | No | Yes | Yes | No | Yes; with limitations. He or she cannot reset passwords for billing, global, and service administrators. |
| Perform billing and purchasing operations | Yes | Yes | No | No | No |
| Create and manage user views | No | Yes | No | No | Yes |
| Create, edit, and delete users and groups, and manage user licenses | No | Yes | No | No | Yes; with limitations. He or she cannot delete a global administrator or create other administrators. |
| Manage domains | No | Yes | No | No | No |
| Manage company information | No | Yes | No | No | No |
| Delegate administrative roles to others | No | Yes | No | No | No |
| Use directory synchronization | No | Yes | No | No | No |

There are also additional roles specific to services that you might use, such as Exchange and SharePoint.

You can read about these roles here at `https://support.office.com/en-us/article/About-Office-365-admin-roles-da585eea-f576-4f55-a1e0-87090b6aaa9d`.

# Summary

In this chapter, you learned about the basic and advanced scenarios of authentication and identities used in Office 365. Cloud identity is the scenario where you only have users in the cloud. Synced identity is where you synchronize your users, groups, and contacts to Microsoft Azure AD. And federated identity combined with synced identity is the one that provides you with the possibility to have a single sign-on experience. You now have more information about how to find the best scenario for identity management to fit your organization.

In the next chapter, you will learn how to configure Office 365 and its services to start consuming based on your project timeline.

# 5
# Configuring Office 365

In this chapter, you will learn how to implement Office 365 in your organization. This chapter will cover the following topics:

- Planning Office 365
- Implementing Office 365

With this foundation, you will learn more about each scenario and which best fits your organization.

## Planning Office 365

All projects, regardless of size, require planning. In `Chapter 2`, *Fundamentals of Office 365*, I advised you to create a project plan with the following phases:

- Start of the project
- Assessment
- Remediation
- Enabling
- Migration
- End phase
- User feedback

You can use this process in all your projects, or just adapt it to your methodology:

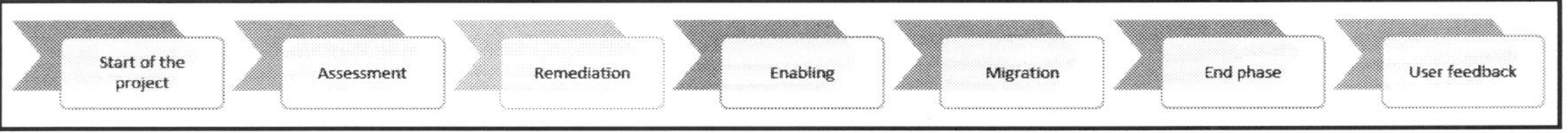

When you are preparing the migration of an enterprise organization to Office 365, it is very important to plan the steps in order for your project to be successful. This sample checklist will help you to start organizing your plan and be prepared for a migration to Office 365.

# Sample checklist

List your deployment goals and bear in mind the following factors:

- Who are your internal and external teams?
- What is the scope of the project?
- What will be the tracking mechanism of the project?
- What are the milestone dates?

Then start making decisions about the deployment:

- Make an inventory of what will be migrated from each workload to Office 365:
    - Users
    - Groups
    - Mailboxes (if it is a mailbox migration)
    - Computers (operating system, Office client version, and patches)
    - File shares (if it is a SharePoint or OneDrive migration)
    - Intranet sites
    - Instant messaging
    - Web conferencing
    - Audio conferencing
    - Voice
    - Third-party applications that are integrated with the current systems

After you have all the data about what type of migration you will perform and the workloads that are to be migrated, you can make decisions that are relevant to the project.

# Implementing Office 365

To start implementing Office 365, you will first need to set up an environment. As described in `Chapter 2`, *Fundamentals of Office 365*, you can use a trial tenant and later add final licenses to it, or you can create a new tenant for the project.

First, you need to set up the tenant, and there are a few basic steps to do this.

# Adding a domain to Office 365

Verify your domain:

1. Sign in to Office 365 and go to the setup wizard at `http://portal.office.com`
2. Choose **Setup** on the **Office 365 Admin center** to start the wizard
3. Enter the domain name you want to use (such as `yourdomainname.com`):

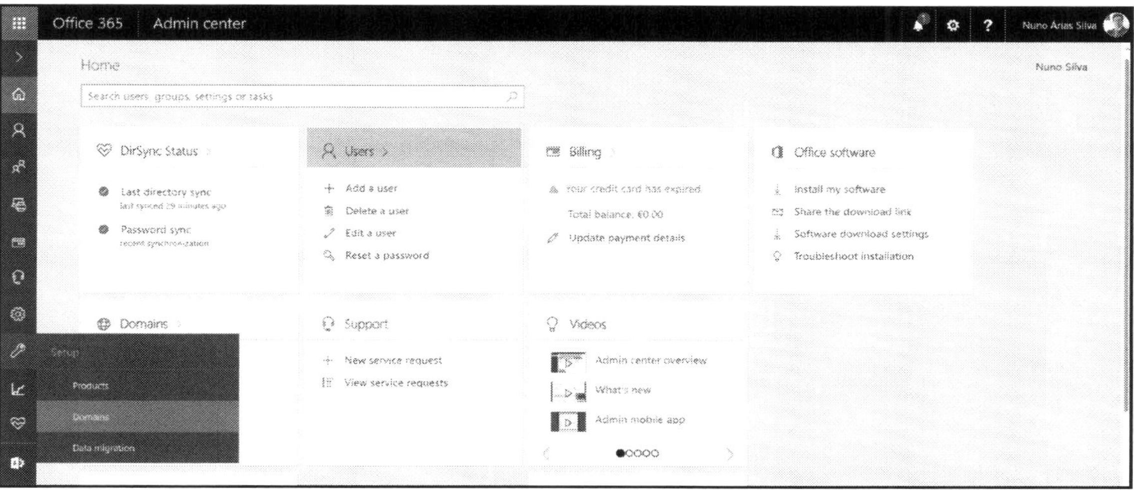

4. You can also go through the **Admin** menu and navigate to **Setup** | **Domains**:

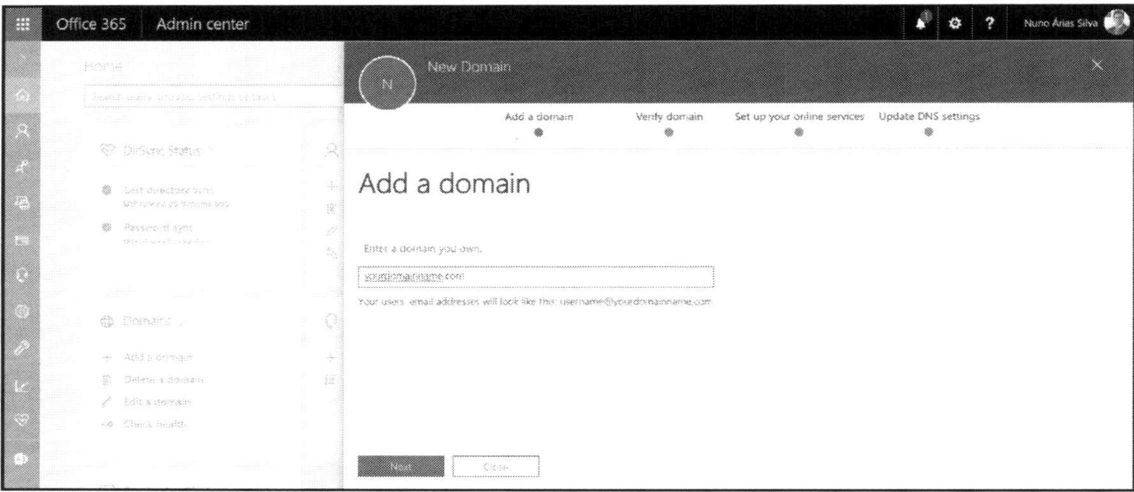


5. Add your domain name (for example, `yourdomainname.com`) and click **Next**
6. After adding the domain, you can use the verification code sent by email or follow the steps in the wizard to add a TXT or MX record (for more information, refer to `https://support.office.com/en-us/article/create-dns-records-at-any-dns-hosting-provider-for-office-365-7b7b075d-79f9-4e37-8a9e-fb60c1d95166?ui=en-USrs=en-001ad=US`), which will verify your own domain:

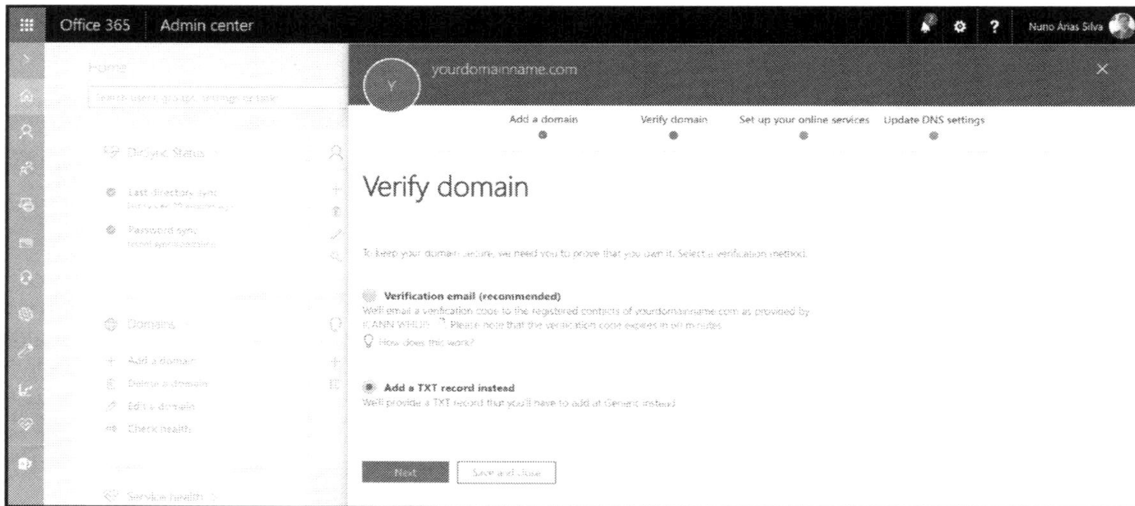

# Configuring application settings

To start using services in Office 365, you will need to configure the application settings for the workloads you are implementing.

The URL `https://support.office.com/en-us/office365admin` is a good place to start.

# Adding users to Office 365

Depending on the identity and authentication scenario you have chosen, as described in `Chapter 4`, *Identities and Authentication*, you now have to configure one of the following options:

- Cloud only
- Directory synchronization
- Federated identity

# Cloud only

This scenario involves the user residing only on Office 365 and Azure AD. It is used mostly in small organizations that do not have an on-premises AD or do not require SSO.

## Using the portal to create a user

To add a user directly to Office 365, you can use the Office 365 Admin portal and create the account individually, add multiple accounts in bulk, or use PowerShell.

To create the account in the portal, go to the Admin center, and click **Add a user**:

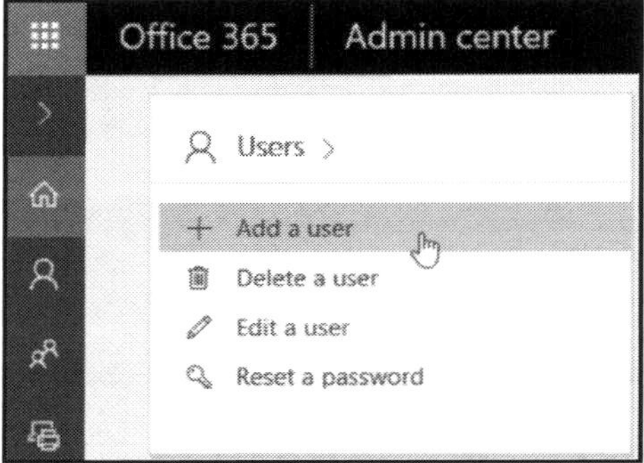


Fill in all the information for the user, as shown in the following screenshot:

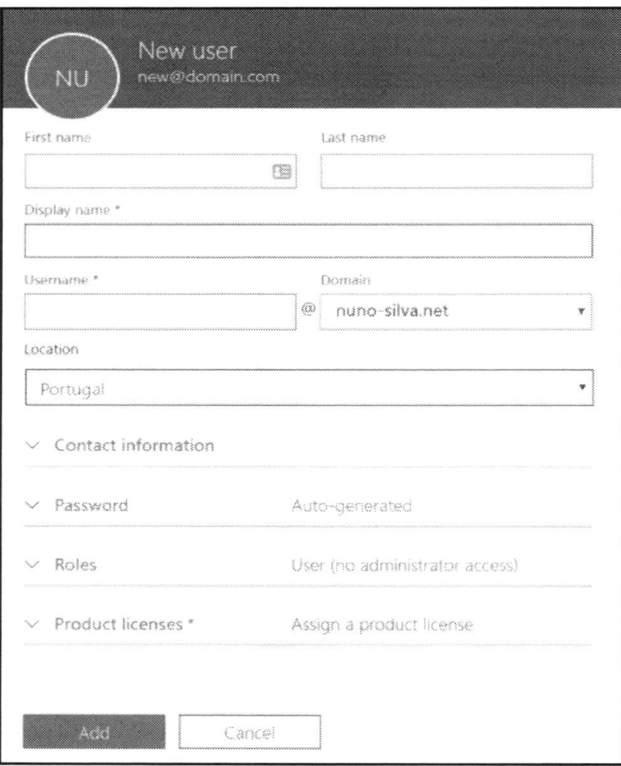

## Using CSV import

If you chose to import from a CSV file, go to **Users**, select **Active users**, and select **Import multiple users** from the **More** drop-down menu:

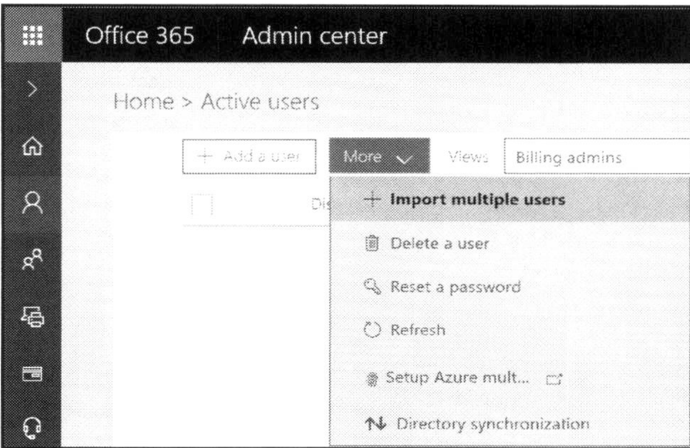


Choose the CSV file to upload to Office 365:

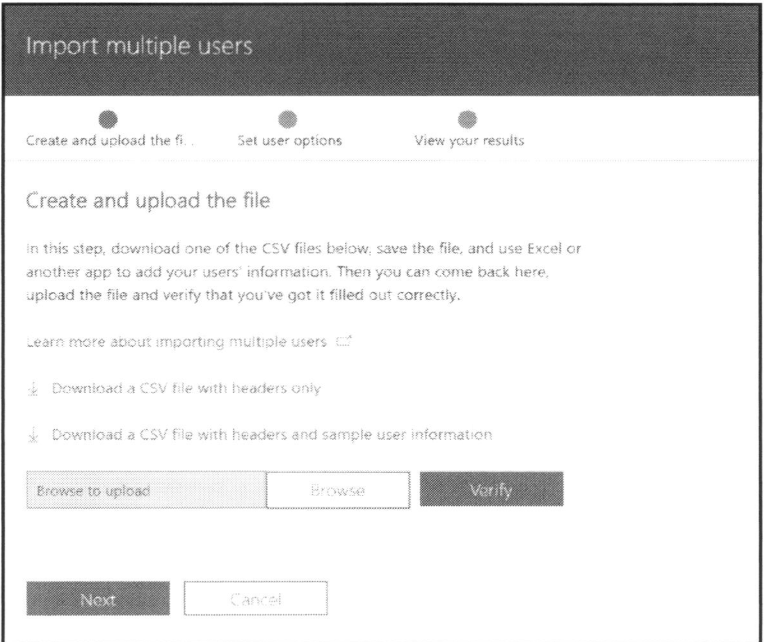

Here is a sample CSV structure:

```
Headers
User Name    First Name    Last Name    Display Name    Job Title
Department    Office Number    Office Phone    Mobile Phone    Fax
Address    City    State or Province    ZIP or Postal Code
Country or Region
Data from one user
test@nuno-silva.net    Chris    Green    Chris Green    IT Manager
Information Technology    123451    212121212    212121211
222121222    City Center    Lisbon    LX    1000    Portugal
```

After you create your file, choose the file and click on the **Verify** button:

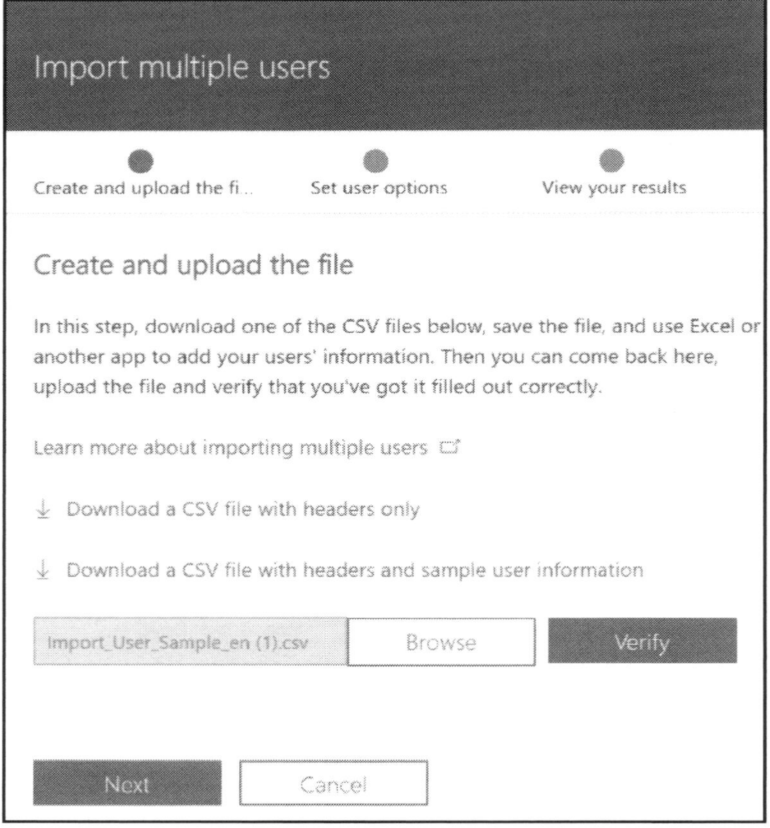

If the file is OK, you will see **Your file looks good**. **Click or tap Next**:

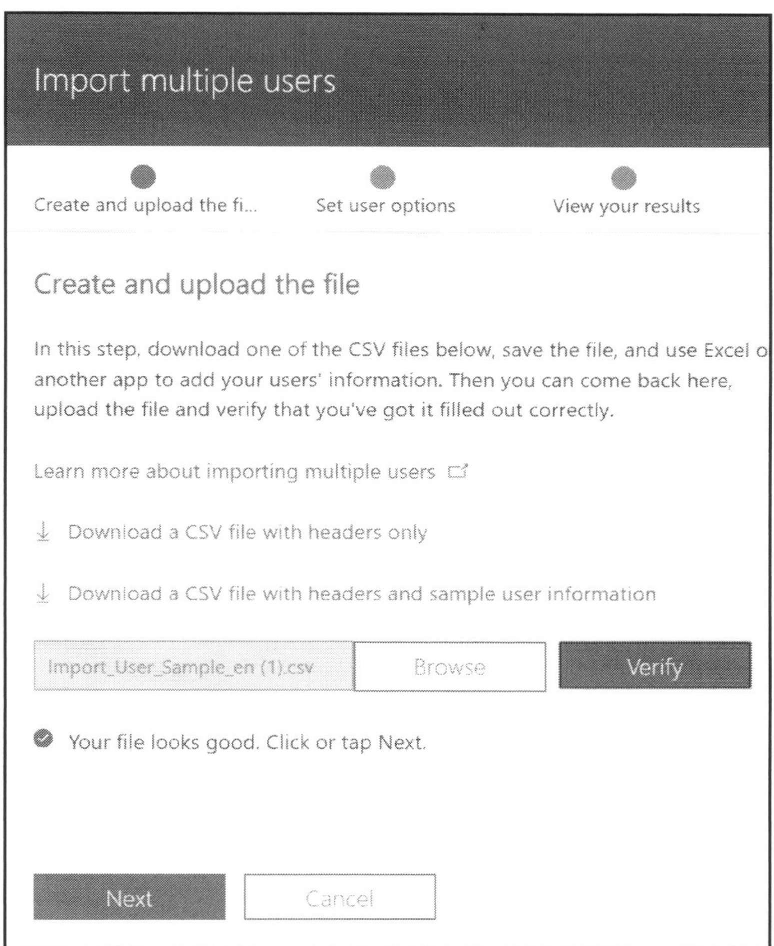

In this example of using an CSV file to import users to Office 365, it was changed the domain name in the CSV file to the example. Change it to your domain name.

Clicking on **Next** will take you to the following screen:

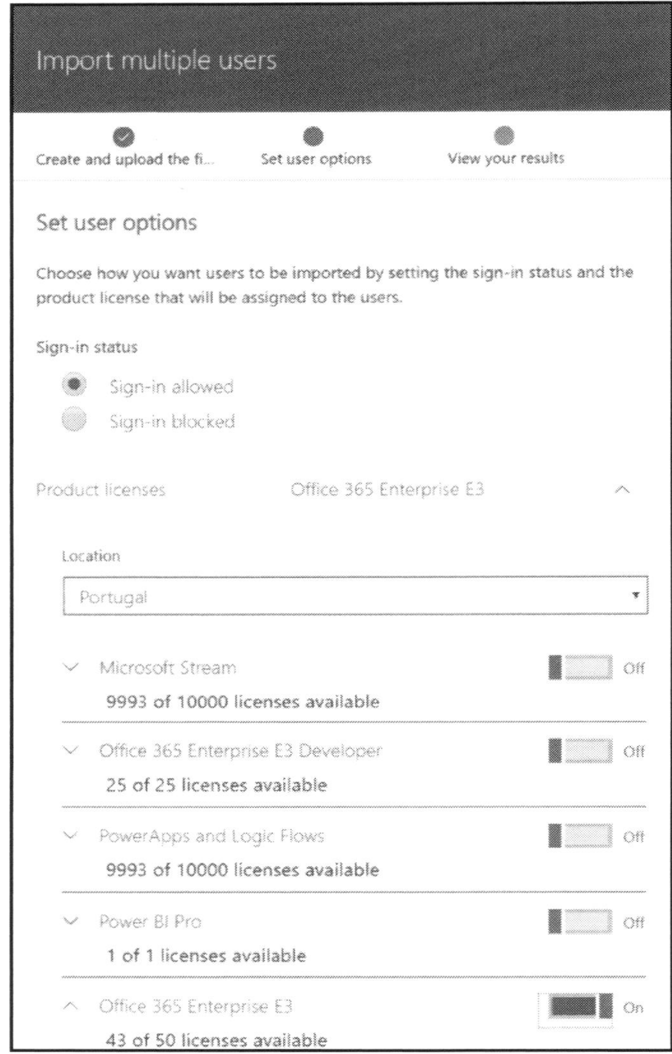


Choose the **Sign-in status**, assign licenses, and click **Next**.

After Office 365 creates the user accounts, it will inform you that the operation has completed successfully. You can then download the results and/or email them to a recipient of your choice.

Click on **Send and close**:

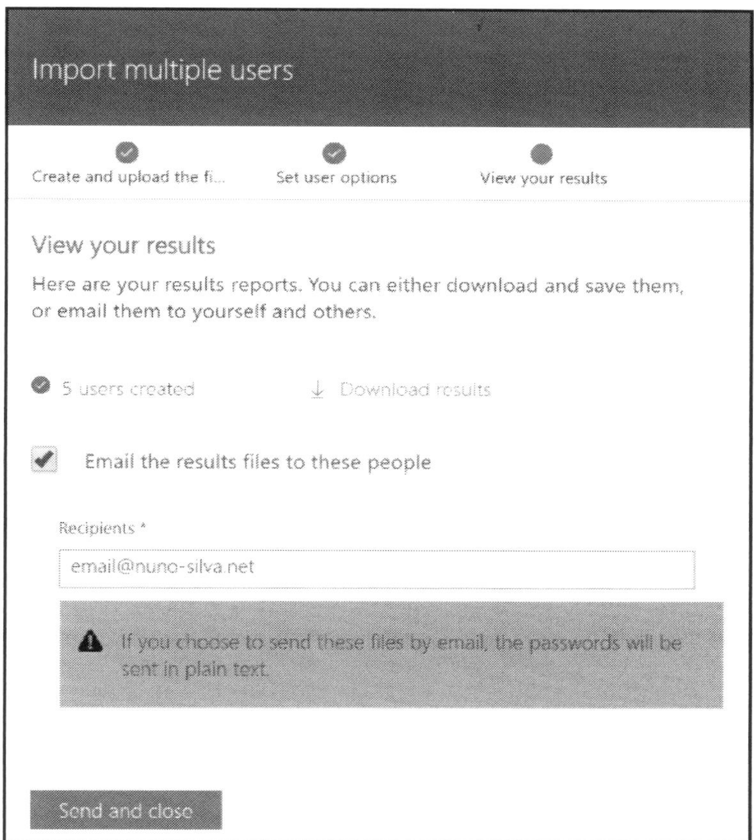


When downloaded, the results will look like the following:

| Display name | Username | Password |
|---|---|---|
| Chris Green | chris@nuno-silva.net | Vuwa4365 |
| Ben Andrews | ben@nuno-silva.net | Xubo9551 |
| David Longmuir | david@nuno-silva.net | Zuno2828 |
| Cynthia Carey | cynthia@nuno-silva.net | Tada4966 |
| Melissa MacBeth | melissa@nuno-silva.net | Bubu2214 |

You will also receive an email with the following information:

**Subject of the email:** New or modified user account information

**Content:**

**Attention:** A user account was created or modified. Retrieve your user's temporary password.

Microsoft

A user account has been created or modified. You can now distribute this information to your user.
The following list contains temporary passwords for newly created or modified user accounts.

Please note:

When distributing IDs and passwords to individual users, be sure to do so in a safe and secure manner
Temporary passwords are valid for 90 days
**User Name:** chris@nuno-silva.net
**Temporary Password:** Vuwa4365

**User Name:** ben@nuno-silva.net
**Temporary Password:** Xubo9551

**User Name:** david@nuno-silva.net
**Temporary Password:** Zuno2828

**User Name:** cynthia@nuno-silva.net
**Temporary Password:** Tada4966

**User Name:** melissa@nuno-silva.net
**Temporary Password:** Bubu2214

Once your end users have successfully signed in with their temporary passwords, they can create new passwords by following the instructions on the sign-in page.

Go to the sign-in page at https://portal.office.com.

Thank you for choosing to host your IT solutions with Microsoft.

Sincerely,
The Microsoft Office 365 Team

This is end of the contents of the email.

After the import, you can access a user account's information, change the data, or just see the data that was created:

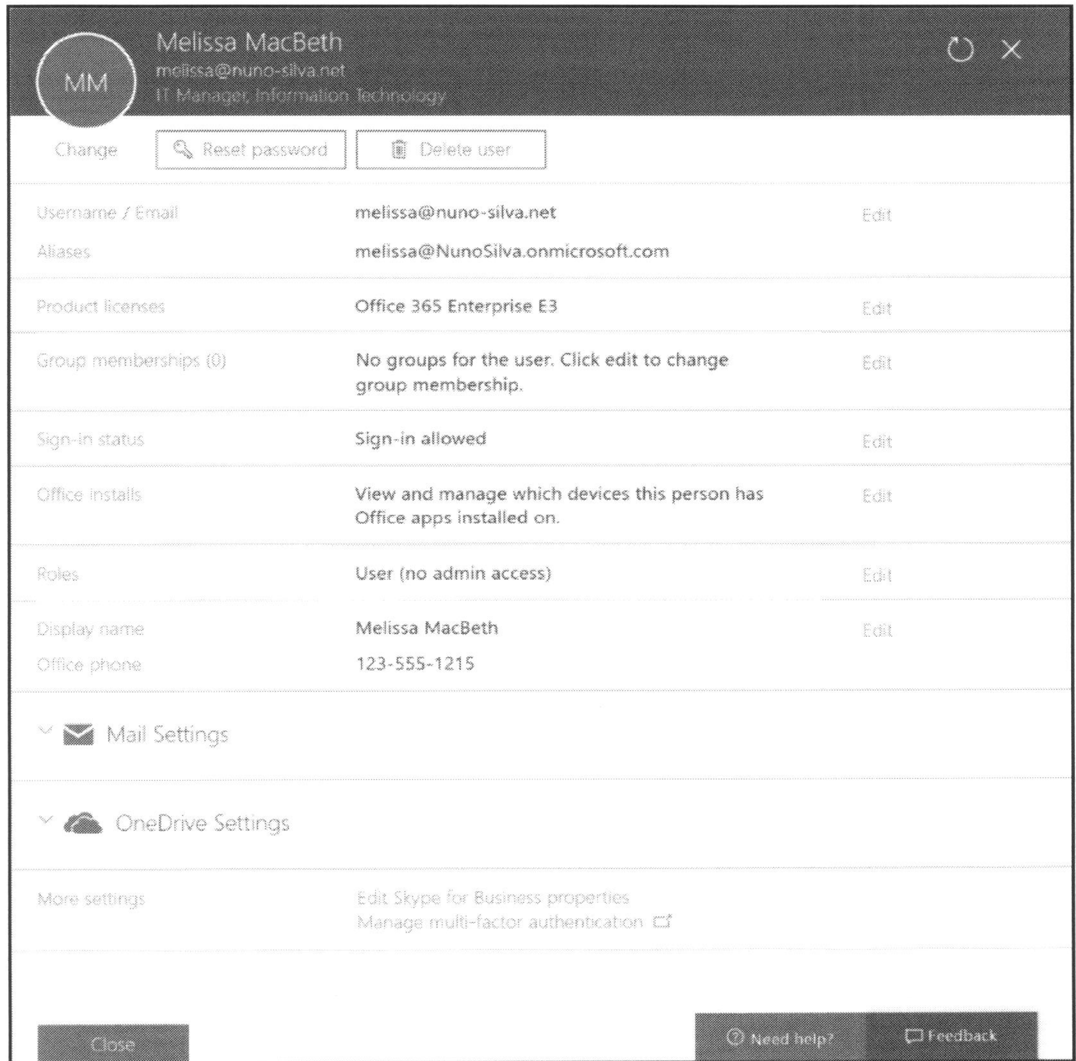

## Using PowerShell

Additionally, you also have the ability to provision accounts with PowerShell, leveraging the Office 365 PowerShell module. To create user accounts in Office 365 PowerShell, you must specify values for a set of properties:

| Property name | Required? | Description |
|---|---|---|
| DisplayName | Yes | The display name of the user |
| UserPrincipalName | Yes | The login name |
| FirstName | No | The first name of the user |
| LastName | No | The last name of the user |
| LicenseAssignment | No | The license plan for the user<br>To check which license plans are available in your tenant, you can use the `Get-MsolAccountSku` command.<br>For more information, see *View licenses and services with Office 365 PowerShell* at `https://docs.microsoft.com/en-us/office365/enterprise/powershell/view-licenses-and-services-with-office-365-powershell`. |
| Password | No | The password for the user. |
| UsageLocation | No | The country where the user resides. This field is used to select the location where the user uses Office 365 the most. |

For more information on creating user accounts with Office 365 PowerShell, visit `https://technet.microsoft.com/library/mt628067.aspx`.

To create users using PowerShell, you need to connect to Office 365. The article at `https://technet.microsoft.com/en-us/library/dn975125.aspx` explains how to connect to Office 365 using PowerShell.

After you install the PowerShell module to connect to Office 365, you can just open PowerShell and use the following commands:

```
$UserCredential = Get-Credential
Connect-MsolService -Credential $UserCredential
```

The screenshot of the preceding command is as follows:

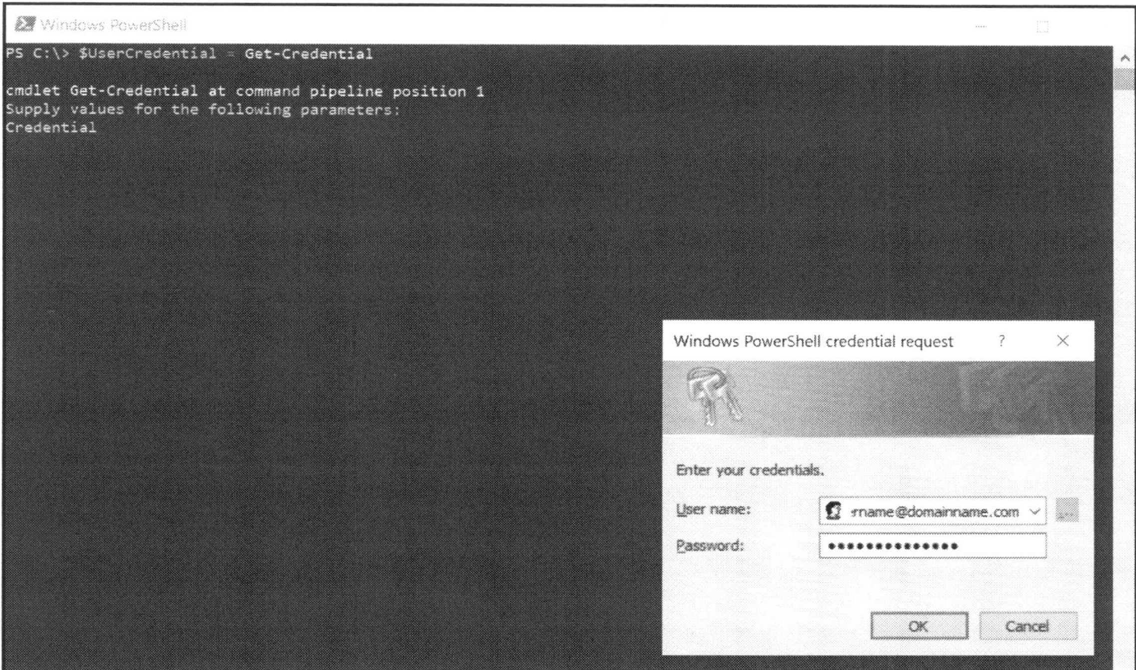

After connecting, you can create a user with the following command, as shown in the following screenshot:

```
new-msoluser -UserPrincipalName user365@o365pt.org -DisplayName "Office 365
User" -FirstName "User" -LastName "365" -UsageLocation "PT" -
LicenseAssignment "NunoSilva:ENTERPRISEPREMIUM"
```

```
Windows PowerShell
PS C:\> get-help new-msoluser -examples

NAME
    New-MsolUser

SYNOPSIS
    Adds a new user to Windows Azure Active Directory.


    -------------------------- EXAMPLE 1 --------------------------

    C:\PS>New-MsolUser -UserPrincipalName user@contoso.com -DisplayName "John Doe" -FirstName "John" -LastName "Doe"

    Returns a user object.

    Description

    -----------

    This command creates a new user.  The user will not have any licenses assigned.  A random password will be
    generated for the user.




    -------------------------- EXAMPLE 2 --------------------------

    C:\PS>New-MsolUser -UserPrincipalName user@contoso.com -DisplayName "John Doe" -FirstName "John" -LastName "Doe"
    -UsageLocation "US" -LicenseAssignment "Contoso:BPOS_Standard"

    Returns a user object.

    Description

    -----------

    This command creates a new user and assigns them a license.





PS C:\> new-msoluser -UserPrincipalName user365@o365pt.org -DisplayName "Office 365 User" -FirstName "User" -LastName "3
65" -UsageLocation "PT" -LicenseAssignment "NunoSilva:ENTERPRISEPREMIUM"

Password UserPrincipalName  DisplayName     isLicensed
-------- -----------------  -----------     ----------
Gof67054 user365@o365pt.org Office 365 User True


PS C:\> _
```

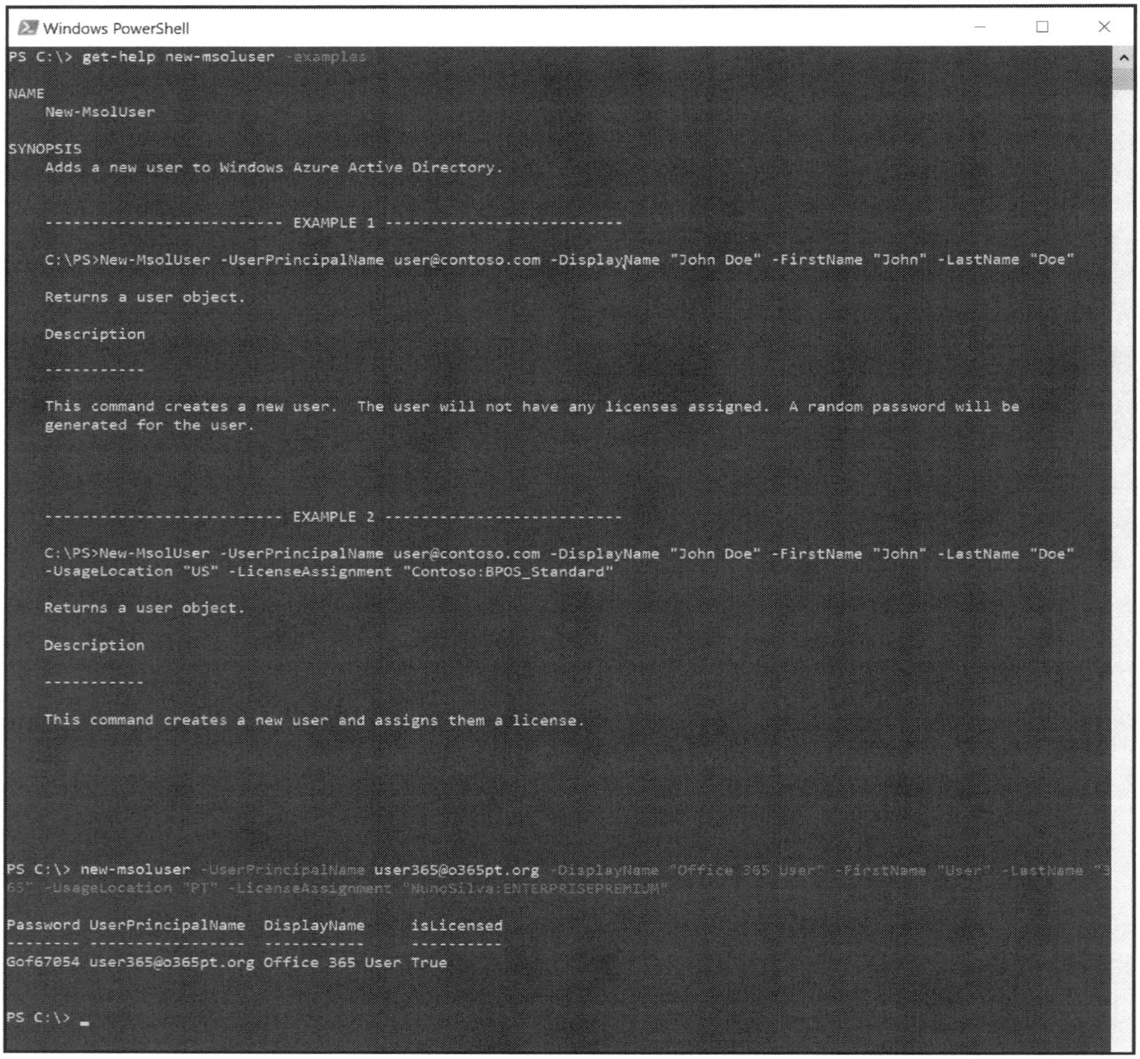

The output of the command will tell you the password, the UPN, the display name, and whether it is licensed.

After creating the user, you can use the following command to view all the information about the user, as shown in the following image.

```
Get-MsolUser -UserPrincipalName user365@o365pt.org | FL
```

When the user is created, a temporary password is generated for the user. By default, the user is required to change it at first login.

Now you can go to the Office 365 portal and try to log in as the user.

Go to `http://portal.office.com` and log in with the username provided:

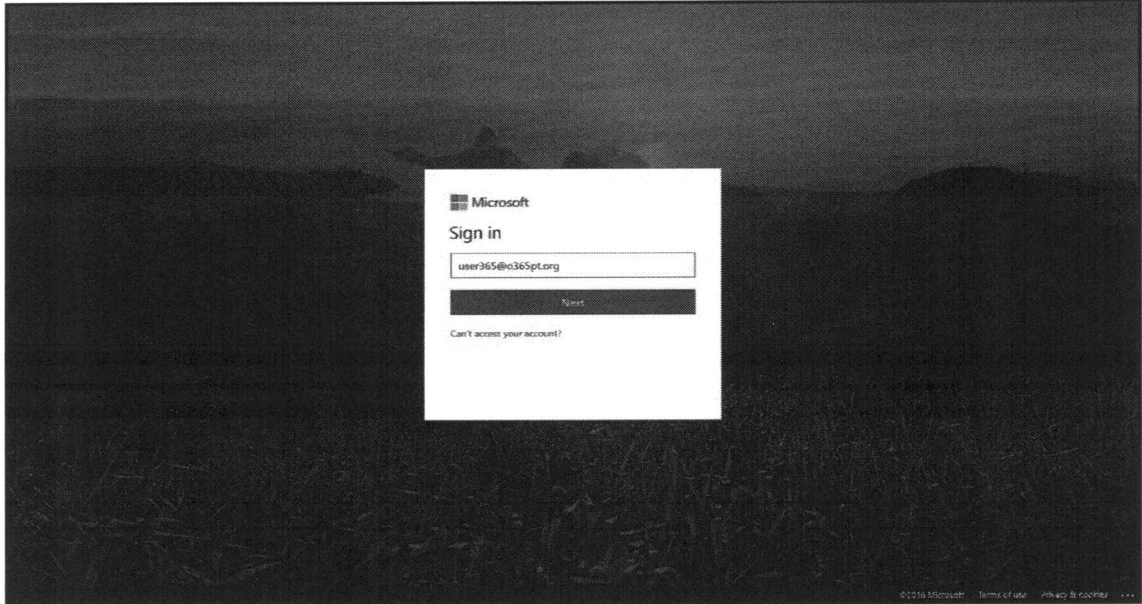

Enter the temporary password of the user:

The Office 365 portal will ask you to change the password at first login, as shown in the following screenshot:

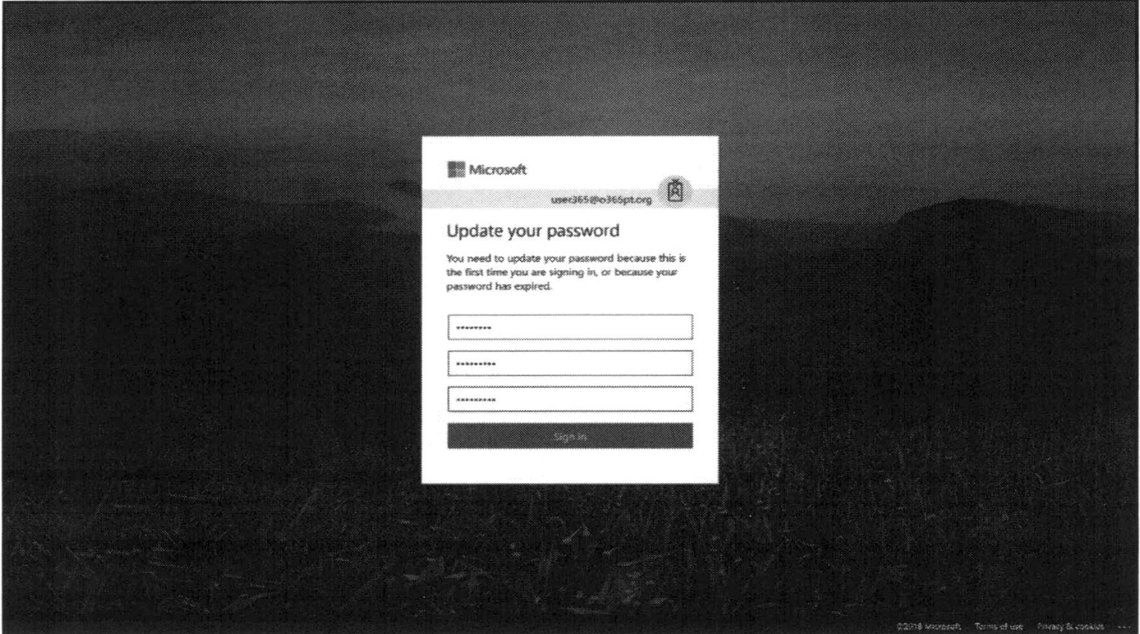

After providing the new password and confirmation, click **Sign in** and you will then be logged in:

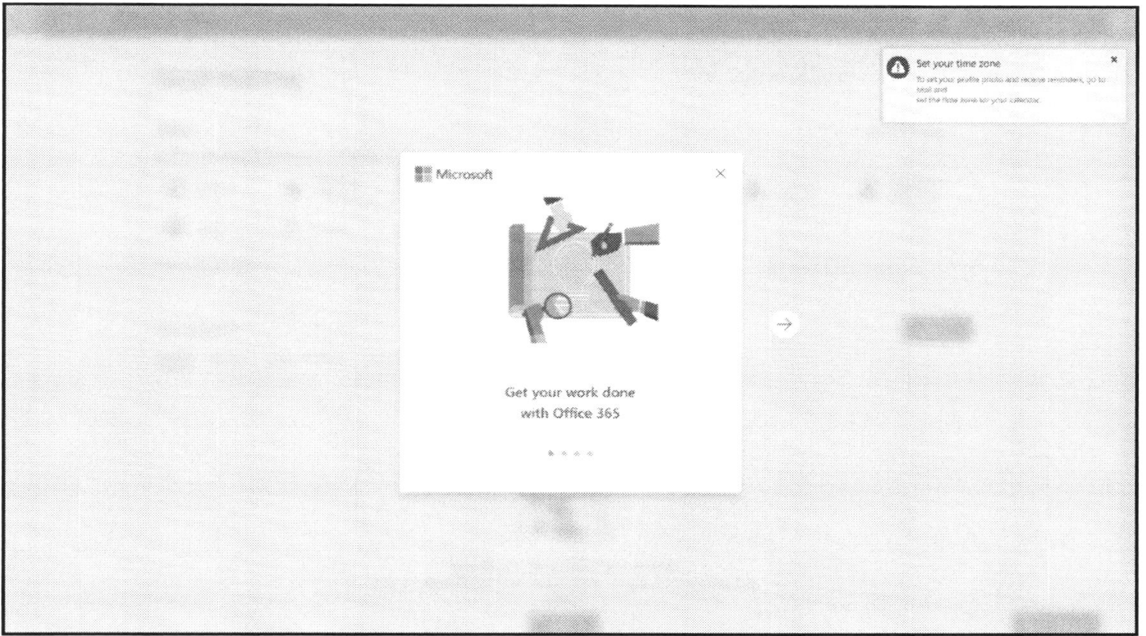

Some services are not immediately configured, and it will take a few minutes for everything to be set up. You can see in the following image that almost all services are available to the user from the start:

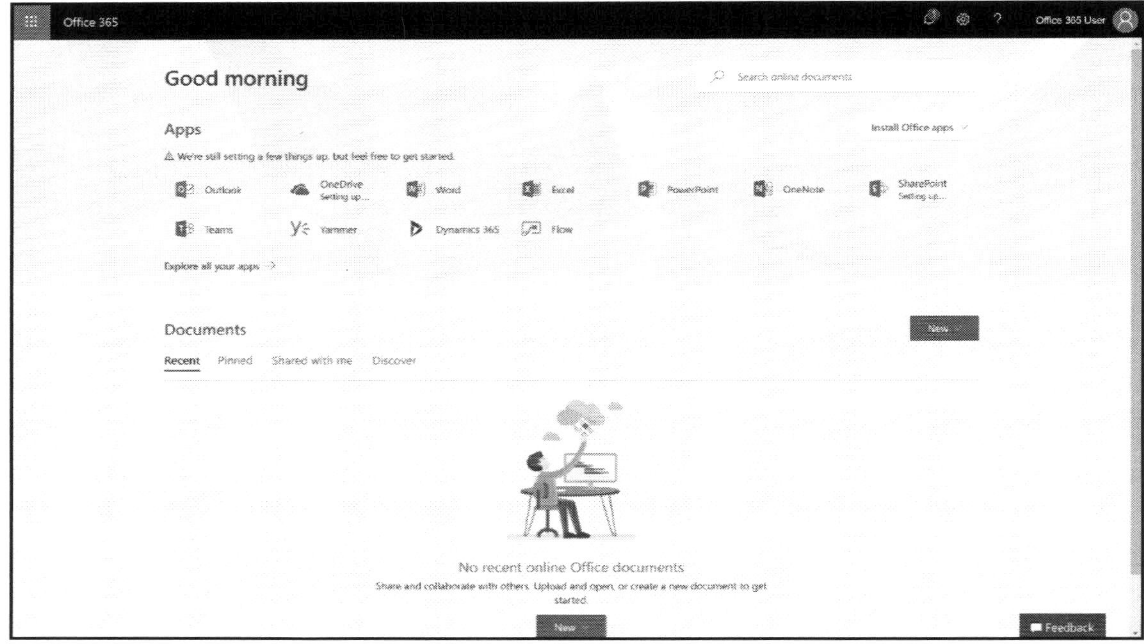


The user can now start working. To test it out, click on **Outlook** to go to the email part of Office 365.

When you first log in to Outlook, it will present you with the following screens. Follow the instructions described in the images:

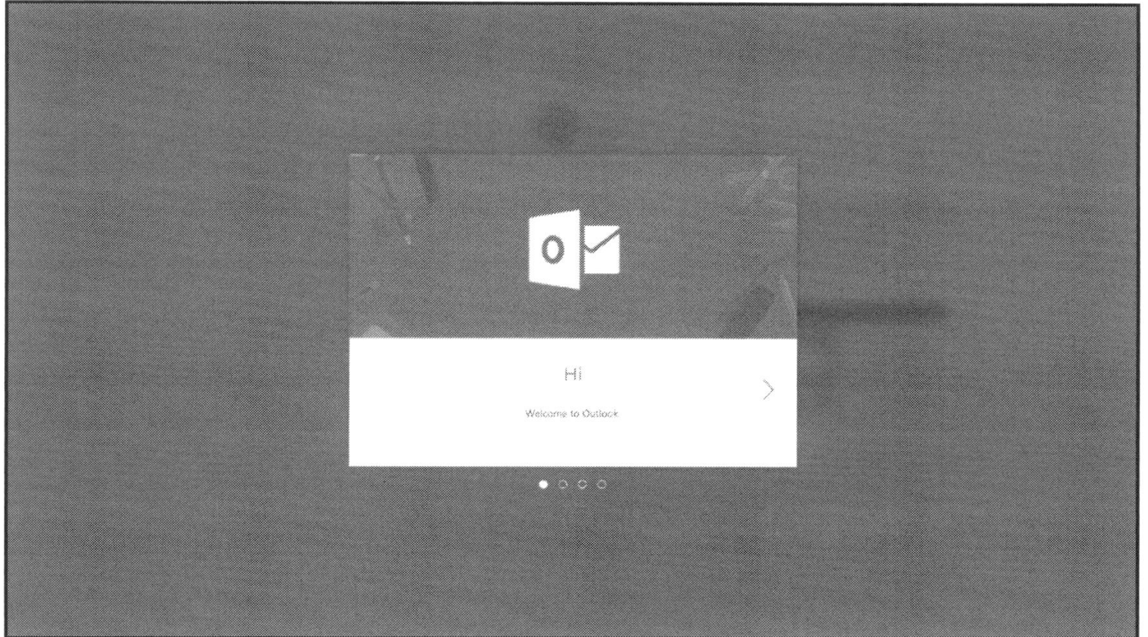

The next screen will help you select the preferred language and time zone:

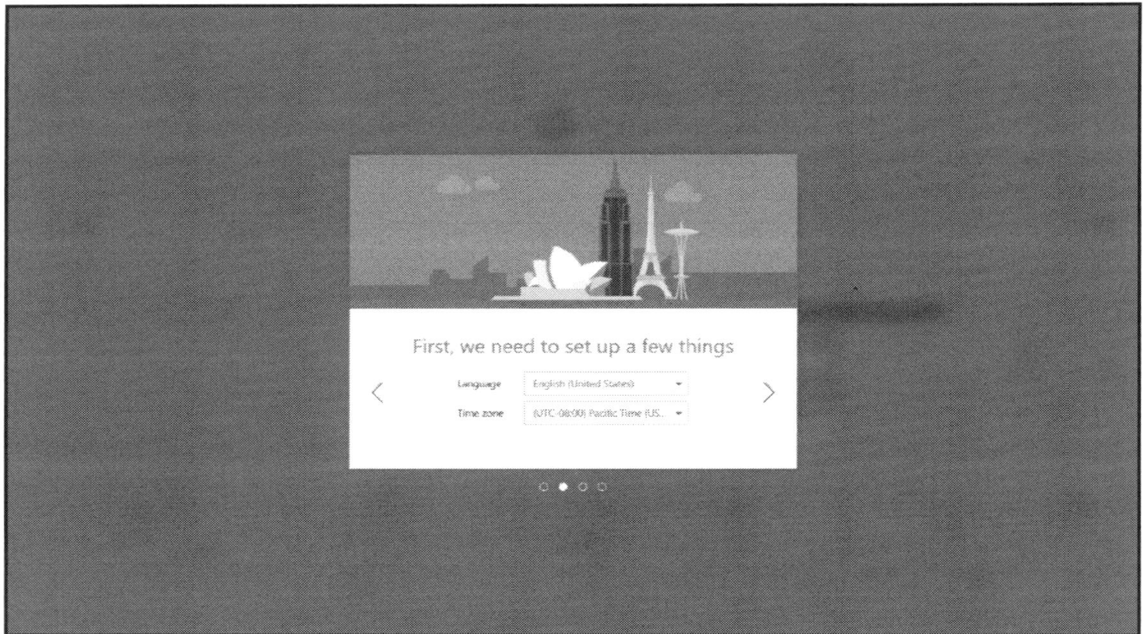

You can select a theme of your choice, as shown in the following screenshot:

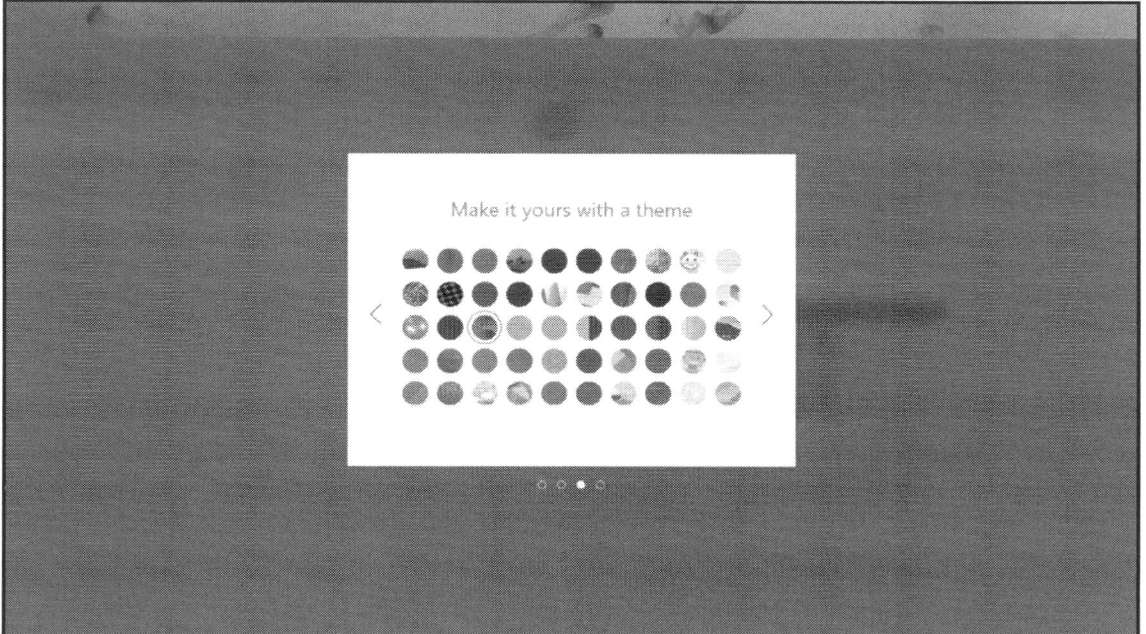

You can customize your signature, as shown in the following screenshot:

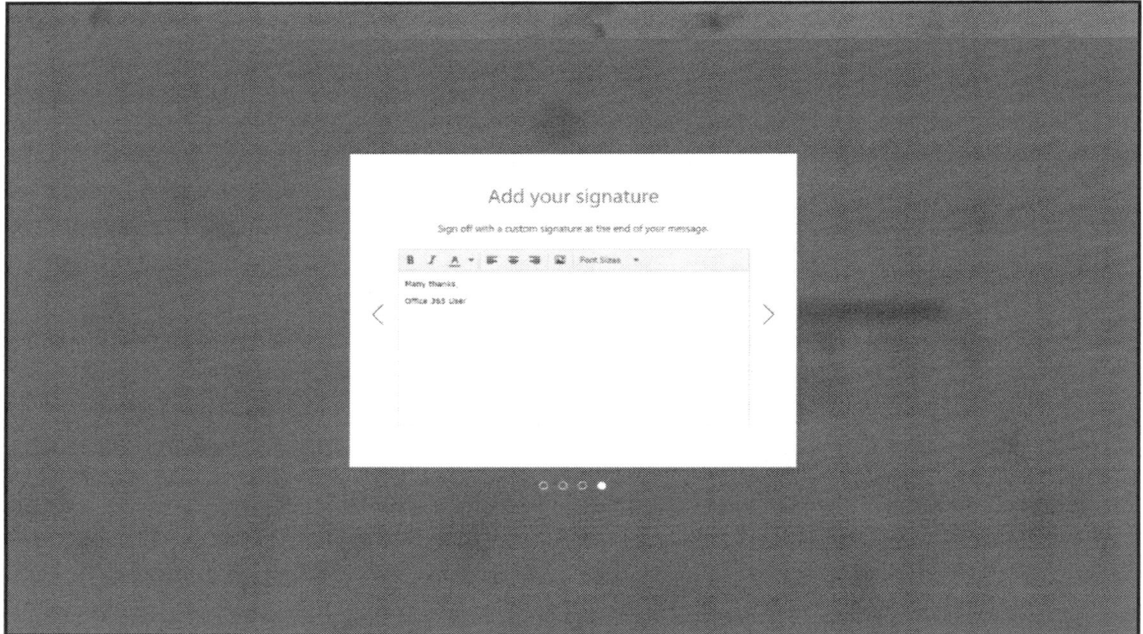

Your new email address is finally set up!

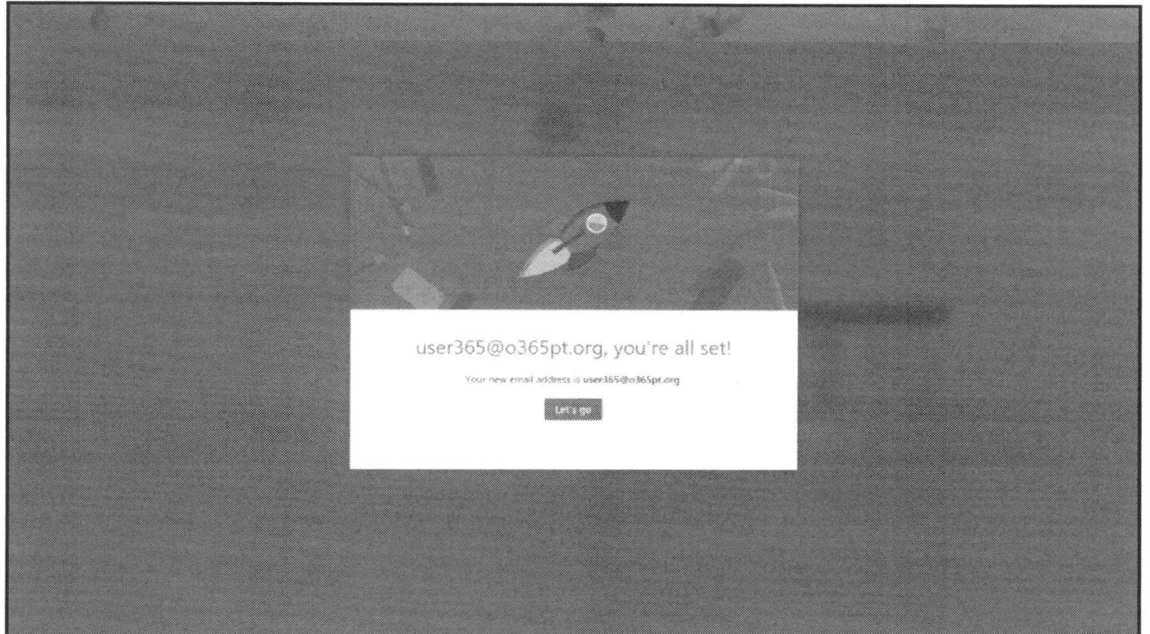

After the first steps are completed, the user is ready to send and receive emails:

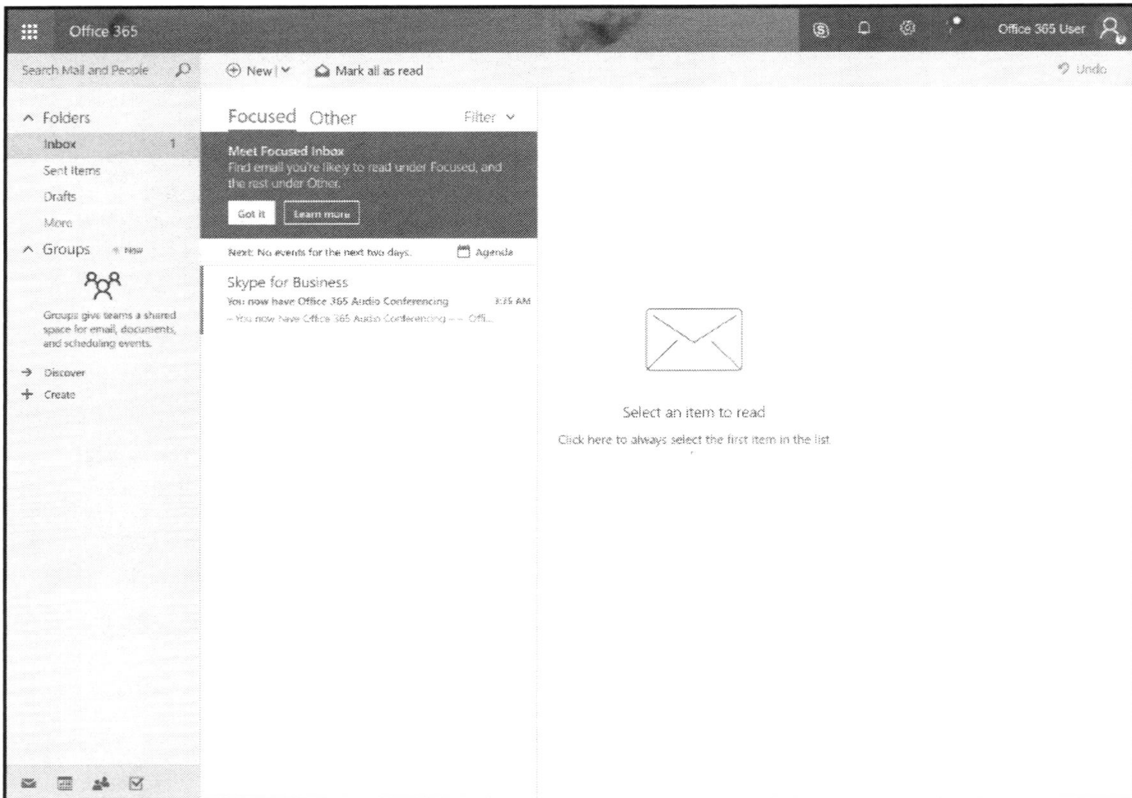

The user can now create new email messages using the **New** button. The right side of the screen will then show an empty email message for the user to add the recipient, subject, and content, as shown in the following image. After composing your email, just click **Send**:

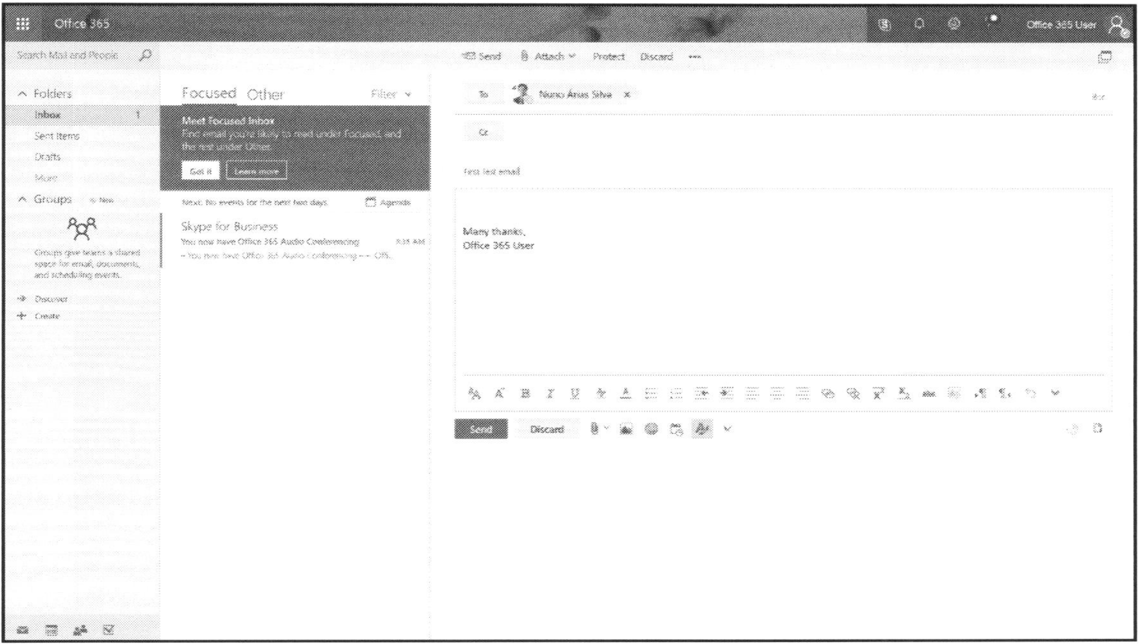

This is the first step of a new user's experience of the Office 365 world:

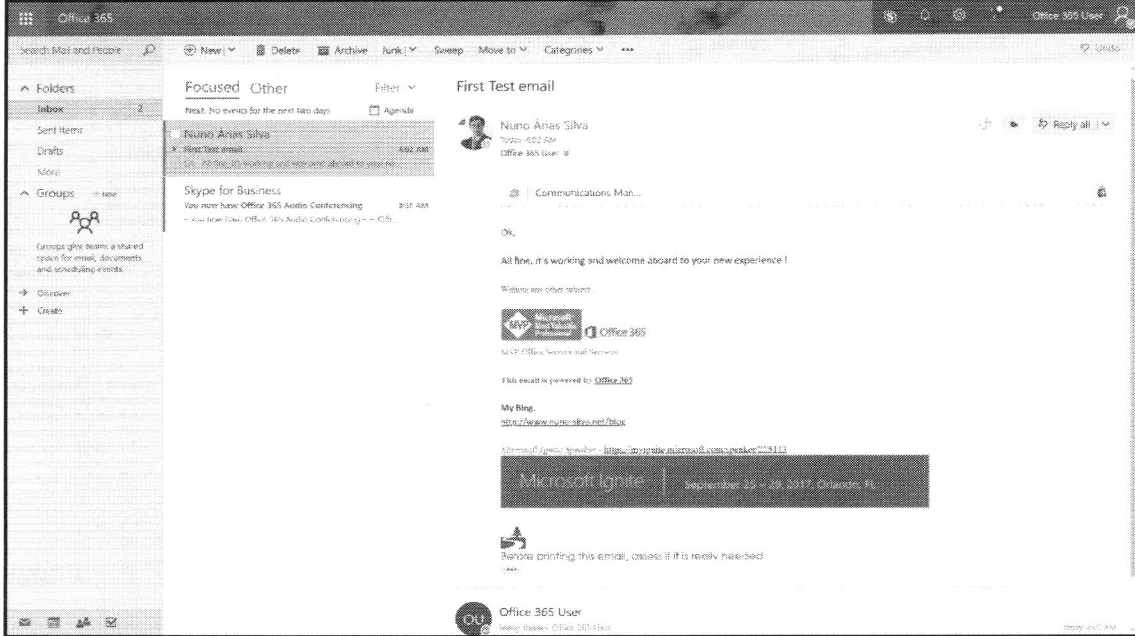


## Directory synchronization

To implement directory synchronization, which is briefly described in `Chapter 4`, *Identities and Authentication*, you need to fulfill a few requirements.

- In a nutshell, these are the prerequisites you'll need to ensure that you have set up:
    - On-premises data prepared and ready
    - On-premises Active Directory
    - Azure AD Connect server
    - SQL Server
    - Accounts
    - Network connectivity
    - Component prerequisites
    - Hardware requirements

To learn about all the prerequisites, go to https://docs.microsoft.com/en-us/azure/active-directory/connect/active-directory-aadconnect-prerequisites.

- **Install Azure AD Connect**. The installation has the following options:
    - Express settings
    - Custom settings

Learn about all the settings at https://docs.microsoft.com/en-us/azure/active-directory/connect/active-directory-aadconnect-select-installation.

- **Plan**:
    - **Design concepts**: Go to https://docs.microsoft.com/en-us/azure/active-directory/connect/active-directory-aadconnect-design-concepts and read the documentation you find there. This article describes the main concepts of Azure AD Connect, such as the source anchor, which must be used when planning an Active Directory synchronization. By following the steps described in the article, you'll be able to select the best approach and synchronization schema for your organization.
    - **Topologies**: Go to https://docs.microsoft.com/en-us/azure/active-directory/connect/active-directory-aadconnect-topologies and read the documentation you find there. This scenario describes the supported topologies when configuring directory synchronization using Azure AD Connect and Azure Active Directory.

Certain combinations of scenarios might not be supported, if they are not described in the article.

- **Manage**:
    - To learn how to manage Azure AD Connect, go to https://docs.microsoft.com/en-us/azure/active-directory/connect/active-directory-aadconnect-whats-next.

The required ports and protocols are shown in the following diagram:

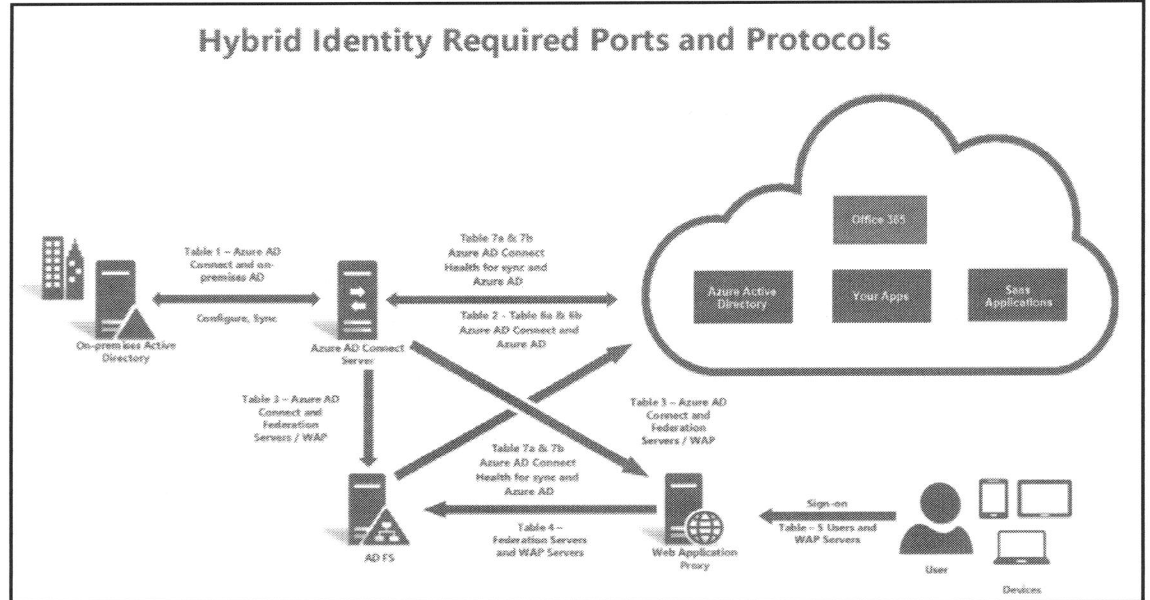

You can learn about all the required ports at `https://docs.microsoft.com/en-us/azure/active-directory/connect/active-directory-aadconnect-ports`.

The express installation is used in most organizations. You can set it up by going to the **Admin center** and, in **Home** | **Active users**, selecting **More** | **Directory synchronization**:

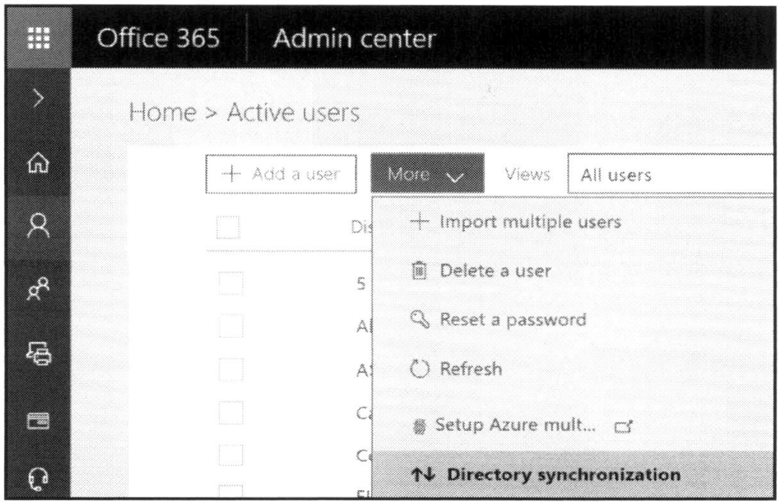


The preceding steps are described at `https://support.office.com/en-us/article/Set-up-directory-synchronization-for-Office-365-1b3b5318-6977-42ed-b5c7-96fa74b08846?ui=en-USrs=en-USad=US`.

## Federated identity

If your organization needs a federated identity, you will still need directory synchronization as a base requirement. You may use your ADFS servers with Office 365 if you already have them in your infrastructure.

To use federated identity, you can also create your infrastructure using Azure AD Connect custom installation. Go to `https://docs.microsoft.com/en-us/azure/active-directory/connect/active-directory-aadconnect-get-started-custom` and skip to the section named *Create a new AD FS form or use an existing AD FS form.*

# Summary

In this chapter, you have learned about the basic planning and how to kick off an implementation of Office 365. You now have more information on how to plan your Office 365 project and how to implement the basic features of Office 365.

In the next chapter, you will learn how to manage Office 365 and its services based on the most common workloads.

# 6
# Managing Office 365

In this chapter, you will learn how to manage Office 365 in your organization. It will cover the following topics:

- Managing basic tasks
- Managing advanced tasks
- Implementing new features

## Office 365 Admin center

After setting up a Microsoft Office 365 tenant, you created a user with global administrator permissions on your tenant. There are several roles and administrative permissions that you can assign to user accounts based on the access requirements for each workload. You can assign, for example, the Exchange administrator role to the person who is managing the Exchange workload and assign the SharePoint administrator to a person of another department to manage SharePoint. With this separation of roles, you have more granular security in your tenant, without giving full access to all the workloads in the tenant. The available roles that you can assign to users are as follows:

- Global administrator
- Billing administrator
- Exchange administrator
- SharePoint administrator
- Password administrator
- Skype for Business administrator
- Service administrator

- User management administrator
- Reports reader
- Dynamics 365
- Dynamics 365 service administrator
- Power BI administrator

More details about these roles are available at `https://support.office.com/en-us/article/About-Office-365-admin-roles-da585eea-f576-4f55-a1e0-87090b6aaa9d?ui=en-US&rs=en-US&ad=US`. All these roles are based on Azure AD, where you can also set them up and assign additional roles, such as the following:

- Billing administrator
- Compliance administrator
- Conditional access administrator
- CRM service administrator
- Device administrator
- Directory reader
- Directory synchronization account
- Directory writer
- Exchange service administrator
- Global administrator/Company administrator
- Guest inviter
- Intune service administrator
- Mailbox administrator
- Password administrator/Helpdesk administrator
- Power BI service administrator
- Privileged role administrator
- Security administrator
- Security reader
- Service support administrator
- SharePoint service administrator
- Skype for Business administrator
- User account administrator

You can find more information at `https://docs.microsoft.com/en-us/azure/active-directory/active-directory-assign-admin-roles-azure-portal`. To access the Office 365 Admin center, go through the following steps:

1. Go to `http://portal.office.com` or directly to `https://portal.office.com/adminportal/home#/homepage`
2. Log in with credentials that have admin privileges
3. Select the **Admin** menu
4. Go to the **Admin centers** drop-down on the left-hand menu:

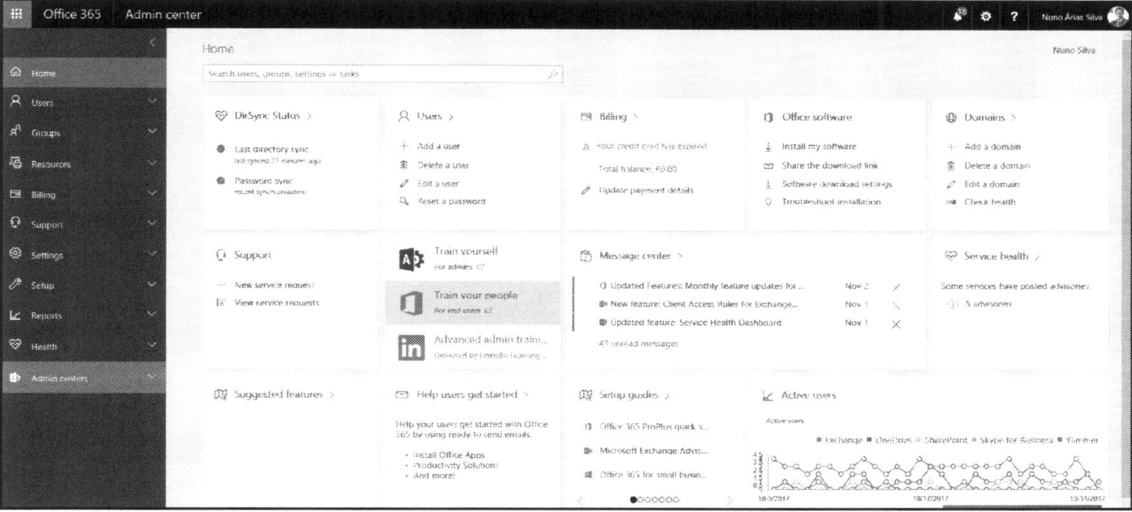


In the home page of the Admin center, you have several options, such as the following:

- **Home**—landing page
- **Users**—manage users
- **Groups**—manage groups
- **Resources**—manage resources
- **Billing**—manage billing

- **Support**—manage support
- **Settings**—manage global settings
- **Setup**—set up services
- **Reports**—manage and view reports
- **Health**—view service health status
- **Admin centers**—manage other services

In each section, you'll find the tasks available to manage each piece of your Office 365 tenant.

# Home

On the home page of Office 365 Admin center, you can directly access several options based on the most used tasks, as well as some useful dashboards. You can perform tasks such as the following:

- Search for users, group settings, or tasks in the search pane
- Check the directory synchronization status
- Go directly to the user management area to create, delete, edit, or reset a password of a user
- Go to the **Billing** section
- Go to **Office software** section
- Manage domains
- Manage support
- Train yourself
- Train your people
- Access advanced administration training on LinkedIn learning
- Check the Message center
- Check the service's health
- View suggested features
- Help users get started
- Access setup guides
- Check a dashboard about the distribution of active users across the workloads

The following screenshot shows the home page of the Office 365 Admin center:

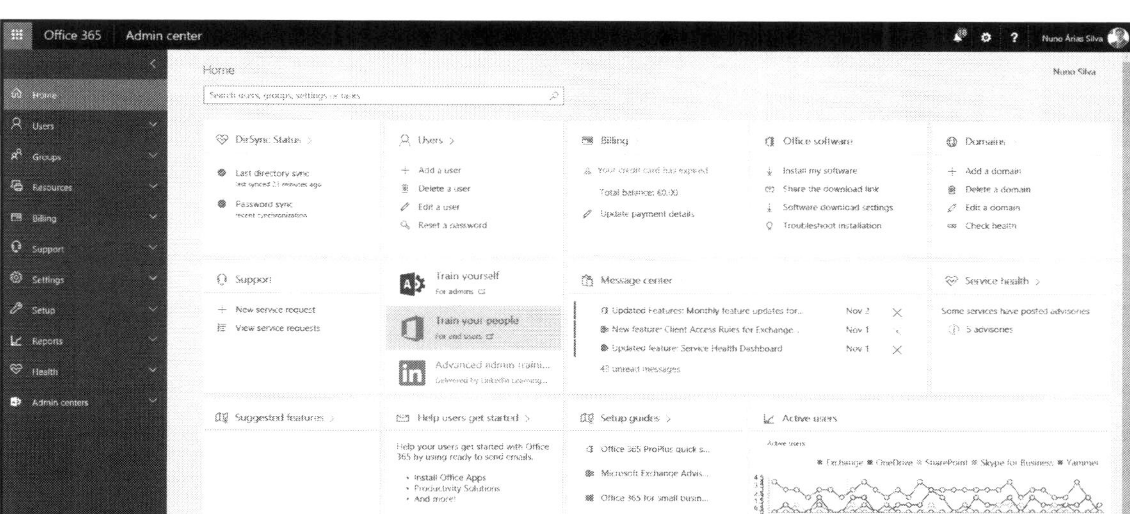

Let us now go through each of the home page's sections.

## Searching for users, groups settings, or tasks on the search pane

In the search pane, you can perform several tasks. Click on the search box and it will give you several suggestions of common search queries:

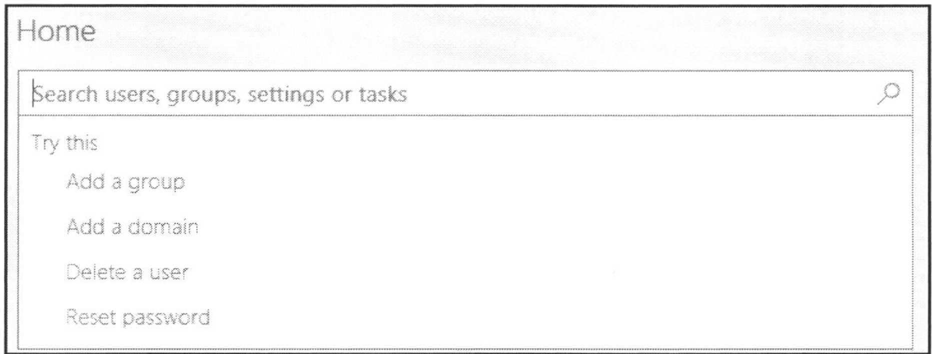

If you start typing the word `add` in the search box, it will provide you with the most common queries containing the `add` word, as you can see in the following screenshot:

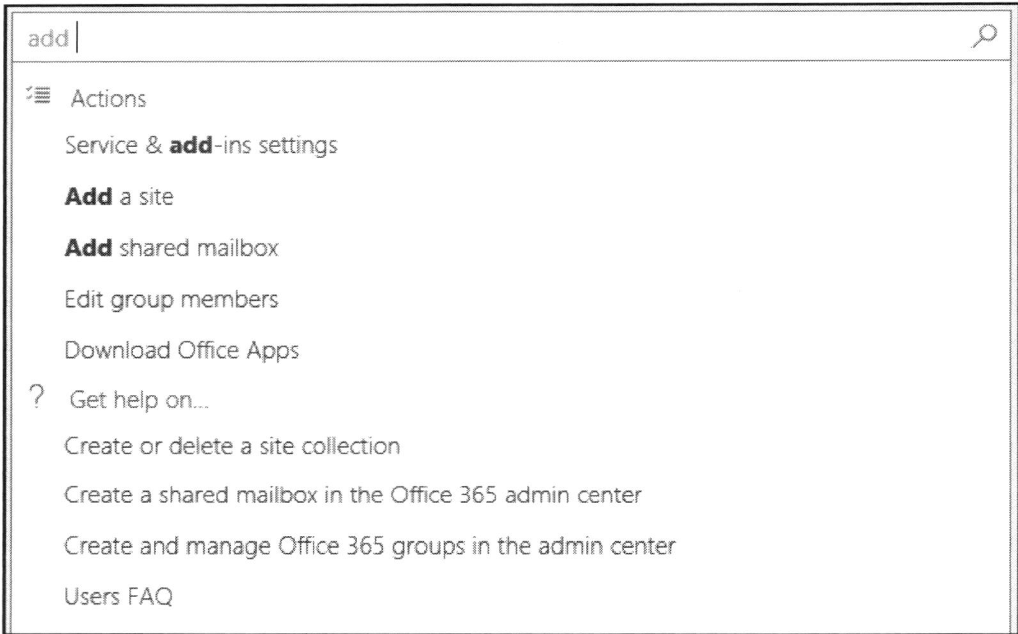


If you try searching for a user using the term `test` (and assuming you have users that contain this word in your directory), it will perform a search as you type and immediately show you the results, as depicted in the following screenshot:

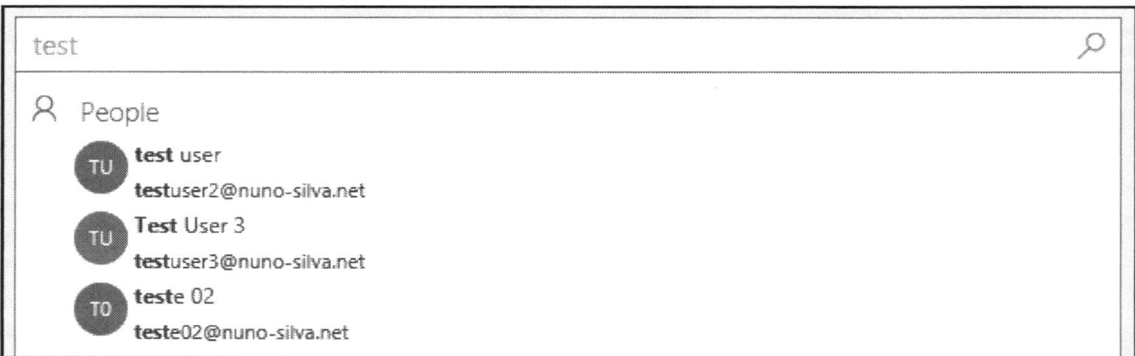

If you place your mouse pointer over a user result, it will show a few of the actions that can be performed over that result on the right-hand side, such as the reset password or edit user icons, as shown in the following screenshot:

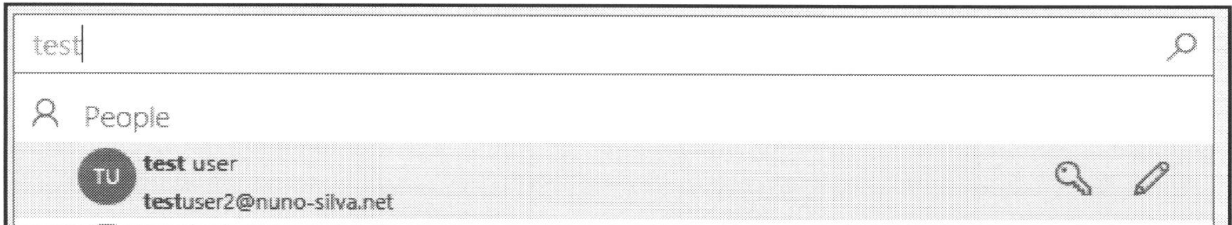


If you click on the edit user icon, you'll be directed to the edit section of that user, as shown in the following screenshot:

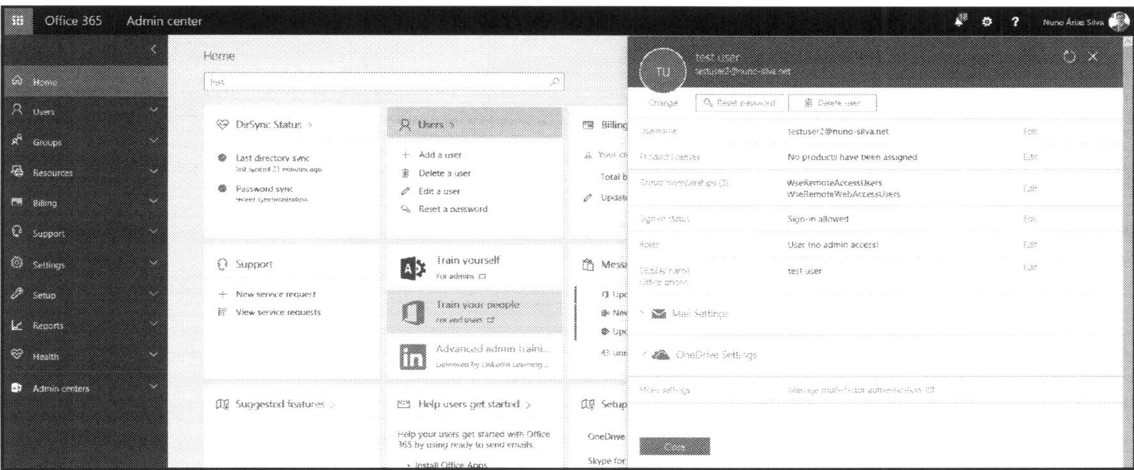

## Directory synchronization status

In the following screenshot, you can see the status about the directory synchronization when is was last synced and if it has any problem:

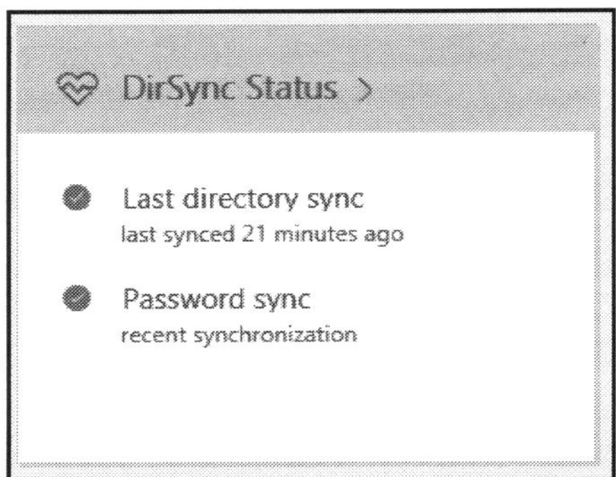


This section shows you a summary of the status of the synchronization with your on-premises AD. When you click on the status, it will take you to the page with the detailed status of the latest directory synchronization execution, as shown in the following screenshot:

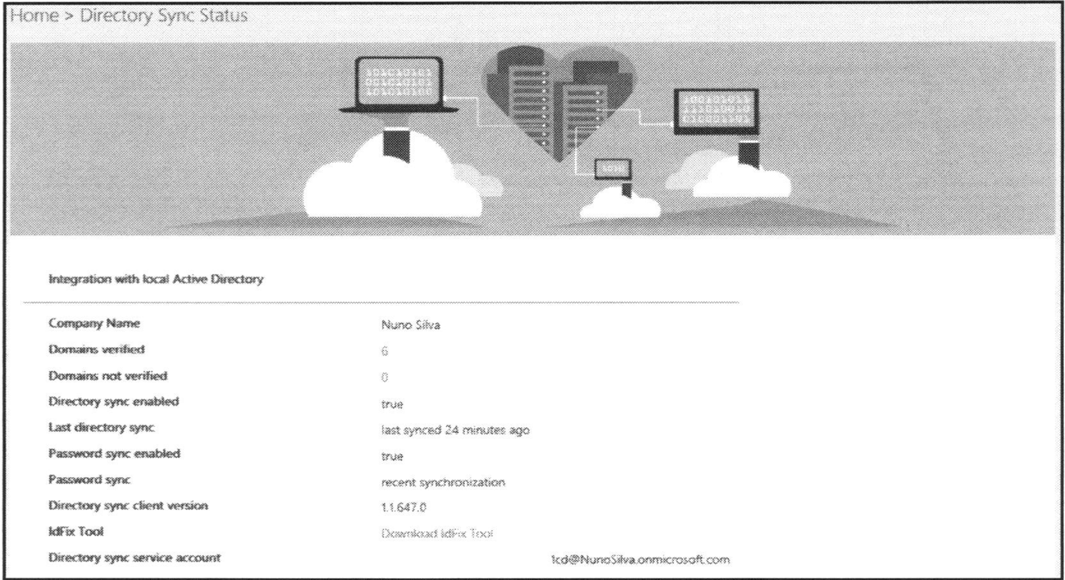

## Going directly to the users section to create, delete, edit, or reset a password of a user

In this section, you can directly perform actions such as the following:

- Adding a user
- Deleting a user
- Editing a user
- Resetting a password

By clicking the **Users** section, you can access the user management area of the portal, where you can perform these tasks, as well as some more advanced ones:

- Add a user
- Import multiple users
- Delete a user
- Reset a user password
- Set up multifactor authentication
- Set up directory synchronization

The following screenshot shows the further options available in the **More** drop-down list:

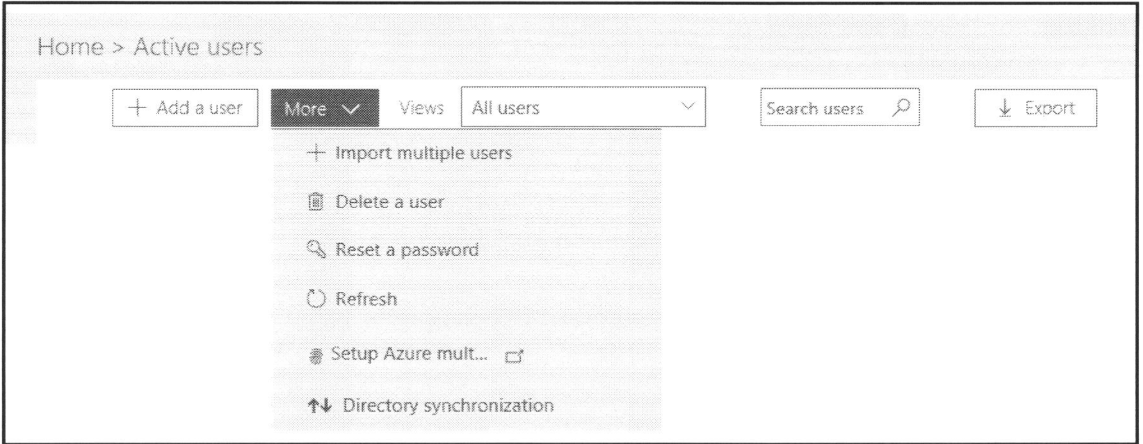

## Going to the Billing section

In the **Billing** widget, you can get a glimpse of your current balance, update your payment details, and view your bill. By clicking the **Billing** section, you are redirected to the **Subscriptions** page inside the billing area of the portal, where you have access to your subscriptions:

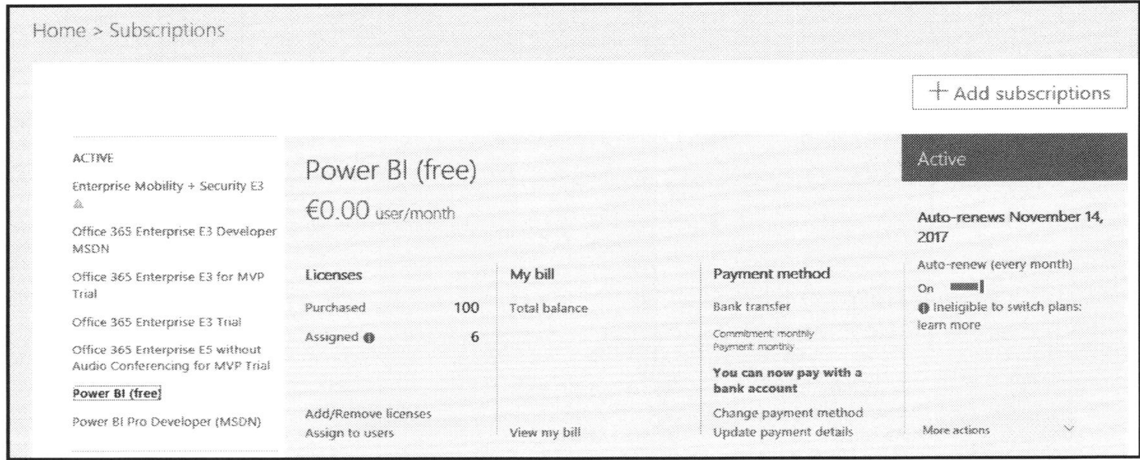


## Going to Office software section

The **Office software** widget allows you to open the **My Software** page, share the download link, update the software download settings, and troubleshoot a software installation. By clicking the button, you'll also land on the My Software page, where you can download Office software from `https://portal.office.com/OLS/MySoftware.aspx`.

*Need help?* Read about it or watch a video at `https://support.office.com/en-US/article/Video-Install-Office-on-your-PC-or-Mac-for-Office-365-for-business-b7071ece-237d-4f84-a67d-d8cf1d1f2e60`.

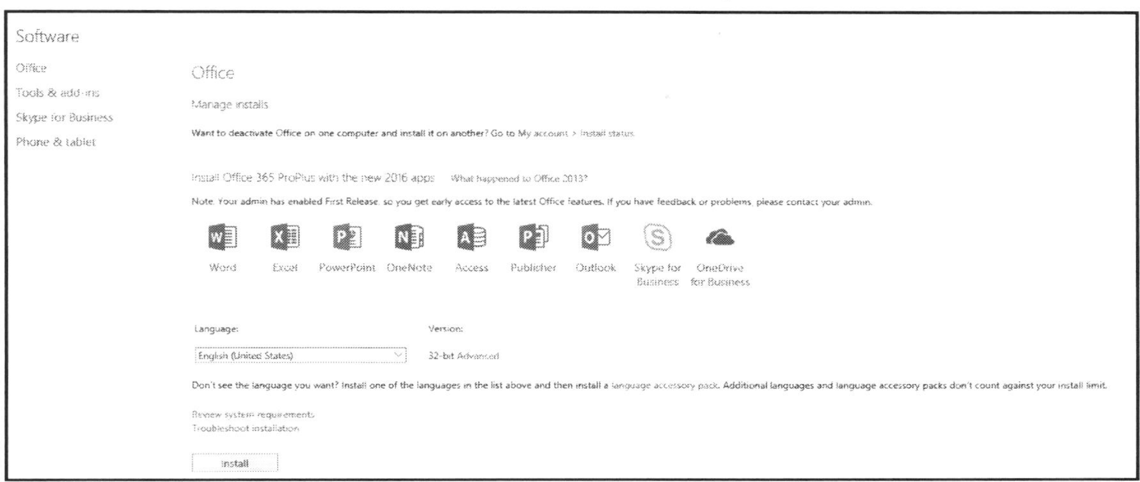


## Managing domains

In the **Domains** widget, you can add a new domain, delete an existing domain, edit a domain configuration, or check a domain's health, without leaving the Admin center homepage. However, if you wish to perform more advanced tasks, you can click on the widget title, which will bring you to the domain management page as shown in the following screenshot:

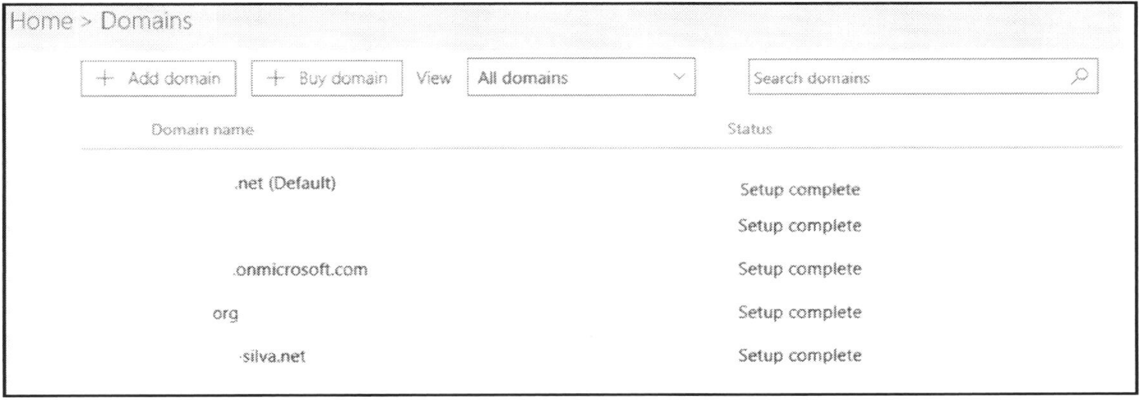

To add your domain, click on the **Add domain** button:

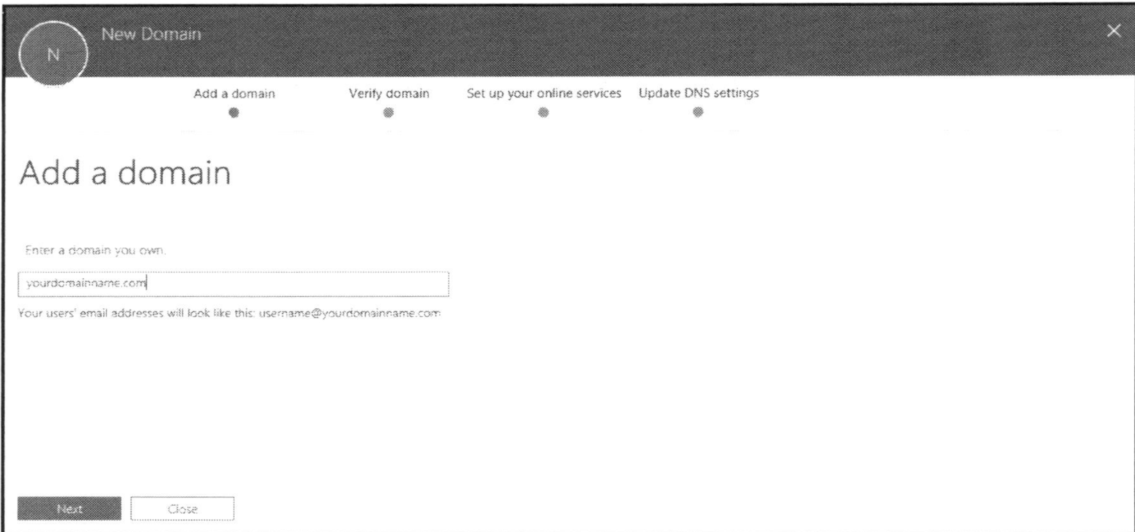


Fill in your domain name, for example, `yourdomainname.com`, and click on the **Next** button. Select the method you wish to use to validate its ownership, and click on the **Next** button, as shown in the following screenshot:

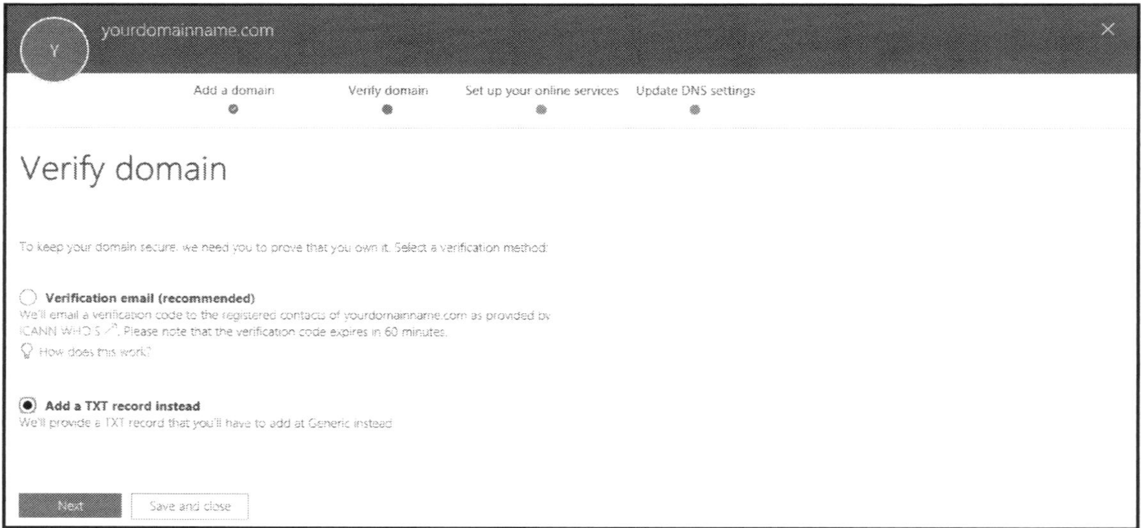

Assuming you wish to validate ownership using a TXT record in your DNS, after you have created the record with the values explained on the page, click on the **Verify** button as shown in the following screenshot:

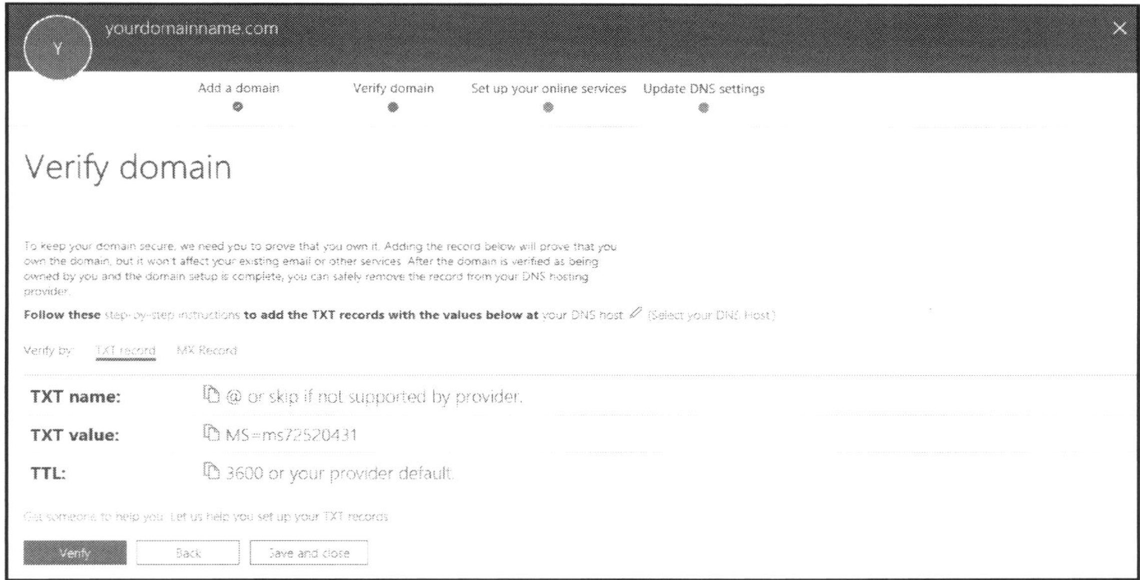


## Managing support

The **Support** widget in the home page allows you to create a new service request or view a service request you have created previously:

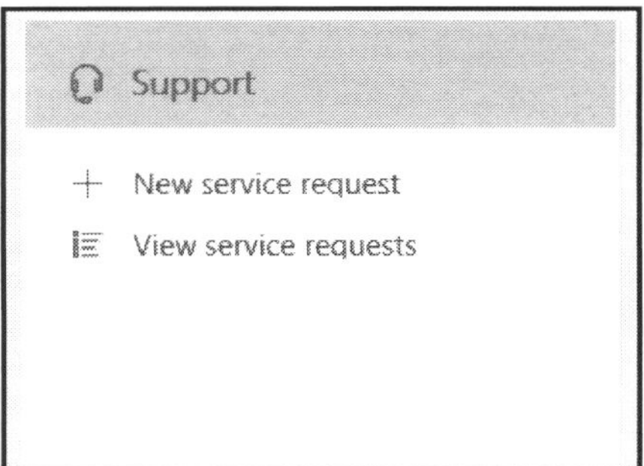

# Train yourself

By clicking the **Train yourself** option in the training widget, you'll be shown the available training lessons. These lessons are as follows:

- **Roadmap**
- **Get started**
- **Setup**
- **Mobile**
- **Communicate**
- **Store and share**
- **Manage**
- **Support**

You can also access this page directly at `https://support.office.com/en-us/article/Office-365-small-business---training-6ab4bbcd-79cf-4000-a0bd-d42ce4d12816?ui=en-USrs=en-USad=US`.

# Train your people

The **Train your people** option in the training widget is meant for end users and takes you to the Office 365 Training center. Here, you can learn more about each of the main client tools in the Office 365 suite:

- **Outlook**: *Outlook for Windows video training* at `https://support.office.com/en-US/article/8a5b816d-9052-4190-a5eb-494512343cca?wt.mc_id=otc_home`
- **OneDrive**: *OneDrive video training* at `https://support.office.com/en-US/article/1f608184-b7e6-43ca-8753-2ff679203132?wt.mc_id=otc_home`
- **Word**: *Word for Windows video training* at `https://support.office.com/en-US/article/7bcd85e6-2c3d-4c3c-a2a5-5ed8847eae73?wt.mc_id=otc_home`
- **Excel**: *Excel video training* at `https://support.office.com/en-US/article/9bc05390-e94c-46af-a5b3-d7c22f6990bb?wt.mc_id=otc_home`

- **PowerPoint**: PowerPoint video training at https://support.office.com/en-US/article/40e8c930-cb0b-40d8-82c4-bd53d3398787?wt.mc_id=otc_home
- **SharePoint**: SharePoint online video training at https://support.office.com/en-US/article/cb8ef501-84db-4427-ac77-ec2009fb8e23?wt.mc_id=otc_home
- **Microsoft Teams**: Microsoft Teams video training at https://support.office.com/en-US/article/4f108e54-240b-4351-8084-b1089f0d21d7?wt.mc_id=otc_home

You'll also have access to a few courses containing multiple lessons, such as the following:

- *Office 365 basics* at https://support.office.com/en-US/article/Start-now-396b8d9e-e118-42d0-8a0d-87d1f2f055fb?wt.mc_id=otc_home
- *Try it with templates* at https://support.office.com/en-US/article/Try-it-0865d155-bd36-407a-82be-929f2cd76f26?wt.mc_id=otc_home
- *Collaborate with Office 365* at https://support.office.com/en-US/article/See-how-ac05a41e-0b49-4420-9ebc-190ee4e744f4?wt.mc_id=otc_home
- *Office tips and tricks* at https://support.office.com/office-training-center/featured-tips?wt.mc_id=OTC_HOME

For quick tips, you can download a few infographics that show interesting use cases when using some of the Office client tools at https://support.office.com/en-us/article/Great-ways-to-work-with-Word-Outlook-and-PowerPoint-6fe70269-b9a4-4ef0-a96e-7a5858b3bd5a?wt.mc_id=otc_home&ui=en-US&rs=en-US&ad=US. Alternatively, you can download the *Office Training Center Bill of Materials*, a searchable list of all learning assets, with almost 400 additional training items at https://www.microsoft.com/en-us/download/details.aspx?id=54088&WT.mc_id=rss_alldownloads_all.

## Advanced admin training on LinkedIn learning

Using the **Advanced admin training on LinkedIn Learning** option, you can access advanced courses for Office 365 administrators and IT pros:

- *Microsoft Cloud: Explore Cloud Services:* `https://support.office.com/en-us/article/Start-training-02ef429a-002e-4990-a152-8a1596ff925d`
- *Office 365: Deployment:* `https://support.office.com/en-us/article/Start-training-1b6d678b-dccc-47e5-9f05-c1e031ba1d29`
- *Office 365: Administration:* `https://support.office.com/en-us/article/Start-training-81d31f7b-2ada-4ecb-83d6-20972025be94`
- *Office 365: Manage Identities Using Azure AD Connect:* `https://support.office.com/en-us/article/Start-training-90991a1d-c0ab-479a-b413-35c9706f6fed`
- *Microsoft Cloud Services: Administer Office 365 and Intune:* `https://support.office.com/en-us/article/Start-training-c1224e20-3d49-4f40-99ee-fd0991880376`
- *Office 365: Troubleshoot Availability and Usage:* `https://support.office.com/en-us/article/Start-training-a72bae2d-6779-49fd-865f-9932293d2912`
- *Office 365 for Administrators: Supporting Users:* `https://support.office.com/en-us/article/Start-training-6373a517-d015-46d6-9713-0d5b18364965`

These are just some of the options-there are many more!

## Message center

The **Message center** widget shows you the latest messages at a glance, and allows you to access the message center area of the portal where you can check all the Office 365 messages:

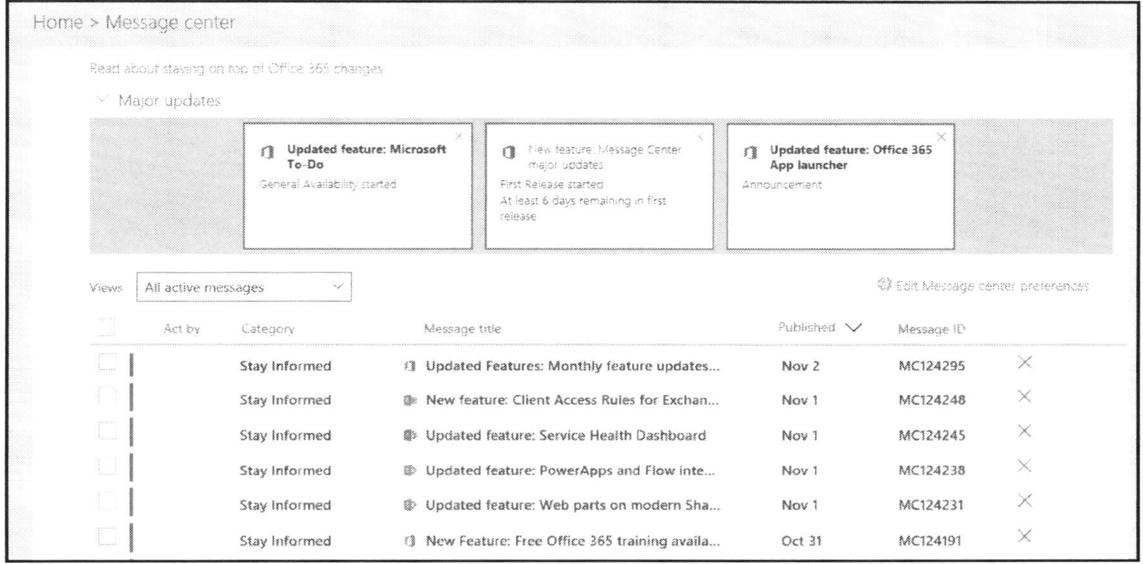

These messages are periodically sent by Microsoft and provide you with information about new features or changes to the Office 365 services or applications:

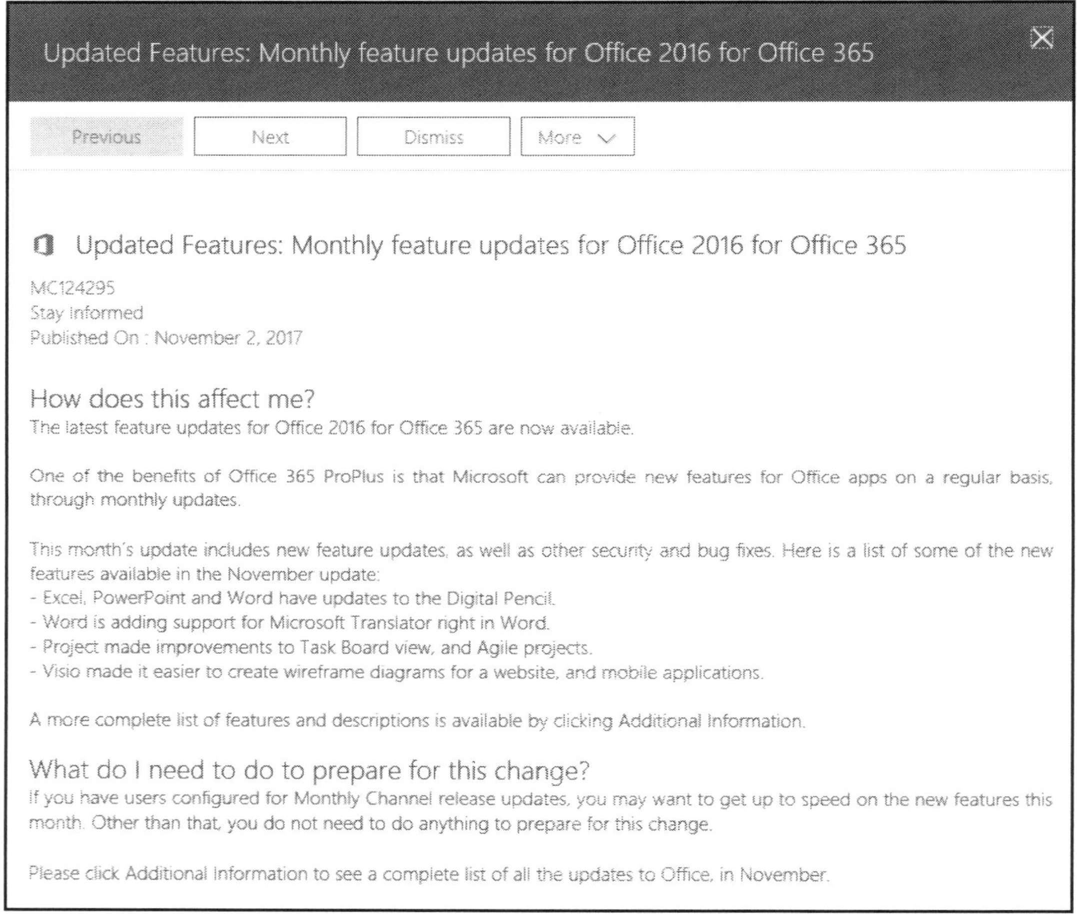


## Service health

In the **Service health** widget, you can see a visual indication of the current health status of the services, which displays advisories and the number of services that might be affected by issues. Clicking on the widget title will bring you to the **Service health** page of the portal, where you can find additional details about the health of each service and any incidents or advisories posted for it:

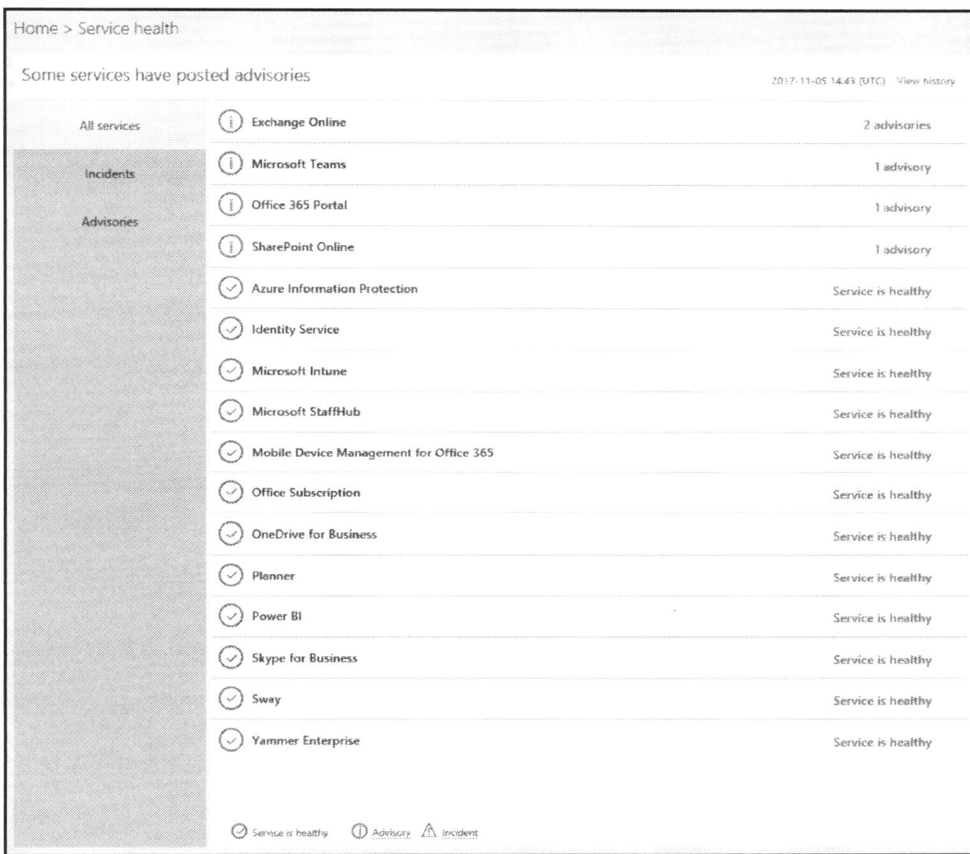


## Suggested features

The **Suggested features** widget shows you small tips and content to help you get the most out of the many workloads of Office 365:

Home > Suggested features

Suggested features: Get more value from your Office 365 subscription!

# Help users get started

The **Help users get started** option gives you the possibility to send prepared emails to all (or a subset) of your users to help them get started with Office 365:

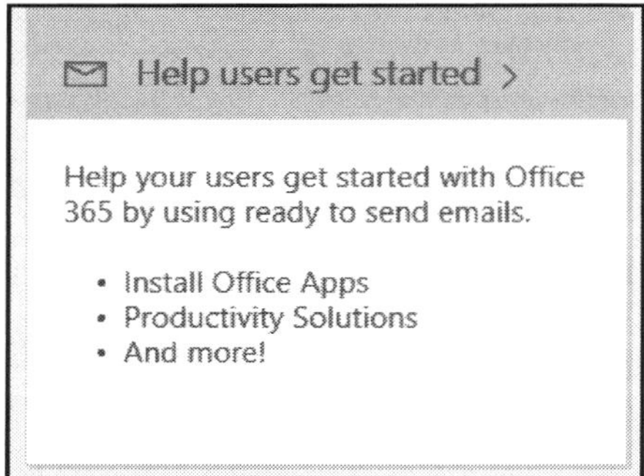


You select one or more users, and an email template to send to them. For example, you can send them an email about the **Productivity library** as shown in the following screenshot:

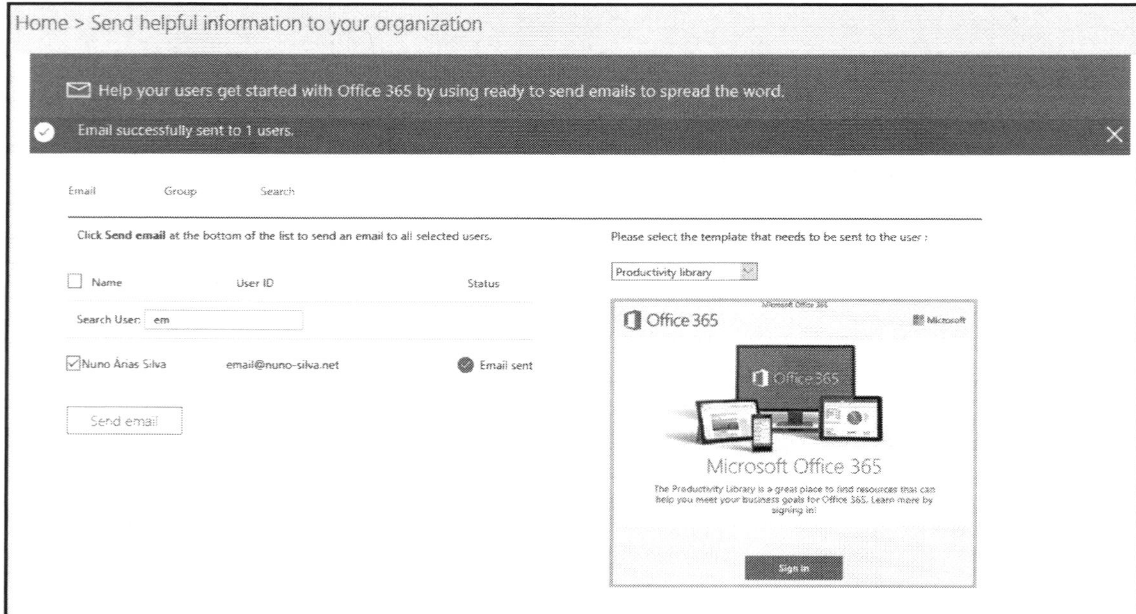

At this point, you will have several templates:

- New Office 365 training
- Office apps
- OneDrive
- Outlook
- Productivity library
- Skype
- Teams

For additional resources, you can also access the Productivity library directly at `https://portal.office.com/onboarding/productivitylibrary#/`.

# Setup guides

In the **Setup guides** widget, you can browse through the existing guides for the many Office 365 services. By clicking the widget's title, you'll be presented with the full list of setup guides, which are specially prepared, self-guided support assets for service setup. As you select the features and options you want to deploy, the guides and advisers will build you a step-by-step setup plan that's customized to your needs. You will get a full set of instructions, videos, reference articles, and scripts.

## Creating content

Express your ideas and data with Word, OneNote, PowerPoint, and Excel. You can find the Office 365 ProPlus quick start guide at `https://aka.ms/OPPquickstartguide`. Use this quick start guide wizard to set up apps such as Word, Excel, PowerPoint, and OneNote for your employees.

## Small business quick start

You can refer to the Office 365 for a small business quick start guide at `https://aka.ms/SmallBusinessQuickstartGuide`. You can get the most from Office 365 business plans with this small business quick start guide.

## Saving, sharing, and coauthoring

You and your team can store, access, and work together on vital content with OneDrive.

You can refer to the SharePoint quick start guide at `https://aka.ms/SPOquickstartguide`.

The SharePoint Online quick start guide for small businesses shows you how to make the most of the SharePoint Online deployment options and steps that work for your organization.

The OneDrive for Business quick start guide is at `https://aka.ms/ODfBquickstartguide`. Set up OneDrive, where your employees can store and access files in the cloud.

## Mail and calendars

Keep yourself and your team on the same page with Outlook. For more information on Microsoft Exchange advisors, you can refer to `https://aka.ms/setupexchangepage`. With these tools, you can set up mail, connect your users, set up auditing, track messages, and help protect email from spam and malware.

*Need to migrate?* You can find more information at `https://aka.ms/sifndc`.

## Chat, online meetings, and voice

Connect with others near and far with Skype for Business and Intune.

For more information on the Microsoft Teams deployment advisor, please refer to `https://aka.ms/teamsguidance`. Microsoft Teams is a chat-based workspace in Office 365. It gives your team a dedicated hub that brings together all their chats, content, people, and tools.

You can find the Skype for Business quick start guide at `https://aka.ms/SfBquickstartguide`. The Skype for Business quick start guide for small businesses will show you how to quickly set up the client, video, IM, and presence functions, and allow external screen sharing for your users.

You can refer to the Yammer quick start guide at `https://aka.ms/yamquickstartguide`. Use this quick start guide to set up your Yammer corporate network so that your employees can keep up with what's happening in your company.

## Security and identity

Refer to the Azure AD basic setup guide at `https://aka.ms/azureadbasic`. Set up the basic edition of Azure AD for features such as group-based access management, self-service password resets, and publishing on-premises web applications.

The Azure AD premium setup guide is available at `https://aka.ms/aadpguidance`. You can set up Azure AD premium for advanced features such as multifactor authentication, **single sign-on** (**SSO**), device registration, security monitoring, and more.

For more information on the Microsoft Intune deployment advisor refer to `https://aka.ms/intuneguidance`. Use Intune to help keep corporate applications, data, and resources secure on devices (such as mobiles, tablets, and PCs).

For more information on the Azure Information Protection deployment wizard refer to `https://aka.ms/azurermsguidance`. Help protect your organization's sensitive information by setting up permissions for accessing and sharing data in your company.

## Videos for IT pros

You may want to refer to a few videos, the links of which are given as follows:

- **Creating content:**
    - Click-to-Run and Office 365 ProPlus: `https://aka.ms/qo45jf`
    - Overview of Office 365 ProPlus: `https://aka.ms/r359zr`
    - Telemetry and Office 365 ProPlus: `https://aka.ms/cjpq52`
- **Saving, sharing, and coauthoring**
    - OneDrive for Business Integrated Advantage: `https://aka.ms/f66hqa`
- **Chat, online meetings, and voice**
    - Skype for Business Enablement quick start: `https://aka.ms/cjfutd`
- **Admin center**
    - Create users in the Admin center: `https://aka.ms/ac-createusers`
    - DNS records and the Admin center: `https://aka.ms/ac-dnsrecords`
    - Verify your domain in the Admin center: `https://aka.ms/ac-verifydns`

- **Walk-throughs for users**
    - Walk-throughs for Office 365 users: `https://aka.ms/usertrainingwizards`

See the walk-throughs for Office 365 user videos for quick, how-to guidance on things such as installing Office 365 apps on mobile devices or syncing files to OneDrive for Business.

## Active users

The **Active users** widget presents you with a simplified version of the distribution over time of your active users for each workload. Clicking the widget title will take you to the usage reports area, where you can find reports such as the following:

- **Office 365**:
    - Activations
    - Active users
    - Office 365 group activity
- **Exchange**:
    - Email activity
    - Email app usage
    - Mailbox usage
- **OneDrive**:
    - OneDrive activity
    - OneDrive usage
- **SharePoint**:
    - SharePoint activity
    - SharePoint site usage
- **Skype for Business**:
    - Skype for Business activity
    - Skype for Business peer-to-peer activity
    - Skype for Business conference organizer activity
    - Skype for Business conference participant activity
    - Skype for Business device usage
    - Skype for Business PSTN usage
    - Skype for Business users blocked

- **Yammer**:
    - Yammer activity
    - Yammer device usage
    - Yammer group activity

You can select a report or just take a look at the main usage stats. The following screenshot shows the main report of active users:

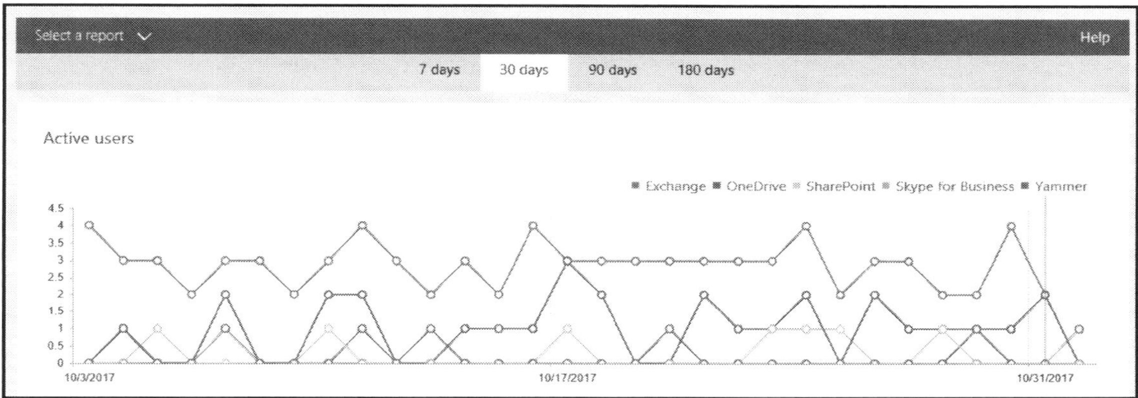


The following screenshot shows the Email, OneDrive, SharePoint and Skype for Business activities:

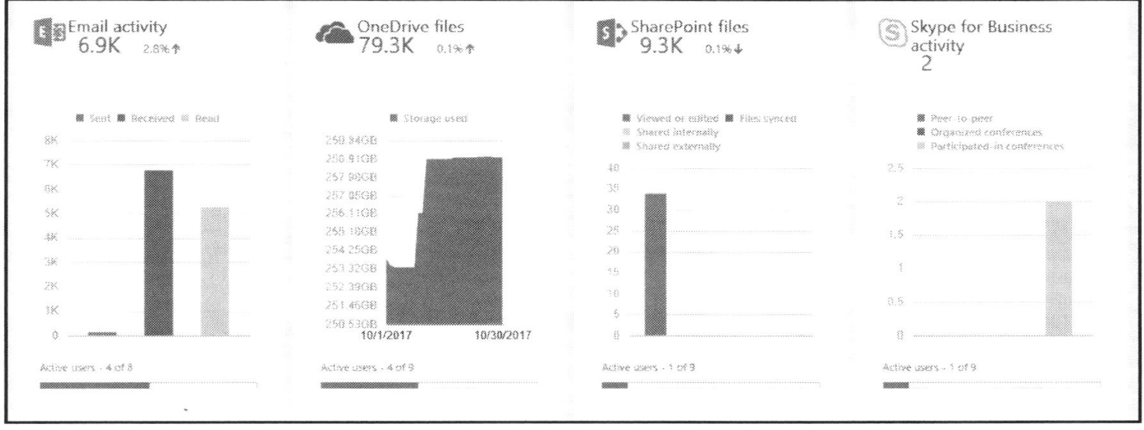

The following screenshot shows the Office activations, Yammer and the link to more reports using Office 365 Adoption preview that is powered by PowerBI:

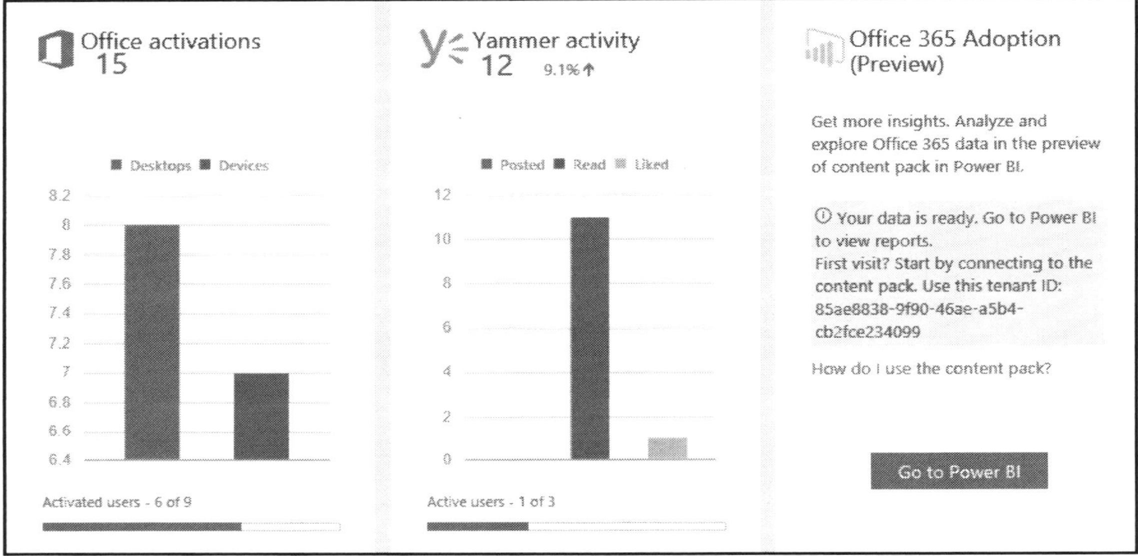


# Office 365 Adoption preview

If you want to have more access to information and insights about service usage, you can use the Office 365 Adoption content pack for Power BI. This invaluable tool will provide you with dashboards such as the ones described in the following screenshot:

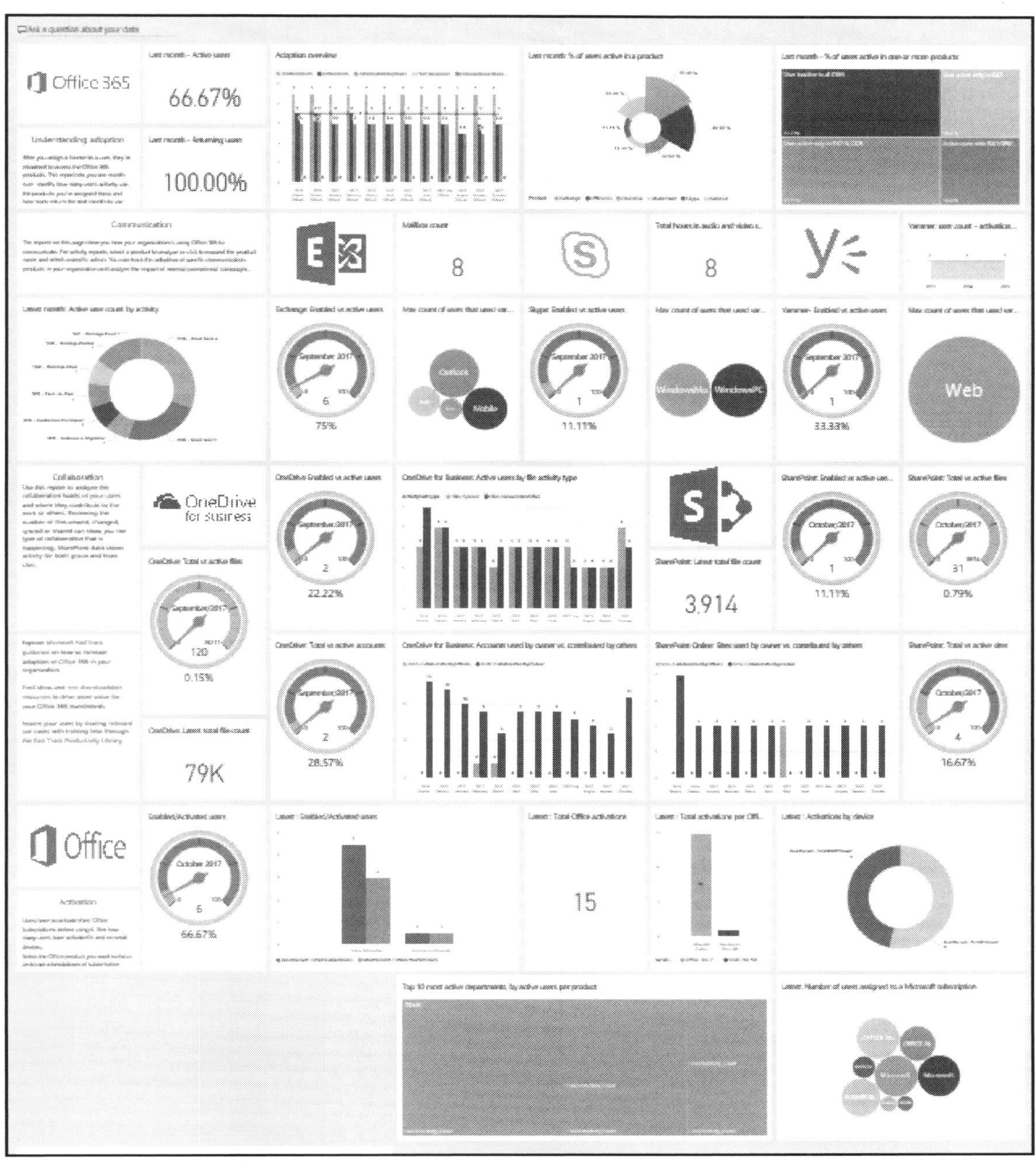
Office 365
66.67%
100.00%
8
8
Outlook
Mobile
Web
75%
11.11%
33.33%
OneDrive for Business
22.22%
3,914
11.11%
0.79%
0.15%
28.57%
16.67%
79K
Office
66.67%
15

The Office 365 Adoption content pack for Power BI provides an extensive set of information about how your organization is using the Office 365 workloads, how they are used, what the usage trends are, and which workloads require attention to foster adoption. You can also use it to make decisions about which licensing needs your organization actually has and which provide a great opportunity for optimization. Since it is a content pack for Power BI, you can also customize the dashboards and set it up in the way that makes the most sense to you. It is truly an invaluable tool.

## What is in the Office 365 Adoption content pack?

- **Adoption**: You can quickly get a big picture view of your Office 365 environment, as well as the license usage in your Office 365 tenant, and use that information to make fast decisions. You can view how many licenses of each product are assigned to the users and which users are using the features of a particular product on Office 365 per month. These metrics are based on a user having used a product at least once.
- **Communication**: You can look at Exchange, Yammer, and Skype for Business data to see how users are communicating. You can easily see whether your organization prefers email, Yammer posts, or Skype calls to stay in the loop and get work done.
- **Collaboration**: Great teams work together, and by analyzing OneDrive and SharePoint site usage patterns, you'll see how users in your organization collaborate.
- **Access from anywhere**: No more wondering which clients and devices are used to connect to email, Skype for Business, or Yammer when users are on the go—you can see that information right here.
- **Storage use**: Track cloud storage consumption for mailboxes, OneDrive, and SharePoint sites to help users stay under limits and to help quantify how much data your organization is storing.
- **Office activation**: When you assign a license for Office, users can install the apps on up to five devices. In this report, you can now easily see the device types on which users have installed Office apps.

You can go to the initial dashboard or you can browse through additional reports, such as the following:

- Adoption overview
- Product usage
- Communication
- Collaboration
- Access from anywhere
- Storage
- Office activation
- Exchange usage
- Skype for Business usage
- Yammer usage
- OneDrive for Business usage
- SharePoint usage
- Exchange—user activity
- Skype for Business—user activity
- Yammer—user activity
- OneDrive—user activity
- SharePoint—user activity
- User adoption by product
- Adoption by department
- Adoption by region
- Assigned licenses

The following are a few examples of the reports that can be compiled in a demo tenant:

- **Adoption overview**: The Adoption overview report is shown in the following screenshot:

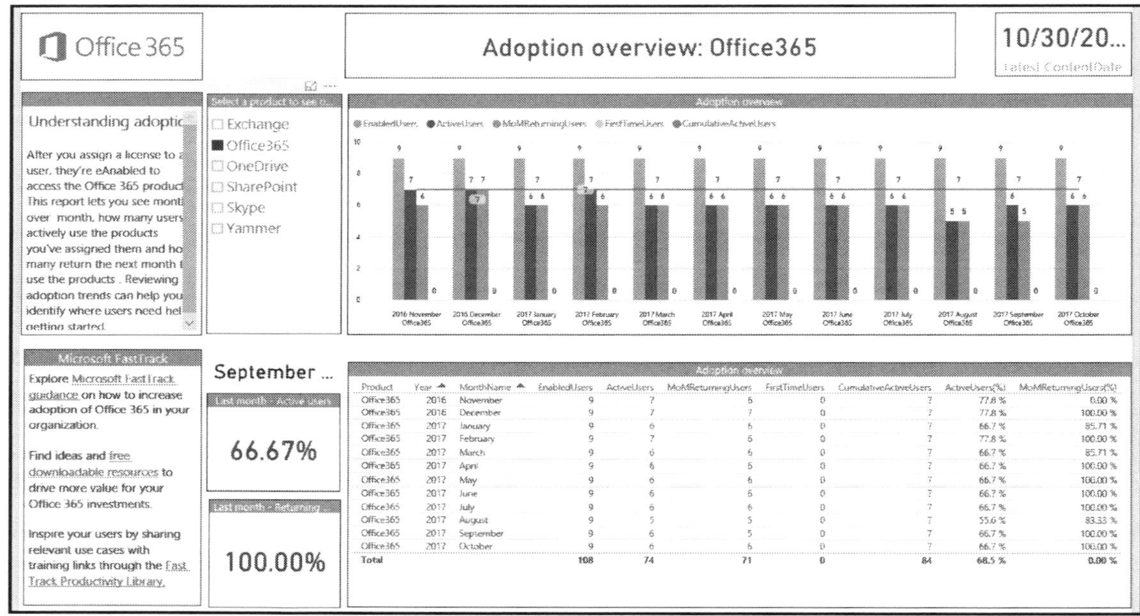

- **Product usage:** The Product usage report is shown in the following screenshot:

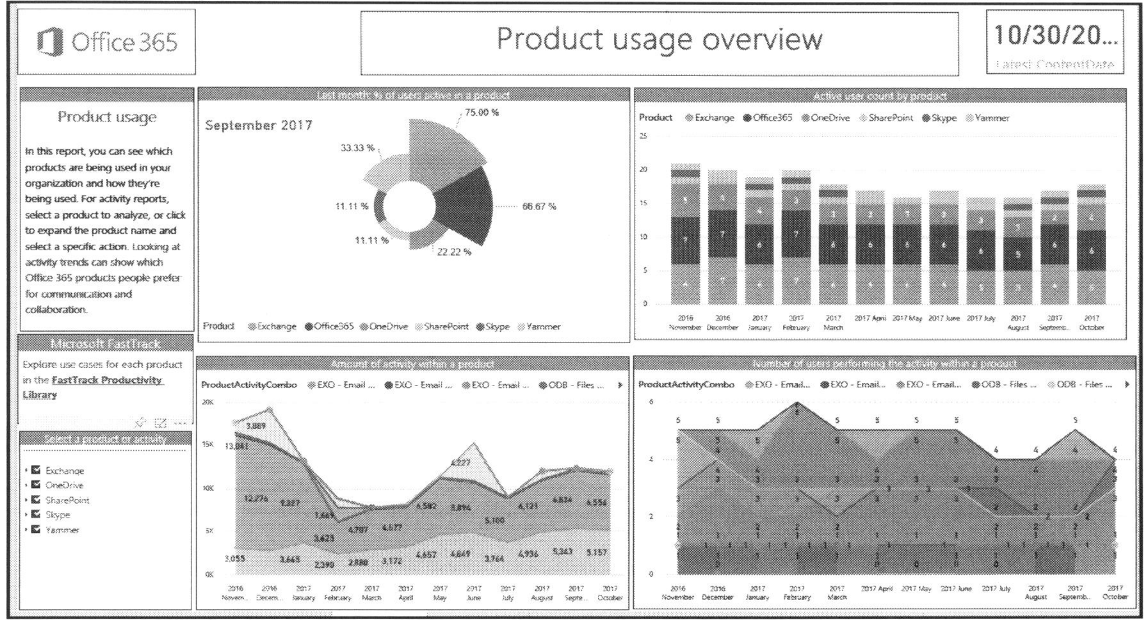

- **Communication:** The Communication report is shown in the following screenshot:

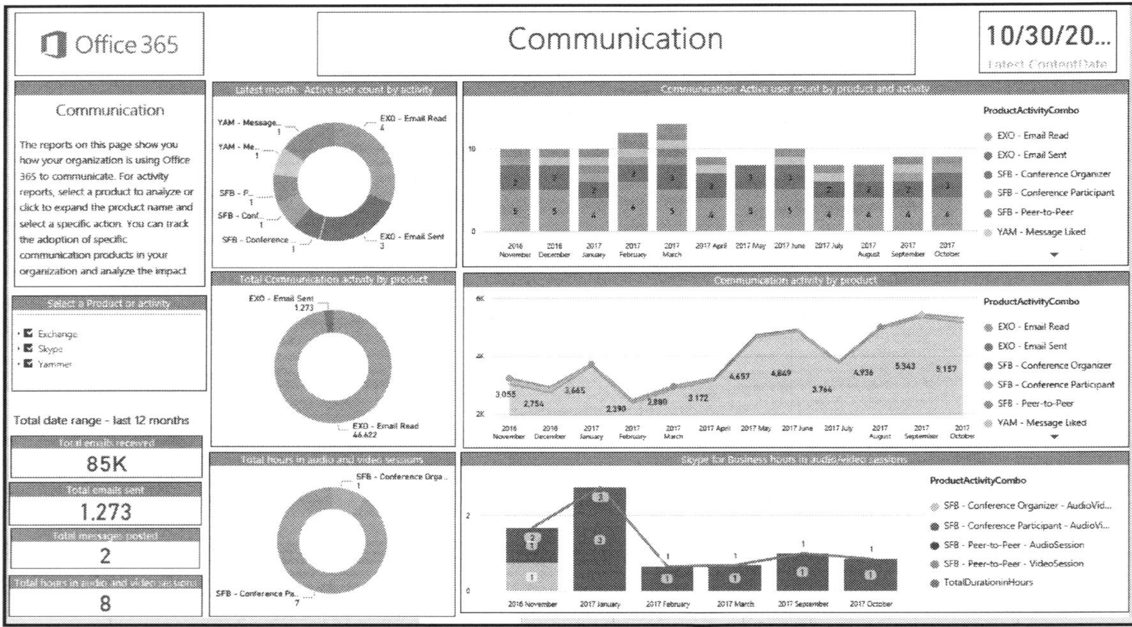

- **Collaboration:** The Collaboration trends are shown in the following screenshot:

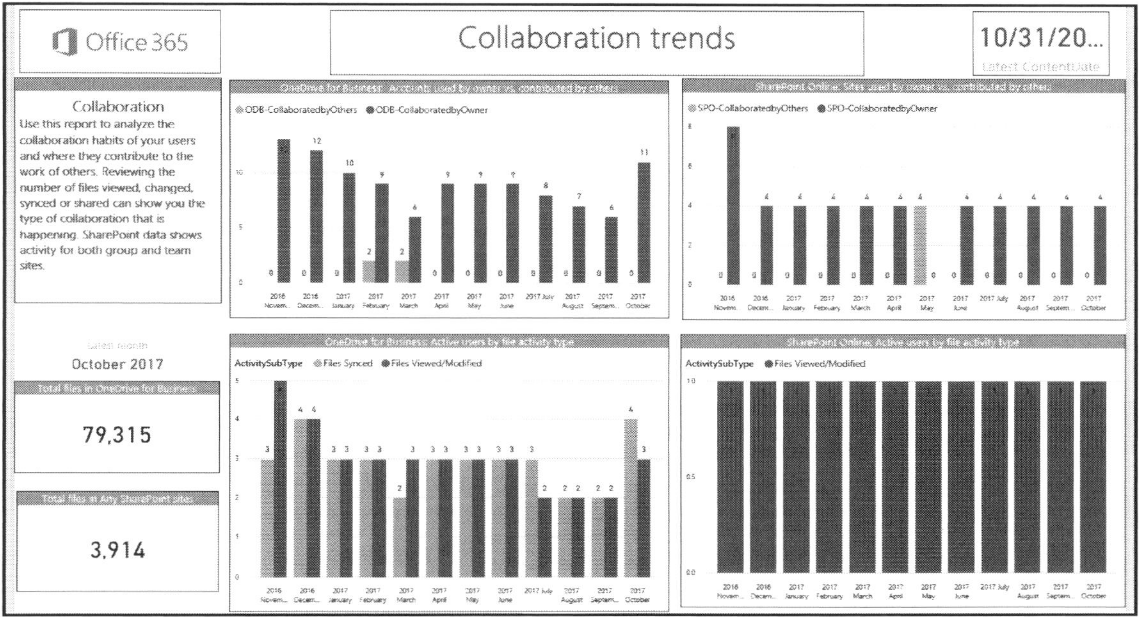

- **Access from anywhere:** The Access from anywhere, on any device report is shown in the following screenshot:

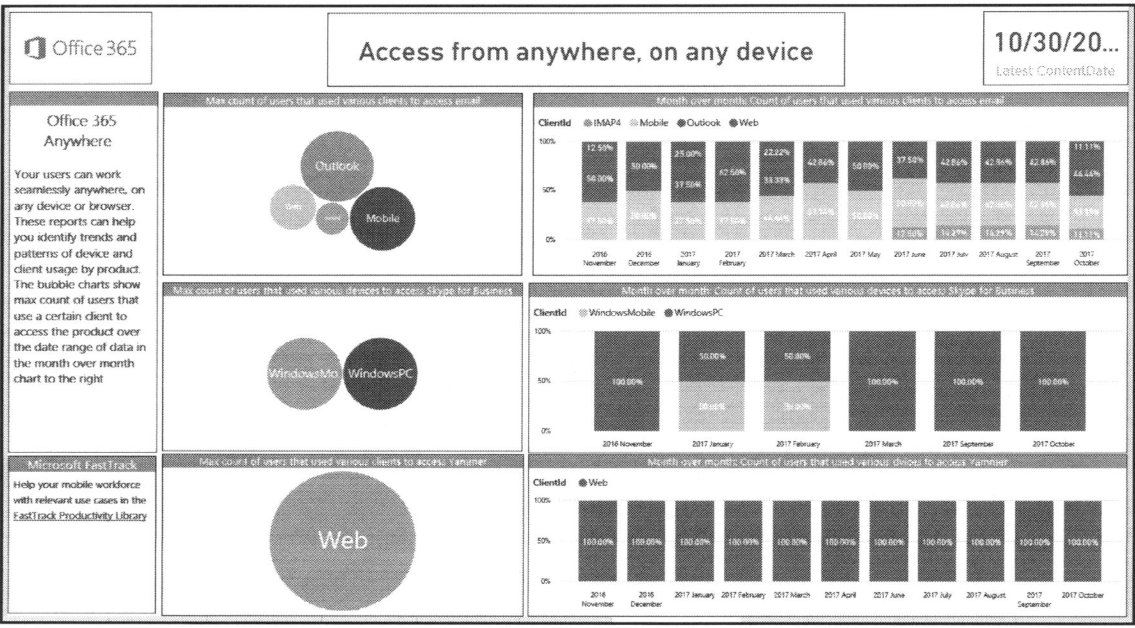

- **Storage:** The report for the amount of storage used is shown in the following screenshot:

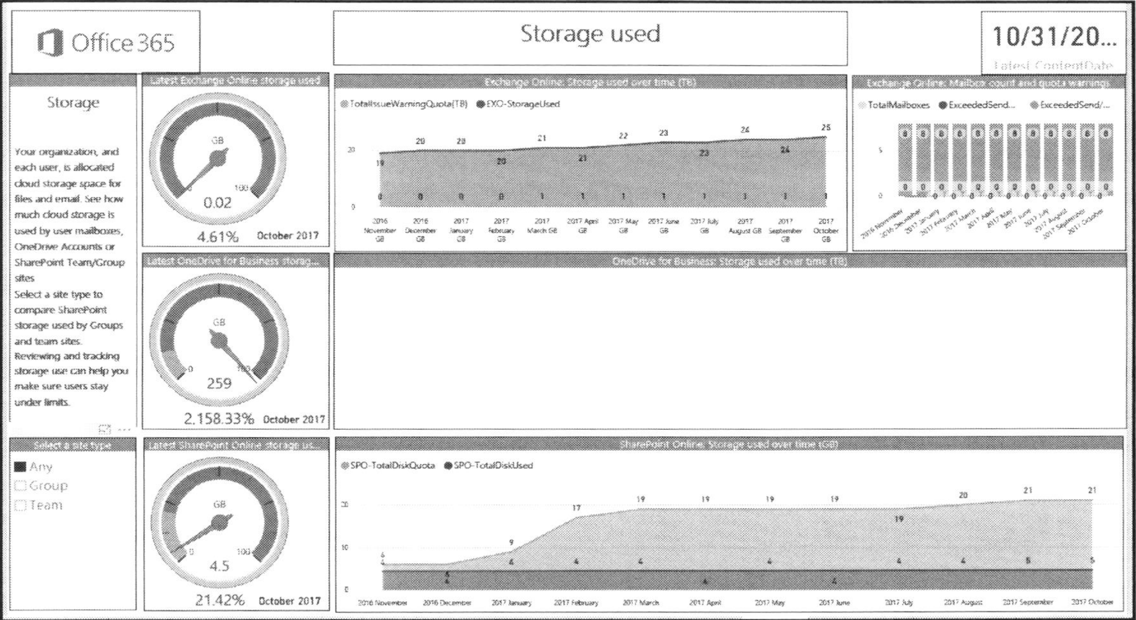

- **Office activation:** The Office activation report is shown in the following screenshot:

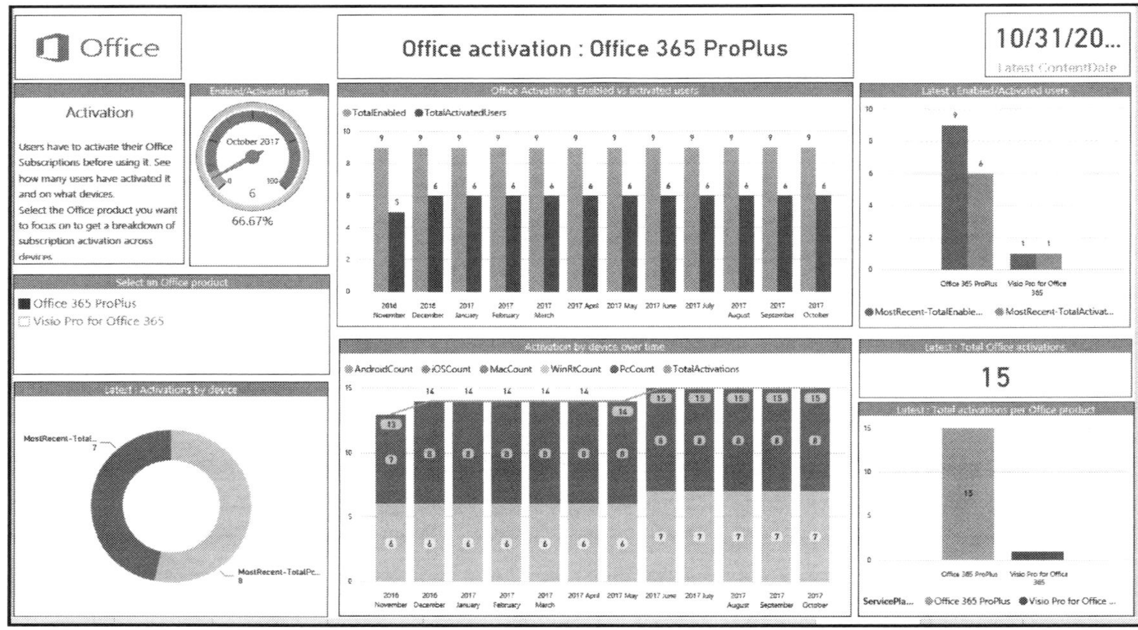

- **Exchange Online usage:** The Exchange Online usage report is shown in the following screenshot:

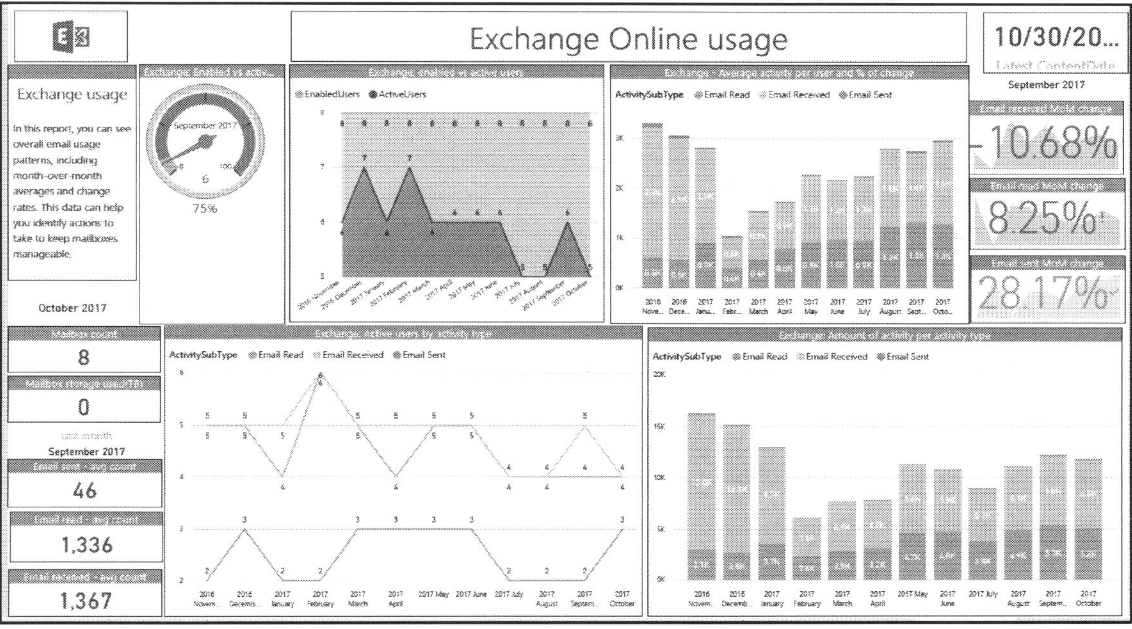

- **Skype for Business usage:** The Skype for Business usage report is shown in the following screenshot:

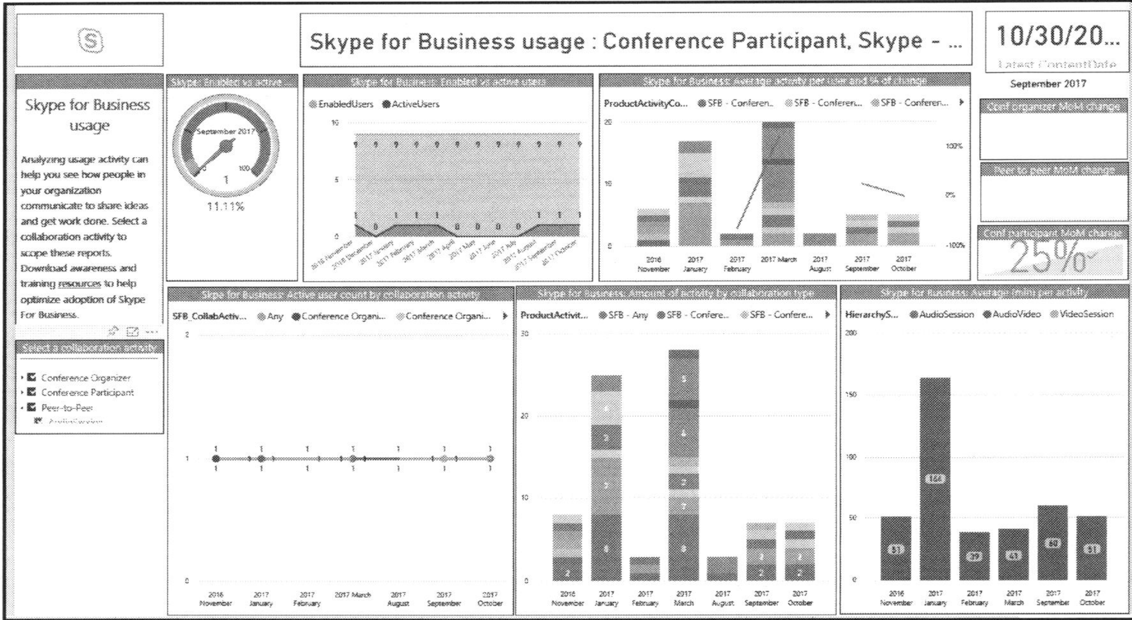

- **Yammer usage:** The Yammer usage report is shown in the following screenshot:

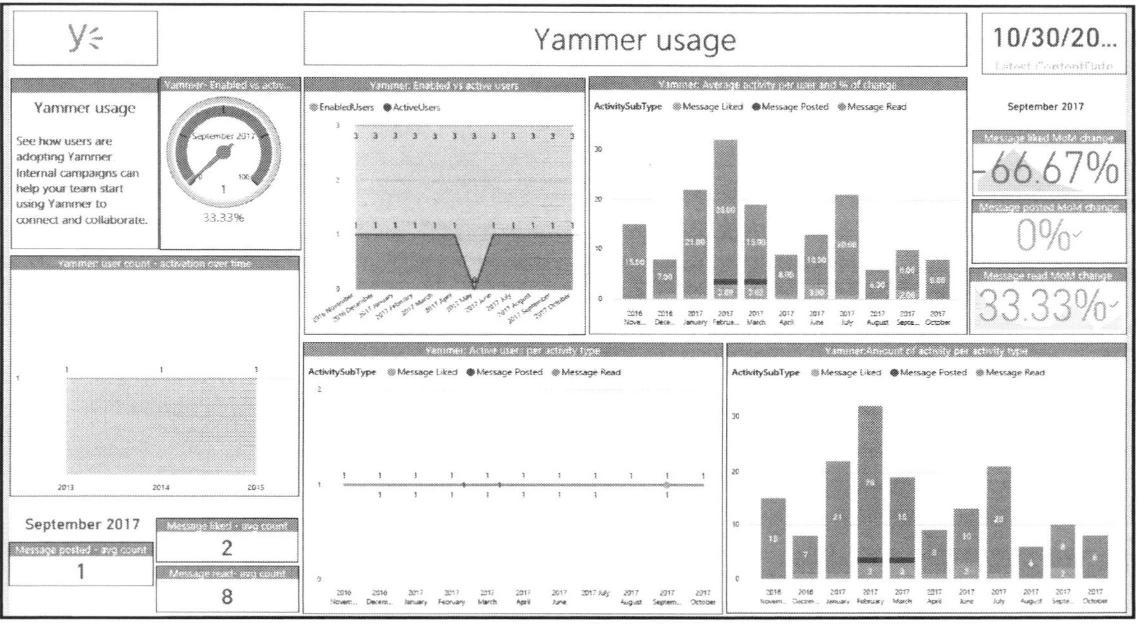

- **OneDrive for Business usage:** The OneDrive for Business usage report is shown in the following screenshot:

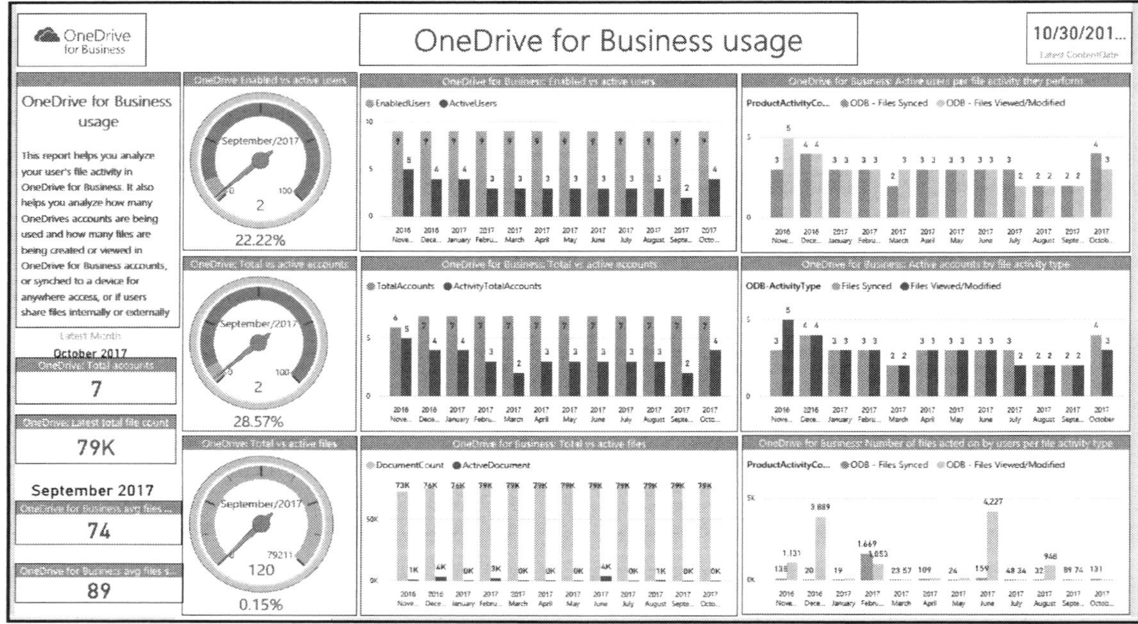

- **SharePoint usage:** The SharePoint usage report is shown in the following screenshot:

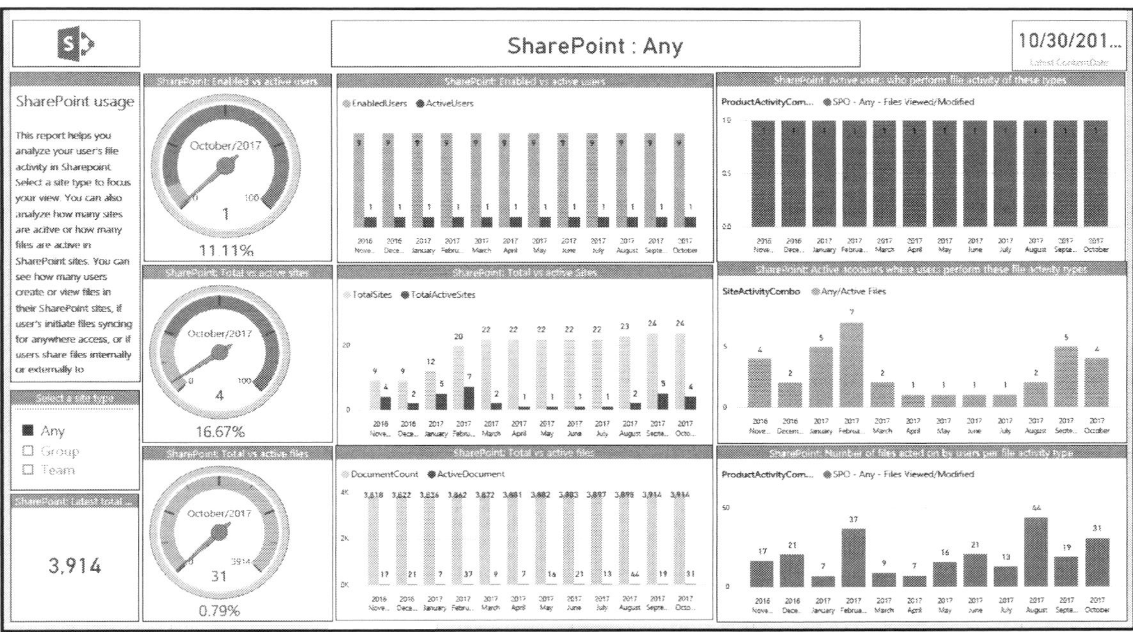

# Users

The first area of the Admin center is the user management area. By clicking the **Users** item in the left-hand navigation menu, you will have access to these sub items as shown in the following screenshot:

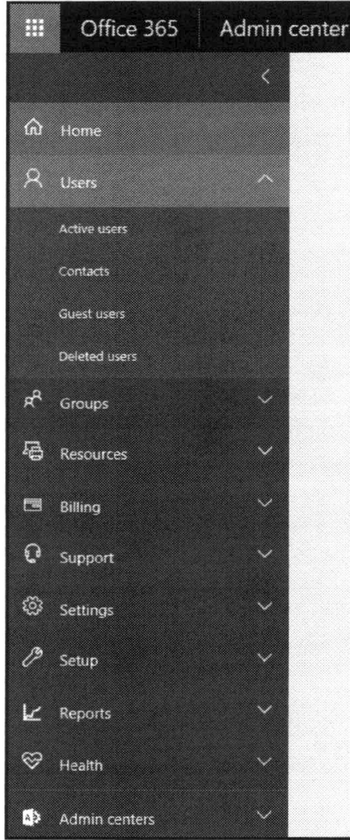


# Groups

The **Groups** area will provide you with access to the following:

- Groups (security groups as well as Office 365 groups)
- Shared mailboxes

# Resources

The **Resources** area allows you to manage the following:

- **Rooms and equipment**
- **Sites**

# Billing

The **Billing** area provides you with access to the following:

- **Subscriptions**
- **Bills**
- **Licenses**
- **Purchase services**
- **Billing notifications**

# Support

The **Support** area allows you to do the following:

- Create a new service request
- View previous service requests
- View customer lockbox requests (if you have E5 licenses)

# Settings

In the **Settings** area, you have access to the following:

- **Services & add-ins**
- **Security & privacy**
- **DirSync errors** (directory synchronization)
- **Organization profile**
- **Partner relationships**

## Services & add-ins

By clicking the **Services & add-ins** option, you can configure detailed options for some of the services of Office 365, which are as follows:

- **Azure multifactor authentication:** Manage your settings for Azure multifactor authentication
- **Bing:** Turn Bing for Business access on or off for your company employees
- **Calendar:** Let people share their calendars with external users
- **Cortana:** Turn Cortana access on or off for your entire organization
- **Directory Synchronization:** Sync users to the cloud, using AD
- **Docs.com:** Manage and update your `Docs.com` settings
- **Dynamics Customer Insights Preview:** Manage and update your Dynamic Customer Insights Preview settings
- **Integrated Apps:** Manage your Integrated Apps settings
- **Mail:** Set up auditing, track messages, and protect email from spam and malware
- **Microsoft Azure Information Protection:** Update your settings for Microsoft Azure Information Protection
- **Microsoft Forms:** Manage and update your Microsoft Form settings
- **Microsoft Teams:** Manage and update your Microsoft Team settings
- **Office 365 Groups:** Control settings for Office 365 groups
- **Office Online:** Let people use third-party hosted storage services
- **Office Software Download Settings:** Control versions and which Office apps are available to download
- **Office Store:** Manage your Office Store settings
- **Reports:** Show anonymous IDs instead of names in all reports or enable the Power BI content pack
- **Sites:** Update your site's settings
- **Skype for Business:** Set up domain exceptions and dial-in conferencing, and allow external sharing
- **StaffHub:** Turn StaffHub on or off for your entire organization
- **Sway:** Manage your Sway settings
- **To-Do:** Manage and update your To-Do settings

# Security & privacy

By clicking the **Security & privacy** option, you can configure the following options:

- **Password policy**
- **Customer Lockbox**
- **Sharing**
- **Let your people reset their own passwords**

The following is a screenshot of the **Security & privacy** option:

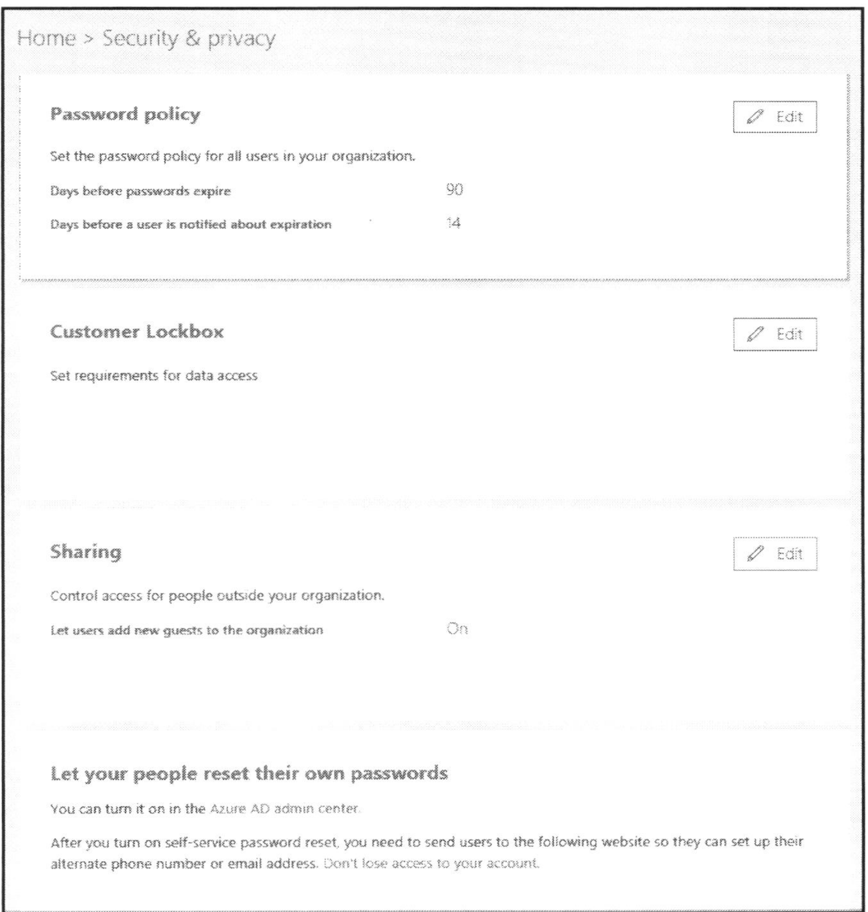

## DirSync errors

The following screenshot shows us the different possible errors for the objects that have been synced:

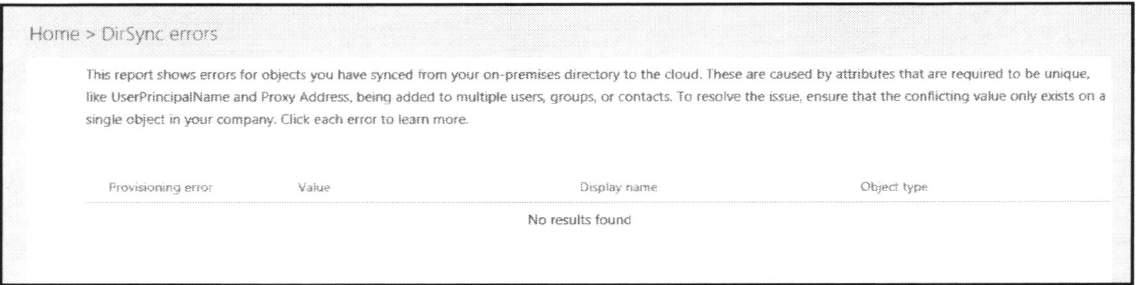


## Organization profile

The **Organization profile** options provide the following properties:

- Release preferences
- Manage custom themes for your organization
- Add custom tiles for your organization
- Provide customized help desk contact information

## Partner relationships

In the **Partner relationships** section, you can view and manage the partners that can help you on your Office 365 environment.

# Setup

The **Setup** area provides access to the following:

- Products (subscribed products and licensed assignments)
- Domains (configured custom domains, with the possibility of adding or buying additional domains)
- Data migration (helpful tools for mailbox migrations, as well as guidance for other workloads)

# Reports

The **Reports** area allows you to access the following:

- The usage report area with all the dashboards, as described previously
- Security and compliance reports, which can be further explored in the **Security & Compliance** center.

# Health

The **Health** navigation item aggregates the following areas:

- Service health page
- Message center
- Directory sync status page

# Admin centers

Some of the other services included in Office 365 have additional administration centers, which you can access through the Admin centers navigation item at the bottom of the left-hand menu:

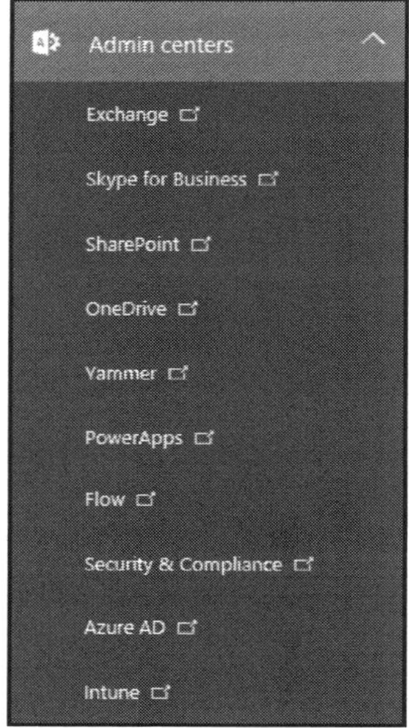


These Admin centers will be discussed in later chapters.

# Summary

In this chapter, you have learned about managing Office 365 services to keep up to date with the state-of-the-art of cloud productivity services. You now have more information on how to manage your Office 365 tenant and services, and how to keep updated with the latest updates of Office 365. In the next chapter, you will learn how to implement Exchange Online.

# 7
# Exchange Online

In this chapter, you will be introduced to Exchange Online. We will cover the following topics:

- Exchange Online in Office 365
- Planning Exchange Online
- Implementing and migrating Exchange Online
- Administering Exchange Online

In the previous chapter, you learned how to manage Office 365 workloads and you got a detailed tour of the Office 365 Admin center portal. In this chapter, we'll go deeper into Exchange Online, one of the core components of Office 365, and you'll learn more about how to plan and execute a good implementation of Exchange Online in your organization.

## Exchange Online in Office 365

Microsoft Exchange Online is the enterprise email service offered by Microsoft and is the most widely used workload of Office 365.

Exchange Online is a service hosted by Microsoft to provide organizations with an email system that can be employed to communicate using email features, schedule appointments using calendar features, create tasks, and organize emails in the inbox or archive them.

Exchange Server is an enterprise-class server that was born in 1996 and is the most widely used email system by organizations around the world. It has many features:

- Routing and transport rules
- Encrypt and secure mail
- In-Place Hold, allowing you to retain the email forever
- eDiscovery, to search content across the whole organization

Microsoft Exchange Online is divided into three main workloads, depending on where the mail is and its destination:

- **Exchange Online Protection** (**EOP**): EOP is the system by Microsoft Services that protects the Exchange system from malware, spam, and other threats.
- **Exchange Online**: Exchange Online is the core component of Exchange and where the main data accessed by the users resides.
- **Exchange Online Archive**: This is a system that is used for archiving email that is not needed in an offline device. In some plans, users have an unlimited space quota for the archive:

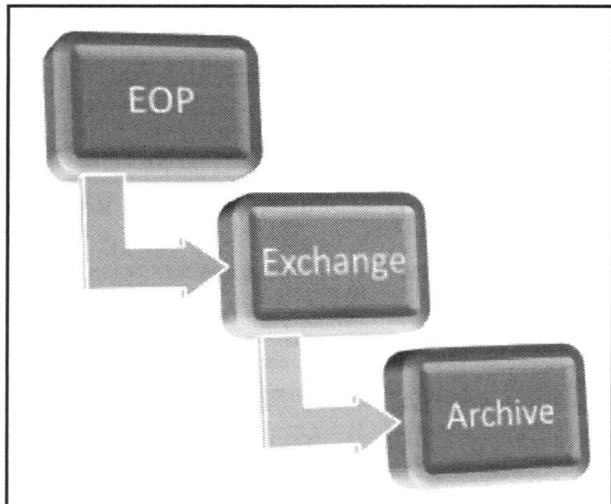

In Exchange Online, you have two subscriptions plans available—**Plan 1** and **Plan 2**. The following table summarizes the main differences between them:

| **Exchange Online Plan** | **Plan 1** | **Plan 2** |
|---|---|---|
| Capacity in primary mailbox | 50 GB | 100 GB |
| Capacity in archive | 50 GB | Unlimited |
| Communications | Not available | Instant messaging |
| Retention and preservation | Not available | In-Place Hold |

It's possible for the same tenant to have different subscriptions and to combine the products needed by each organization to accommodate their needs, at any point in time. A user may only be assigned to a single plan within the same workload. For instance, a user may not be assigned to both Exchange Online Plan 1 and Plan 2.

You can switch licenses at any time, but it is advised that the switch operation is performed simultaneously and not in two steps, to avoid removing and then adding the license. Performing these operations simultaneously (that is, atomically) will avoid, for example, the deletion of the mailbox and then a reconnection to the same user, which can cause some issues for the end user. When you remove a license, you have 30 days to recover that data; otherwise, the data will be lost and will not be recoverable. 30 days after deletion, it is not possible to recover any data from that mailbox.

# EOP

EOP is a service that is integrated in Office 365.

This system was created to protect the Exchange system, and it holds the responsibility of protecting, filtering, and ensuring the hygiene of your email, as an outer layer before messages hit the end user's inbox.

Because it operates at an outer level, before the core of Exchange is reached, it constitutes a powerful protection that mitigates several risks. This system was created as a distributed computational system, across all Microsoft data centers, to have the ability to scan, protect, and deliver the legitimate email in the fastest possible way.

# Exchange Online

Microsoft Exchange Online is the system where all the main user actions happen. It is where the users have their inboxes, calendars, and other objects, and where they access the features they need for their daily tasks, either using a smartphone, tablet, or other device, such as a PC.

Exchange Online establishes some limits to avoid problems that could impact your reputation. For example, it's only possible to send 30 messages per minute from a user's mailbox. If you need to send email in bulk, for a marketing campaign for example, it is advised that you rely on third-party services or use a different system in another infrastructure.

# Exchange Online Archive

The Microsoft Exchange Online Archive is the system that allows the end user to archive the emails that they do not need to keep online. This will store the user's older email in an *Online Archive*, which, as the name states, is only available if you have internet access to Office 365. For example, if you use the Outlook desktop and you have offline cache set to active for your primary mailbox, you will not have access to the archive if you are working offline, without internet access.

In Exchange Plan 2, you have unlimited storage in Exchange Online Archive.

To access the Exchange Online Admin center:

1. Go to `https://portal.office.com`
2. Select the **Admin** option
3. On the Admin center, in the **Admin centers** section, select the **Exchange** option, as shown in the following screenshot:

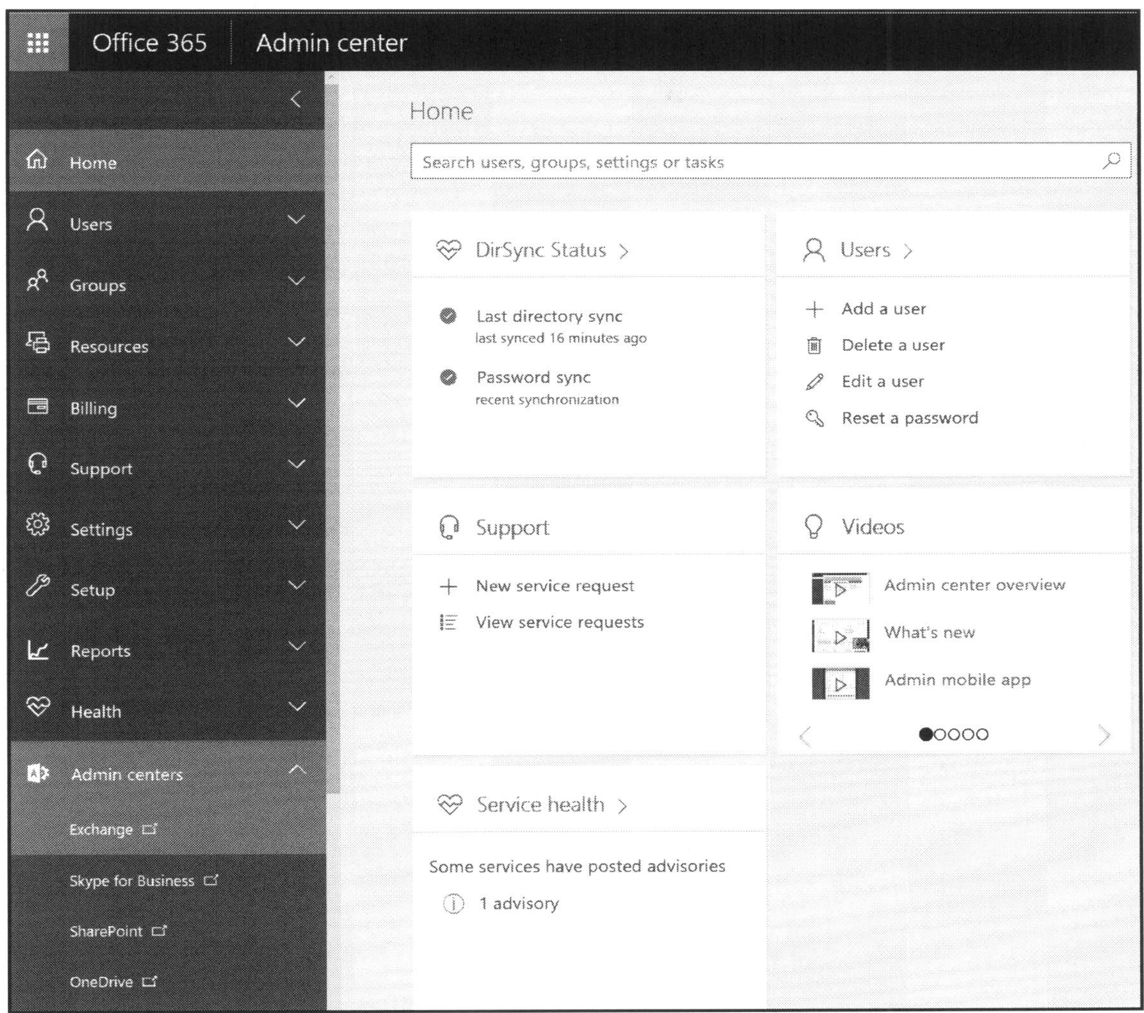

Office 365
Admin center
Home
Users
Groups
Resources
Billing
Support
Settings
Setup
Reports
Health
Admin centers
Exchange
Skype for Business
SharePoint
OneDrive
Home
Search users, groups, settings or tasks
DirSync Status
Last directory sync
last synced 16 minutes ago
Password sync
recent synchronization
Users
Add a user
Delete a user
Edit a user
Reset a password
Support
New service request
View service requests
Videos
Admin center overview
What's new
Admin mobile app
Service health
Some services have posted advisories
1 advisory

4. After connecting to Exchange Online admin, you will have access to a central place where you can manage the Exchange platform:

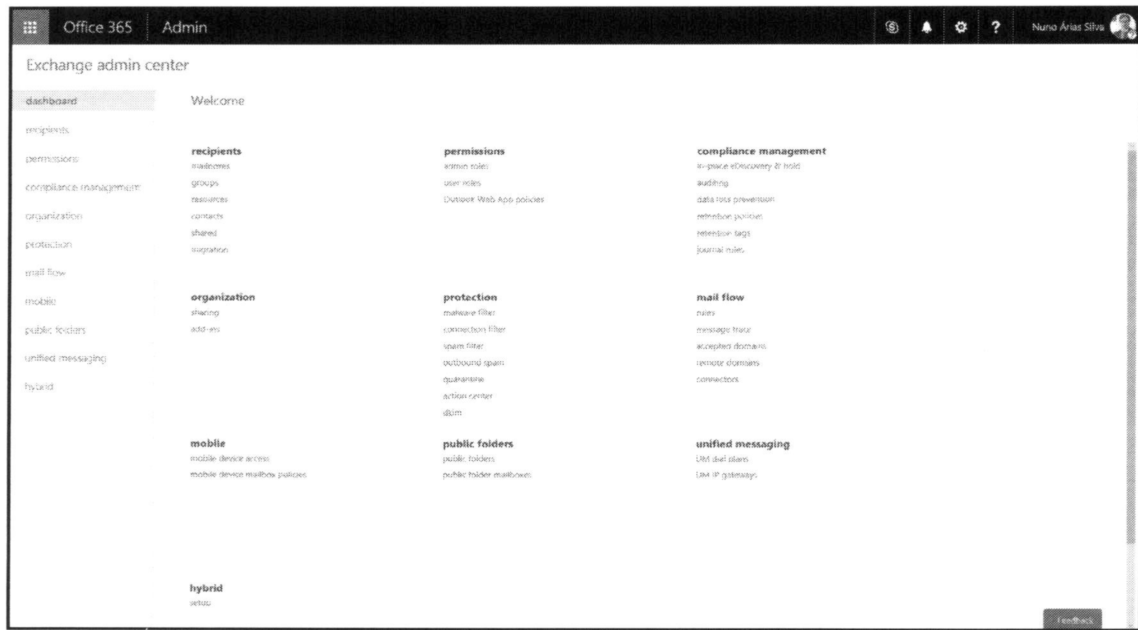


In the next section, we will see how to plan an implementation of Exchange Online.

# Planning Exchange Online

In each project or subproject, it is always advised to carefully plan using best practices, depending on the type of implementation or migration that you require.

You will need to know the core functions and capabilities of Exchange and its requirements.

The best way to start is to use the **Microsoft Exchange Server Deployment Assistant**. This tool is an effective way to start the planning of your project. It is available at `https://technet.microsoft.com/en-us/office/dn756393.aspx`. As shown in the following screenshot, it supports several scenarios:

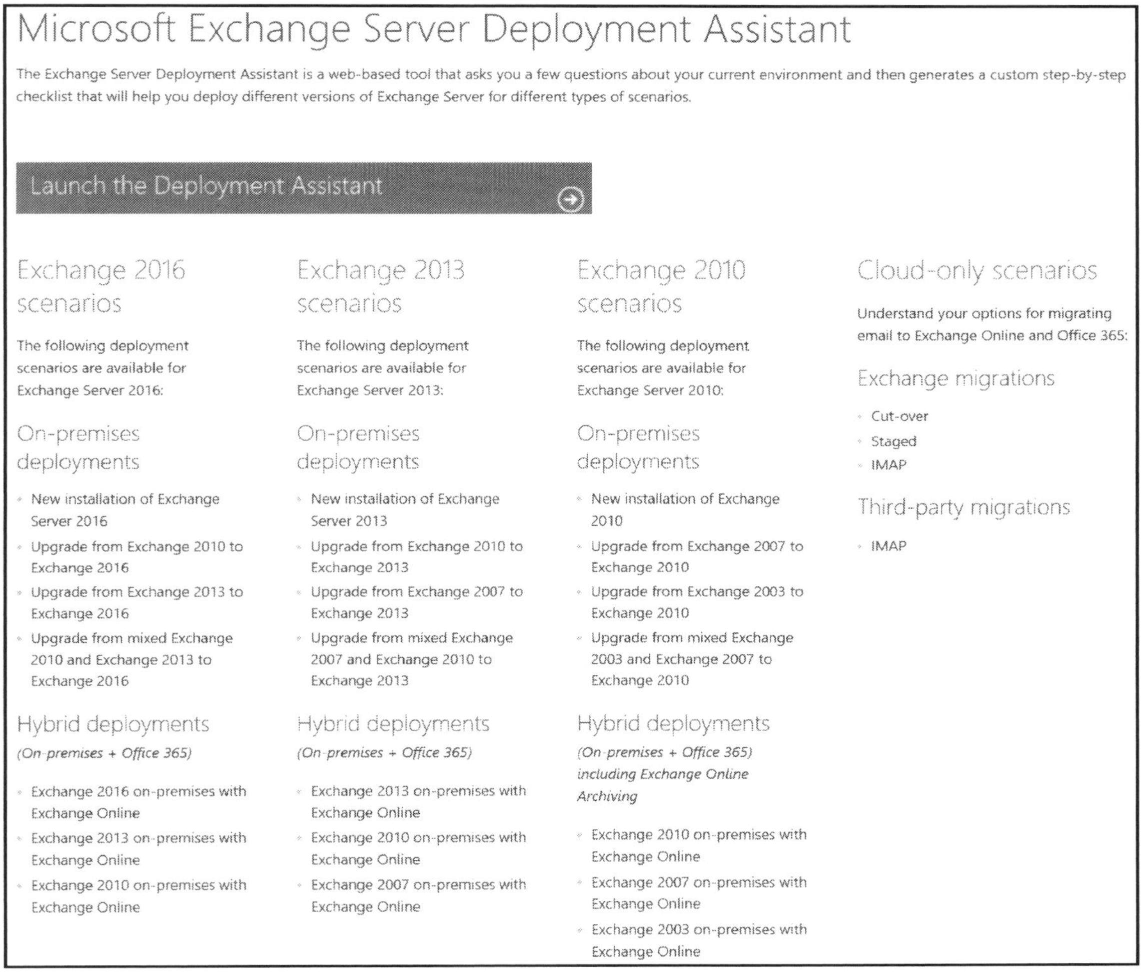

# Microsoft Exchange Server Deployment Assistant

The Exchange Server Deployment Assistant is a web-based tool that asks you a few questions about your current environment and then generates a custom step-by-step checklist that will help you deploy different versions of Exchange Server for different types of scenarios.

Launch the Deployment Assistant

## Exchange 2016 scenarios

The following deployment scenarios are available for Exchange Server 2016:

### On-premises deployments

- New installation of Exchange Server 2016
- Upgrade from Exchange 2010 to Exchange 2016
- Upgrade from Exchange 2013 to Exchange 2016
- Upgrade from mixed Exchange 2010 and Exchange 2013 to Exchange 2016

### Hybrid deployments

*(On-premises + Office 365)*

- Exchange 2016 on-premises with Exchange Online
- Exchange 2013 on-premises with Exchange Online
- Exchange 2010 on-premises with Exchange Online

## Exchange 2013 scenarios

The following deployment scenarios are available for Exchange Server 2013:

### On-premises deployments

- New installation of Exchange Server 2013
- Upgrade from Exchange 2010 to Exchange 2013
- Upgrade from Exchange 2007 to Exchange 2013
- Upgrade from mixed Exchange 2007 and Exchange 2010 to Exchange 2013

### Hybrid deployments

*(On-premises + Office 365)*

- Exchange 2013 on-premises with Exchange Online
- Exchange 2010 on-premises with Exchange Online
- Exchange 2007 on-premises with Exchange Online

## Exchange 2010 scenarios

The following deployment scenarios are available for Exchange Server 2010:

### On-premises deployments

- New installation of Exchange 2010
- Upgrade from Exchange 2007 to Exchange 2010
- Upgrade from Exchange 2003 to Exchange 2010
- Upgrade from mixed Exchange 2003 and Exchange 2007 to Exchange 2010

### Hybrid deployments

*(On-premises + Office 365) including Exchange Online Archiving*

- Exchange 2010 on-premises with Exchange Online
- Exchange 2007 on-premises with Exchange Online
- Exchange 2003 on-premises with Exchange Online

## Cloud-only scenarios

Understand your options for migrating email to Exchange Online and Office 365:

### Exchange migrations

- Cut-over
- Staged
- IMAP

### Third-party migrations

- IMAP

Exchange Server Deployment Assistant is a tool that was developed to help the implementation of Exchange scenarios, either on-premises, cloud, or hybrid. This tool asks you a few questions within the scenario that you have in place or your future scenario, and it will give you a checklist of the tasks you must perform. It also provides you with an estimate of how much effort you'll need to spend on your project to help you calculate the required investment.

At the time of writing, the deployment assistant supports the following scenarios:

- Exchange 2016
- Exchange 2013
- Exchange 2010
- Cloud-only
- Hybrid

In the following example, we will use Exchange 2016 in a hybrid deployment (on-premises and Office 365) scenario in the deployment assistant.

When we start the deployment, the assistant allows us to choose **Hybrid**, as shown in the following screenshot:

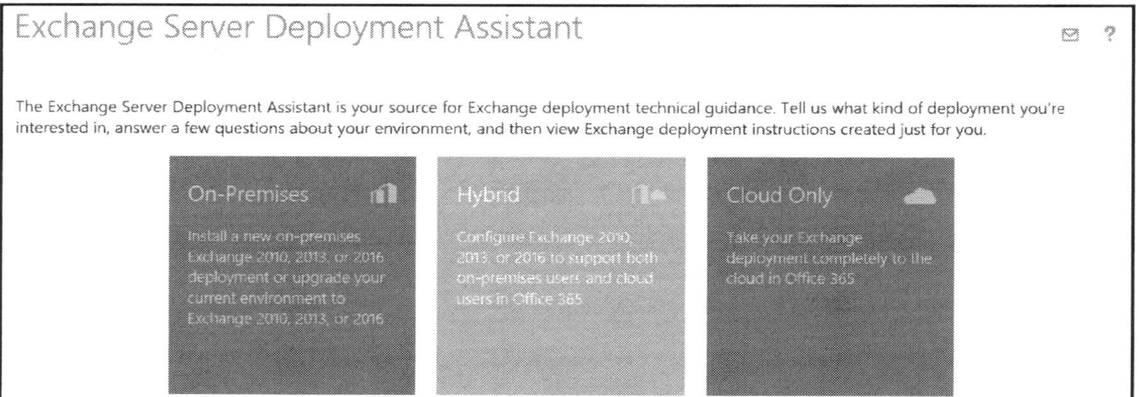

All the processes described later are the result of content provided by Microsoft within the results of the wizard of Exchange Deployment Assistant, and were changed to reflect this scenario as an example of the configuration that I have done. Refer to `https://technet.microsoft.com/en-us/library/hh529921`.

Next, we are going to select Exchange 2016 hybrid.

Then, select the **Exchange Server 2016** as the **Current on-premises environment** option:

Exchange Server Deployment Assistant
Welcome
Deployment Options
Choose your deployment type
Current on-premises environment
Current on-premises environment
What is your current on-premises Exchange environment?
Exchange Server 2016
Exchange Server 2013
Exchange Server 2010
I don't have Exchange Server installed in my on-premises organization

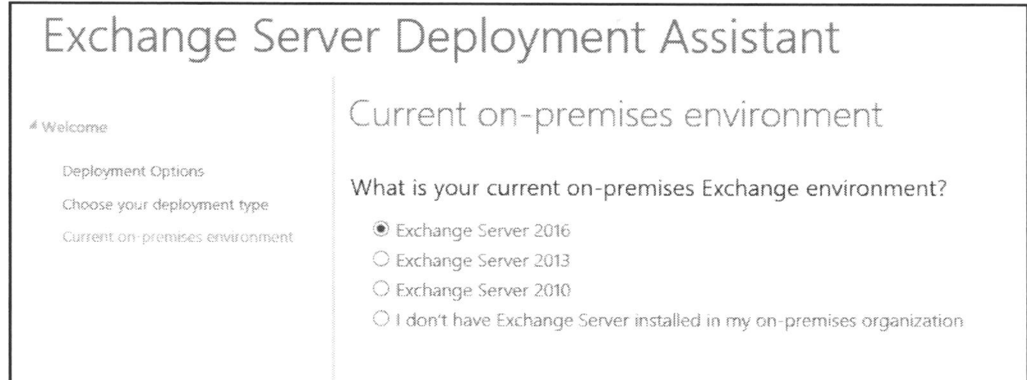

We are going to select the first scenario, but you will need an Office 365 plan that is supported for the hybrid scenario, such as enterprise, government, nonprofit, or education:

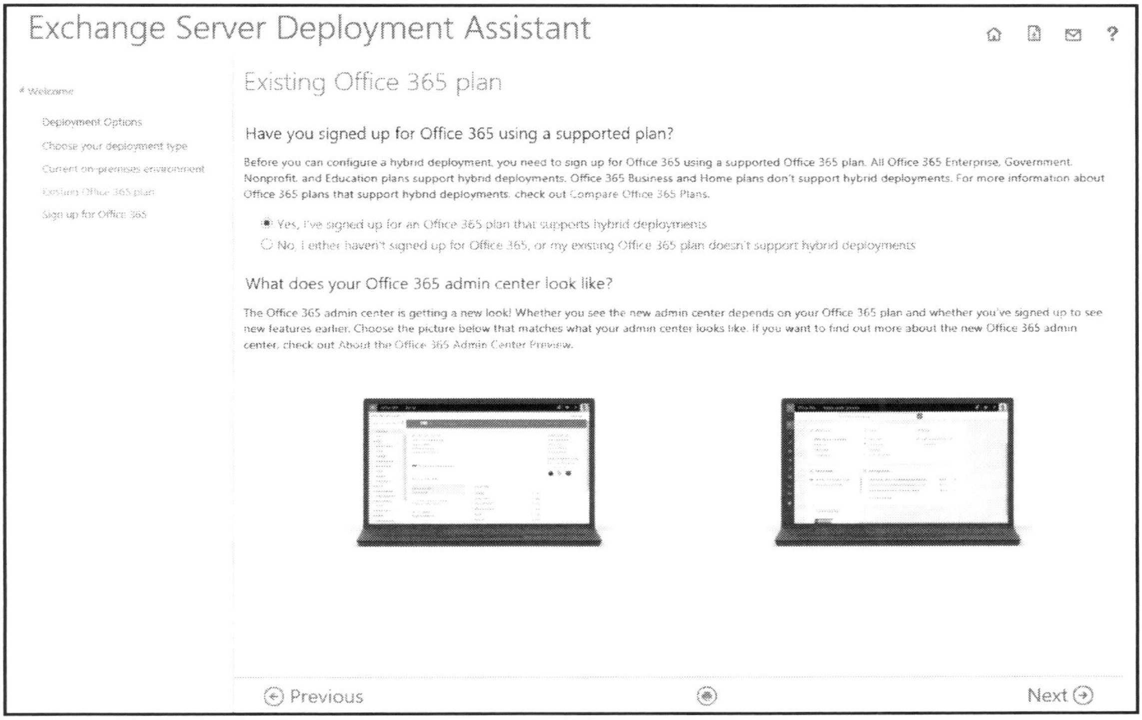
Exchange Server Deployment Assistant
Welcome
Deployment Options
Choose your deployment type
Current on-premises environment
Existing Office 365 plan
Sign up for Office 365
Existing Office 365 plan
Have you signed up for Office 365 using a supported plan?
Before you can configure a hybrid deployment, you need to sign up for Office 365 using a supported Office 365 plan. All Office 365 Enterprise, Government, Nonprofit, and Education plans support hybrid deployments. Office 365 Business and Home plans don't support hybrid deployments. For more information about Office 365 plans that support hybrid deployments, check out Compare Office 365 Plans.
Yes, I've signed up for an Office 365 plan that supports hybrid deployments
No, I either haven't signed up for Office 365, or my existing Office 365 plan doesn't support hybrid deployments
What does your Office 365 admin center look like?
The Office 365 admin center is getting a new look! Whether you see the new admin center depends on your Office 365 plan and whether you've signed up to see new features earlier. Choose the picture below that matches what your admin center looks like. If you want to find out more about the new Office 365 admin center, check out About the Office 365 Admin Center Preview.
Previous
Next

Next, you'll be asked to select the authentication method. Select the **Password synchronization (recommended)** radio button, as shown in the following screenshot:

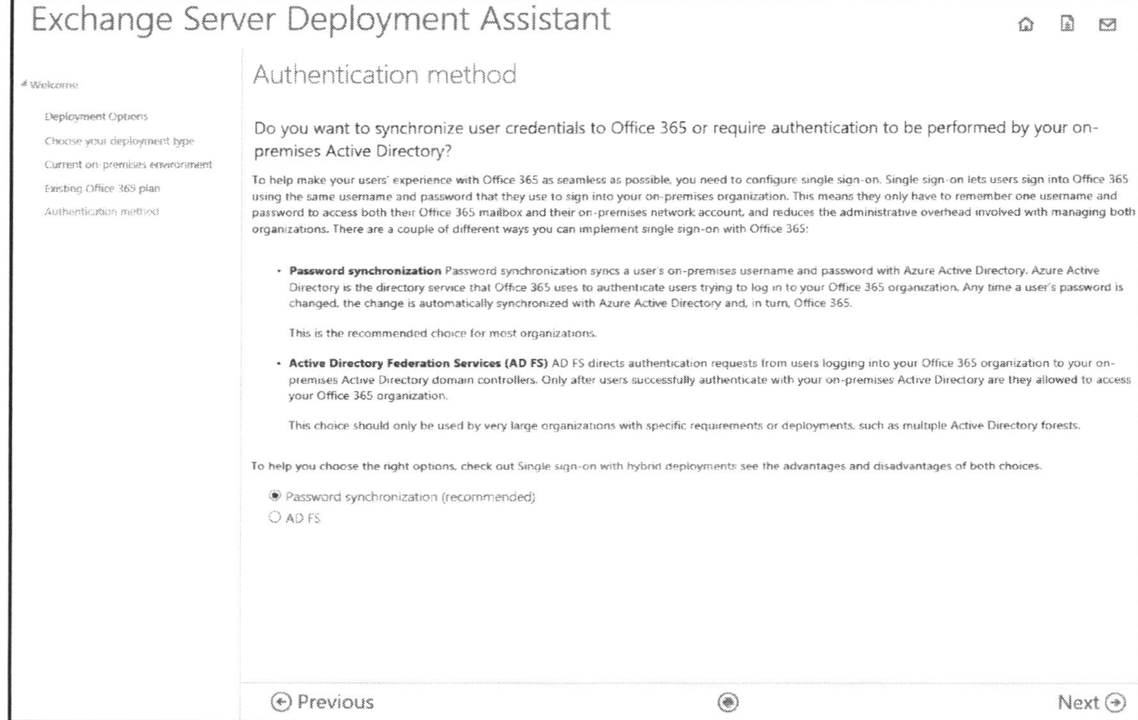

In the Edge Transport question, to keep this scenario simple, just select a scenario that does not require edge servers by clicking on the **No** radio button:

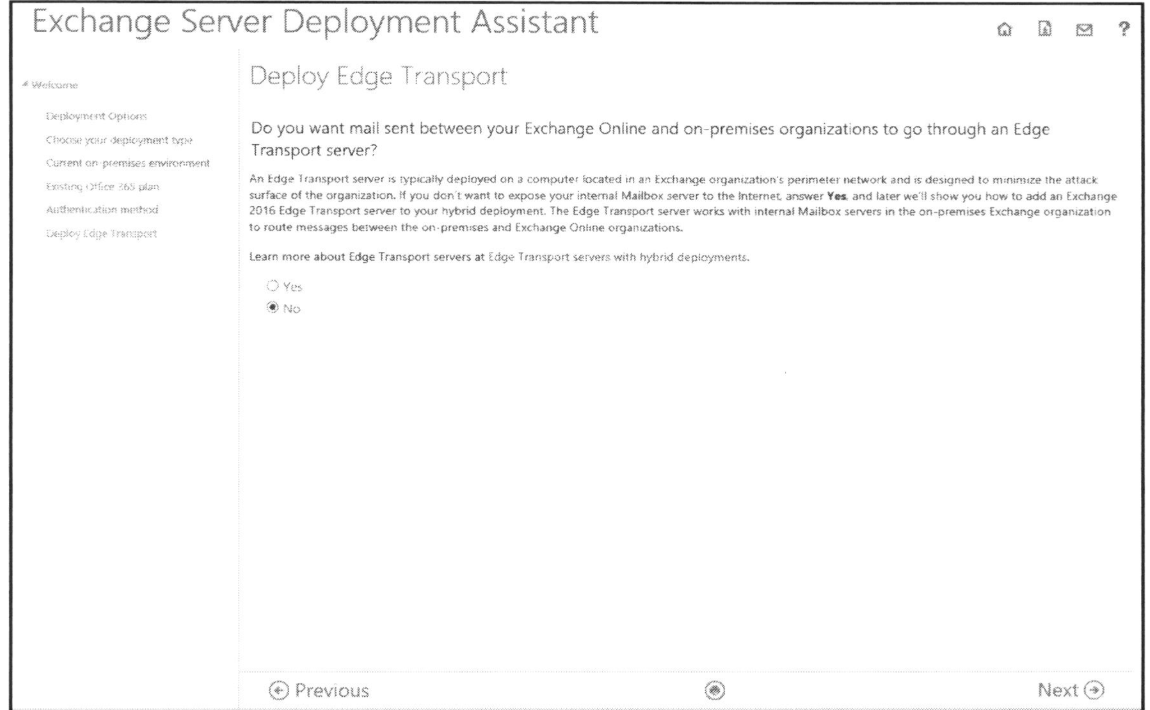

Then, we are asked how the inbound messages should be routed, through the on-premises email server or through Office 365. Select the option to route the messages through Office 365:

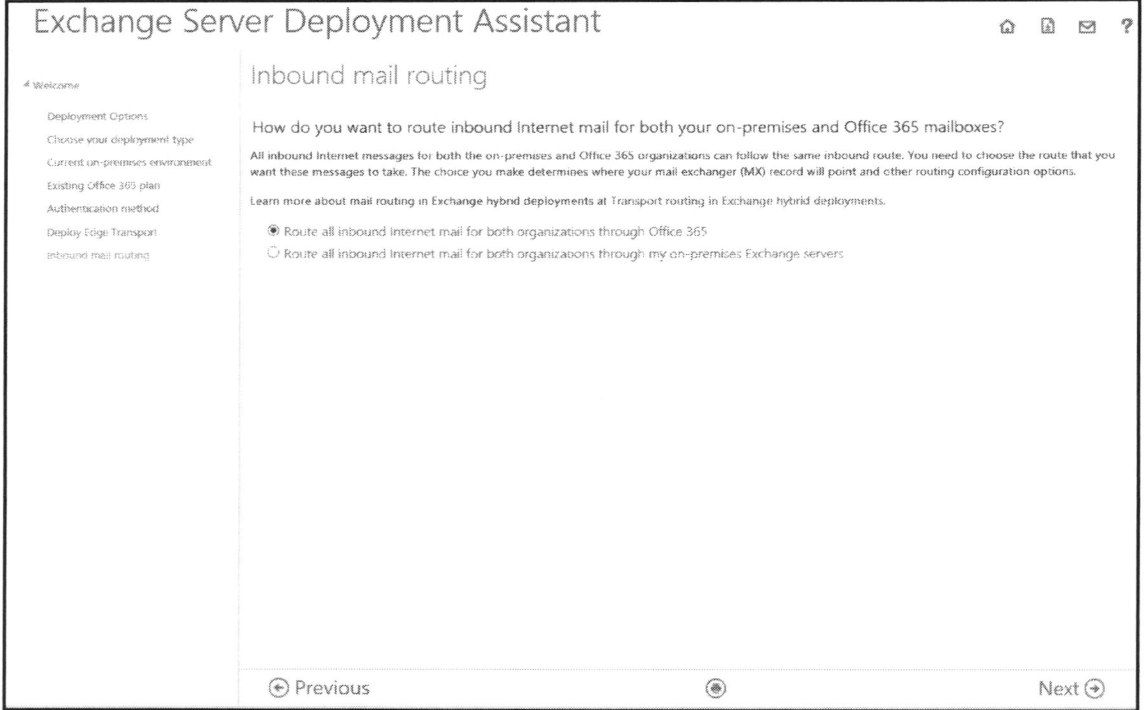


After clicking on the **Next** button, we will see the checklist with the steps to deploy this scenario:

This will be the deployment scenario demonstrated throughout this chapter. I use my domain name, `nuno-silva.net`, in all the examples.

The following is a summary of the deployment options.

The Exchange Server Deployment Assistant is the best way to know the most appropriate scenario for your organization as well as to guide you throughout the deployment of Exchange. With this tool, you only need to answer some questions about the Exchange environment, and the deployment assistant will provide you with the instructions to deploy that scenario. If you do not have experience within Exchange deployments, it is advised that you contact a partner to design your scenario and to deploy your Exchange workload. The partners have extensive experience from years deploying Exchange scenarios in complex architectures that you can leverage, avoiding surprises and issues with your deployment.

The scenario that will be described in the following sections is the hybrid scenario using Exchange 2016 connected to Office 365 with Azure AD Connect with password sync.

All the processes described later are the result of content provided by Microsoft within the results of the wizard of Exchange Deployment Assistant, and some variables has been changed according the scenario and is an example configuration. Refer to `https://technet.microsoft.com/en-us/library/hh529921`.

# Implementation and migration Exchange Online

The implementation and migration steps are explained in the following sections.

## Some notes before starting

In a hybrid deployment, it is recommended that you create a complete plan of the deployment. It is also advised that, before starting to configure the environment, you carefully read the deployment assistant's output to know what steps will be necessary, where you'll need to go, and what configurations you need, based on the scenario you have selected. This includes components such as networks, security certificates, and firewall rules. If you are not familiar with some of these topics, it is always advised to find a partner with experience, because any missteps might cause trouble down the road.

To successfully configure your organization for a hybrid deployment, you need to sign up for Office 365 using a supported subscription plan. In the beginning of this book, we gave you the instructions to sign up for Office 365.

# What is a hybrid deployment?

Hybrid deployment is a connection between your Exchange organization that is on-premises and Exchange Online. This connection is a federation that is done by **Hybrid Configuration Wizard** (**HCW**) that performs several steps:

- The configuration of SMTP connectors between Office 365 that gives the mail flow in both ways using your certificate with TLS.
- The implementation of the global address list is shared between the two organizations.
- The federation of free/busy that gives you the possibility to have the availability in calendars between users connected on each Exchange organization (on-premises and online).
- You can continue to use `http://webmail.yourorganization.com`, where you can change `yourorganization.com` to your public internet domain name as you did before hybrid. When a user has their mailbox moved to Office 365, it will also be connected to Office 365.
- When you have ActiveSync, the users will be automatically redirected when their mailbox moves between organizations.
- Using **Exchange Web Service** (**EWS**), you have the ability to do a remote move between your mailboxes' organizations.
- If your hybrid is Exchange 2013 or 2016, you can use your Exchange Admin center to manage both Exchange organizations.

It is not possible to have the primary in the cloud and the archive on the premises. You can learn more about Exchange Online Archiving at `https://technet.microsoft.com/en-us/library/archive-features-in-exchange-online-archiving.aspx`.

# Hybrid deployment components

In a Hybrid deployment, you will have several components as follows:

- **On-premises servers**: Exchange servers and AD Connect has requirements to implement Exchange hybrid
- **Office 365**: Your tenant where your Exchange Online is
- **HCW**: This is where you configure the connection between your environments

Learn more about *Hybrid Configuration wizard* at `https://technet.microsoft.com/en-us/library/hh529921`.

Learn more about *Sharing and Collaboration* at `https://technet.microsoft.com/en-us/library/exchange-online-sharing-and-collaboration.aspx`.

- **Azure AD synchronization**: Azure AD Connect synchronizes your on-premises directory to Azure AD to support a hybrid Exchange. It synchronizes several objects, such as users, distribution groups, security groups, and contacts. With this synchronization, you will have a unique **Global Address List (GAL)** available to the users. Keep in mind that when you have a hybrid Exchange environment, your on-premises objects are the source authority system. Azure AD Connect is a software component that is installed on an on-premises server separate to domain controllers and Exchange environments.

Learn more about Azure AD Connect at `https://docs.microsoft.com/en-us/azure/active-directory/connect/active-directory-aadconnect-prerequisites`.

# Hybrid deployment example

The following scenario was created for this book. This is an example architecture topology that provides you with an overview of a typical Exchange 2016 environment. `Nuno Silva` is a single-forest, single-domain organization with two domain controllers and one Exchange 2016 server installed with the latest supported rollup update. Remote `Nuno Silva` users use Outlook on the web to connect to Exchange 2016 over the internet to check their mailboxes and access their Outlook calendar and using ActiveSync on mobile devices also.

The following figure shows the scenario:

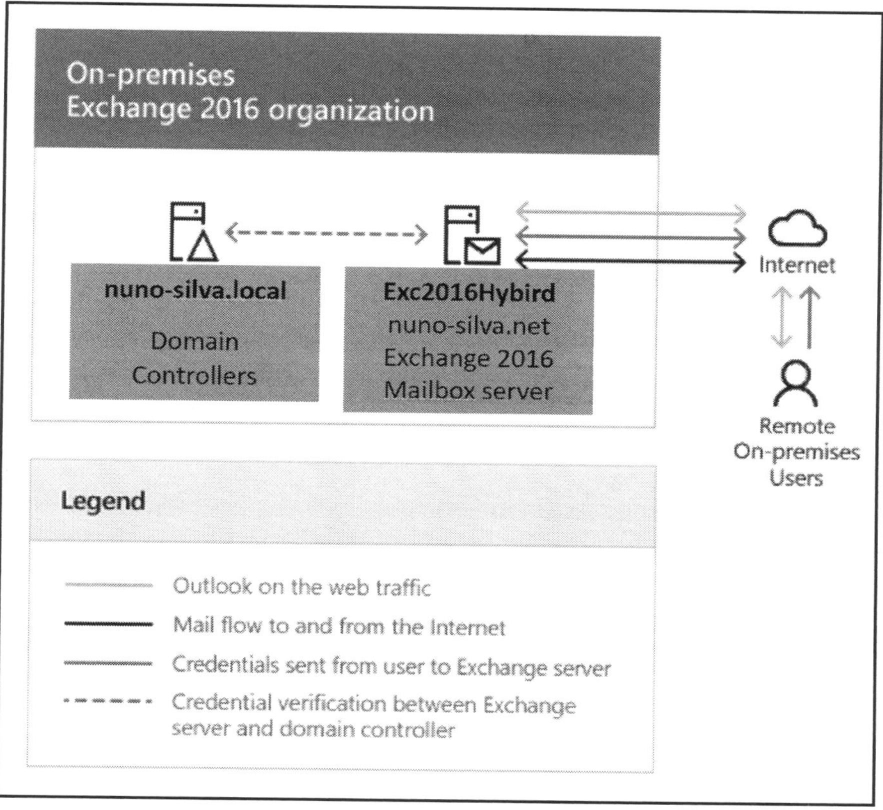

The following figure represents the scenario as an example of my configuration:

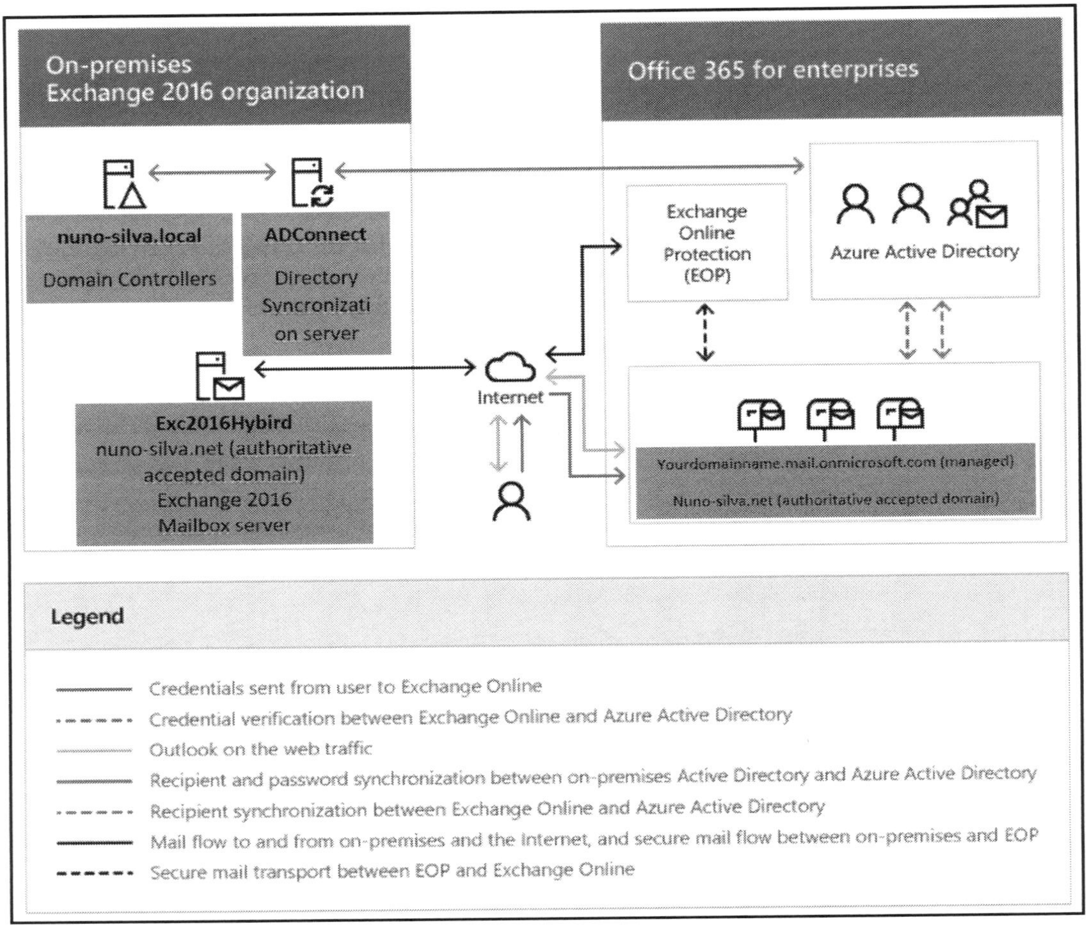

## Directory synchronization and SSO

AD synchronization between the on-premises and Office 365 organizations is performed every 30 minutes by a server on your on-premises, running Azure AD Connect, and it is a requirement for configuring a hybrid deployment.

To know about certificates, bandwidth, mail flow, and information rights management, refer to `https://technet.microsoft.com/en-us/library/mt595771(v=exchg.150).aspx`.

It is advised that you always review all the requirements before starting.

## Troubleshooting hybrid deployments

Configuring a hybrid deployment with the Hybrid Configuration wizard greatly minimizes the potential that the hybrid deployment will experience problems. However, there are some typical areas outside the scope of the Hybrid Configuration wizard that, if misconfigured, may present problems in a hybrid deployment. Sometimes, there can be minor configuration issues that prevent your hybrid deployment features from working as expected.

Check out the following resources to resolve some common hybrid deployment configuration issues:

- *Troubleshoot a hybrid deployment* at `https://technet.microsoft.com/en-us/library/jj659053`
- *Troubleshooting free/busy issues in Exchange hybrid environment* at `https://support.microsoft.com/en-us/help/10092/troubleshooting-free-busy-issues-in-exchange-hybrid-environment`

# Administering Exchange Online

In this section, I will show you how to administer Exchange Online. Based on the steps created before, you will see the following parts:

- AD Connect
- Exchange Hybrid
- Exchange Online

# AD Connect

After the installation of AD Connect using Express install option, you can read the instructions at link `https://docs.microsoft.com/en-us/azure/active-directory/connect/active-directory-aadconnect-get-started-express`.

Go to the **Start** Menu and select the **Synchronization service** option. This program shows the history of your synchronization between your on-premises AD and Azure AD, as shown in the following screenshot:

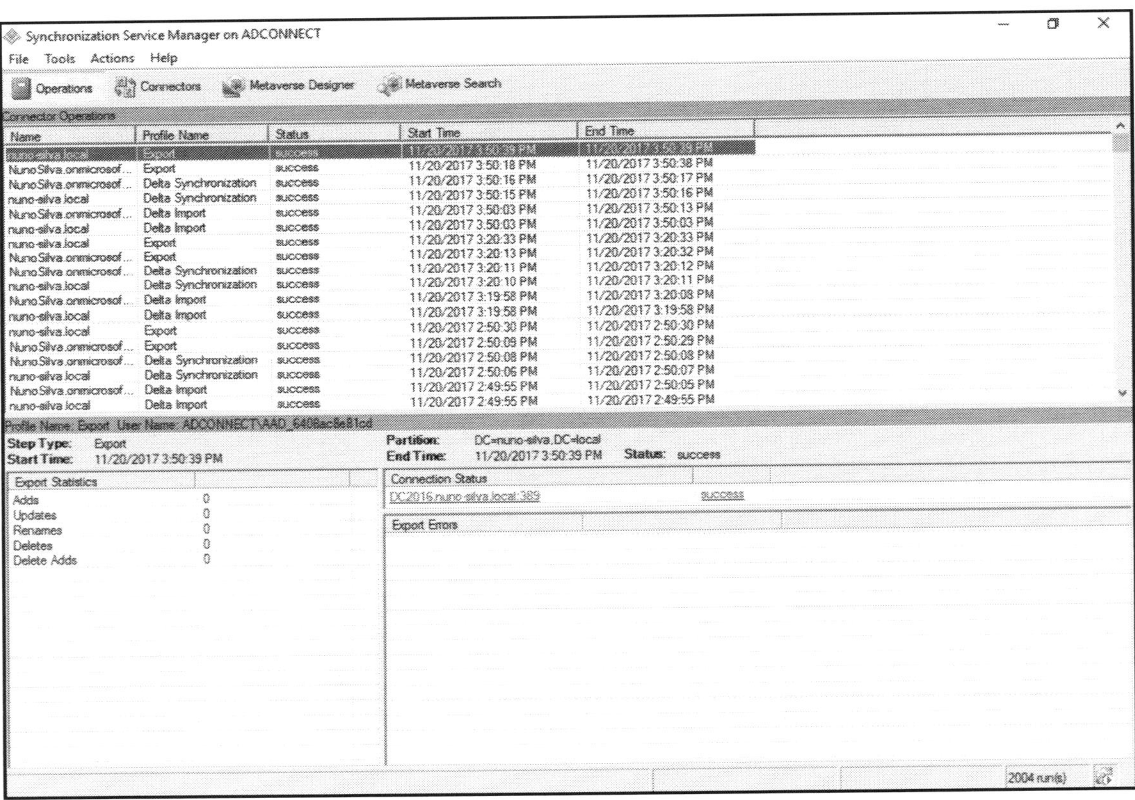

AD Connect by default will run every 30 minutes. To do a Delta synchronization, you can create a script in PowerShell, as shown in the following screenshot:

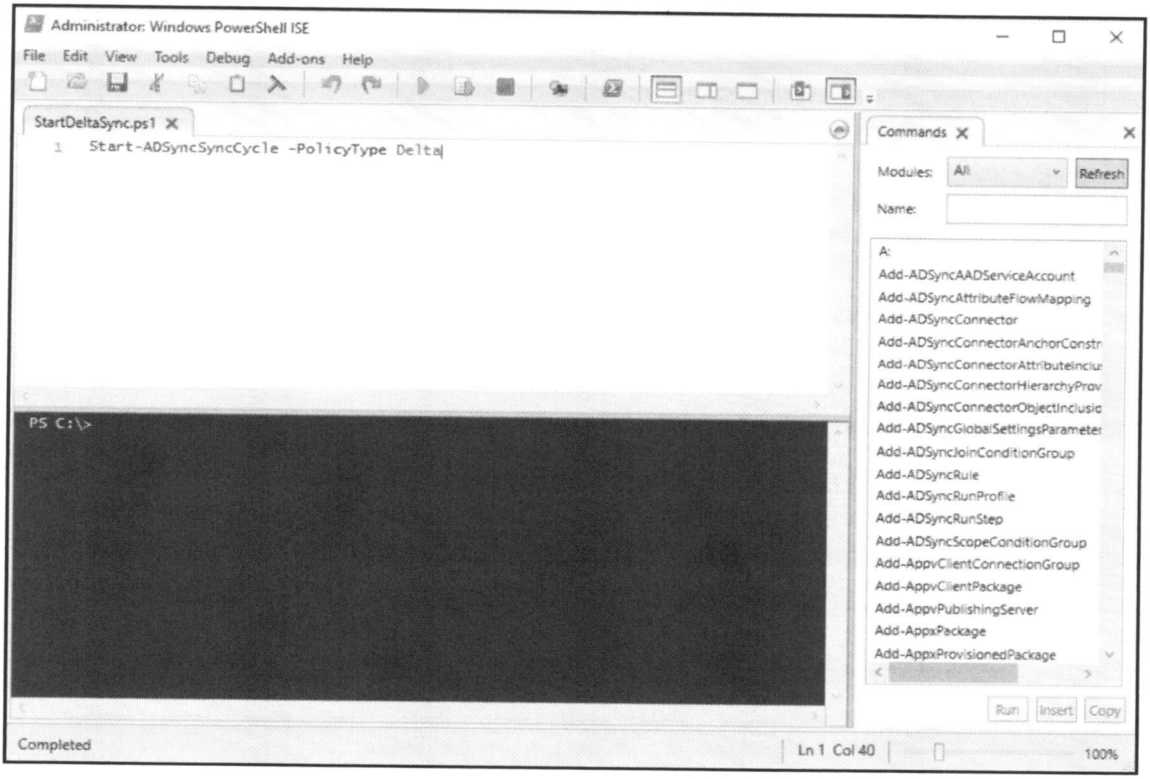

Create a file with the `.PS1` extension and write the following script:

```
Start-ADSyncSyncCycle -PolicyType Delta
```

You will have access to the main content of AD Connect and architectures at `https://docs.microsoft.com/en-us/azure/active-directory/connect/active-directory-aadconnect`.

# Exchange hybrid

To manage your Exchange hybrid after the setup of hybrid Exchange, refer to `https://yoururlofexchange.domain.com/ecp`, where change `yoururlofexchange.domain.com` to your public internet domain name.

After logging in, you will have access to your Exchange Admin center:

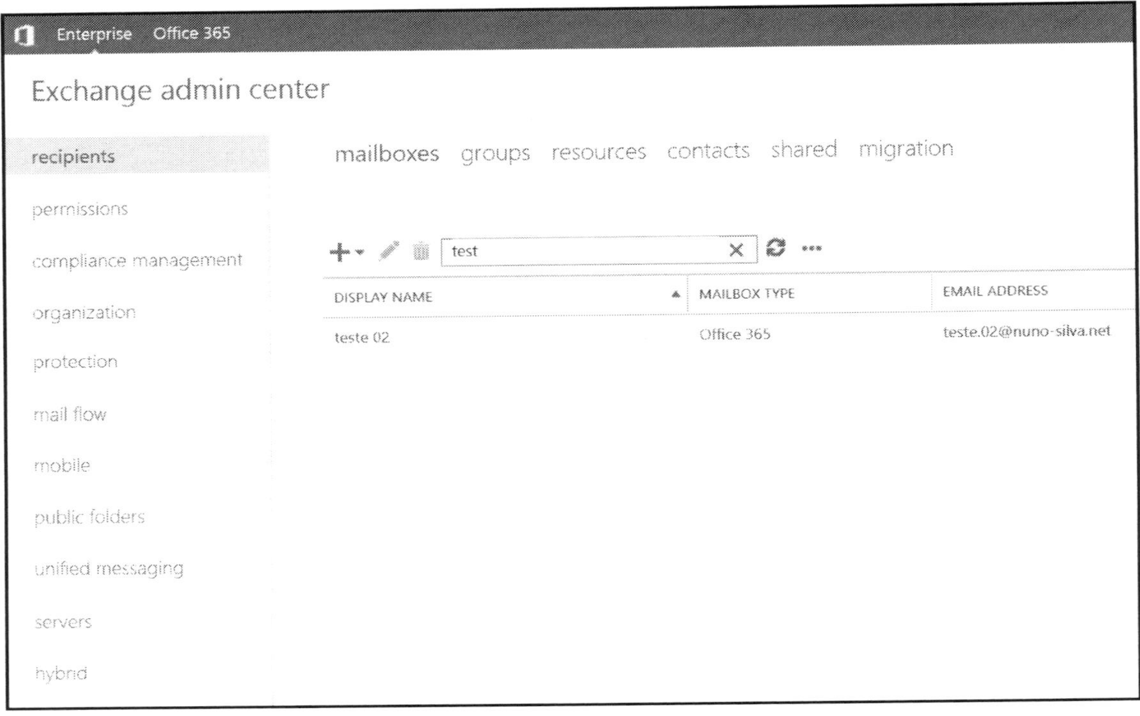

# Exchange Online

To administer Exchange Online, go to `http://portal.office.com` and select the **Admin** option, then go to **Admin centers** | **Exchange**, as in the following screenshot:

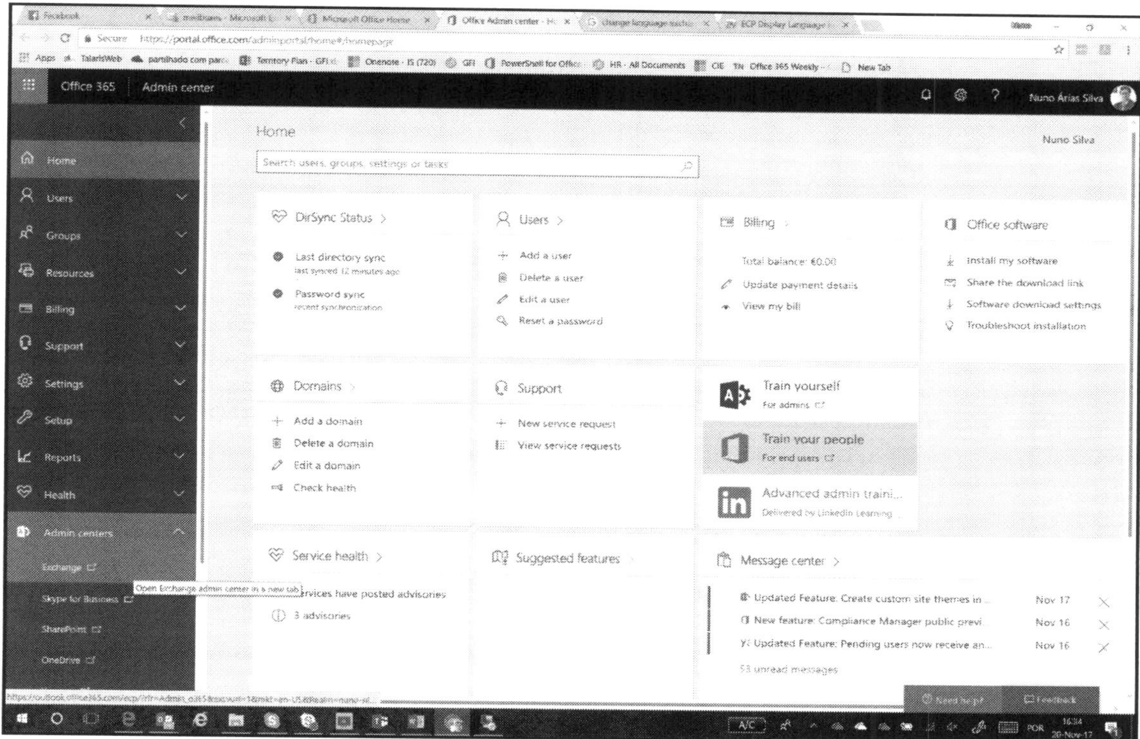

If you are already in your on-premises Exchange, you have the **Office 365** tab on the top, as seen in the following screenshot:

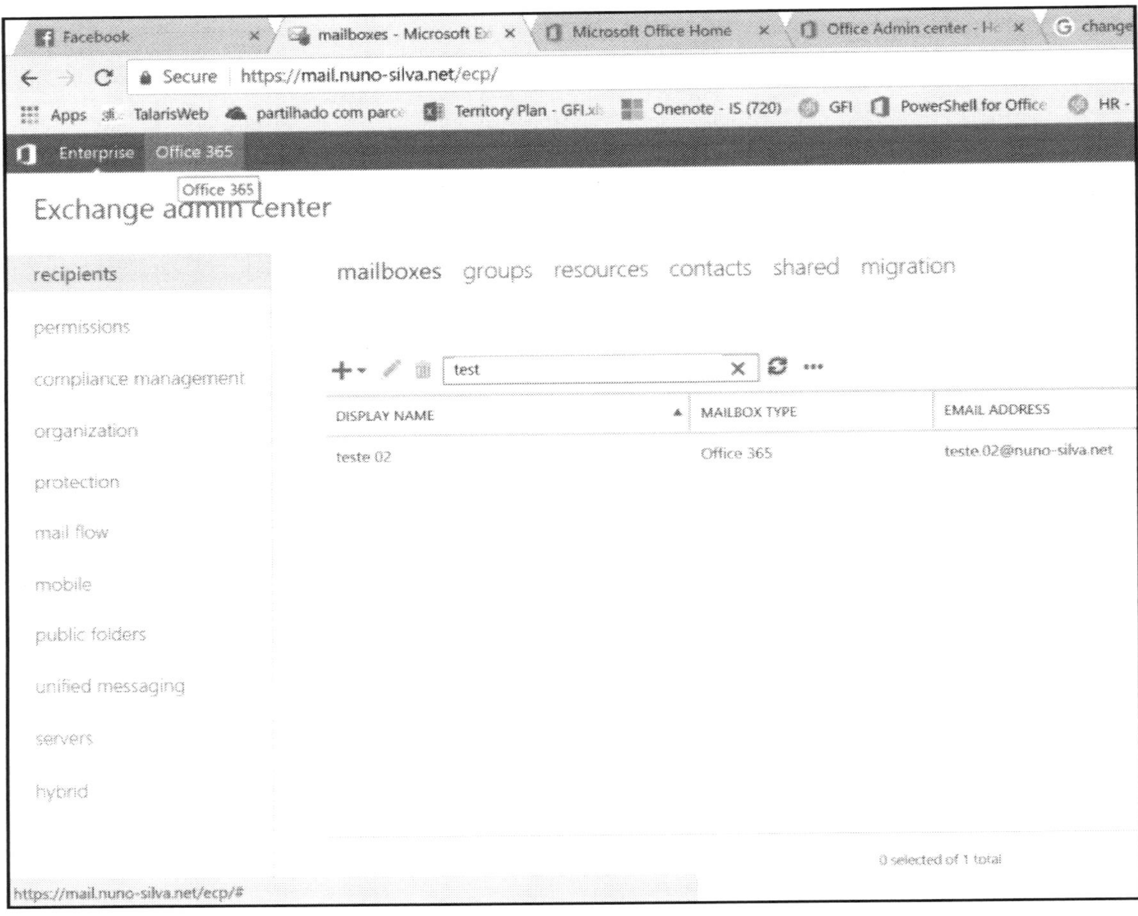


Select **Office 365** to go directly to Exchange Online administrative center.

# Summary

In this chapter, you learned about basic planning and started to implement Exchange Online.

You now have more information on how to plan your Exchange Online project and how to implement the base of Exchange Online.

In the next chapter, you will learn how to implement SharePoint Online, one of the most widely used workloads in Office 365.

# 8
# SharePoint Online

This chapter will be an introduction to SharePoint Online. It will cover the following topics:

- Implementing SharePoint Online
- Architecture of SharePoint Online
- Administering SharePoint Online

With this foundation of knowledge, you will learn more about how to implement SharePoint Online in your organization.

## Implementing SharePoint Online

Microsoft SharePoint Online is an online platform that allows organizations to have a central location in which to collaborate. This can be formed using the intranet, extranet, or other collaboration portals. With SharePoint Online, all types and sizes of organizations have a central point where the end users have access to important data. In this way, data can be accessed from any browser and any device, enabling your workers to collaborate in a modern way from any location, drastically increasing their productivity. Organizations that use SharePoint Online have productivity services that they can use to build collaboration sites, manage their business, and use a central portal to organize their organization's data. They need to own a platform that can be scalable and customized to their specific needs. When you create an Office 365 tenant, the SharePoint Online service is populated with some basic portals.

To access your SharePoint central administration, go to `http://portal.office.com` and go through the following steps:

1. Select the **Admin** option from the home page:

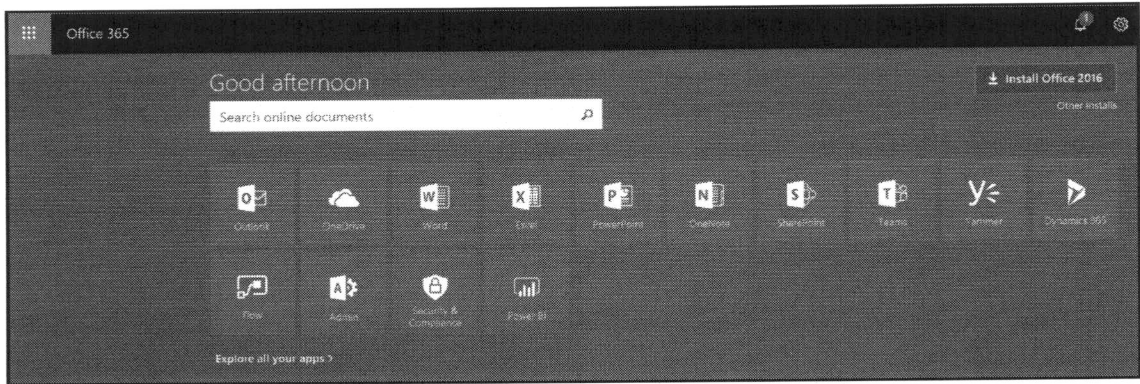


You can also access it from the menu on the upper left:

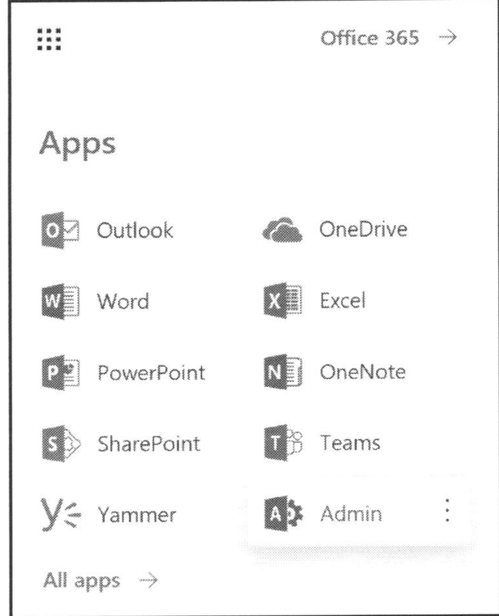

2. Go to the admin part of your Office 365 to access the **Admin centers** section. Then go to the **SharePoint** option as shown in the following screenshot:

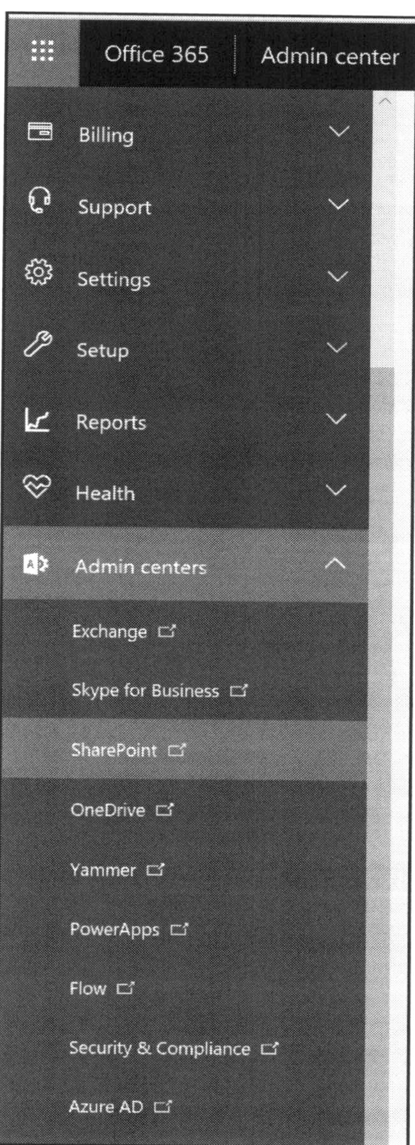

3. You can go directly to your SharePoint admin center using `https://yourtenantname-admin.sharepoint.com`:

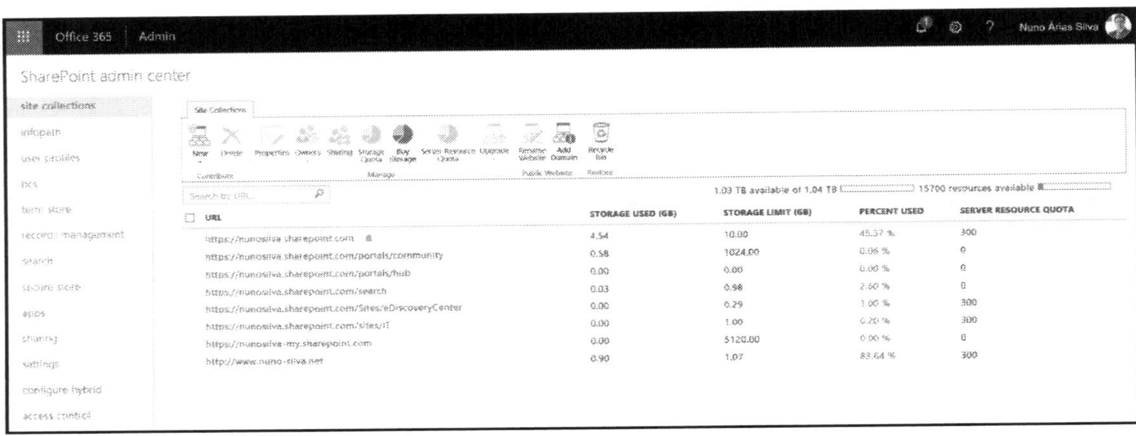


## Site collections

The first thing you'll see after accessing the SharePoint Online admin center is the list of site collections. Let's take a closer look at each of these sites:

- `Yourtenantname.sharepoint.com`: The home URL such as `https://yourtenantname.sharepoint.com` is your starting point for SharePoint Online, and is where your top root site for the default site collection is. This is the place where you can create your organization's intranet.

- `Yourtenantname.sharepoint.com/portals/hub`: The `portals/hub` URL is where you can find your Office 365 Video portal videos that are currently being migrated to Microsoft Stream. If you use Office 365 Video, you should migrate to Microsoft Stream. You can read more at `https://docs.microsoft.com/en-us/stream/migrate-from-office-365`. The following screenshot shows the video portal that is arranged with channels to your organization:

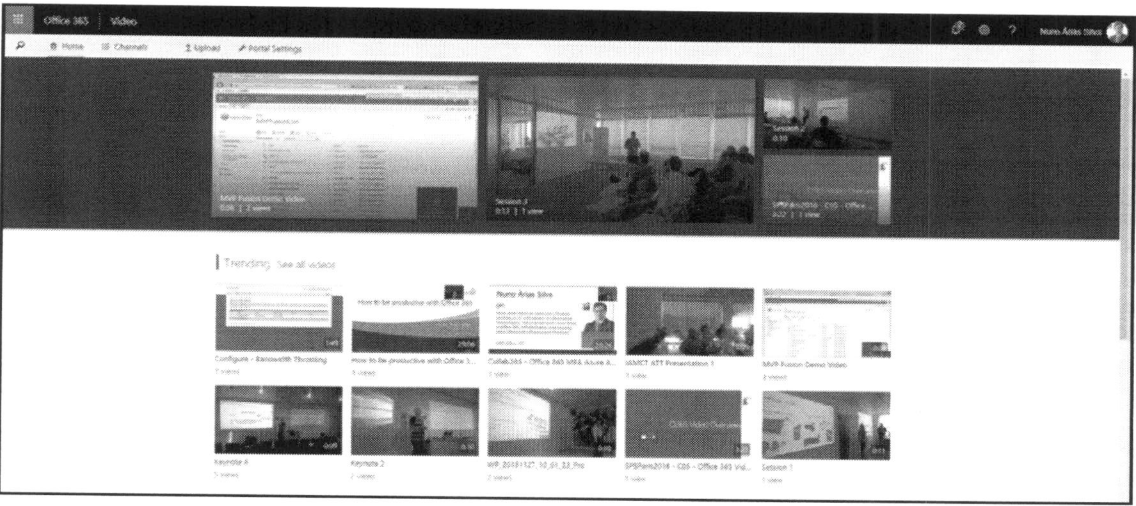

The following screenshot is the stream portal, where you have the new Office 365 service where Microsoft will migrate all your content to, from Office 365 Video:

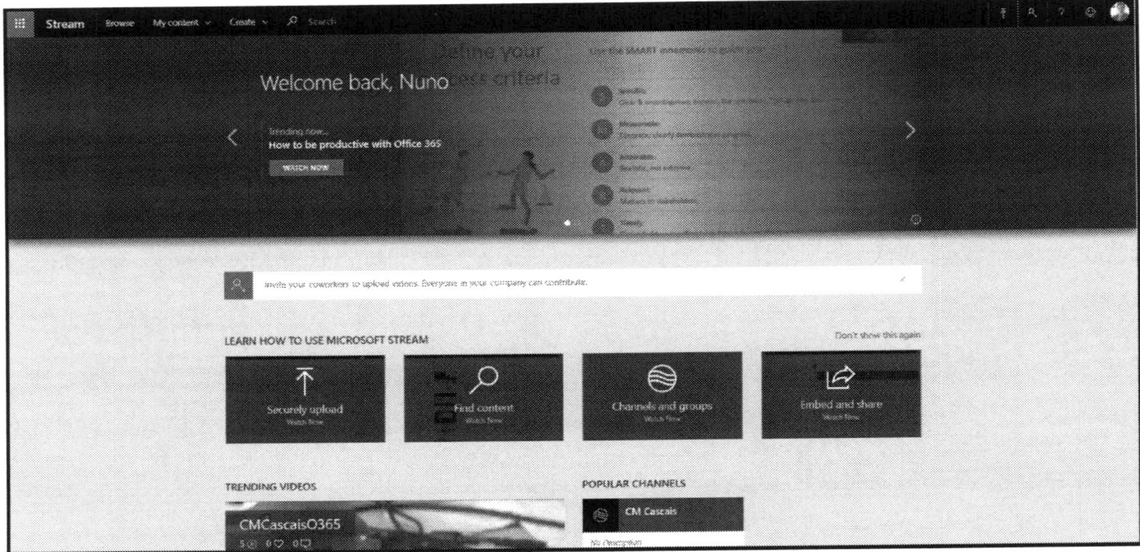


- `Yourtenantname.sharepoint.com/portals/community`: The `portals/community` URL is where you will have your community site. Let's see how to create a collected site using the community site template. Go to site admin and create a new site collection. Fill in all the requested properties, such as the following:
    - **Title**
    - **Web Site Address**
    - **Template Selection**:
        - **Select a language**
        - **Select a template**
    - **Time Zone**
    - **Administrator**
    - **Storage Quota**
    - **Server Resource Quota**

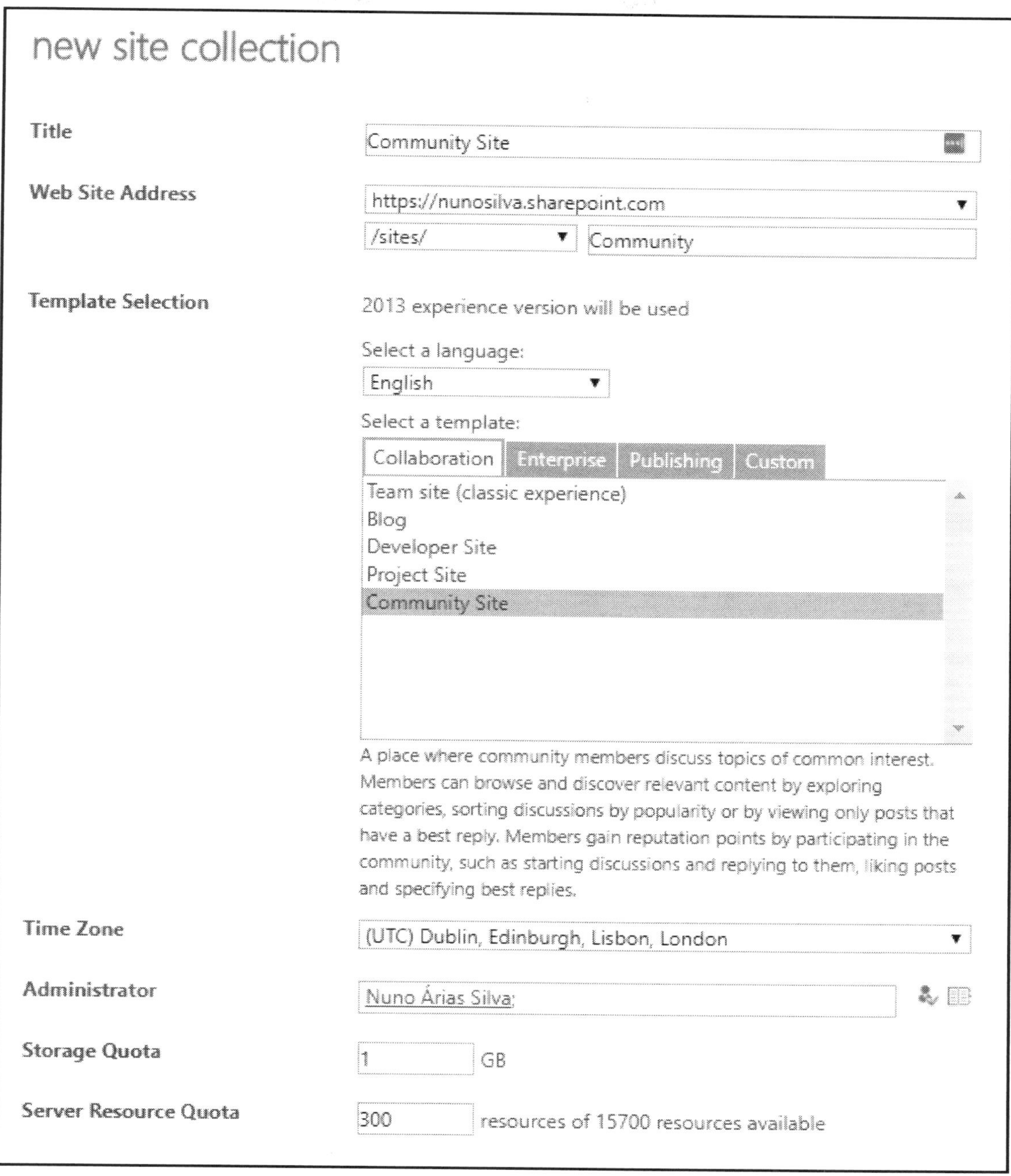

new site collection
Title
Community Site
Web Site Address
https://nunosilva.sharepoint.com
/sites/
Community
Template Selection
2013 experience version will be used
Select a language:
English
Select a template:
Collaboration
Enterprise
Publishing
Custom
Team site (classic experience)
Blog
Developer Site
Project Site
Community Site
A place where community members discuss topics of common interest. Members can browse and discover relevant content by exploring categories, sorting discussions by popularity or by viewing only posts that have a best reply. Members gain reputation points by participating in the community, such as starting discussions and replying to them, liking posts and specifying best replies.
Time Zone
(UTC) Dublin, Edinburgh, Lisbon, London
Administrator
Nuno Árias Silva;
Storage Quota
1
GB
Server Resource Quota
300
resources of 15700 resources available

The preceding screenshot shows the page where you can create a new site collection. In this case, it is a community site. Wait for a few moments while the site is created as shown in the following screenshot:

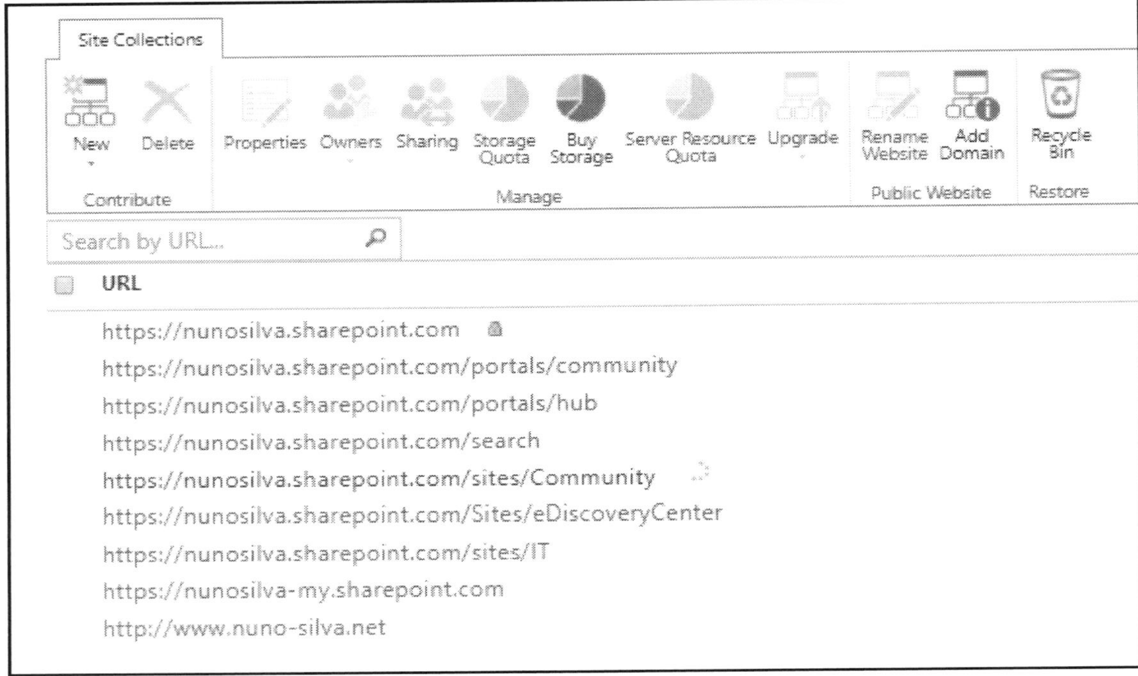

After the site has been created, it will look like the following screenshot:

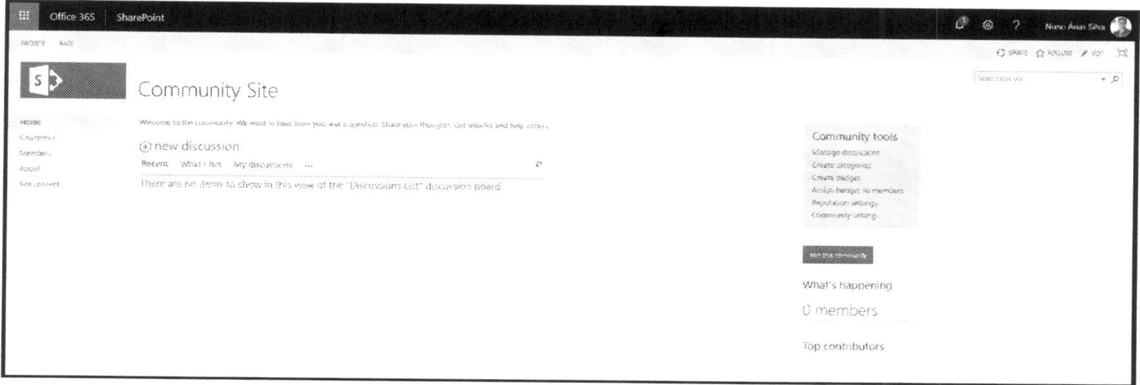


You can see the whole process of creating a community site at `https://support.office.com/en-us/article/Create-a-community-8b6bb936-7ebc-4e60-b8ab-2d4897499af9`.

- `Yourtenantname.sharepoint.com/search`: The `/search` URL is where the **Search** in the SharePoint and the search center reside. It's also where you can issue your search queries:

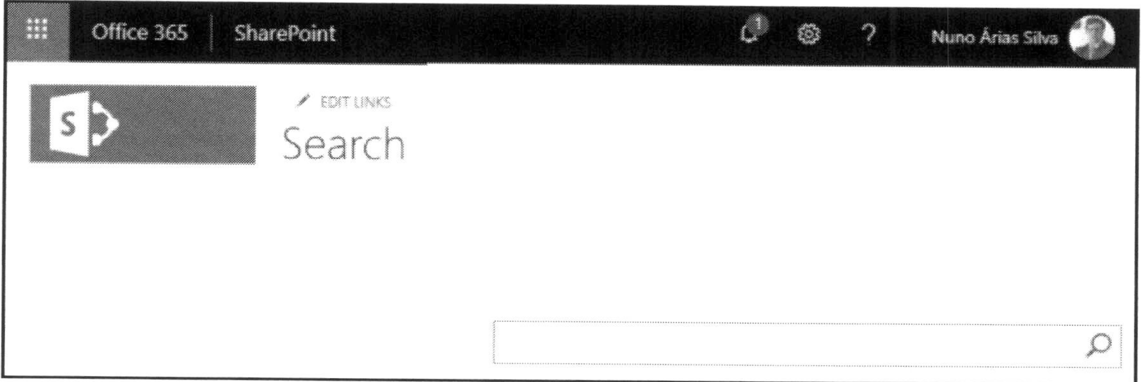

After you type, for example, `test`, you can see all the contents that have the `Test` keyword as shown in the following screenshot:

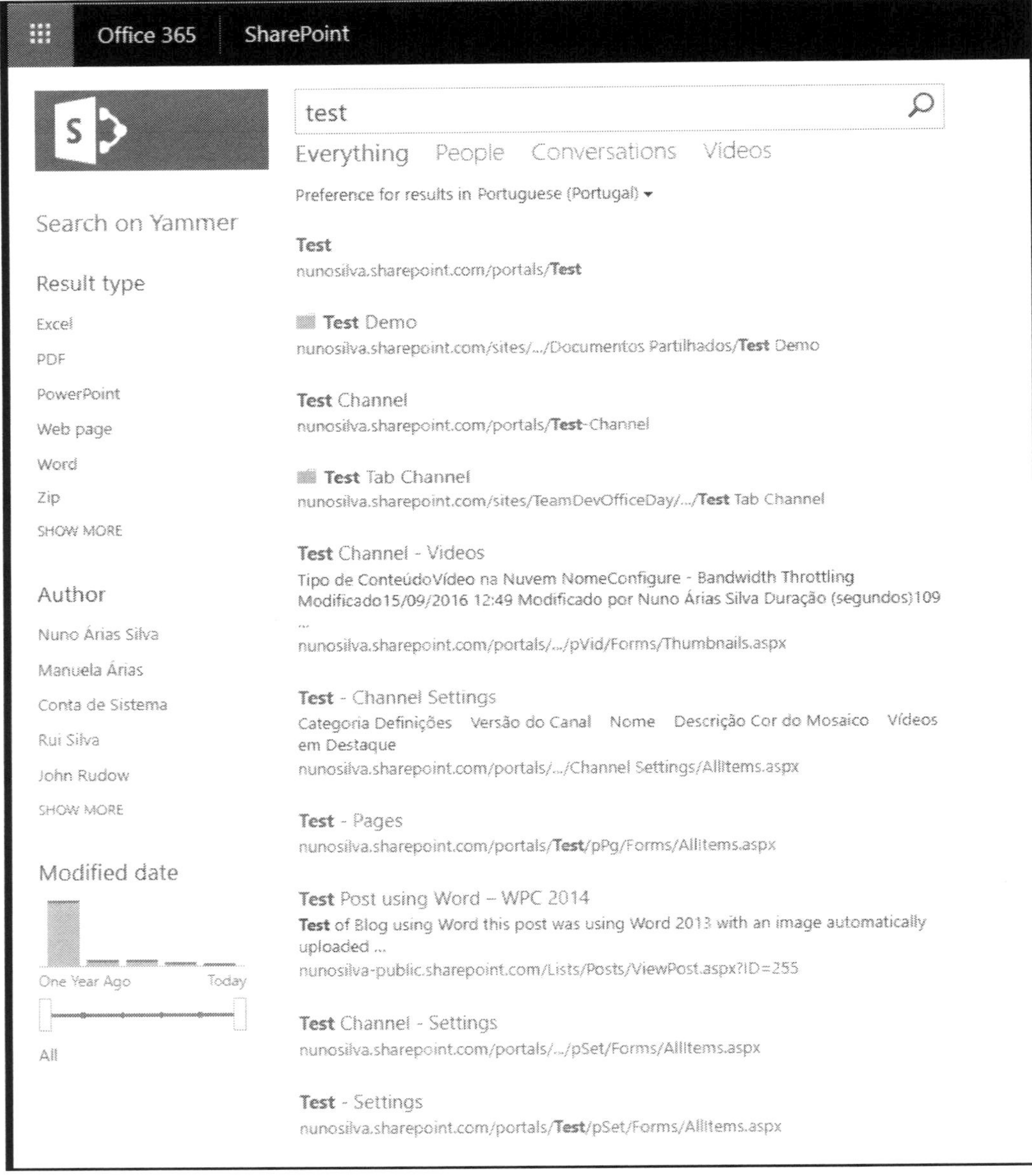

- `Yourtenantname.sharepoint.com/sites/CompliancePolicyCenter`: The `/sites/CompliancePolicyCenter` is the URL that is used for your compliance policy center, where you can configure information-management policies that will be applied to your content. You can, for example, create a policy that will delete all documents that are more than 10 years old:

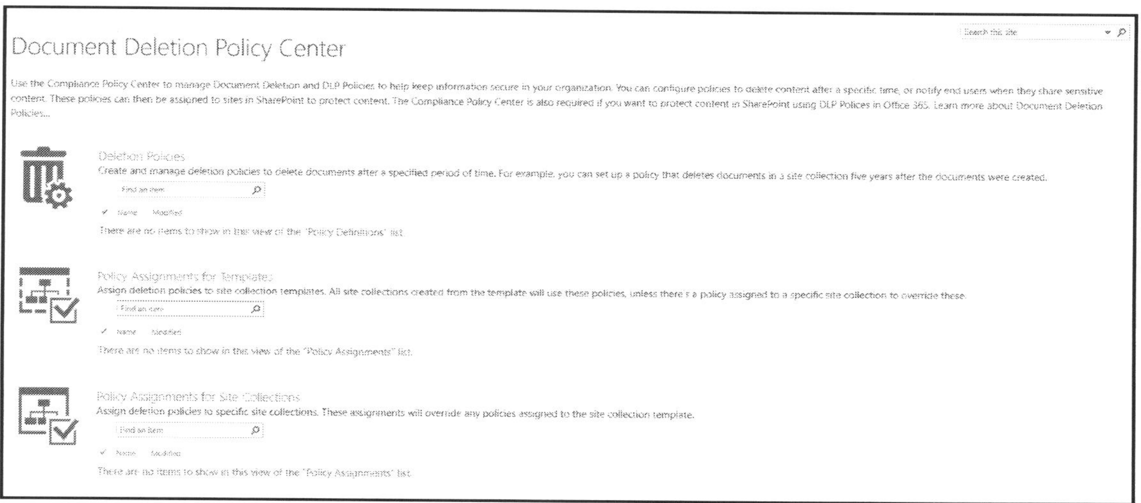


To learn more, go to `https://support.office.com/en-us/article/Overview-of-document-deletion-policies-55e8d858-f278-482b-a198-2e62d6a2e6e5?ui=en-USrs=en-USad=US`.

- `Yourtenantname-my.sharepoint.com`: The `-my.sharepoint.com` URL is where your OneDrive for Business resides:

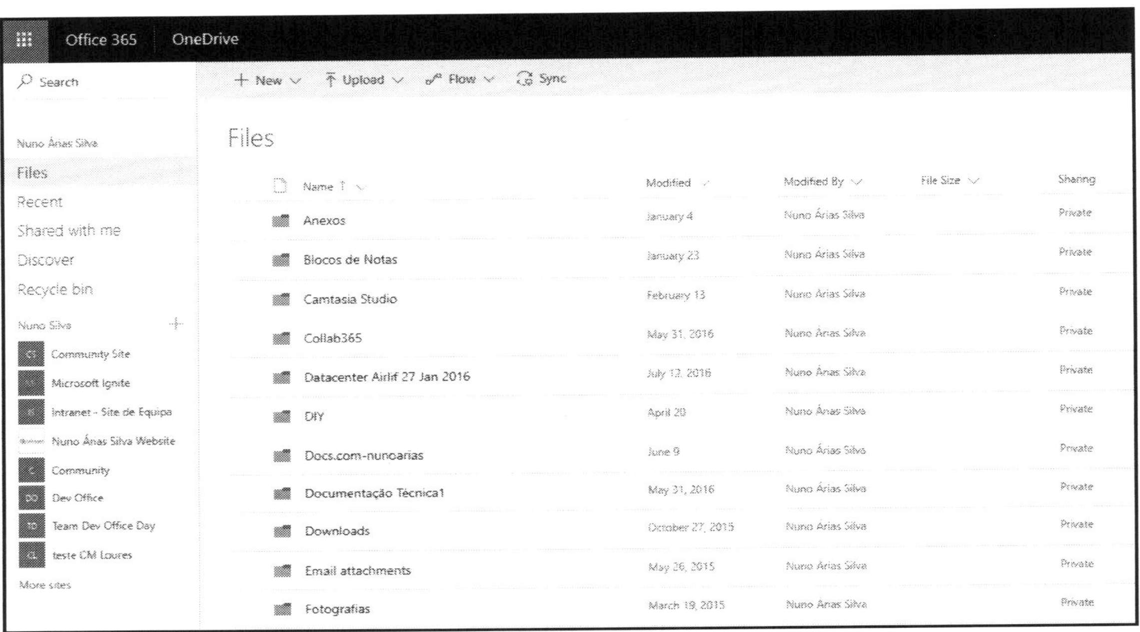


OneDrive for Business is the enterprise-class file storage service for your personal files, and it resides in SharePoint Online. To access your personal OneDrive, you can go to `http://yourtenantname-my.sharepoint.com` or you can use the OneDrive client on your machine or device. You can download the client at `https://onedrive.live.com/about/en-us/download/`.

- `Yourtenantname-public.sharepoint.com`: Public websites have been retired by Microsoft. The following screenshot shows how they used to look:

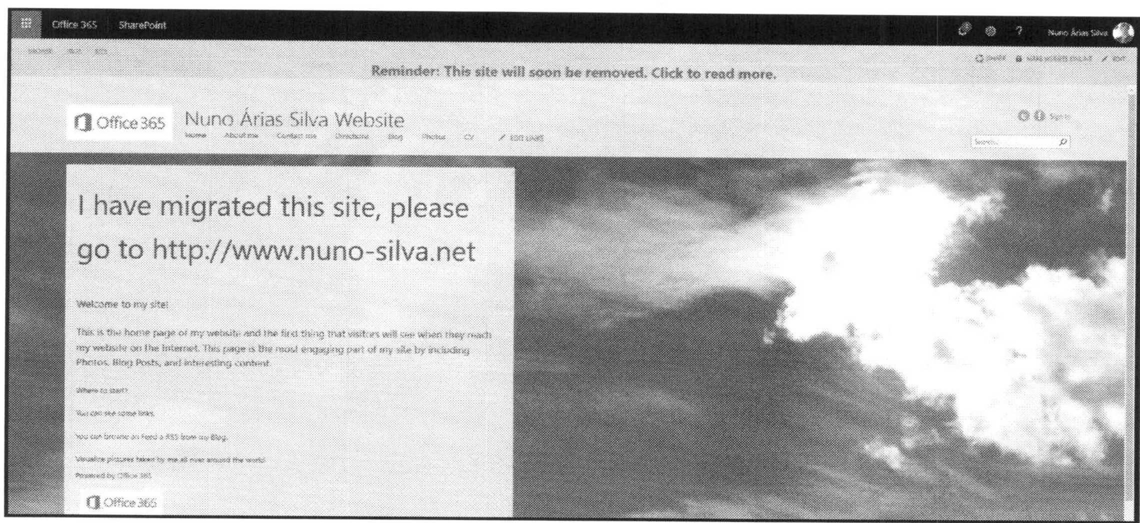


I have used the public website feature for several years, and I have now migrated to a solution that has more capabilities and that is more scalable. On April 1 2018, Microsoft deleted the content of the site, and I have written an article that was widely used by customers that needed to migrate their content to a new and more scalable platform. You can read my article to learn how to migrate your content to a new solution using Azure, WordPress, and SQL Database on Azure. You can find the article at `https://www.nuno-silva.net/blog/post/10723/migrate-sharepoint-public-website-to-wordpress-on-azure-with-sql`.

# Architecture of SharePoint Online

SharePoint can be deployed in different topologies:

- SharePoint Online
- Hybrid
- Azure/IaaS
- On-premises

The following image shows how responsibilities are split between Microsoft and the customer depending on the selected topology:

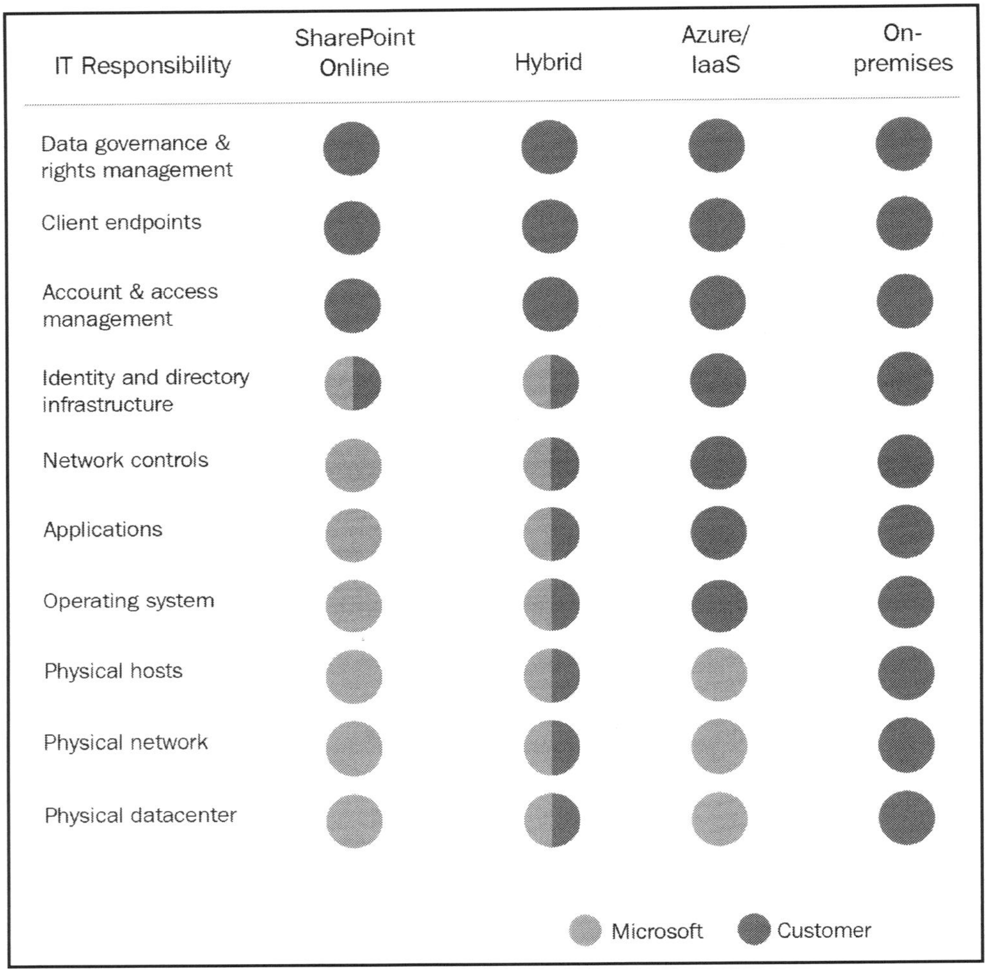

| IT Responsibility | SharePoint Online | Hybrid | Azure/ IaaS | On-premises |
|---|---|---|---|---|
| Data governance & rights management | | | | |
| Client endpoints | | | | |
| Account & access management | | | | |
| Identity and directory infrastructure | | | | |
| Network controls | | | | |
| Applications | | | | |
| Operating system | | | | |
| Physical hosts | | | | |
| Physical network | | | | |
| Physical datacenter | | | | |

Microsoft Customer

## SharePoint Online

SharePoint Online is a **software as a service** (**SaaS**) product that comes with your Office 365 tenant. The following image depicts a typical scenario in most organizations that uses SharePoint Online, with synchronized users to Azure AD and the source of the identity being the on-premises AD:

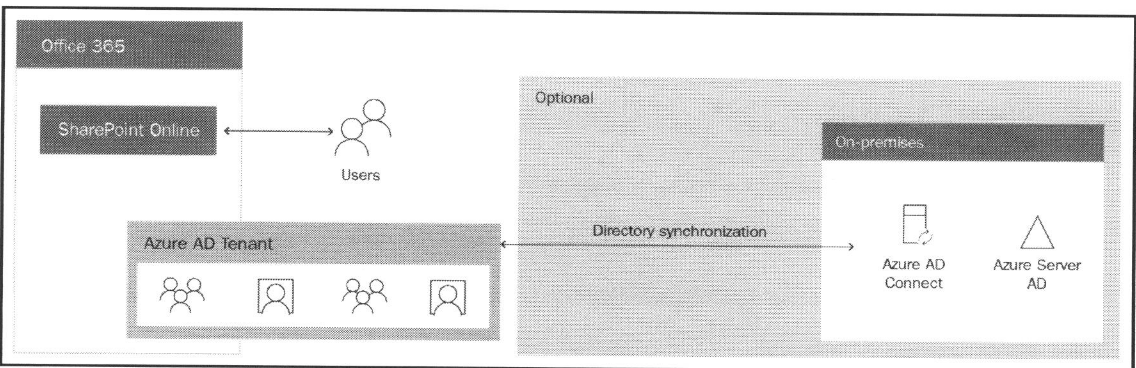


## SharePoint in Azure or an on-premises hybrid

A SharePoint hybrid is a way to integrate your SharePoint Server 2016 on-premises farm with your SharePoint Online tenant by sharing some of the components of the two". You can deploy your on-premises farm either in your data center or on Azure as an **infrastructure as a service** (**IaaS**).

# SharePoint hybrid

The following image represents an organization that has SharePoint on-premises and is connected to SharePoint Online so that it can have capabilities such as integrated searches:

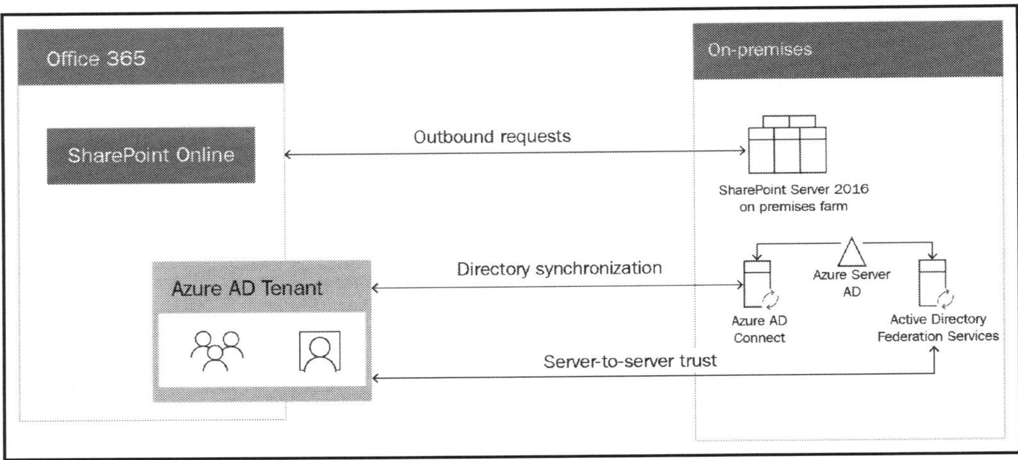


# SharePoint on Azure

Alternatively, some customers use an on-premises SharePoint infrastructure deployed on Azure instead of their own datacenter. Consider the following image:

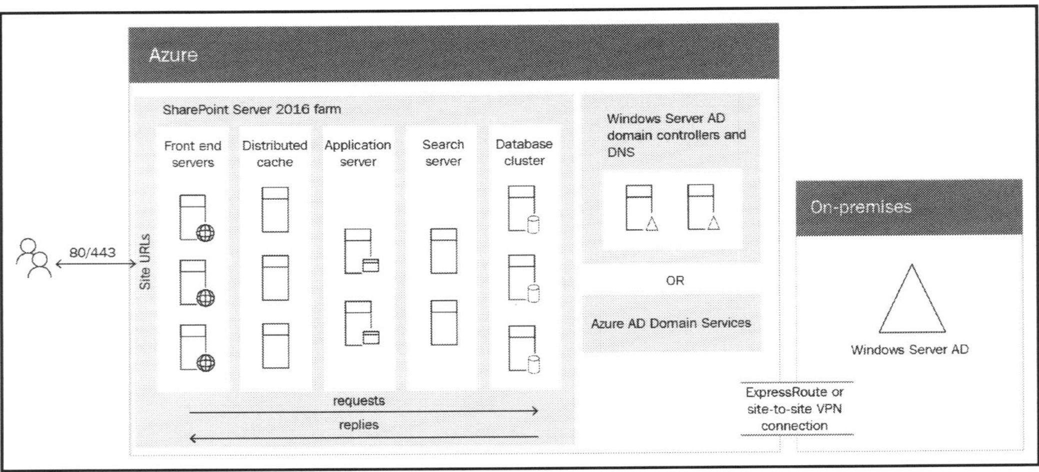

## SharePoint on-premises

A SharePoint on-premises architecture is where SharePoint is only deployed on the on-premises infrastructure datacenter or on an IaaS cloud provider:

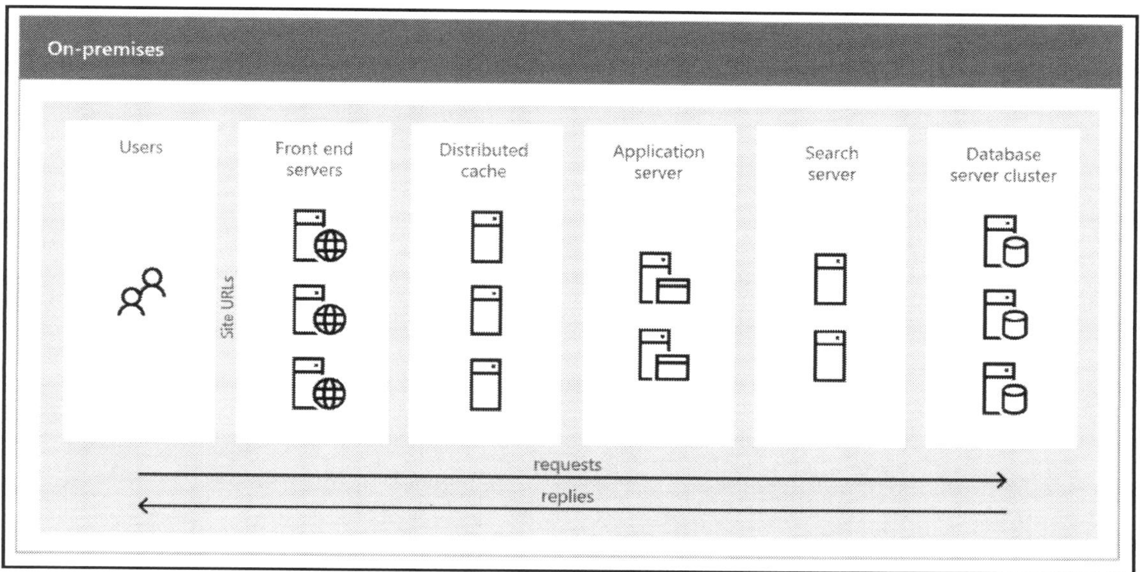


You can deploy SharePoint in several different topologies, such as completely on-premises or in Azure, but the basic architecture described in the hybrid scenario will have the same requirements for your on-premises infrastructure in your data center, or for Azure as an IaaS. You can see more at `https://technet.microsoft.com/en-us/library/cc263199(v=office.16).aspx`.

## Features

SharePoint Online, like other services following the **software as a service** (**SaaS**) model, has some differences between an on-premises farm installation and its online service brother. To best understand all of the functionalities in each SharePoint plan, go to `https://technet.microsoft.com/en-us/library/sharepoint-online-service-description.aspx`.

# Capabilities

SharePoint Online is a service that leverages the capabilities of the SharePoint platform in the cloud, but it differs in some areas when compared with the on-premises version. It can aid collaboration between people in your organization, and has the following capabilities:

- Enterprise portal
- Intranet sites
- Extranet sites
- Content management for managing files and synchronization with OneDrive
- Search portal
- Rich-editing online, with coediting and authoring, viewing, and sharing
- Enterprise workflow with capacities extended by Microsoft Flow

# Administering SharePoint Online

To administer SharePoint Online, as described earlier, you can go to your admin URL at, for example, `https://yourtenantname-admin.sharepoint.com`. In the SharePoint Online admin center, you have a variety of tools that you can use to set your options according to the needs of your organization. For instance, this is where you can configure tenant settings and implement a hybrid SharePoint. In the admin center, you can configure several components:

- Site collections:
    - Create
    - Manage
    - Delete
    - Change Permissions
    - Change Storage
- Manage and configure features:
    - InfoPath
    - User profiles:
        - People
        - Organizations
        - My Site settings
    - Business Connectivity Services
    - Term Store

- Records Management
- Search
- Secure Store
- Apps
- Sharing
- General Settings
- Configure Hybrid
- Access Control

With these options in the admin center, you can configure your settings based on the requirements of your organization.

Now, we will look at the options available in the Admin center based on the configuration settings.

## Site collections and their various options

In the site collections pane, you have the following options;

- **Create**: To create a new site collection, click on the **New** drop-down, then select **Private Site Collection**, and follow the instructions based on the type of site that you need:

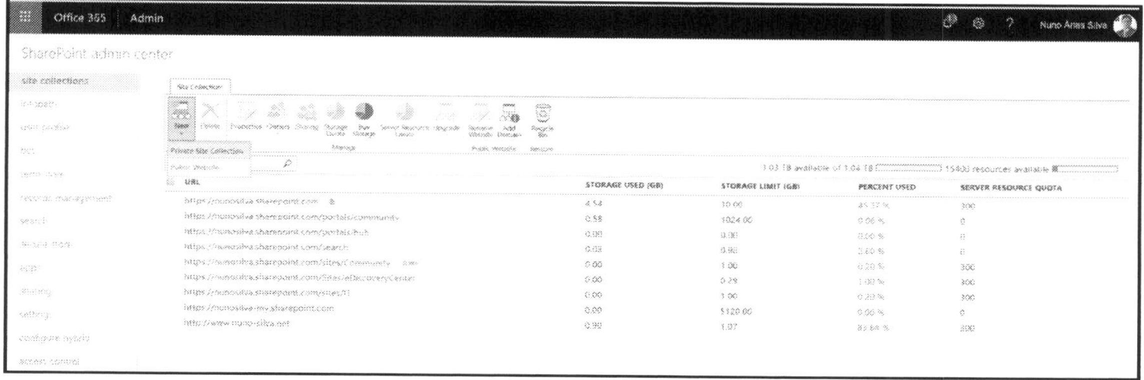

- **Manage**: To manage a site, select a site and choose from options such as **Properties**, **Owners**, **Sharing**, and **Storage Quota** to change its properties as you see fit:

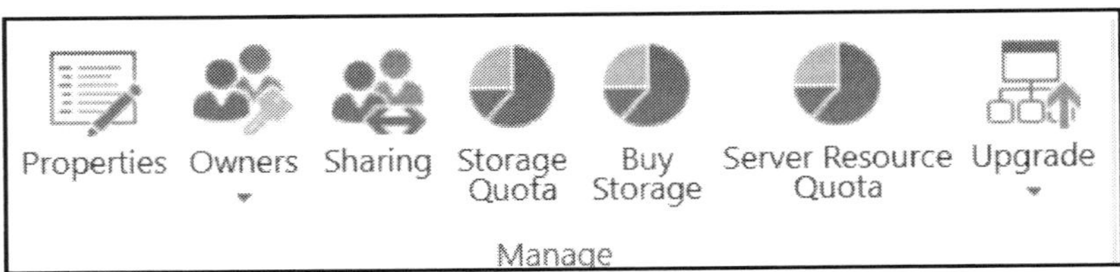


- **Delete**: To delete a site collection, select it and click on the **Delete** button. When you click **Delete**, the following message will be shown stating that you have 30 days to recover the site from the recycle bin:

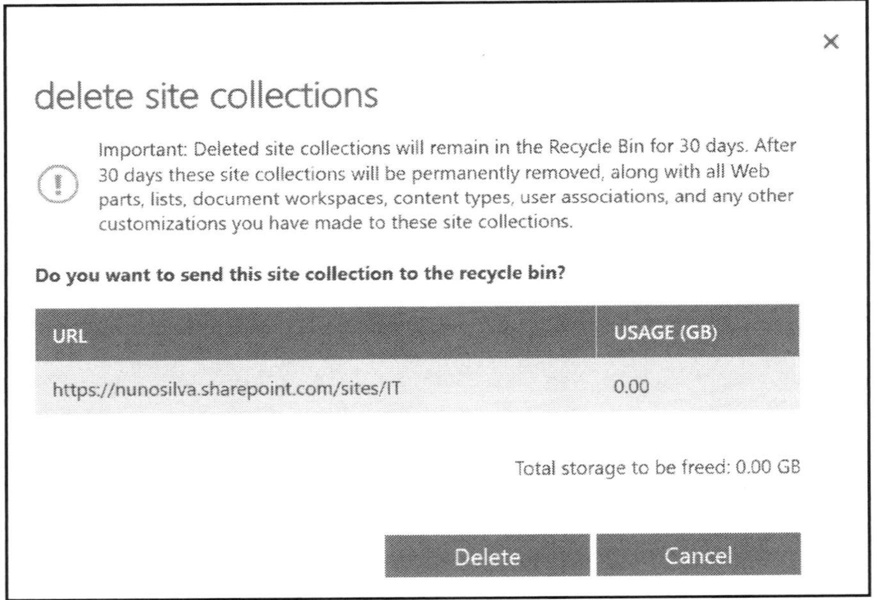

# Managing and configuring features

The managing and configuring features are as follows:

- **InfoPath**: To manage InfoPath, select the **InfoPath** from the left-hand menu:

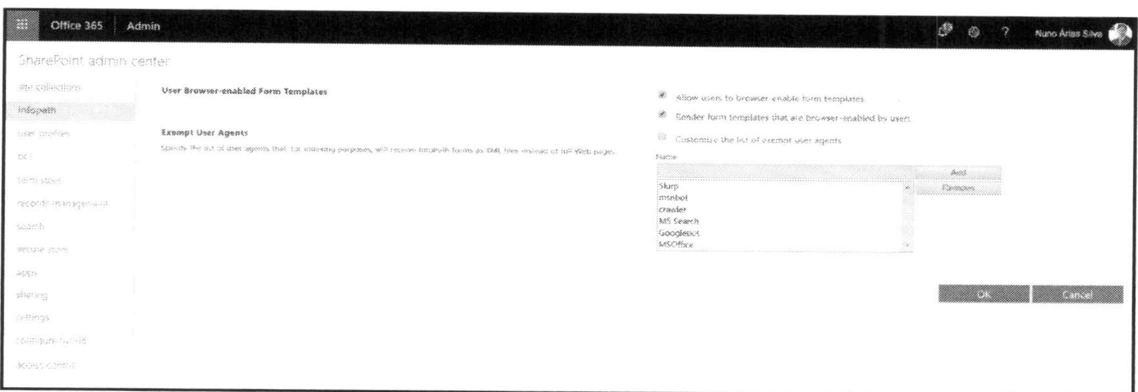


The InfoPath will be supported until 2023. You can learn more about it at `https://blogs.office.com/en-us/2014/01/31/update-on-infopath-and-sharepoint-forms/`.

After the InfoPath section, you have the following options:

- **user profiles**: To manage user profiles, you have several options, such as the following:
    - **People:** In this option, you can manage the following:
        - User properties
        - User profiles
        - User sub-types
        - Audiences
        - User permissions
        - Policies
    - **Organizations:** In this option, you can manage the following:
        - Organization properties
        - Organization profiles
        - Organization sub-types

- **My Site Settings:** In this option, you can manage the following:
    - Setup My Sites
    - Configure trusted host locations
    - Manage promoted sites
    - Publish links to Office client applications
    - Managing social tags and notes

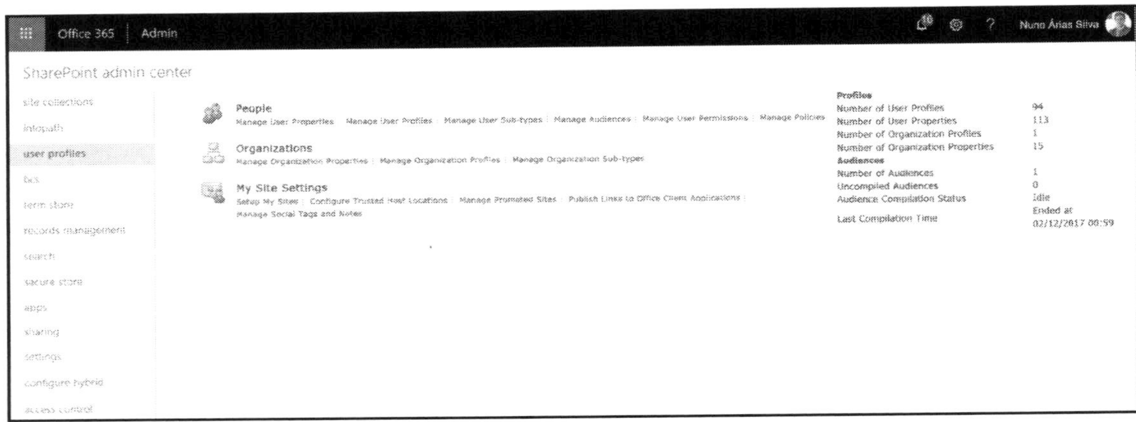


- **bcs**: To manage **Business Connectivity Services** (**BCS**), you have several options, such as the following:
    - **business connectivity services**:
        - **Manage BDC Models and External Content Types**

- **connection settings for apps**:
    - **Manage connections to online services**
    - **Manage connections to on-premises services**

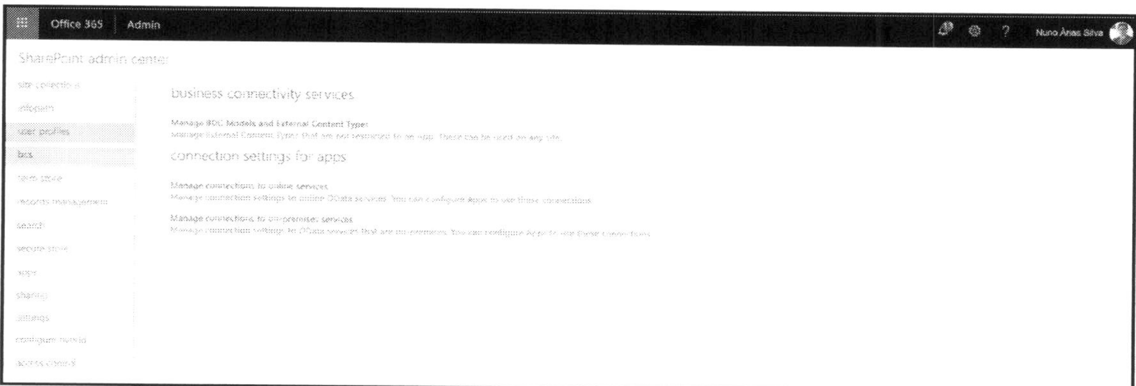


- **term store**: In the **term store** option, you can manage the taxonomies used in your tenant:

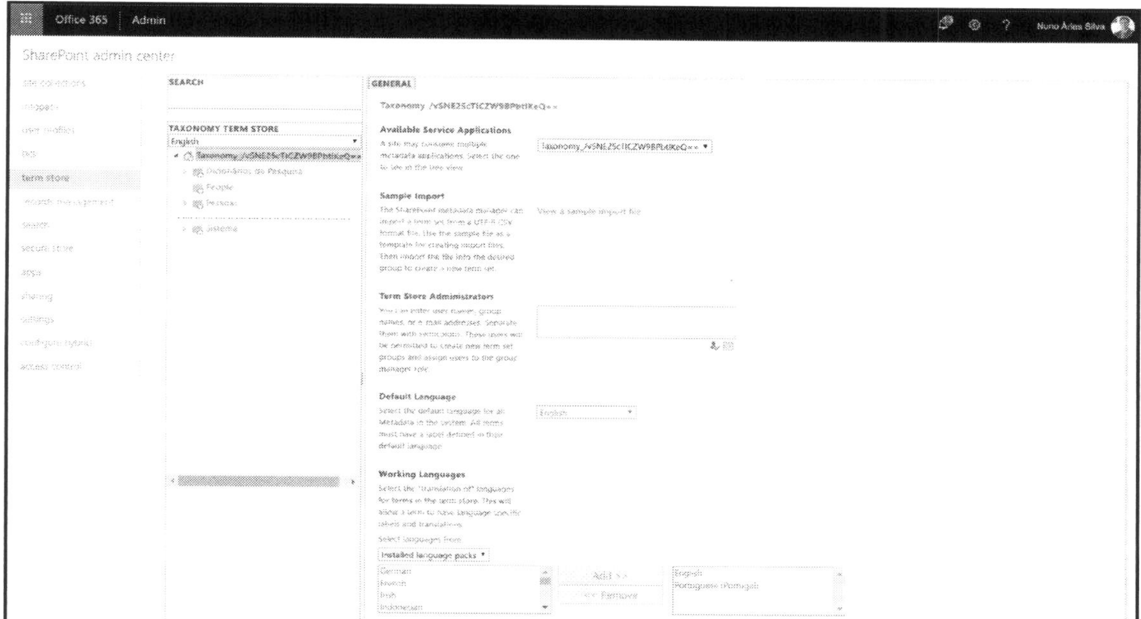

- **records management**: In this option, you can manage the record location using the menu on the left:

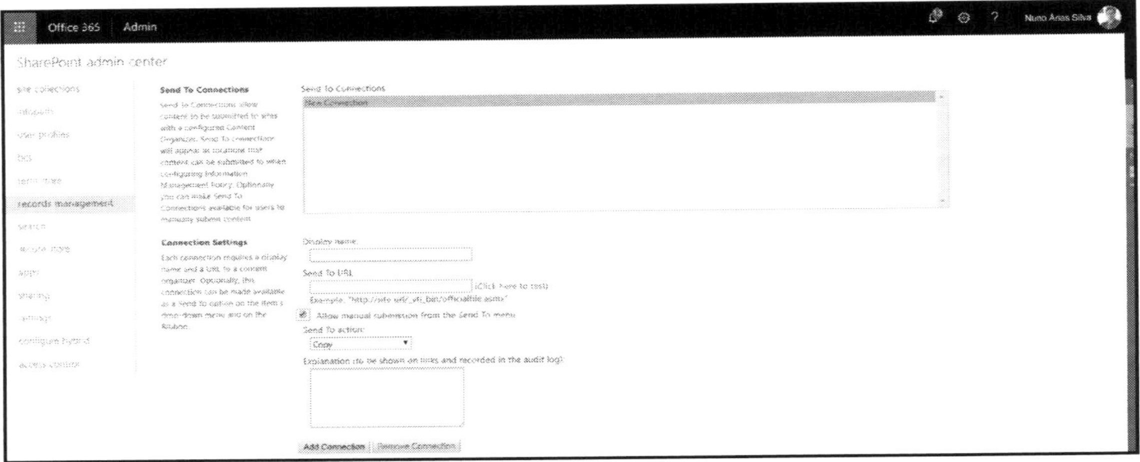

- **search**: In the **search** section, you can manage the following:
  - **Manage Search Schema**
  - **Manage Search Dictionaries**
  - **Manage Authoritative Pages**
  - **Query Suggestion Settings**
  - **Manage Result Sources**
  - **Manage Query Rules**
  - **Manage Query Client Types**
  - **Manage Remove Search Results**
  - **View Usage Reports**
  - **Search Center Settings**
  - **Export Search Configuration**
  - **Import Search Configuration**
  - **Crawl Log Permissions**

- **secure store**: In this section, you can manage target applications as shown in the following screenshot:

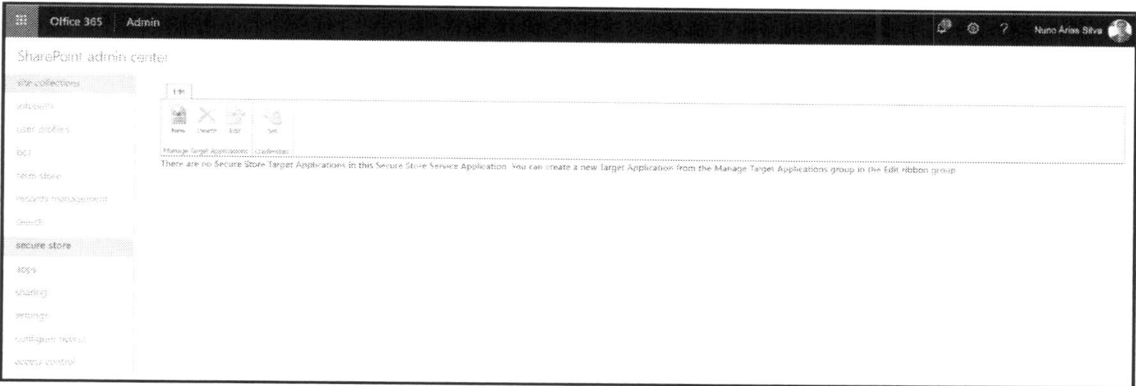


- **apps**: In this section, you can manage apps using the following options:
    - **App Catalog**
    - **Purchase Apps**
    - **Manage Licenses**
    - **Configure Store Settings**
    - **Monitor Apps**
    - **App Permissions**
- **sharing**: In this section, you can set your sharing options for your tenant. You can configure the following:
    - **Sharing outside your organization**
    - **Who can share outside your organization**
    - **Default link type**
    - **Default link permission**
    - **Additional settings**
    - **Notifications**

The following configuration is recommended when you share information outside your organization:

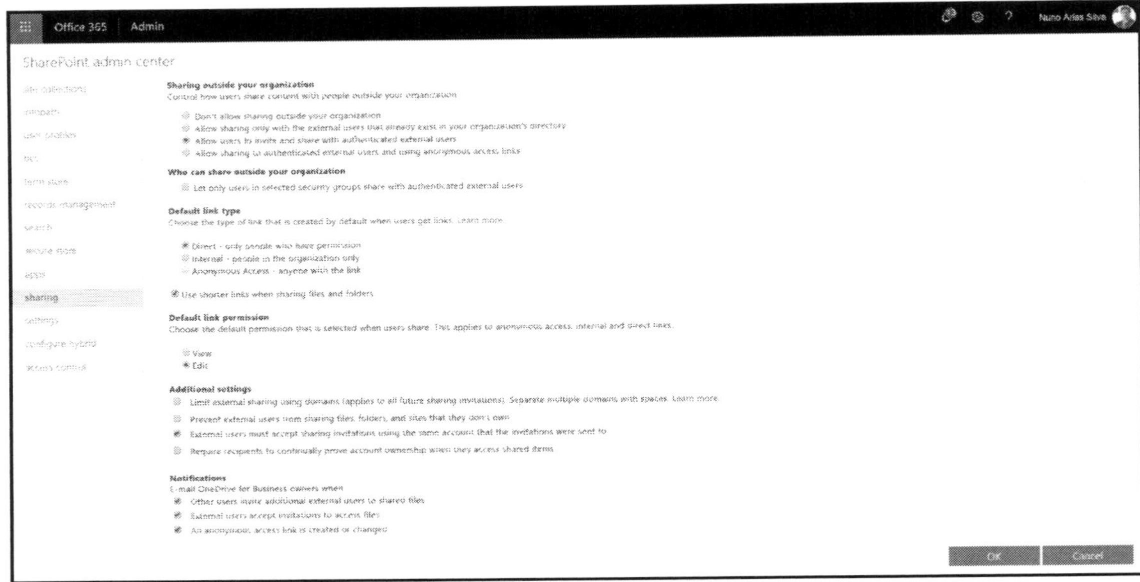

You can be more precise in the permissions you give than the recommendation we have shown here.

# General settings

In the **settings** option, you can configure the following:

- **Show or Hide Options**
- **Site Collection Storage Management**
- **OneDrive for Business Experience**
- **OneDrive Sync Button**
- **SharePoint Lists and Libraries Experience**
- **Postpone deletion of SharePoint Online public websites**
- **Admin Center Experience**
- **Office Graph**
- **Enterprise Social Collaboration**
- **Streaming Video Service**
- **Site Pages**
- **Global Experience Version Settings**
- **Information Rights Management (IRM)**
- **Site Creation**
- **Subsite Creation**
- **Custom Script**
- **Preview Features**
- **Connected Services**
- **Access Apps**
- **Mobile Push Notifications - OneDrive for Business**
- **Mobile Push Notifications - SharePoint**
- **Comments on Site Pages**

# Configure hybrid

This section is where you start to configure you hybrid SharePoint to leverage SharePoint Online features in your on-premises SharePoint deployment:

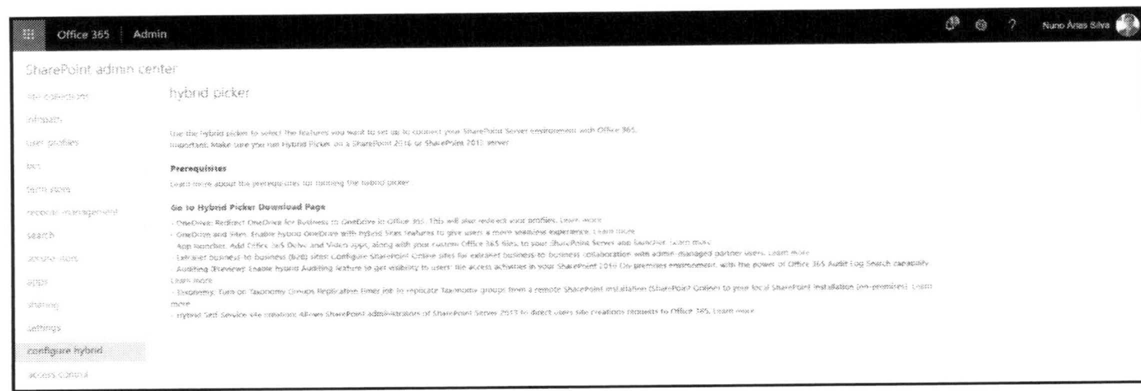


When you go to Hybrid Picker, download `https://configure.office.com/scenario.aspx?Sid=54`, you will have access to the Hybrid configuration:

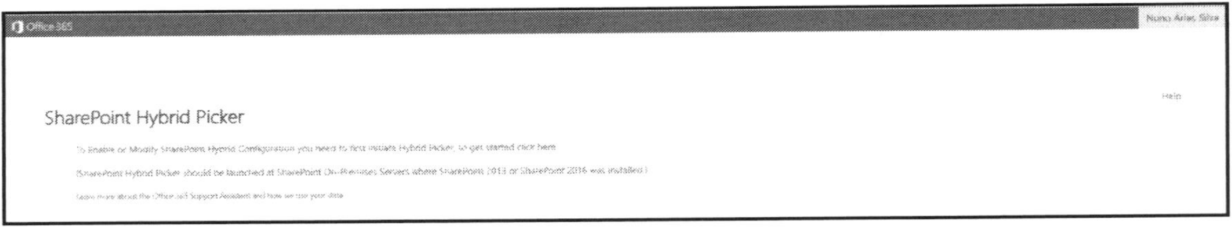

To access to the Hybrid Picker you need to have an Office 365 and be administrator at least for SharePoint.

# Access control

In the **access control** section, you can configure the following settings:

- **Restrict access based on device or network location**:
    - **Unmanaged devices**
    - **Apps that don't use modern authentication**
    - **Control access based on network location**

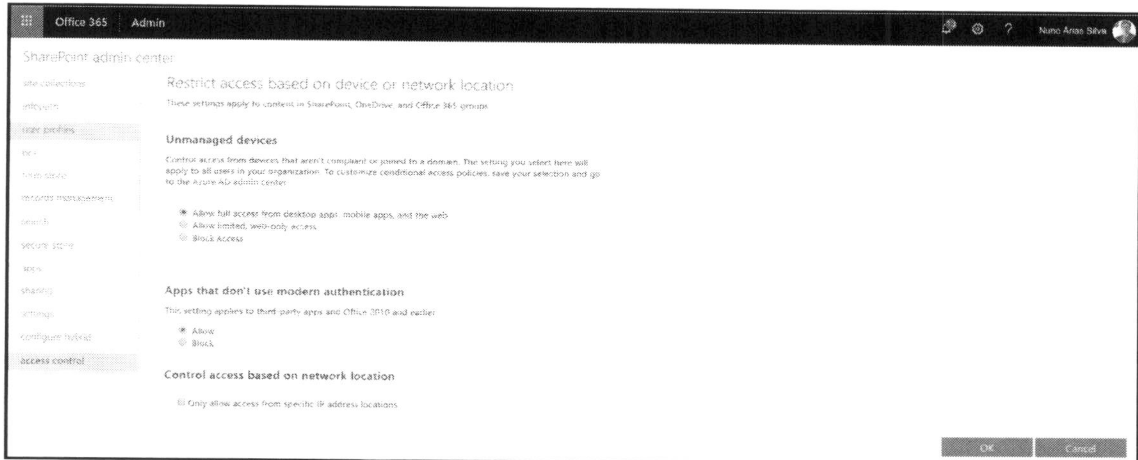


# OneDrive admin center

OneDrive for Business is a part of SharePoint, but has a separate admin center that can be accessed directly at `https://admin.onedrive.com`. In this admin center, you can configure the following options:

- **Sharing**
- **Sync**
- **Storage**
- **Device Access**

- **Compliance**
- **Notifications**

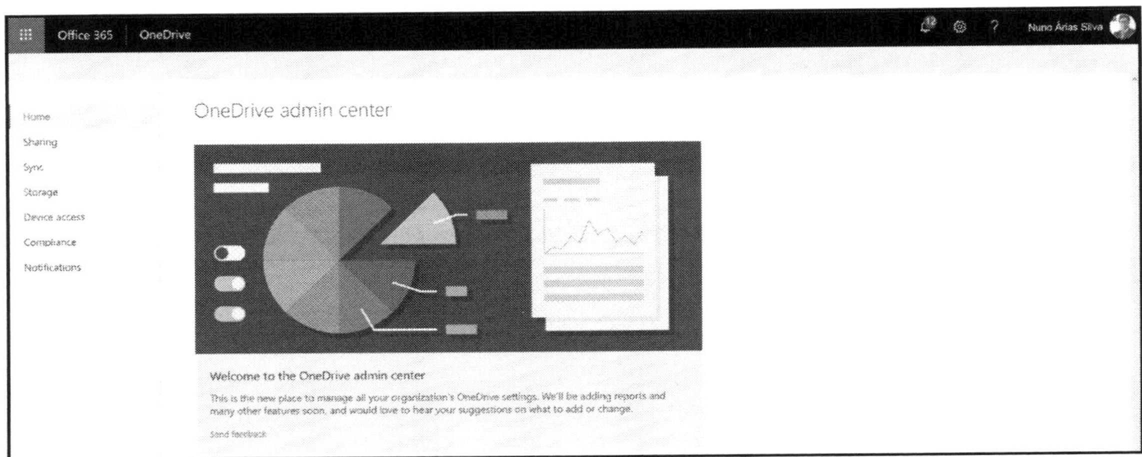


Now we will look at the options that we can configure in the OneDrive Admin center.

# Sharing

In the **Sharing** section, you can configure the following:

- **Links**
- **External Sharing**

The following two screenshots show the recommended settings to use when setting up an organization in which you want to be able to share documents and sites outside of Office 365 and the SharePoint Online environment:

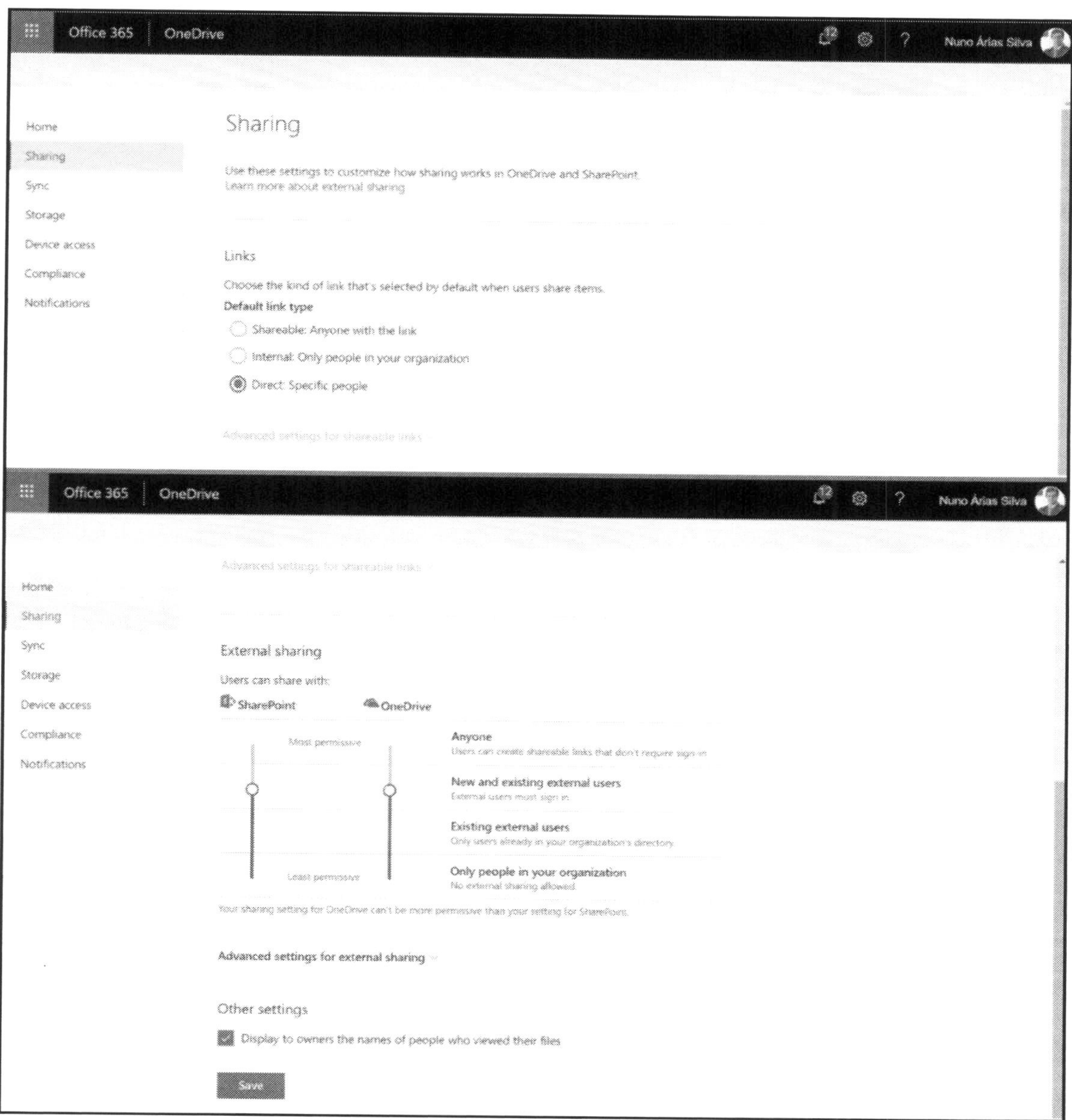

# Sync

The **Sync** setting helps you control the syncing of files in OneDrive and SharePoint. You can configure the various options as shown in the following screenshot:

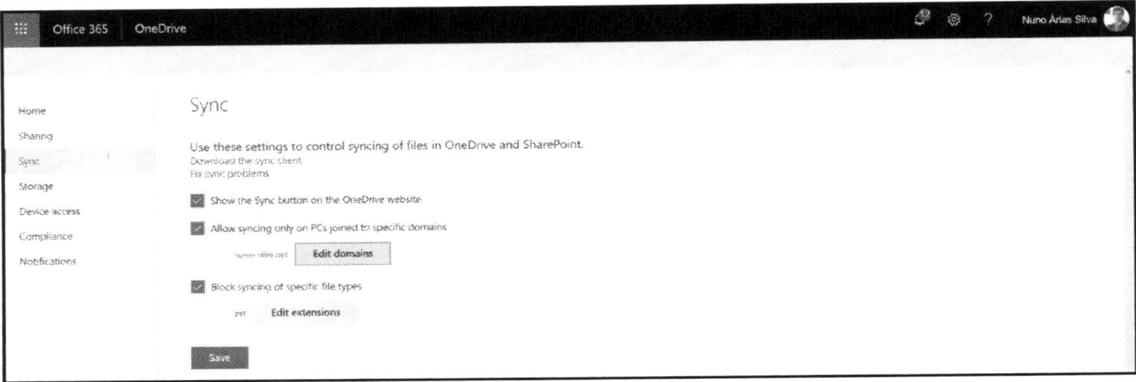


# Storage

You can use the **Storage** section to specify the storage limits for all users. You can configure the options as shown in the following screenshot

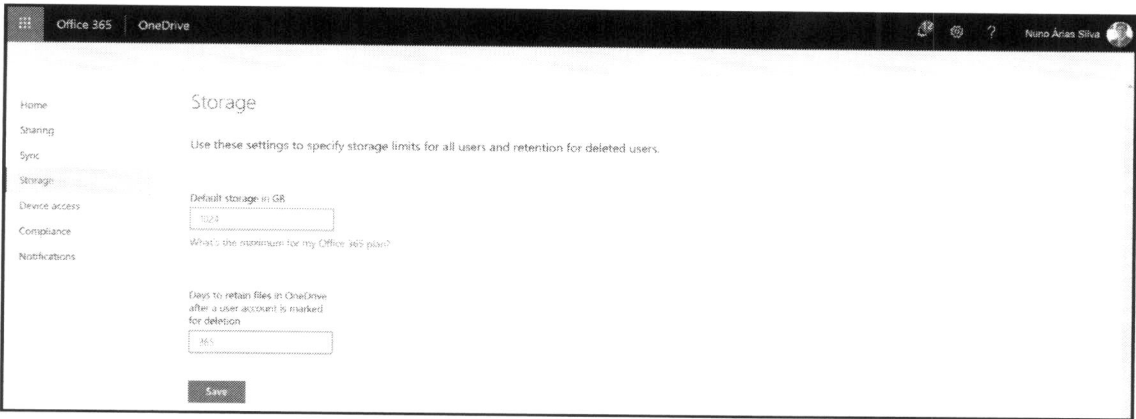


## Device access

The **Device access** section helps you control the access of each device. You can configure the following options as shown in the following screenshot:

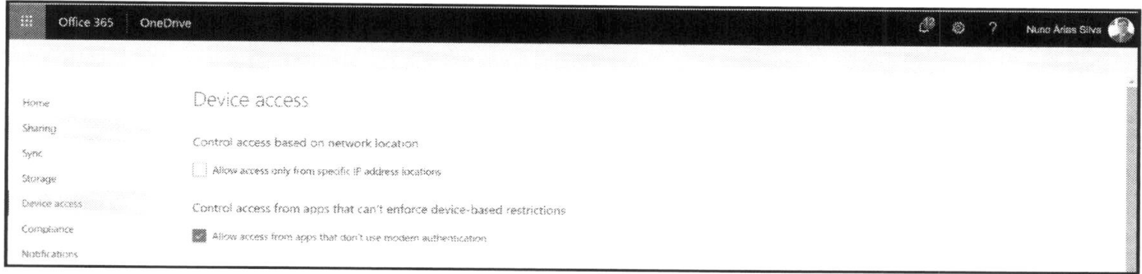

The **Device access** option, has the following settings for your mobile applications management:

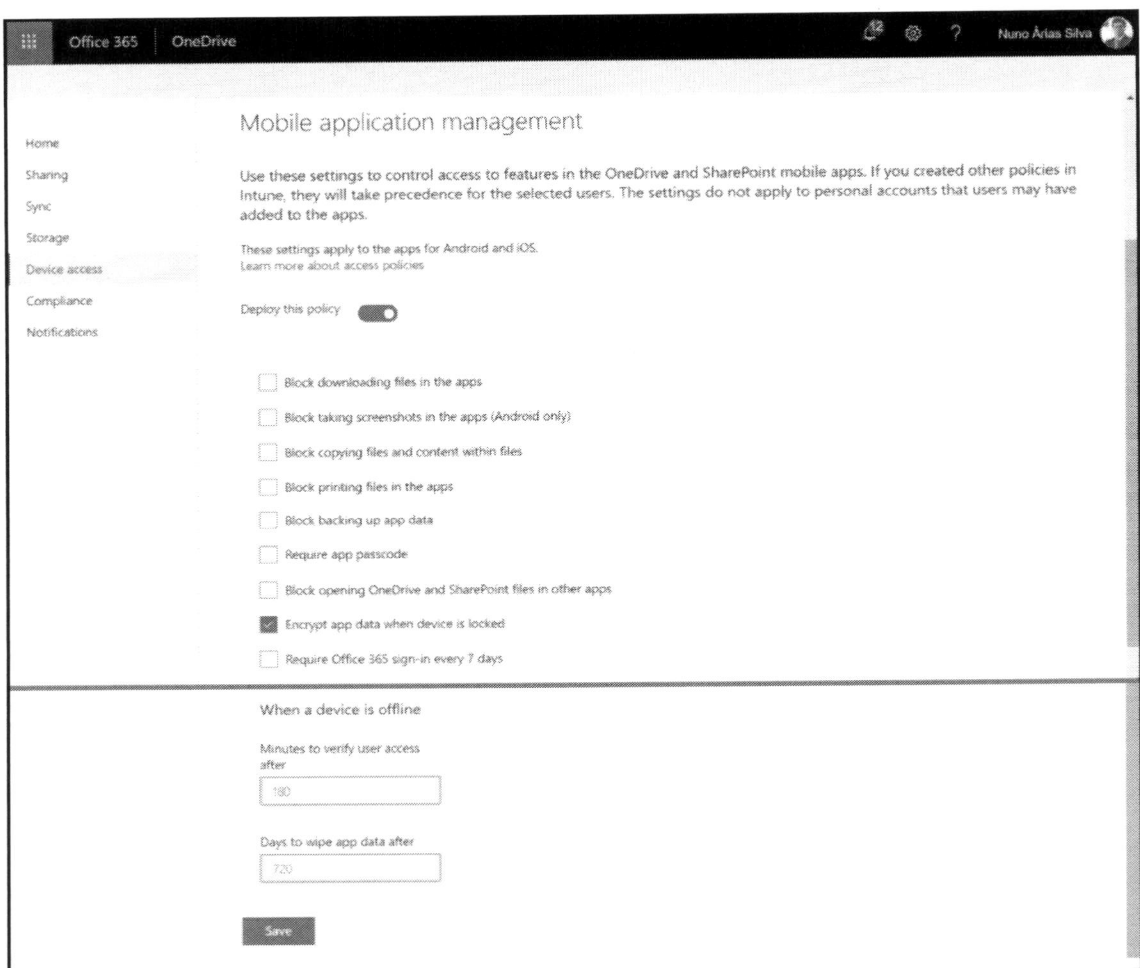


## Compliance

The **Compliance** section helps you keep a check on all the legal, regulatory or technical standards that you may need to meet. In the **Compliance** section, you can configure the options as shown in the following screenshot:

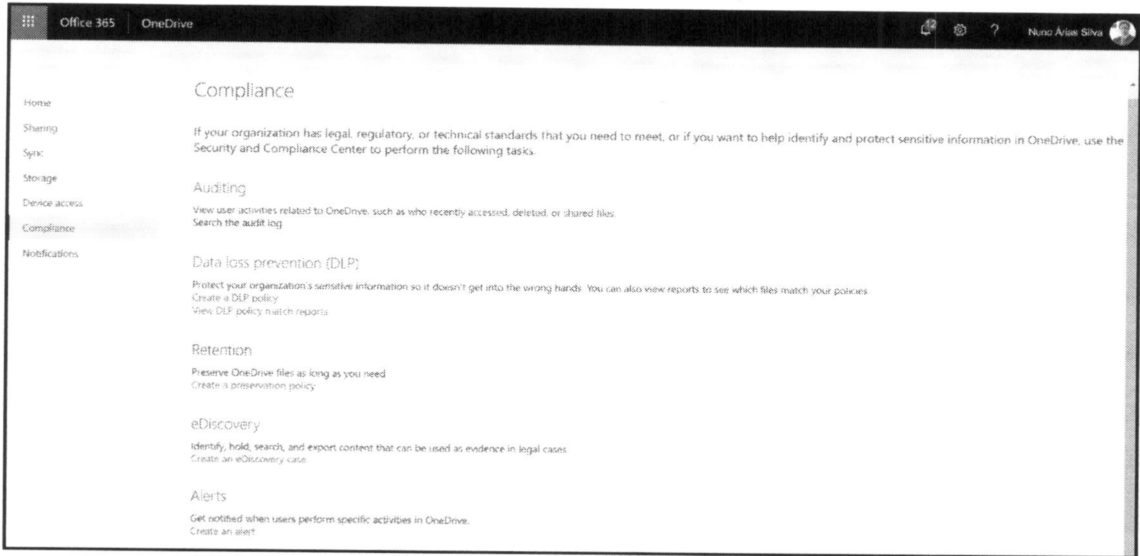


# Notifications

You can use the **Notifications** section to control the various notifications that you receive. The following is a screenshot of the options that you can configure in the notification section:

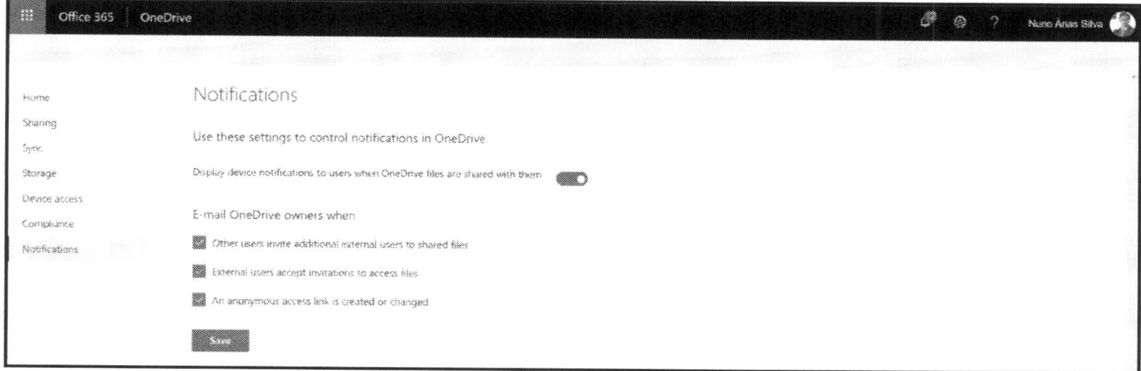

# Summary

In this chapter, you have learned about the basic planning and implementation of SharePoint. You now have more information on how to plan your SharePoint Online project and how to implement the basics of SharePoint Online. In the next chapter, you will learn how to implement Skype for Business Online, another of Office 365's most popular tools.

# 9
# Skype for Business

In this chapter, you will learn about Skype for Business Online. The chapter will cover the following topics:

- Implementation of Skype for Business
- Architecture of Skype for Business
- Administration of Skype for Business

With this base, you will learn more about how to implement Skype for Business Online.

Skype for Business includes the following features:

- **Instant Messaging** (**IM**) and presence
- Web conferencing
- Audio conferencing
- PBX
- Broadcast

Skype for Business gives you the possibility to perform the following:

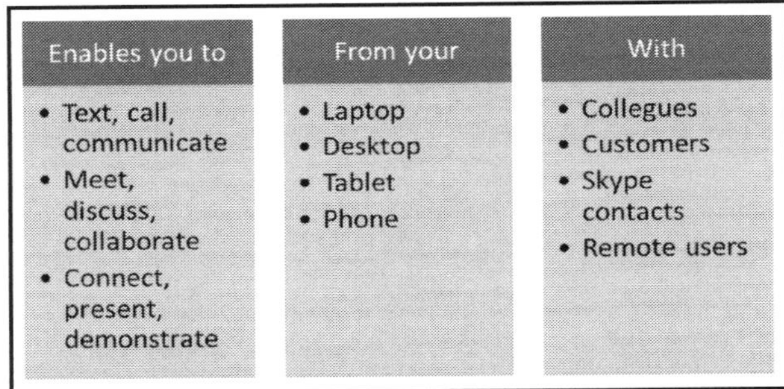


# Implementing Skype for Business

In the near future, customers of Skype for Business Online will be migrated to Microsoft Teams and this chapter will show you how to implement and manage Skype for Business Online while it's still supported.

Skype for Business Online is the easiest product to implement if you use a cloud-only scenario. Go to: `https://portal.office.com/Domains/AddDomainWizard.aspx?Scenario=AdvancedSetup`.

To implement Skype for Business Online, first you will need to set up your domains:

1. Provide a domain name as shown in the following screenshot:

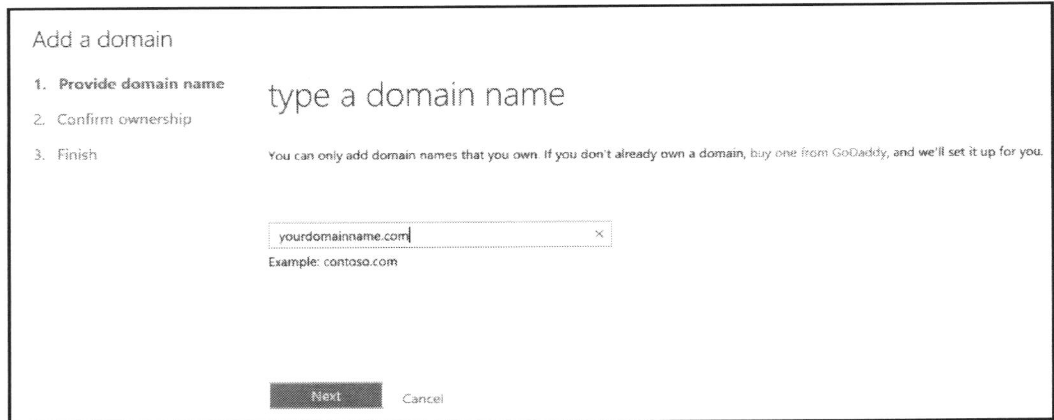

2. The next step is to confirm the ownership.
3. Follow the instructions to validate your domain name:

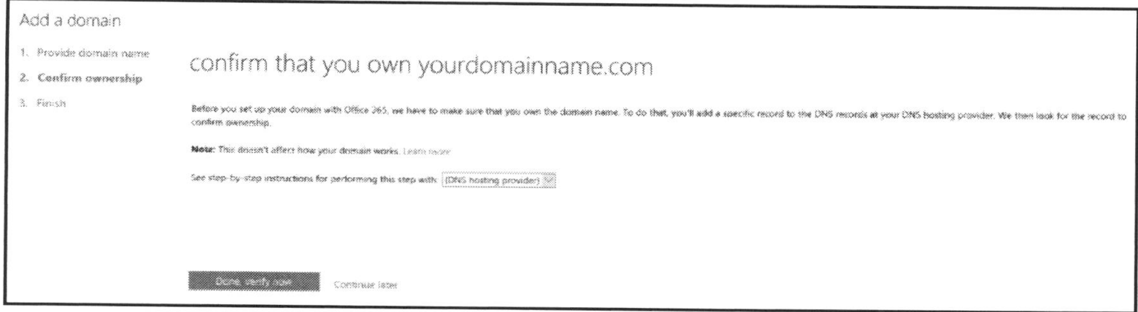


To confirm the ownership of your domain, you will need to create a record on your public DNS:

- If you do not have access to your public DNS, or it is under the responsibility of another team, you will need to ask the team responsible to create the DNS record to validate your domain as proof that you are the owner.
- When you receive the DNS record from the team or external DNS provider, you can go back to the Office 365 portal and click on the **Done, verify now** button.
- Microsoft will need to validate that you are the owner of the domain name. To accomplish this, it is necessary to create the record, as shown in the following table:

To validate the domain, you only need to create one of the following DNS records.

| **Record type (choose one)** | Alias or hostname | Destination or points to address | TTL |
|---|---|---|---|
| TXT | `@` or `yourdomainname.com` | `MS=ms123456789` | 1 hour |
| MX | `@` or `yourdomainname.com` | `ms123456789.msv1.invalid.outlook.com` | 1 hour |

If you have access to your public DNS infrastructure or DNS provider, you can create the DNS record asked by the Office 365 portal.

The direct link to add domains can be found at `https://portal.office.com/Domains/AddDomainWizard.aspx?Scenario=AdvancedSetup`.

4. After having registered the domain, follow the instructions to add the DNS records required for Skype for Business, as shown in the following screenshot:

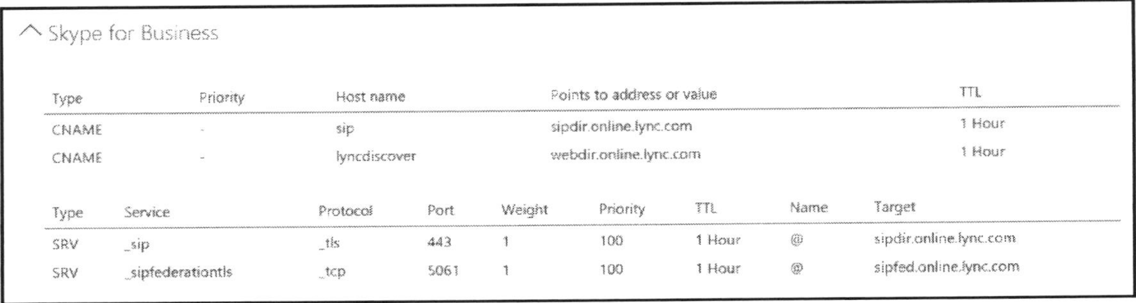

Skype for Business

| Type | Priority | Host name | Points to address or value | TTL |
|---|---|---|---|---|
| CNAME | - | sip | sipdir.online.lync.com | 1 Hour |
| CNAME | - | lyncdiscover | webdir.online.lync.com | 1 Hour |

| Type | Service | Protocol | Port | Weight | Priority | TTL | Name | Target |
|---|---|---|---|---|---|---|---|---|
| SRV | _sip | _tls | 443 | 1 | 100 | 1 Hour | @ | sipdir.online.lync.com |
| SRV | _sipfederationtls | _tcp | 5061 | 1 | 100 | 1 Hour | @ | sipfed.online.lync.com |

After validating your domain, you just need to add a license to the users within your domain name and Skype for Business Online is all set.

If you are using a split DNS (separate DNS servers provided for internal and external networks), you will need to set them up on both DNS infrastructure zones. The complete setup guide can be found at `https://support.office.com/en-us/article/Set-up-Skype-for-Business-Online-40296968-e779-4259-980b-c2de1c044c6e`.

5. Go to the Office 365 portal `http://portal.office.com` and then to the **Admin** section as shown in the following screenshot:

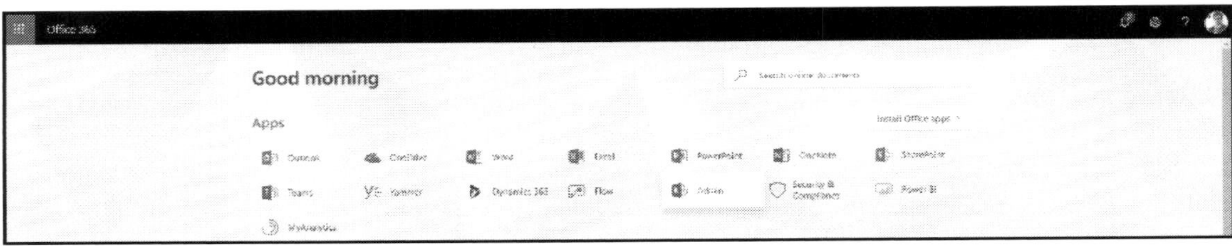

6. Go to the **Users** section and create a user and provide the Skype for Business License.
7. In the **Active users** pane, you will find the **Add a user** option. Click on it as shown in the following screenshot:

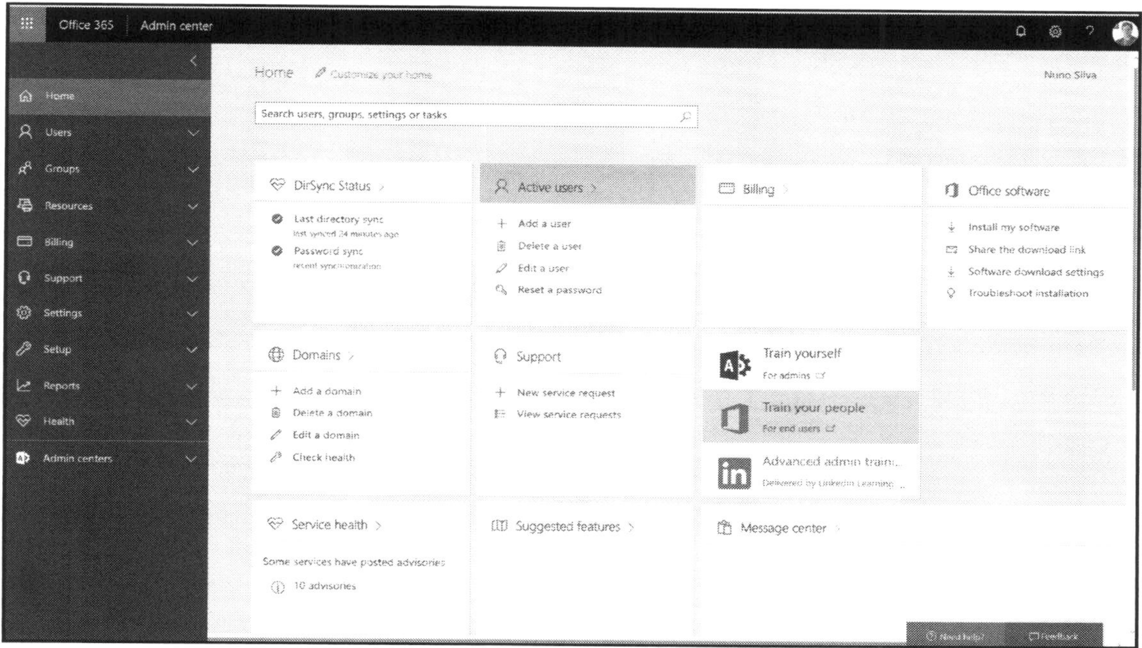

8. Fill in the **First name**, **Last name**, **Display name**, and **Username** fields and select the domain and location as shown in the following screenshot:

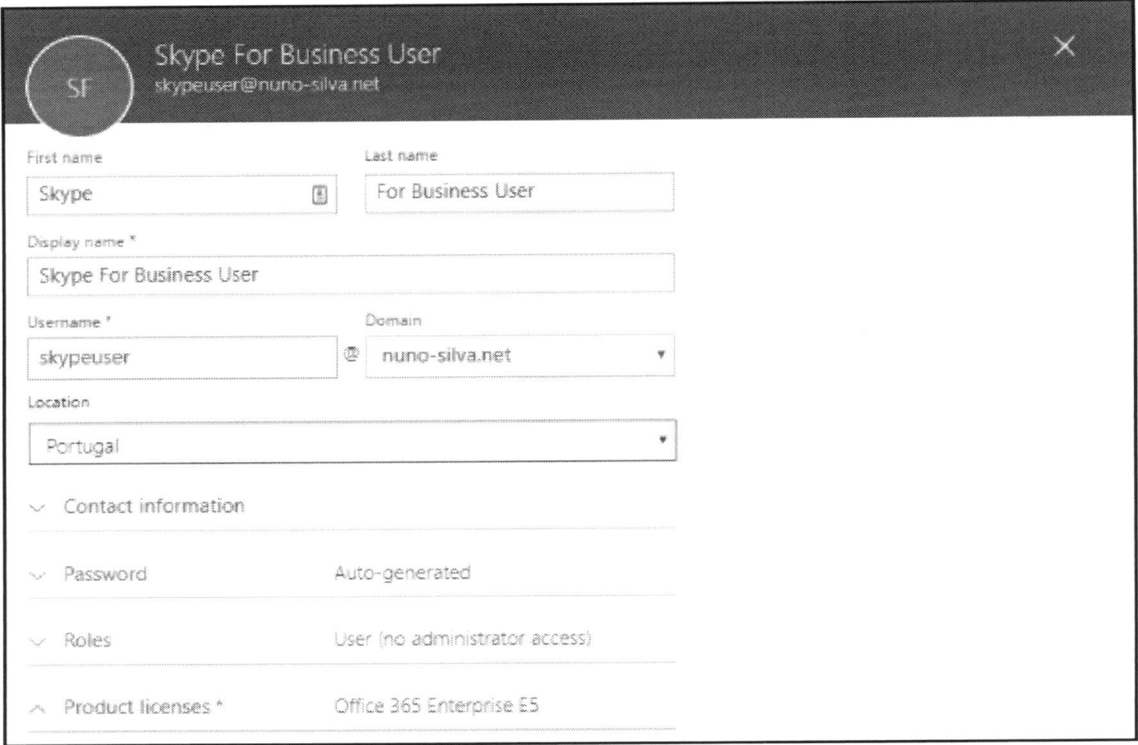

9. Now we need to select the Skype for Business license. We should only select Skype for Business features, as shown in the following screenshot and select as shown in the following screenshot:

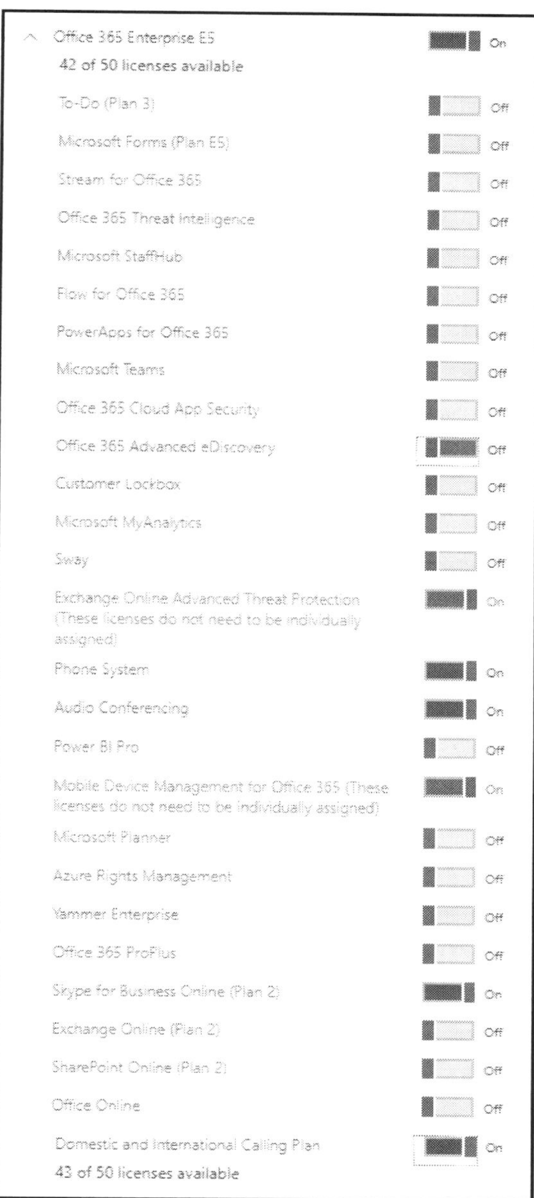

10. After the user is created, the Office 365 portal shows the information about the result of the operation:

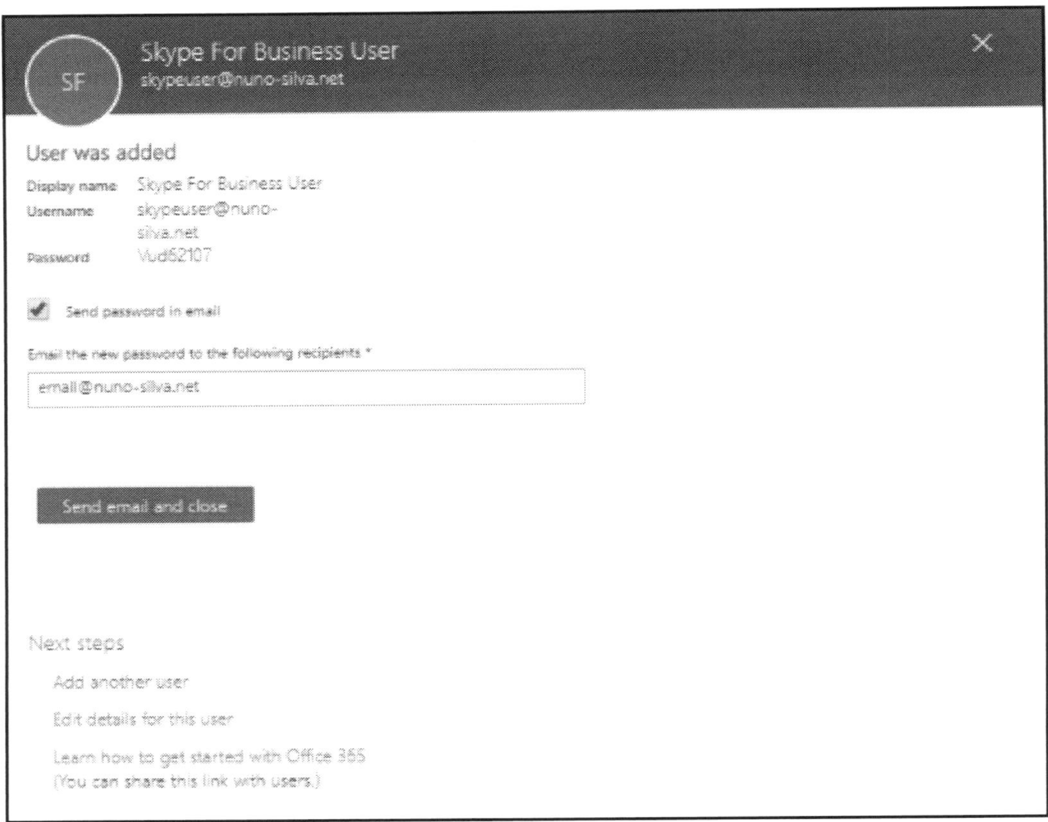

11. Now let's log in with the user by going to `http://portal.office.com` and filling in the username:

12. Click the **Next** button, fill in the password, and click on the **Sign in** button:

13. Since the user only has a Skype for Business license, you must install the Skype for Business client on your desktop. In the Office 365 portal, select the **Install Office apps** drop-down:

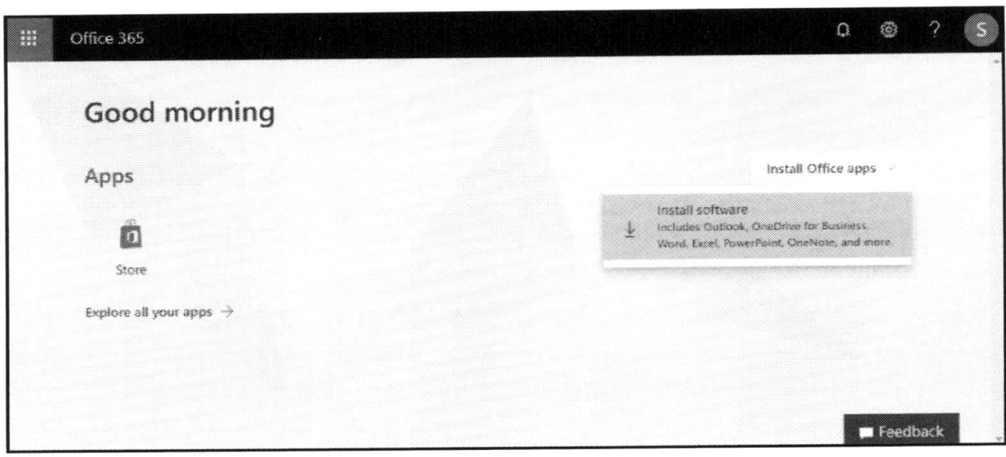


14. Select the version required and click on the **Install** button:

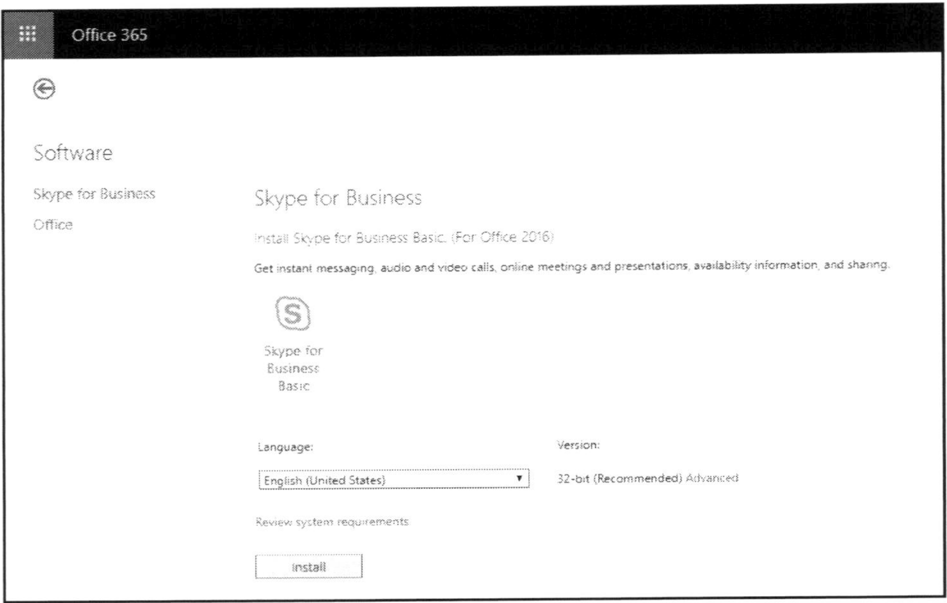

15. After installing the Skype for Business client and the user has logged in, he/she can start using the service:

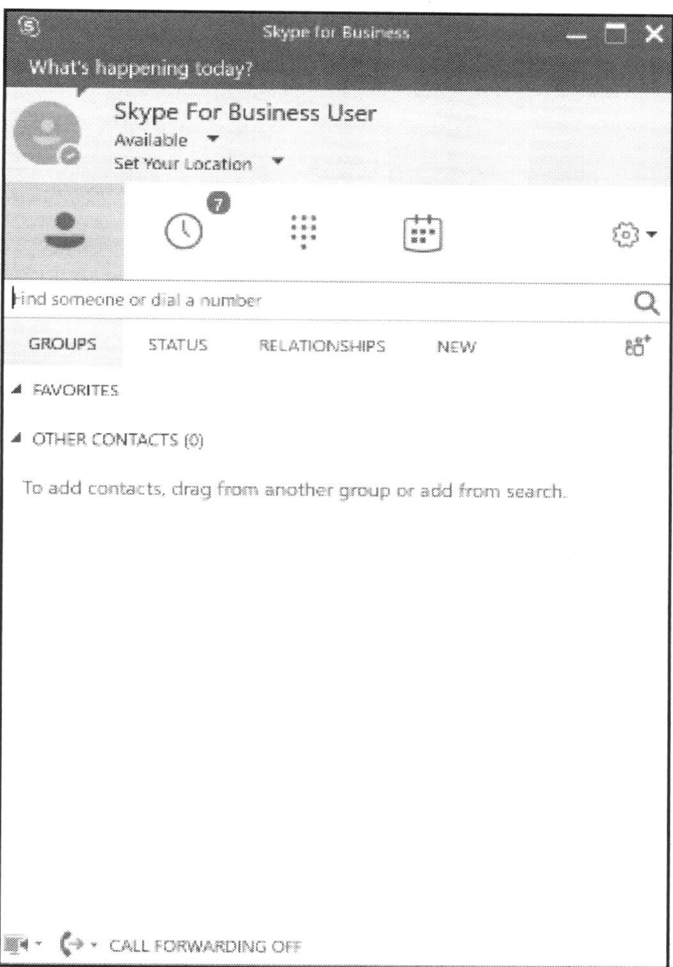

16. The user can now search for a contact and start a conversation:

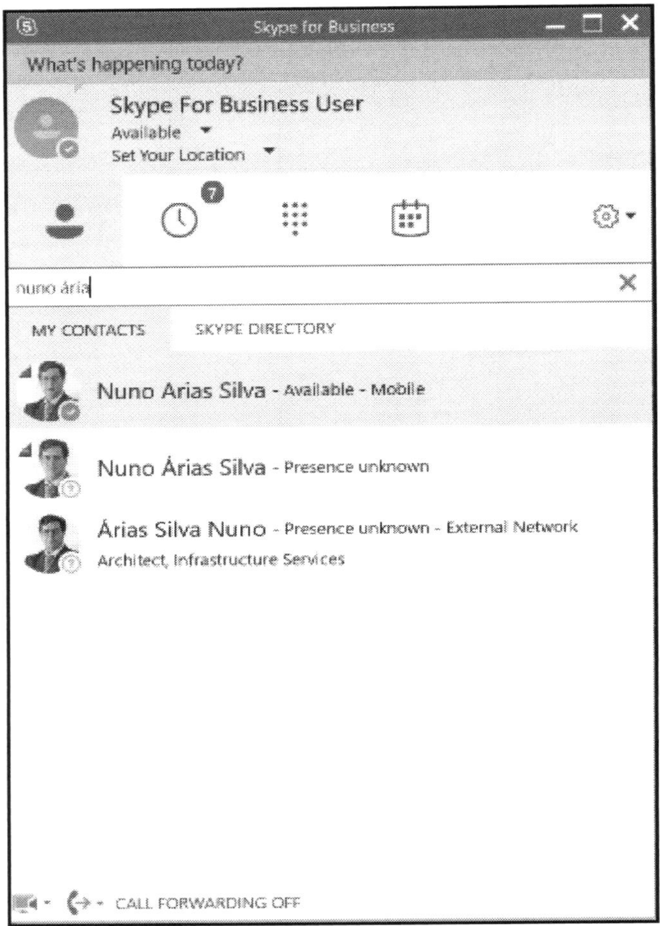


# Architecture

Regarding the architecture of Skype for Business Online, there are three models:

- Cloud only
- Skype for Business on-premises
- Skype for Business hybrid

## Cloud only

The cloud-only model is used as **Software-as-a-Service** (**SaaS**). Microsoft has your identity and manages the Skype for Business infrastructure. You can also have some add-ons, such as Microsoft's cloud-hosted **Private Branch Exchange** (**PBX**) and the **Public Switched Telephone Network** (**PSTN**) calling service:

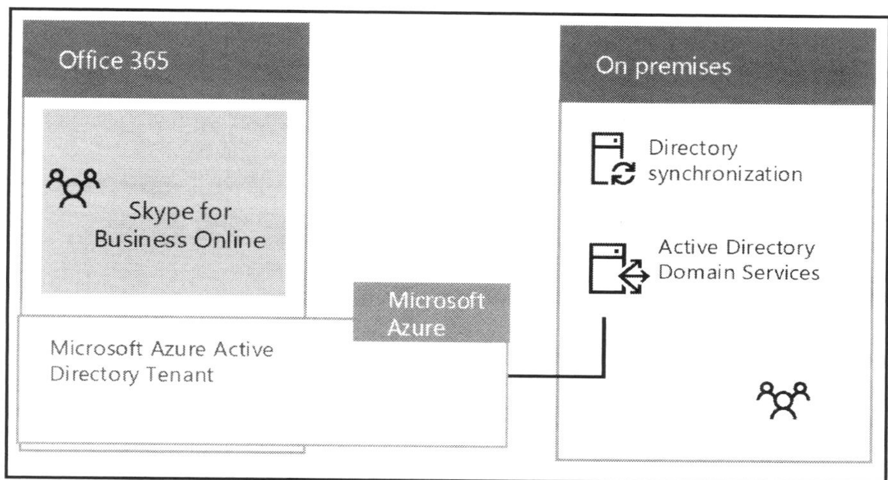


In cloud-only scenarios, organizations use the Skype for Business service only on the Microsoft infrastructure.

You can learn more at `https://docs.microsoft.com/en-us/skypeforbusiness/skype-for-business-online`.

# Skype for Business on-premises

Your installation and your architecture are maintained on-premises in a datacenter that your organization controls:

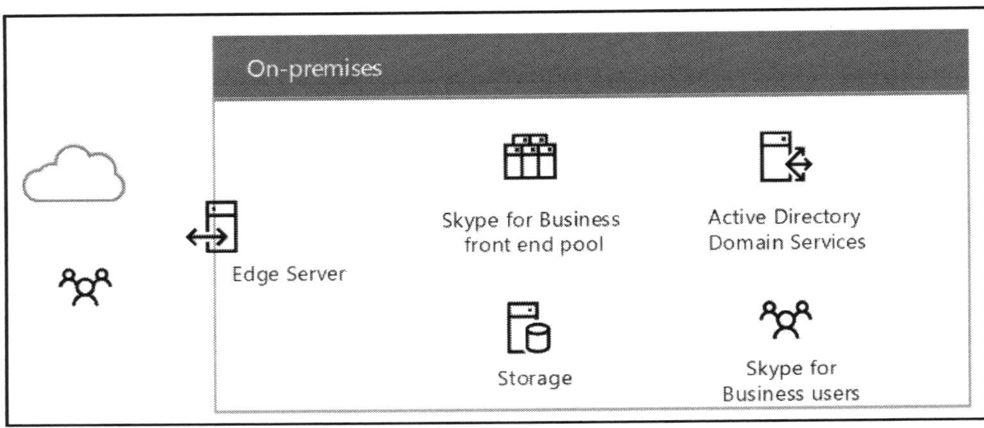


In this scenario, customers have Skype for Business deployed in their infrastructure in their on-premises servers. You can learn more about this at `https://docs.microsoft.com/en-us/skypeforbusiness/plan-your-deployment/topology-basics/reference-topologies`.

The following image is a reference topology used for small organizations:

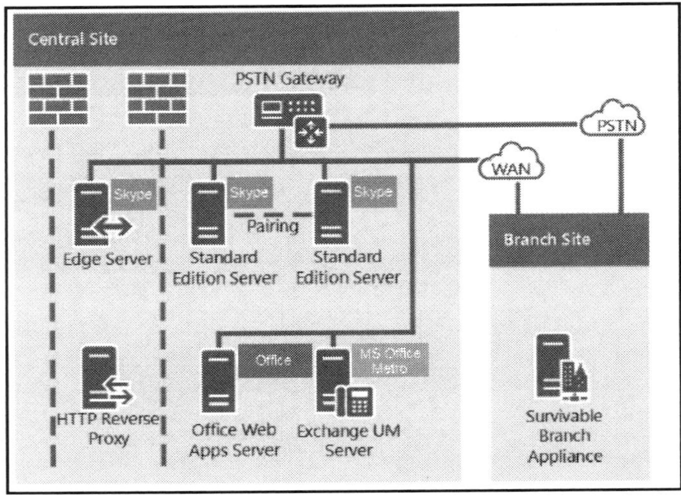

You can read more about how to start to plan your Skype for Business on-premises at `https://docs.microsoft.com/en-us/SkypeForBusiness/plan-your-deployment/plan-your-deployment`.

## Skype for Business hybrid

The third scenario is the hybrid Skype for Business, where you have your on-premises connected to the online Skype for Business:

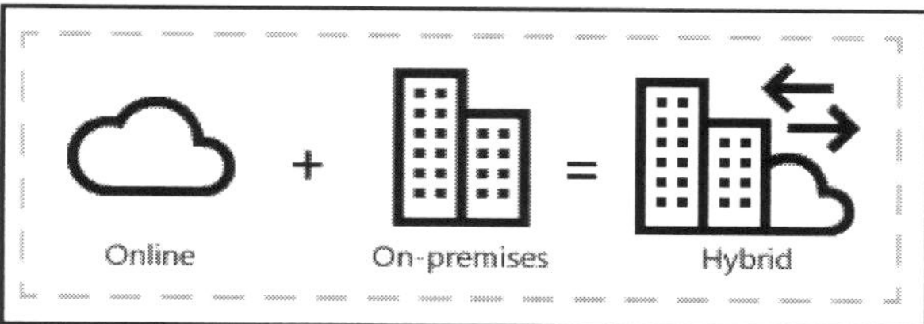


Skype for Business hybrid is a combination of the cloud and on-premises scenarios:

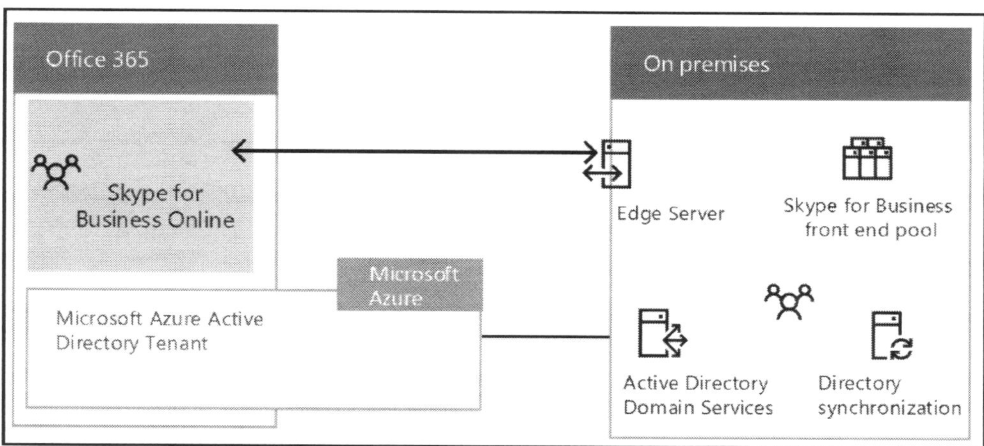


For a complete plan to implement Skype for Business Online in the hybrid mode, visit `https://support.office.com/en-us/article/Plan-your-Skype-for-Business-hybrid-deployment-255f0395-1bfa-4360-9cf6-f0d1d82453a4`.

To learn more about how to implement Skype for Business in a hybrid deployment, visit `https://docs.microsoft.com/en-us/skypeforbusiness/skype-for-business-hybrid-solutions/skype-for-business-hybrid-solutions`.

# Administering Skype for Business

To administer the Skype for Business cloud-only scenario, from the admin section of Office 365, go to the **Skype for Business** admin center as shown in the following screenshot:

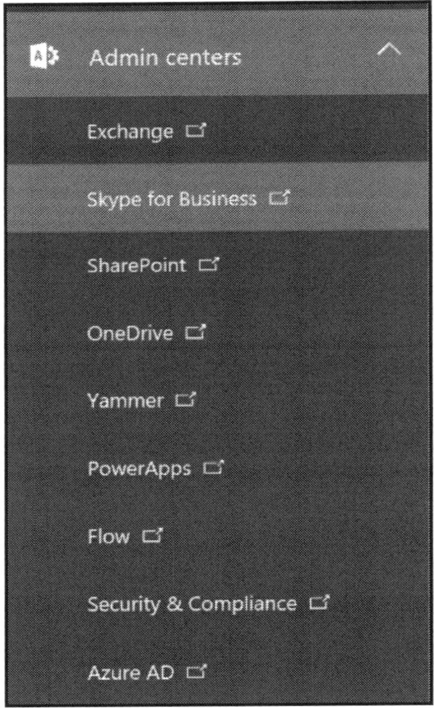

After entering the admin center of Skype for Business, you will have access to the following dashboard:

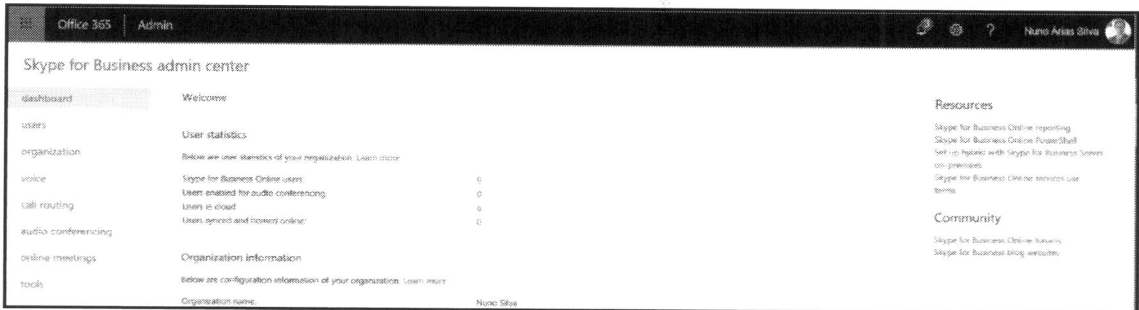


We can see in the following screenshots, the various options are as follows:

- **users:** For Skype for Business user, you can set the following options:
    - **general**: The following screenshot displays the general options that the users can select the Skype for Business features:

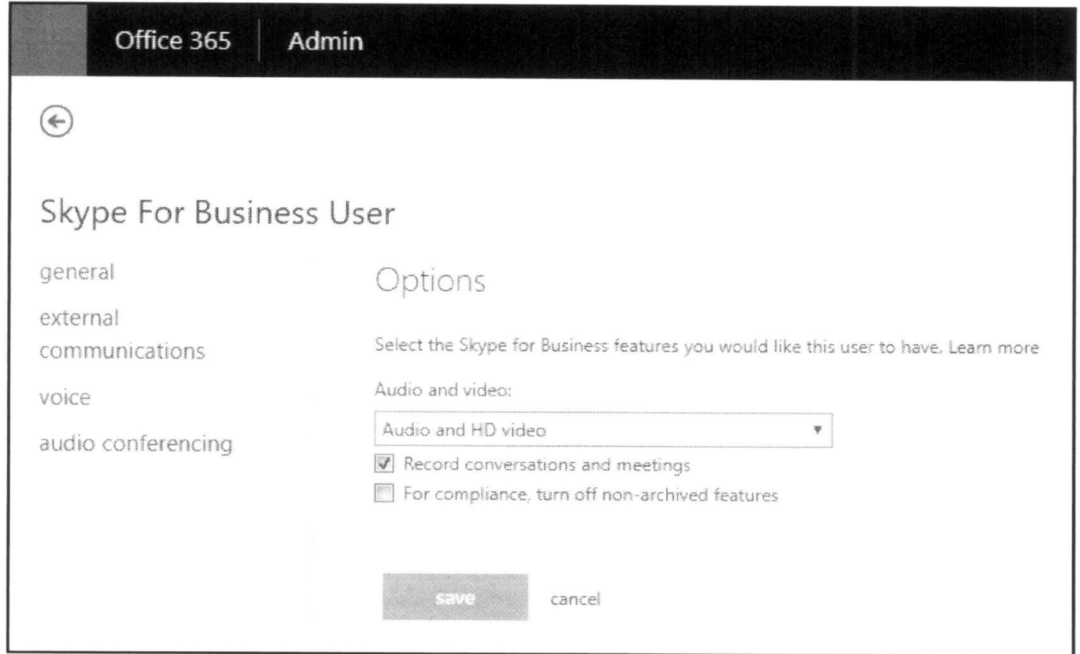

- **external communications**: The following screenshot displays the external communications options where the users can choose people outside the organization they can communicate with:

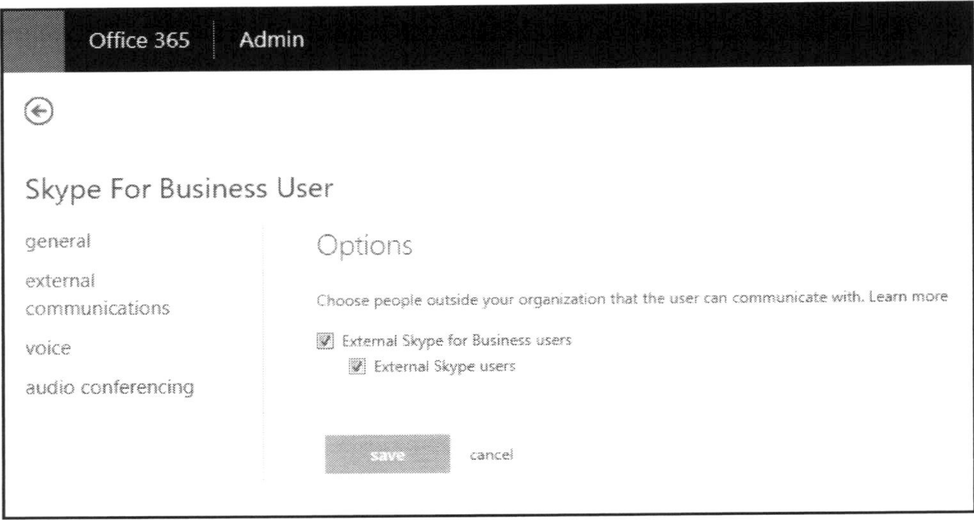


- **voice**: The following screenshot displays the voice options:

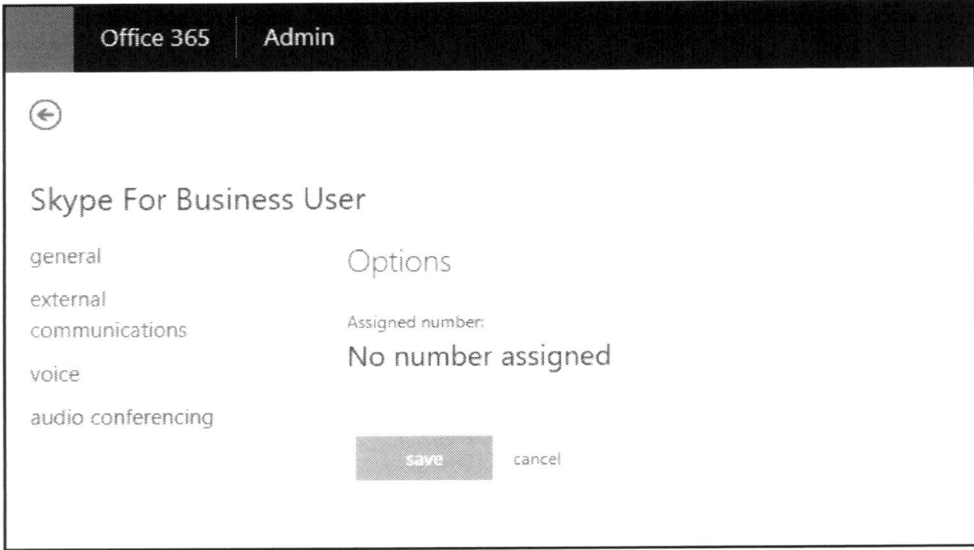

- **audio conferencing**: The following screenshot displays the audio conferencing options where the users can acquire the licenses for the Skype for Business audio conferencing service and so on:

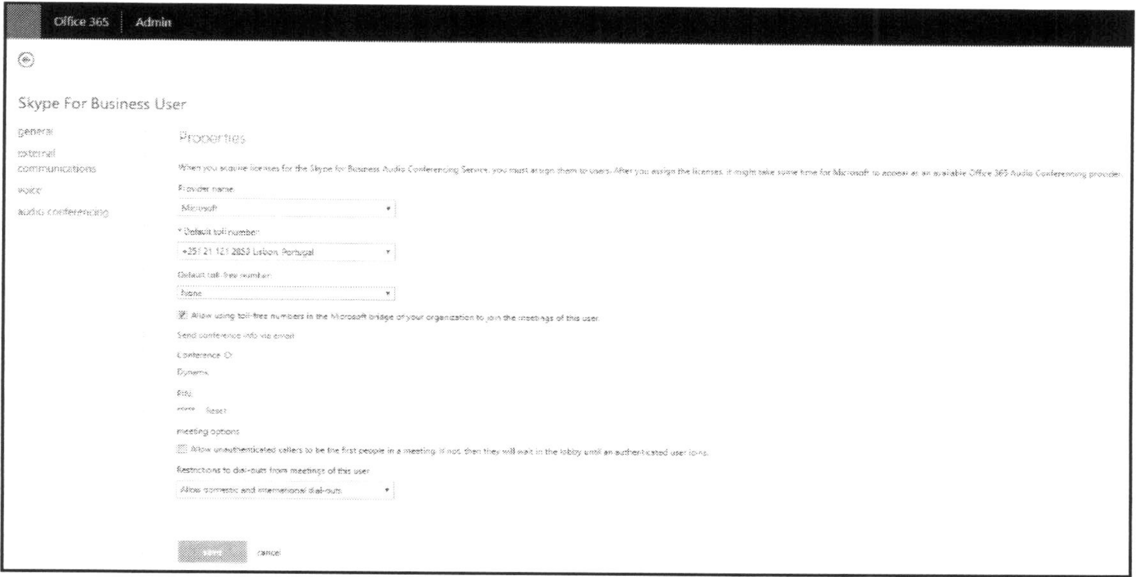

- **organization**: In the **organization** section, we can see several options as shown in the **general** tab:

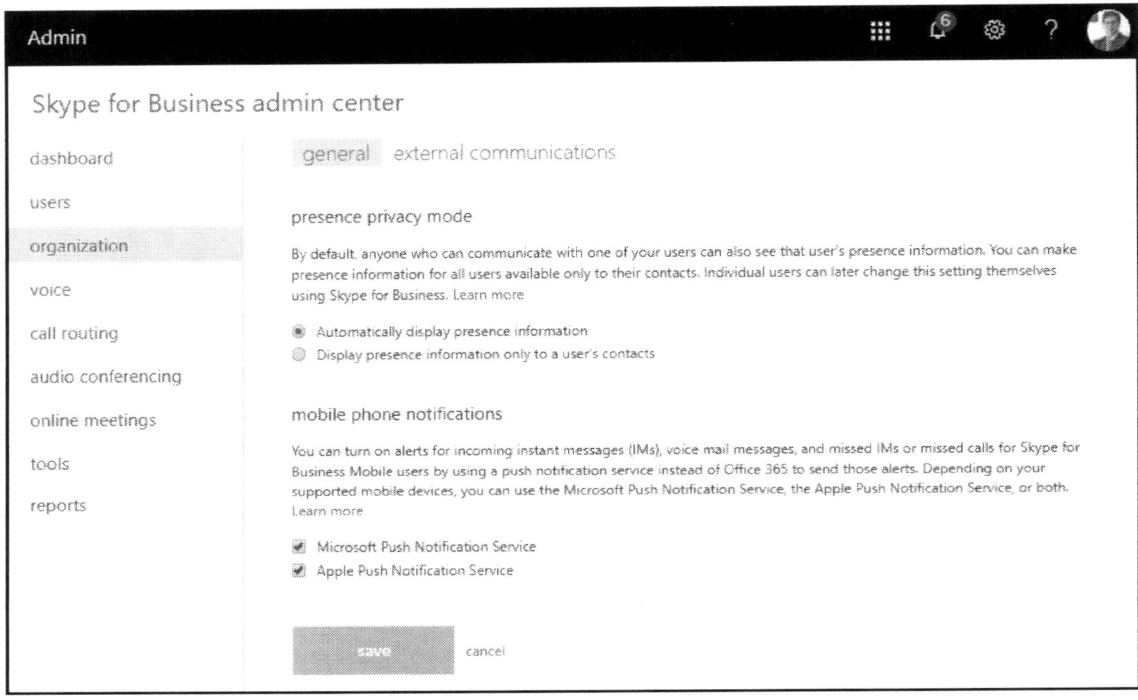

The **external communications** tab is where you can configure the external access:

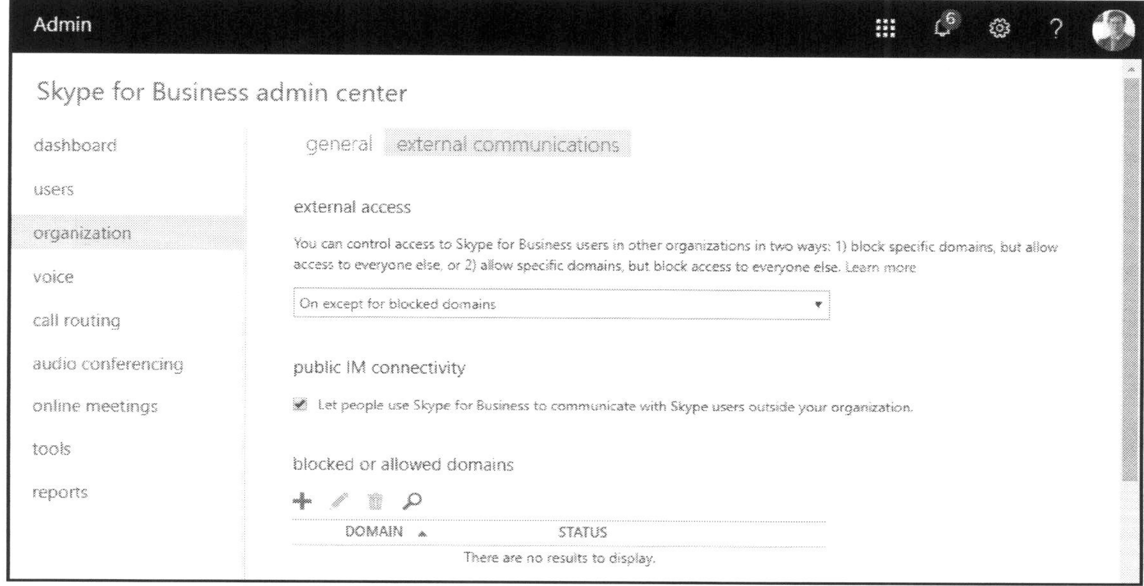

- **voice**: In the **voice** section, we have the configuration of the **phone numbers**, **port orders**, **voice users**, **emergency locations**, and **on premises PSTN** tabs:

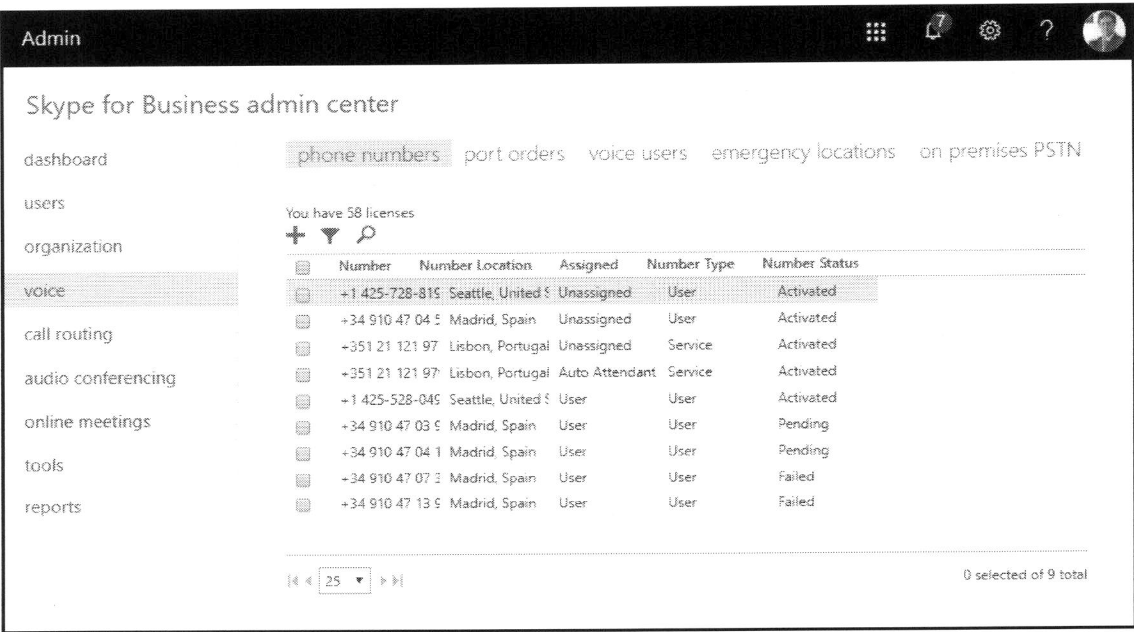

We can go to voice users, select a user, and assign it a number. Click on the **Assign number** link, as shown in the following screenshot:

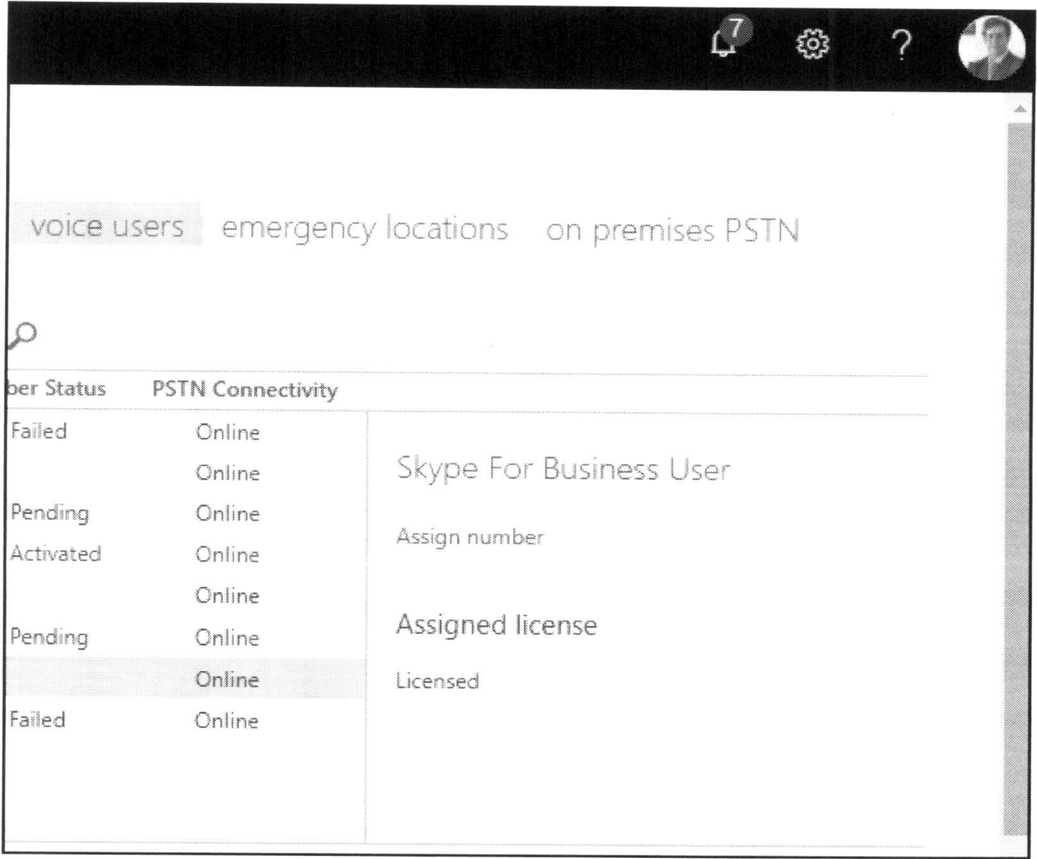

Now you can select a number and emergency location and click on the **save** button:

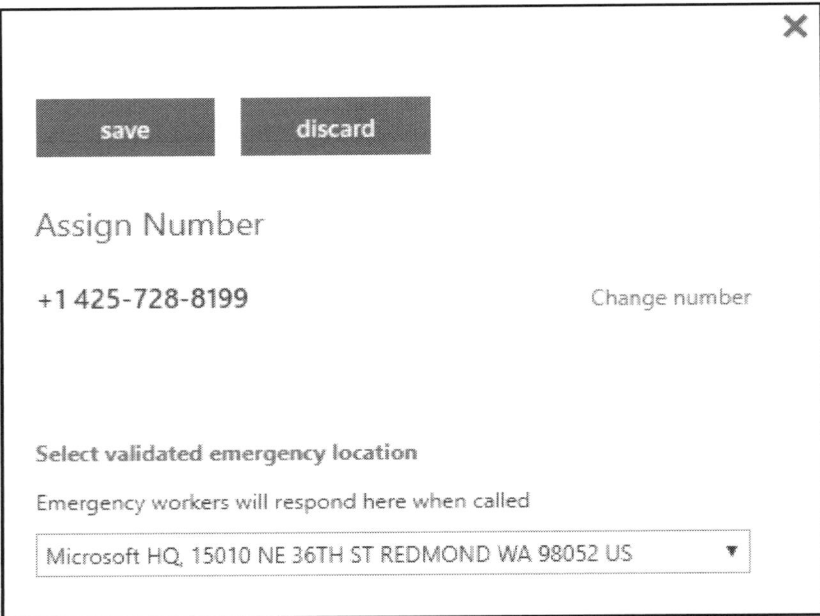

Now the user can start using the number as shown in the following screenshot:

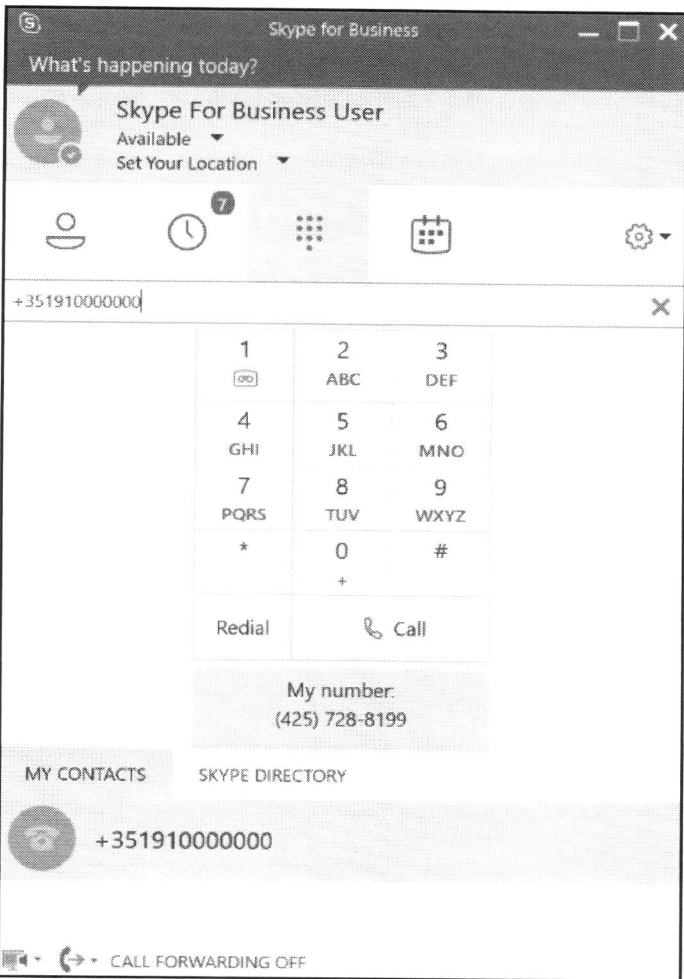

- **call routing**: In the **call routing** section, you can configure the **auto attendants** and **call queues** options:

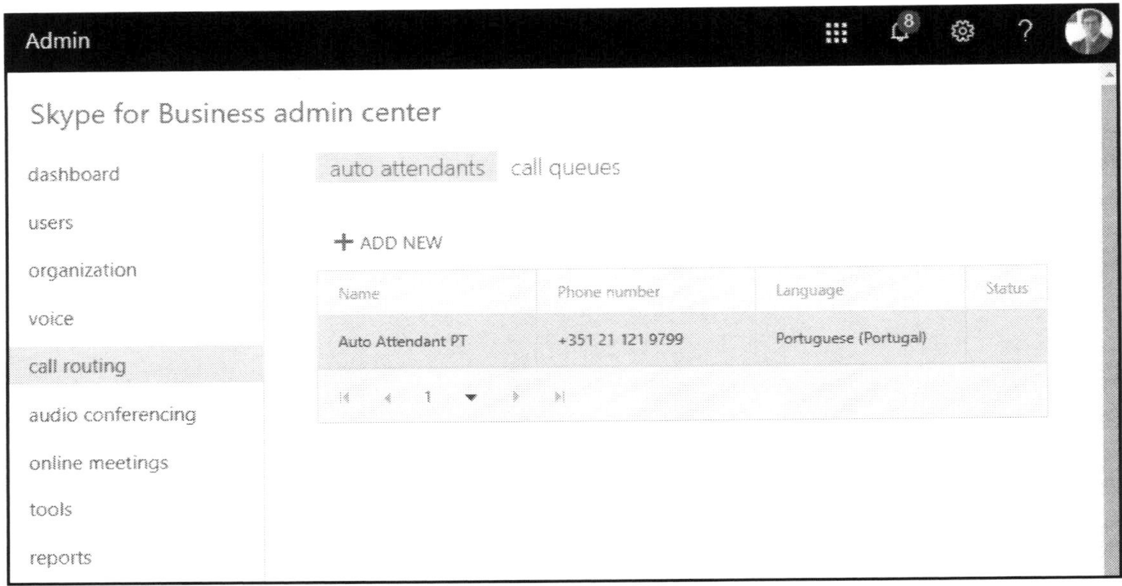


To create an auto attendant, click on the **Add new** button and fill in the general information as shown in the following screenshot:

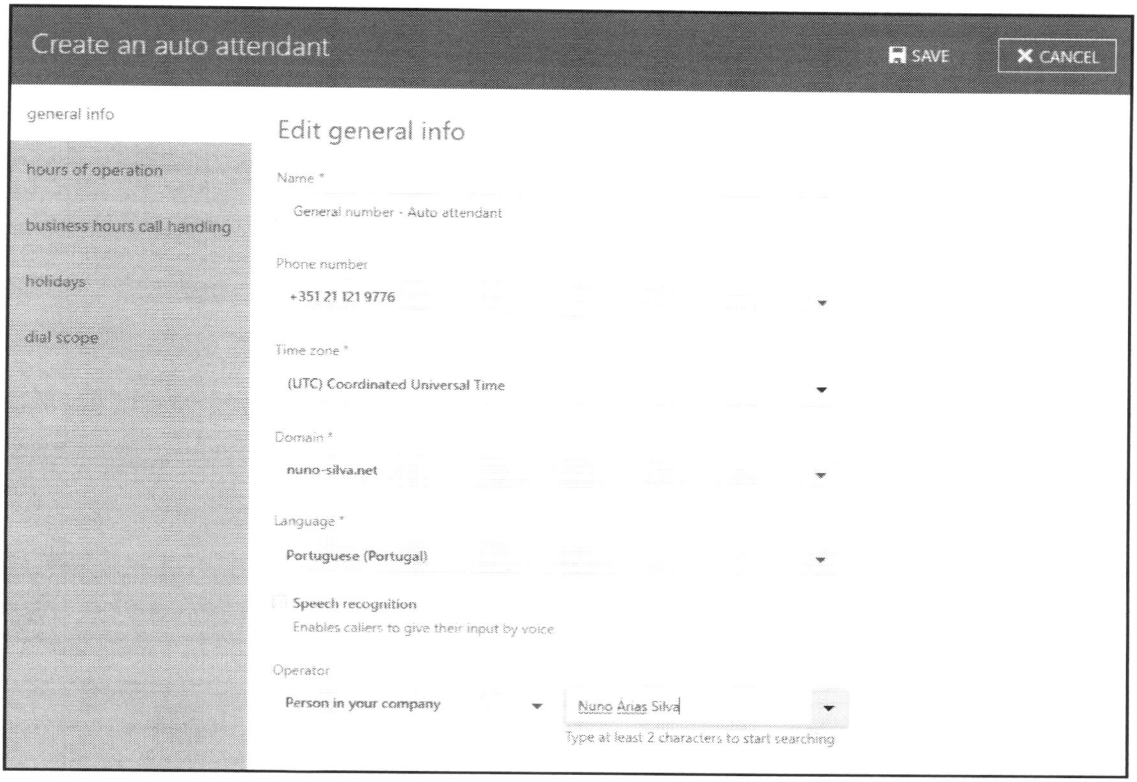

Create an auto attendant
SAVE
CANCEL
general info
hours of operation
business hours call handling
holidays
dial scope
Edit general info
Name *
General number - Auto attendant
Phone number
+351 21 121 9776
Time zone *
(UTC) Coordinated Universal Time
Domain *
nuno-silva.net
Language *
Portuguese (Portugal)
Speech recognition
Enables callers to give their input by voice
Operator
Person in your company
Nuno Arias Silva
Type at least 2 characters to start searching

Select the hours of operation as follows:

Create an auto attendant
SAVE
CANCEL
general info
hours of operation
business hours call handling
holidays
dial scope
Select hours of operation
24/7
Custom

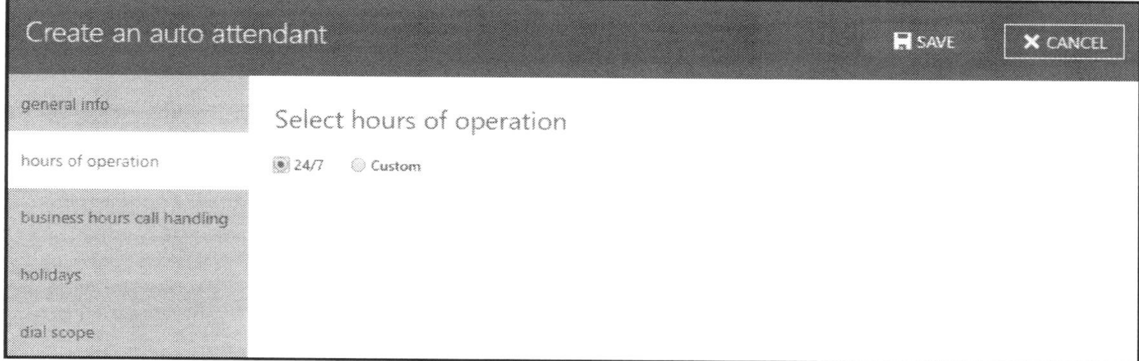

Select the options required in the **Business hours call handling** section:

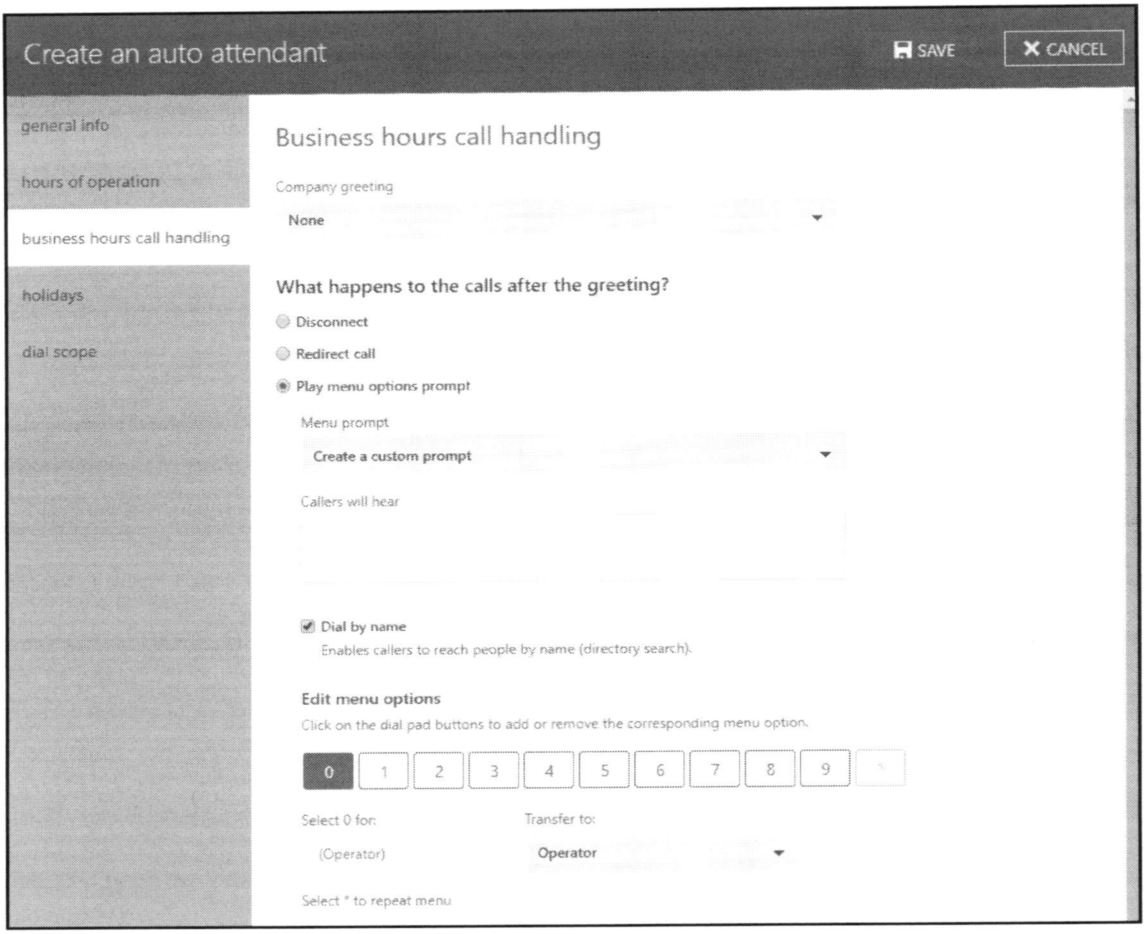

Create an auto attendant
SAVE
CANCEL
general info
hours of operation
business hours call handling
holidays
dial scope
Business hours call handling
Company greeting
None
What happens to the calls after the greeting?
Disconnect
Redirect call
Play menu options prompt
Menu prompt
Create a custom prompt
Callers will hear
Dial by name
Enables callers to reach people by name (directory search).
Edit menu options
Click on the dial pad buttons to add or remove the corresponding menu option.
0 1 2 3 4 5 6 7 8 9
Select 0 for:
Transfer to:
(Operator)
Operator
Select * to repeat menu

Specify the holidays as shown in the following screenshot:

You can only change this setting after saving.

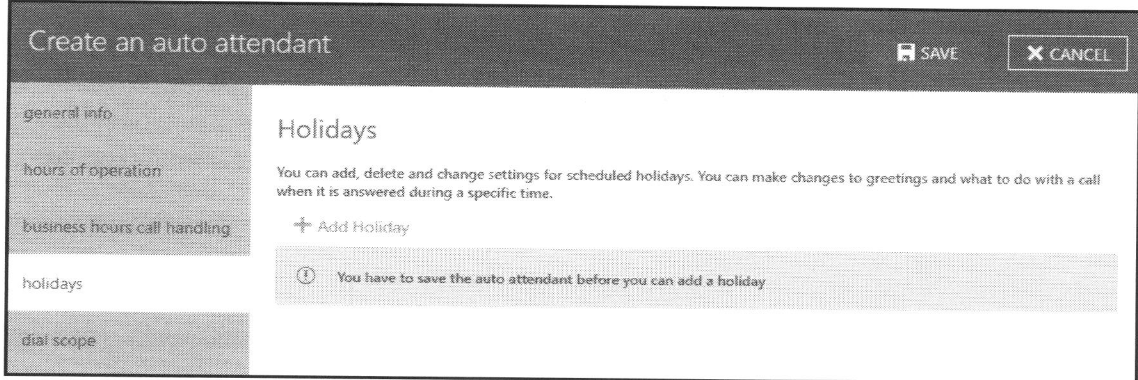


Select the **dial scope** option and click on the **Save** button:

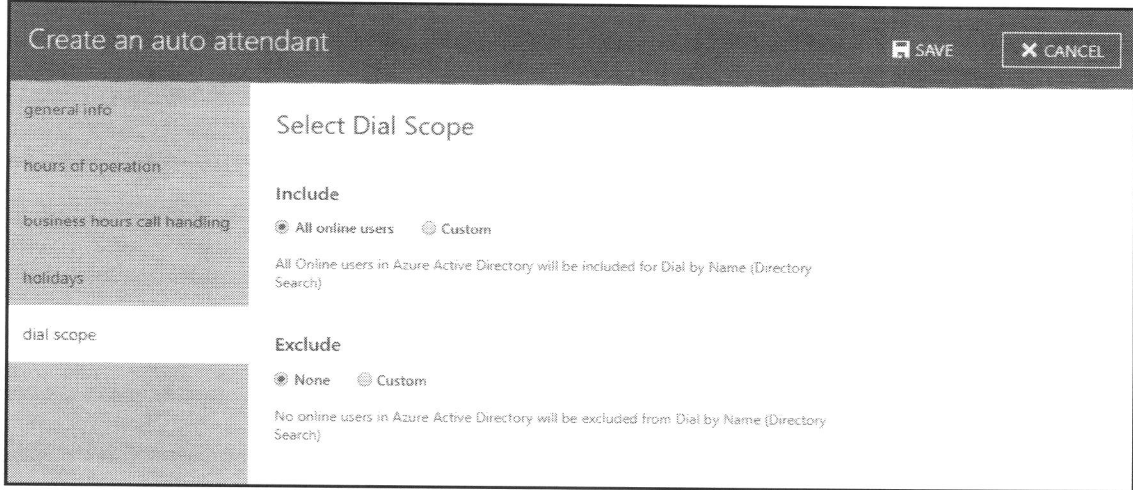


While the auto attendant is being created, do not close the screen:

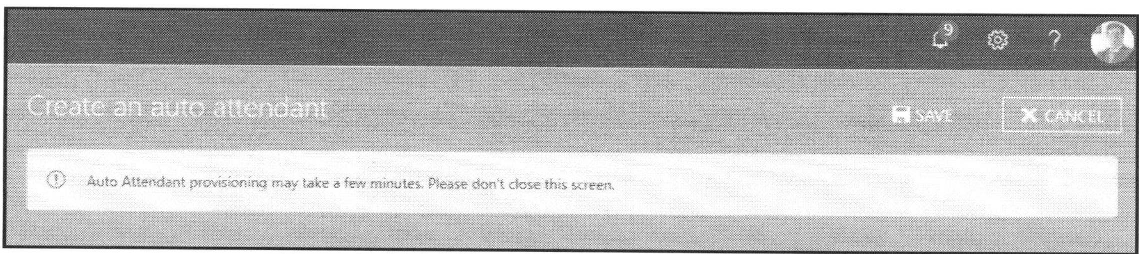

After the creation, we can test, edit, or delete the auto attendant:

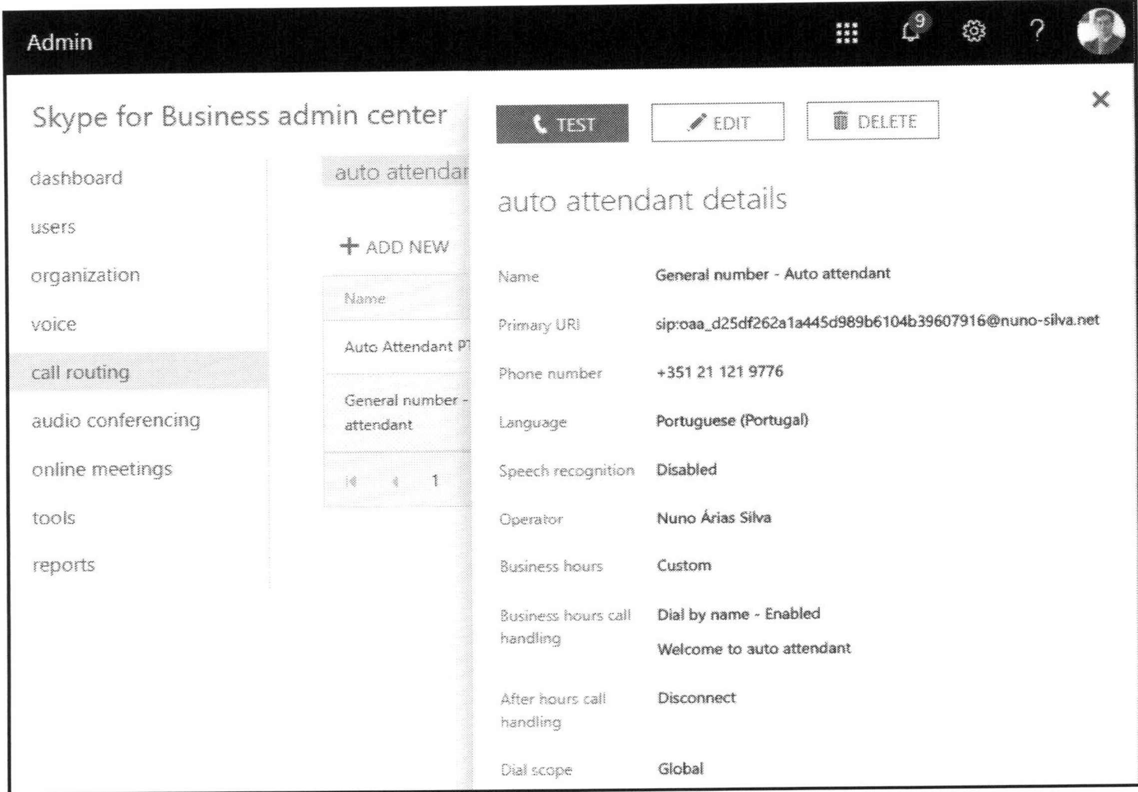


If you are using the Skype for Business Client, when you click on the **Test** button, it will pop up the ability to do the call. Click on **Click to call**:

And, as we can see in the following screenshot, the call is connecting:

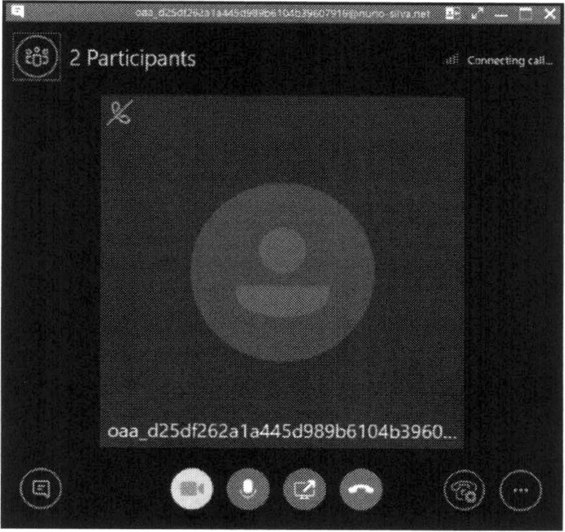

After you call, you can confirm that the auto attendant is working:

After the auto attendant greets you, it will transfer the call to the user, as shown in the following screenshot:

Then the user can answer the call:

- **audio conferencing**: In the admin portal, we can also use the **Microsoft bridge** tab on **audio conferencing** section:

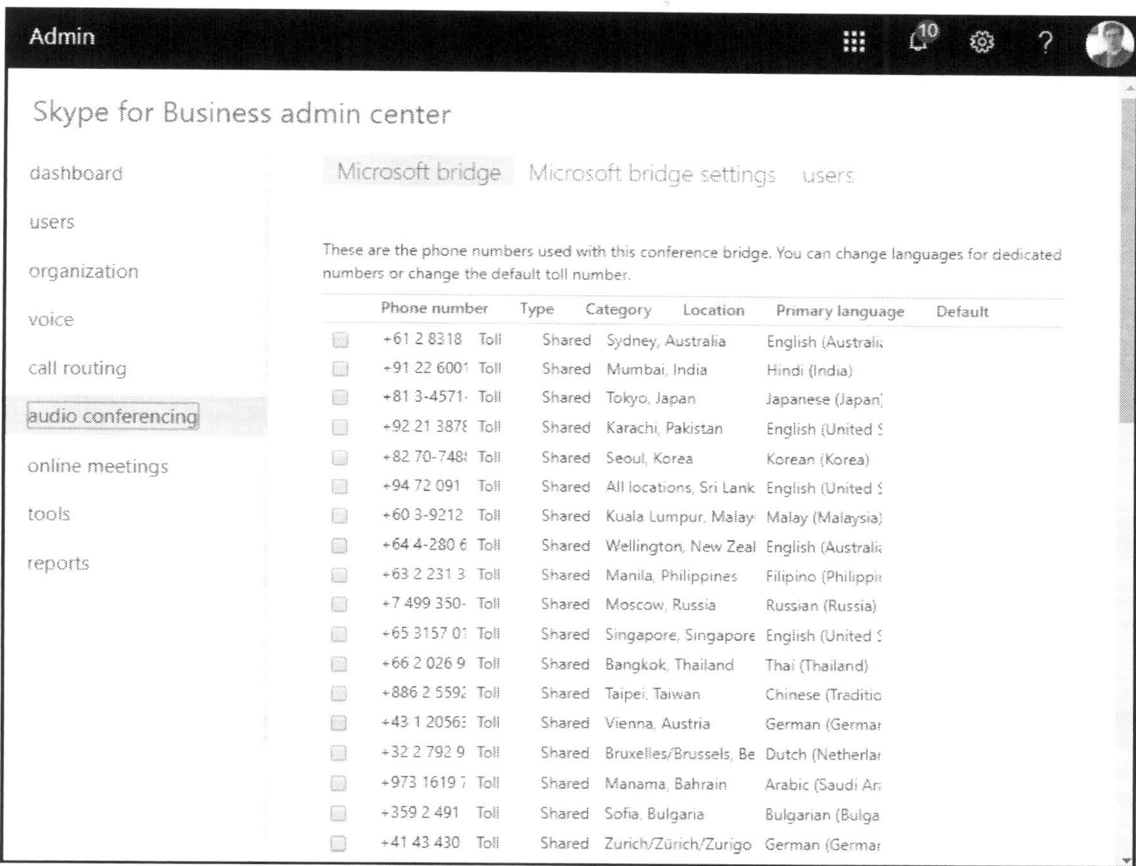

You can also set your **Microsoft bridge settings** options:

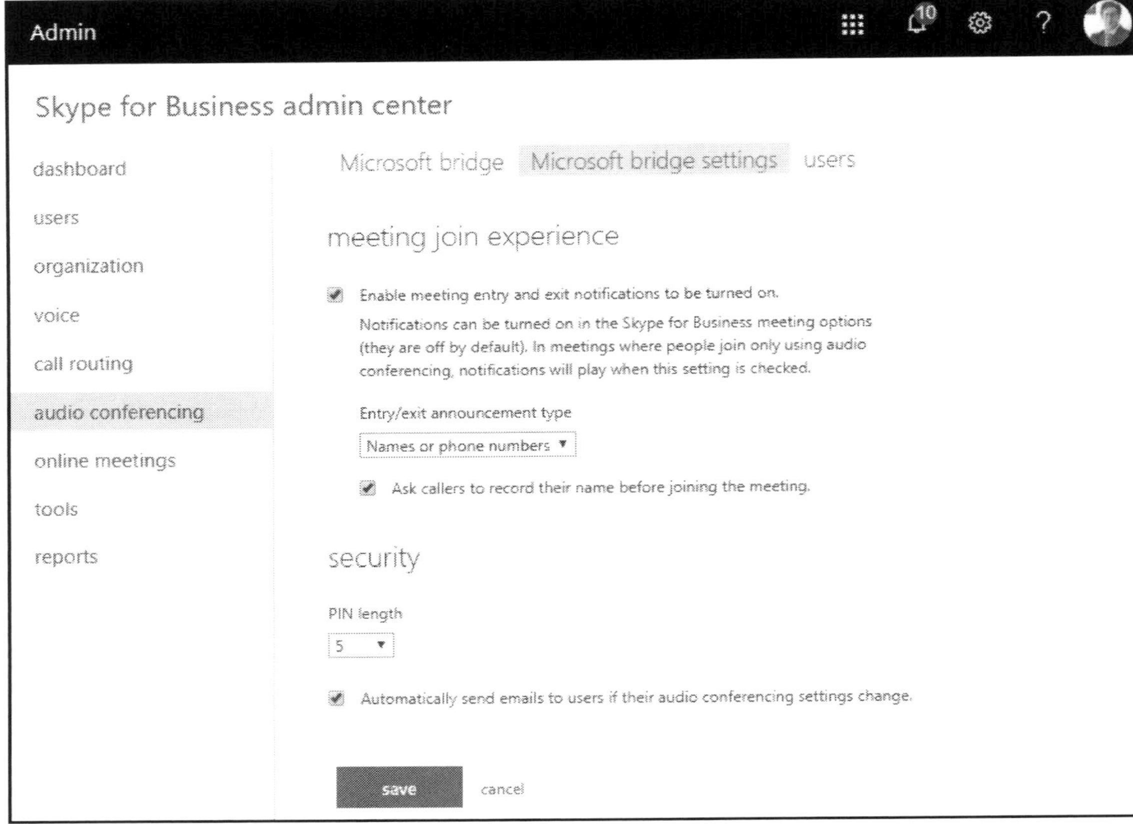

You can search for a user and change their settings:

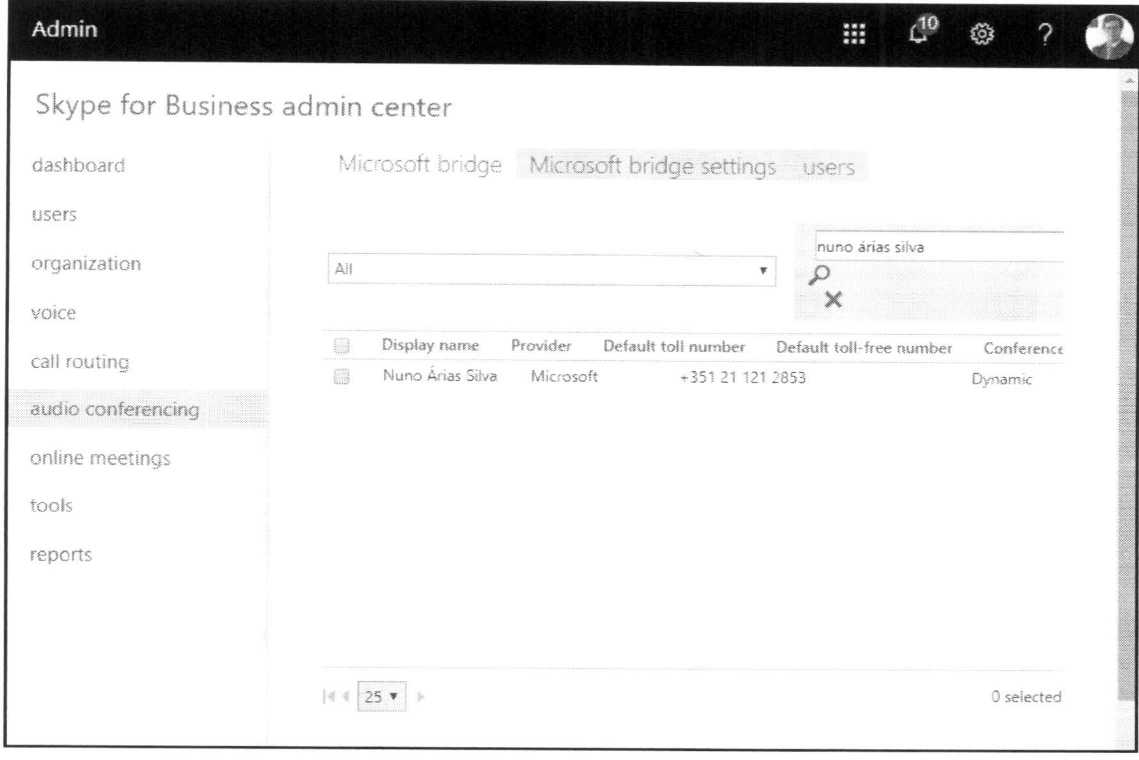

- **online meetings**: In this section, you can set meeting invitation information as shown in the following screenshot:

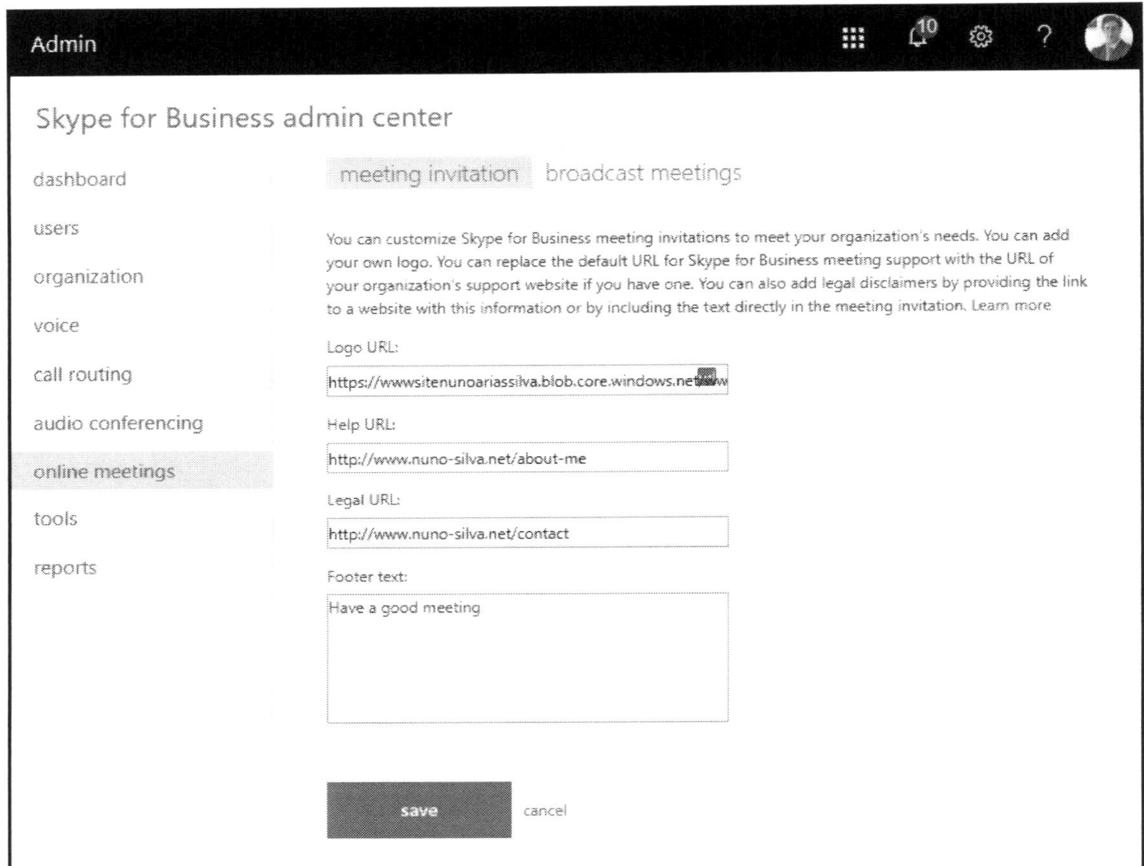

In the **broadcast meetings** tab, you can set the settings for this service:

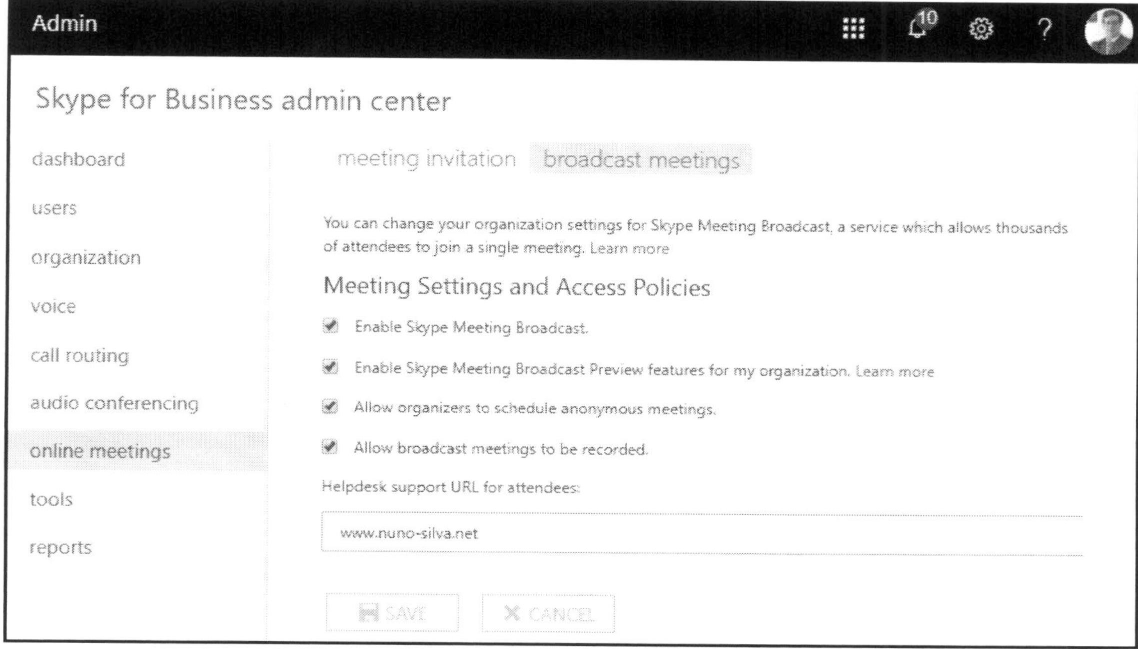

- **tools**: In this section will help you troubleshoot and provide useful tools for implementation:

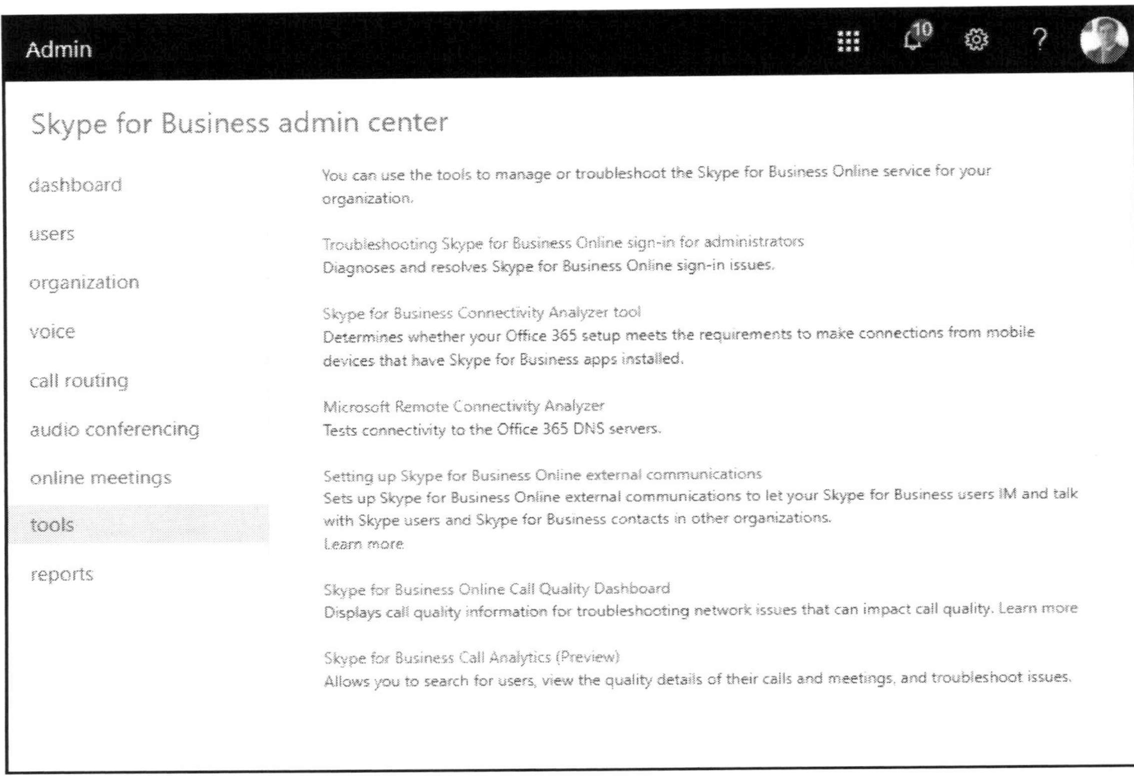

- **reports**: In this section, you have the PSTN usage details:

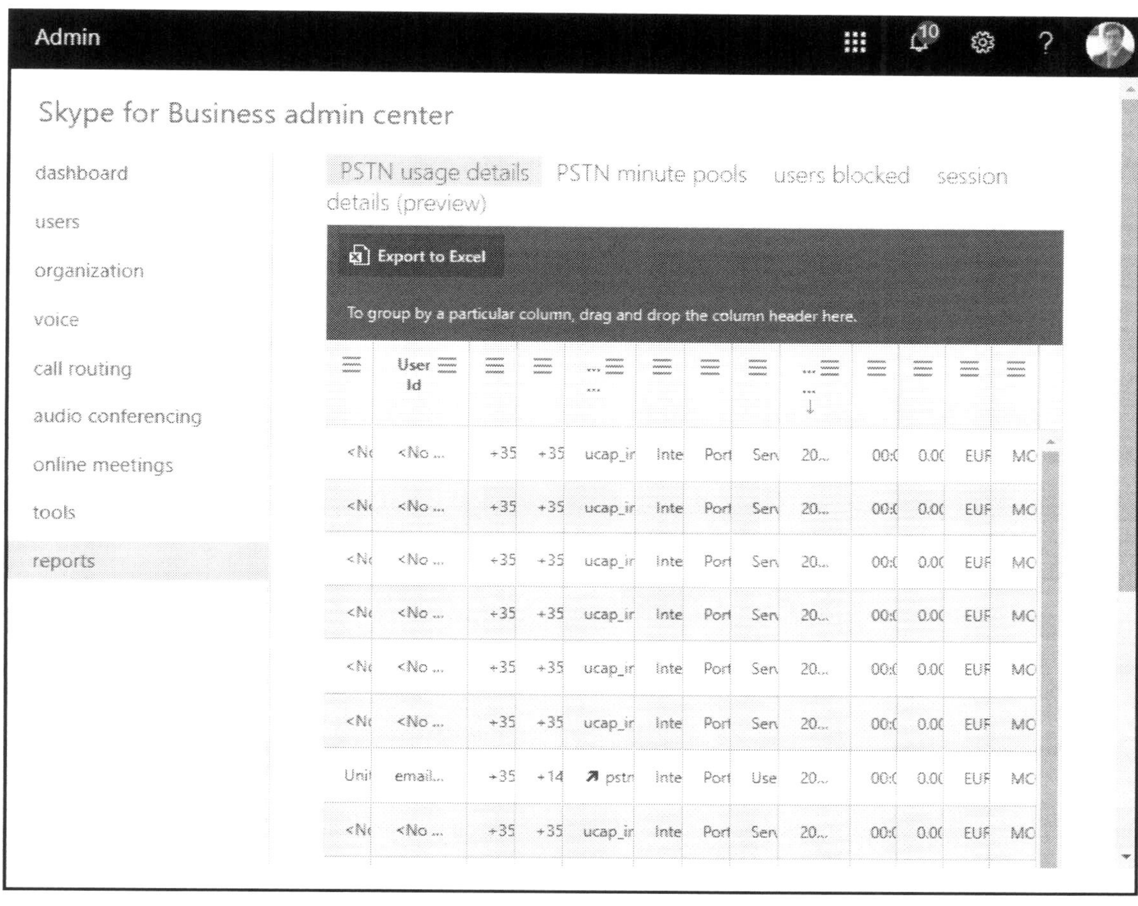

The following screenshot shows the **PSTN minute pools** details:

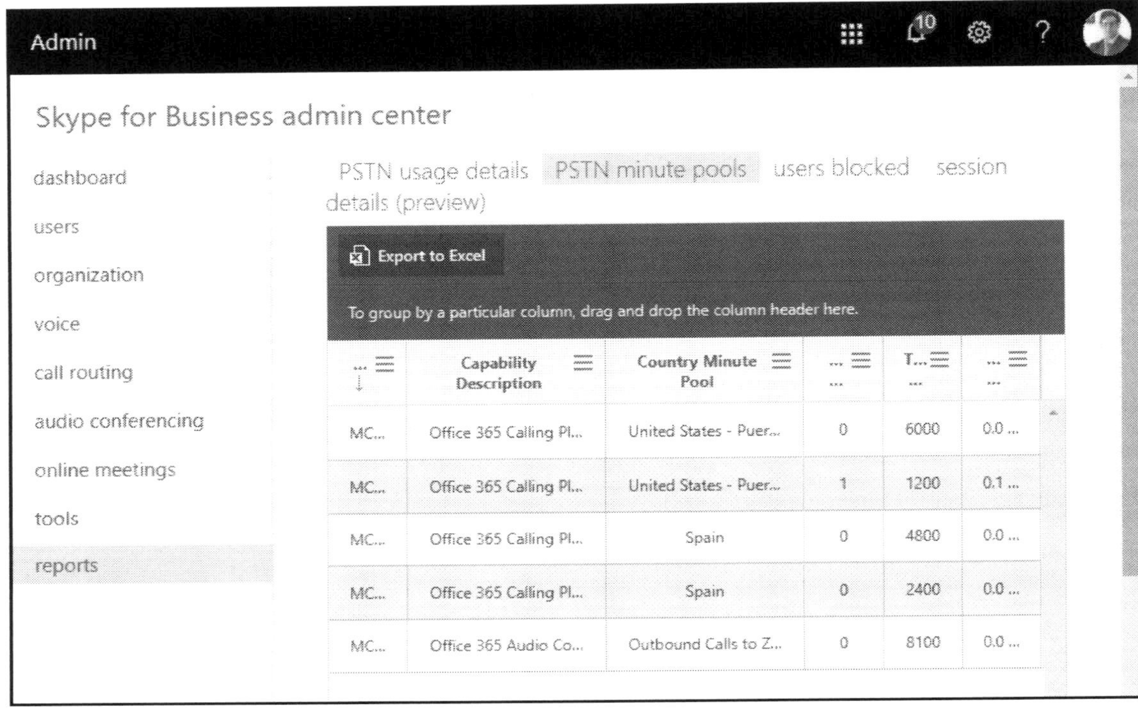

The following screenshot displays the blocked users details:

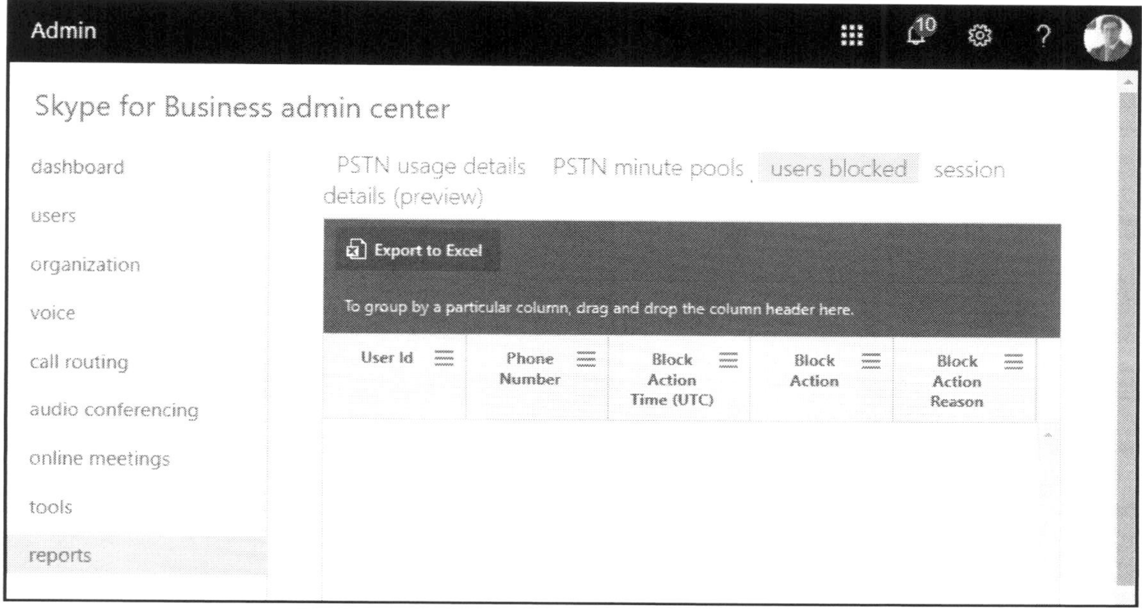

The following screenshot displays the various session details:

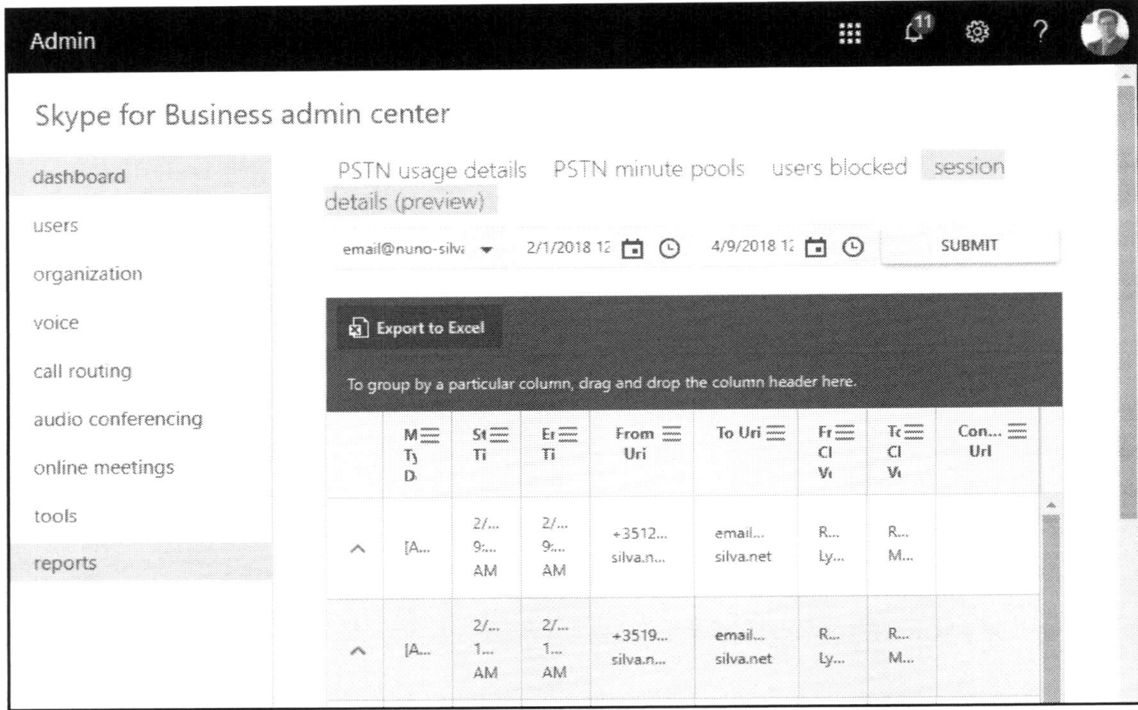


To see the complete admin help, visit the link at `https://support.office.com/en-us/article/Skype-for-Business-Online-in-Office-365---Admin-Help-4307bdbf-6097-458d-9a6a-048112695c59`.

# Summary

In this chapter, you have learned about the basic planning and how to start to implement Skype for Business Online.

You now have more information on how to plan your Skype for Business Online project and how to implement the basics of Skype for Business Online.

In the next chapter, you will learn how to implement Microsoft Teams, which is also one of the fastest growing tools in Office 365.

# 10
# Working with Microsoft Teams

In this chapter, you will be introduced to Microsoft Teams. We will cover the following topics:

- Implementing Microsoft Teams
- Extending Microsoft Teams

With this foundation, you will learn more about how to implement Microsoft Teams.

## Implementing Microsoft Teams

Using Microsoft Teams is an easy way to be more productive on a daily basis. You can use Microsoft Teams to interact with people inside and outside of your organization, by creating a team and creating channels.

With this new way to collaborate, you can have conversations, files, channels, SharePoint pages, mentions, calls, video calls, chats, planners, emails, OneNote notebooks, PowerPoint presentations, Word documents, Excel workbooks, and more, all dedicated to your team or channel in just one place.

To be more productive on a daily basis, we need to focus on the tasks that are related to our team or project in one place. With all the different tools that we use to collaborate, it is difficult to find the information if we use several channels to communicate, for example, email, chat, and file sharing.

When you use Microsoft Teams, you can have your data spread across different technologies and devices, and access it all on Windows, macOS, Android, iOS, or the internet.

These new technologies will allow you to have more time to concentrate on other things, such as creating new projects, adopting new technologies, and becoming more productive. Microsoft Teams helps organizations to build a better world!

In the following figure, you can see where Microsoft Teams fits in your organization:

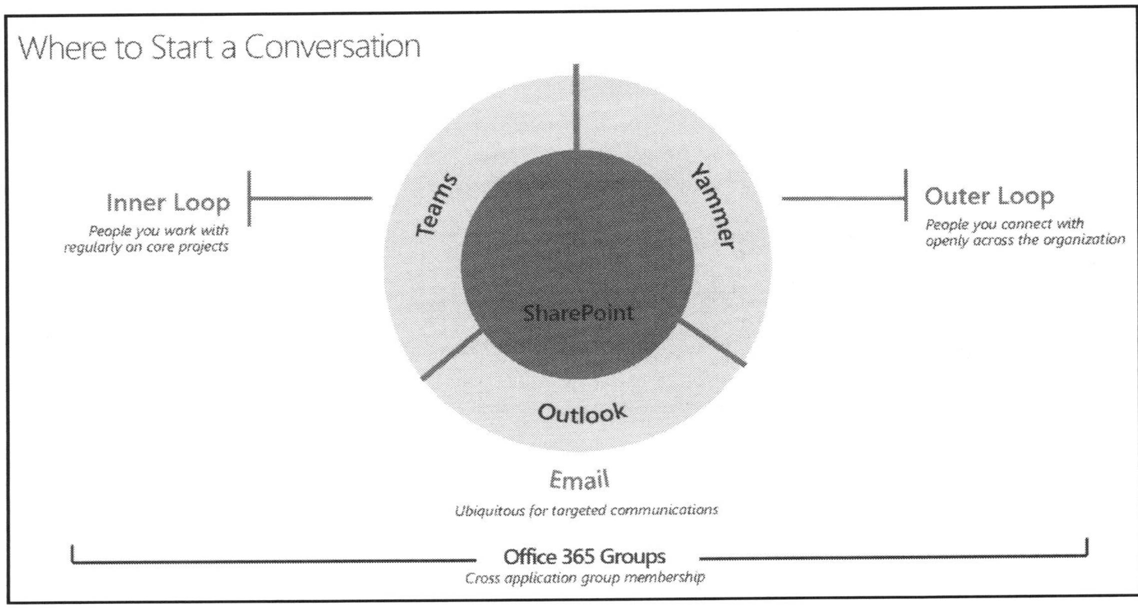


Microsoft Teams is the digital transformation of an open space, office environment that adopts easy connections with people, and it helps each other to work together and build relationships using new technologies and a new way of collaboration.

# Planning Microsoft Teams

In each project, you will need to plan according to what your implementation will be.

*What should you do today?* The following diagram represents the answer:

Check out these *Pilot Essentials* resources at `https://go.microsoft.com/fwlink/?linkid=859067` to run teams and Skype for Business side by side.

You can use these *User Readiness* resources at `https://go.microsoft.com/fwlink/?linkid=859044` to drive value through user adoption.

# Overview of Microsoft Teams

Microsoft Teams is part of Office 365 and has many technologies used on Office 365, such as Exchange Online, groups, and SharePoint, that leverage teams as a productivity tool to have a central workplace to be more productive on a daily basis. You also have the capabilities of chat in a central place that together will give the chance of working together no matter where you are and on what device you are working.

Microsoft Teams has the source of identities on Azure AD, which is the base authority of other services in Office 365. At the creation of a team, it will create an Office 365 Group, an Exchange Online group mailbox, and a SharePoint Online team site.

The chat capacity that you have in Microsoft Teams will interact with many other services, such as the integration with Skype for Business. In Microsoft Teams, you have the experience of Skype for Business with more and more functions coming in the next few months.

You can view the *Office 365 Roadmap* at `https://aka.ms/skype2teamsroadmap` or at `https://products.office.com/en-US/business/office-365-roadmap?filters=%26freeformsearch=Teams`.

You can also develop bots, add tabs to each channel, and connectors as an extension to Microsoft Teams to connect and be more productive, and have an central place connected to external content of Microsoft Teams.

To access Microsoft Teams, go to `http://teams.microsoft.com`.

When you log in to Microsoft Teams for the first time, Microsoft Teams will show you a screen informing you that Microsoft is setting up teams for you. After a few seconds, it will ask you to create your first team. Fill in the name and description and click on the **Create a team** button, or, if you don't want to create a new team right now, skip this step:

If you create a new team, it will ask you to add members to it, as shown in the following screenshot. Search for the users and click on the **Add** button:

After you have defined your team members, click on the **Close** button.

When you first log in to Microsoft Teams, it will show you a few hints to help you work better:

1. Review the **Bring your team together** option and click on the **Next** button
2. Review the **Chat 1:1 and with groups** option and click on the **Next** button
3. Review the **Connect through online meetings** option and click on the **Next** button
4. Review the **Files, notes, apps, and more, all in one place** option and click on the **Next** button

5. Review the **You're ready**! option, where you can view a video to learn more about Microsoft Teams, and then click on the **Let's go** button:

Here, you'll find your first view of Microsoft Teams. You can click on the **Download** button to install a Desktop version of Microsoft Teams:

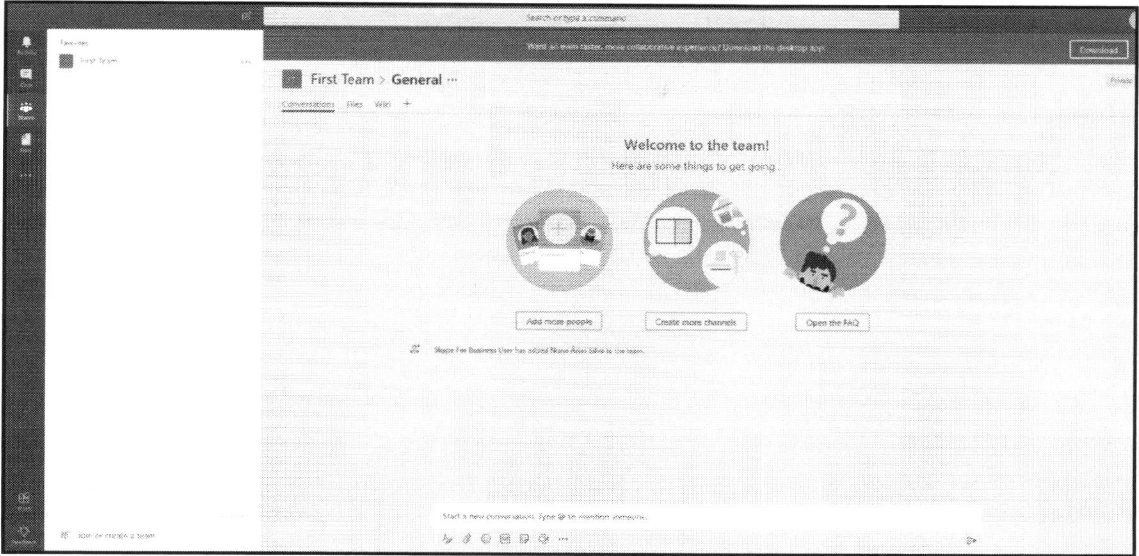


# Microsoft Teams and Office 365

In Office 365, there are applications that use Office 365 Groups; each application is intended to best fit where the user is working depending on the needs and the audience.

These tools are:

- **Microsoft Teams**: Centralized app that users need to work on a team model together
- **Outlook**: An enterprise tool that is used to send and receive email and organize more personal work, it have normally structured data, based on email communications, calendar and contacts
- **Yammer**: This is an enterprise-class social network
- **Skype for Business**: Real-time communication software with presence and unified communications
- **SharePoint Online**: A central place to have intranet, documents, and lists

It is advised that you have a journey to implement Microsoft Teams using a methodology that helps your organization launch a successful project. Use the following phases to implement a project with each phase to deploy Microsoft Teams:

- Technical and legal evaluation
- Assess/prepare
- IT pilot
- Business pilot
- Rollout

In each project, you need three basic tasks to be successful:

- Plan
- Deliver
- Operate

Without those simple phases, you cannot leverage Microsoft Teams to the next level. The Microsoft Teams journey is shown in the following figure:

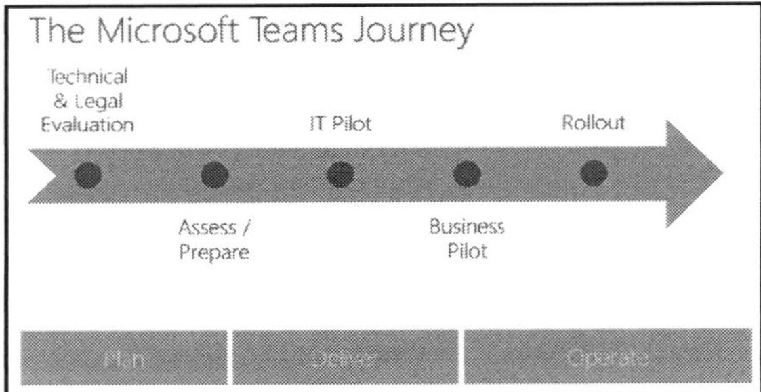


# Clients for Microsoft Teams

To access Microsoft Teams, you have web-based and desktop-based clients as well as mobile clients:

- **Web-based client**: For the web-based client, you can use `http://teams.microsoft.com` for the web version of Microsoft Teams; it has almost all functions that the desktop version has. Real-time communications are not available at the time of writing this book. View the roadmap of Microsoft Teams to see the updated features and delivery dates.

- **Desktop clients**: Microsoft Teams has desktop clients for Windows and macOS. You have 32-bit and 64-bit versions as well. With this version, you have a fully functional client that has access to real-time communications, such as video, calls, and meetings. To download the clients, go to `https://teams.microsoft.com/downloads` and select your desktop app.
- **Mobile clients**: The mobile apps for Microsoft Teams are available for Android, iOS, and Windows Phone, and they are geared at users participating in the chat-based conversations while on the go and allow users to have peer-to-peer audio calls. The supported mobile platforms for Microsoft Teams' mobile apps are as follows:
    - **Android**: 4.4 or higher
    - **iOS**: 10.0 or higher
    - **Windows Phone**: Windows 10 mobile

To download the clients, go to `https://teams.microsoft.com/downloads` and select your mobile app.

# Office 365 licensing for Microsoft Teams

The following Office 365 subscriptions will enable users for Microsoft Teams:

- Office 365 Business Essentials
- Office 365 Business Premium
- Office 365 Enterprise E1
- Office 365 Enterprise E3
- Office 365 Enterprise E4—existing subscriptions only (retired plan)
- Office 365 Enterprise E5

Microsoft Teams is also available for nonprofit organizations.

Microsoft Teams are available in multiple Office 365 plans, and there is no difference in features on the core components. The only difference is on compliance that is tied on the E3 or E5 subscriptions.

Within any subscription that has Microsoft Teams available, you will have access to all clients, such as desktop, mobile, and web.

# Microsoft Teams license

When you enable an eligible license plan of Office 365, the **Microsoft Teams** license is enabled by default. The Office 365 individual user license assignment can be seen in the following screenshot:

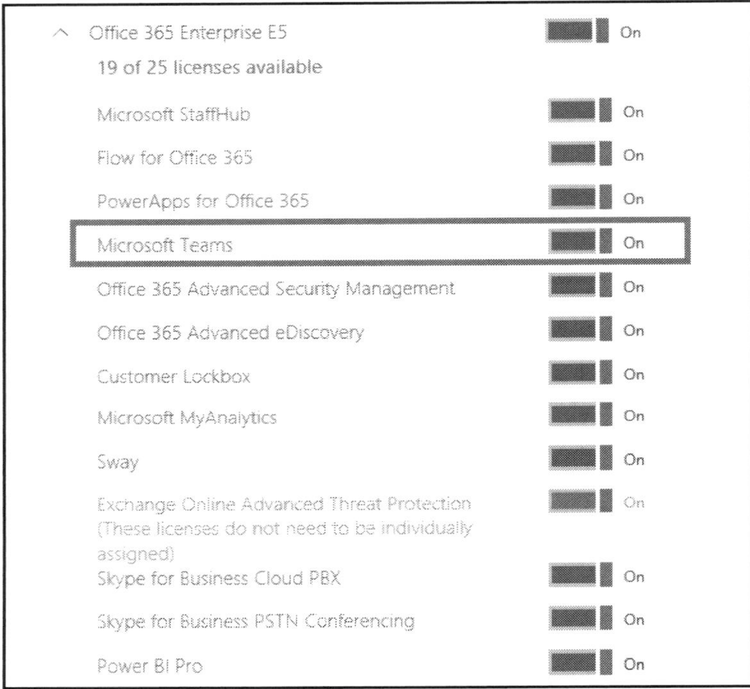


Microsoft Teams is enabled by default on Office 365 for the whole organization, but if you need to do a proof of concept on a few users or a department, you will need to disable all users that are not part of your proof of concept, or you can use a separate tenant to test it.

## Tenant-level configuration

If you need to configure Microsoft Teams in Office 365, you can enable or disable it for the whole organization. Remember that it is enabled by default.

If you need the complete instructions for how to disable or enable Microsoft Teams on Office 365, refer to `https://docs.microsoft.com/en-us/microsoftteams/enable-features-office-365`.

If you need to change some configurations, you can do it by going to `http://portal.office.com` and then to the admin center. Expand the **Settings** drop-down menu and click on the **Service & add-ins** option and then you will find Microsoft Teams. Also, you can go directly to `https://portal.office.com/adminportal/home#/Settings/ServicesAndAddIns`.

In the following three screenshots, you have the settings to configure Microsoft Teams:

- The **General** and **Email integration** settings:

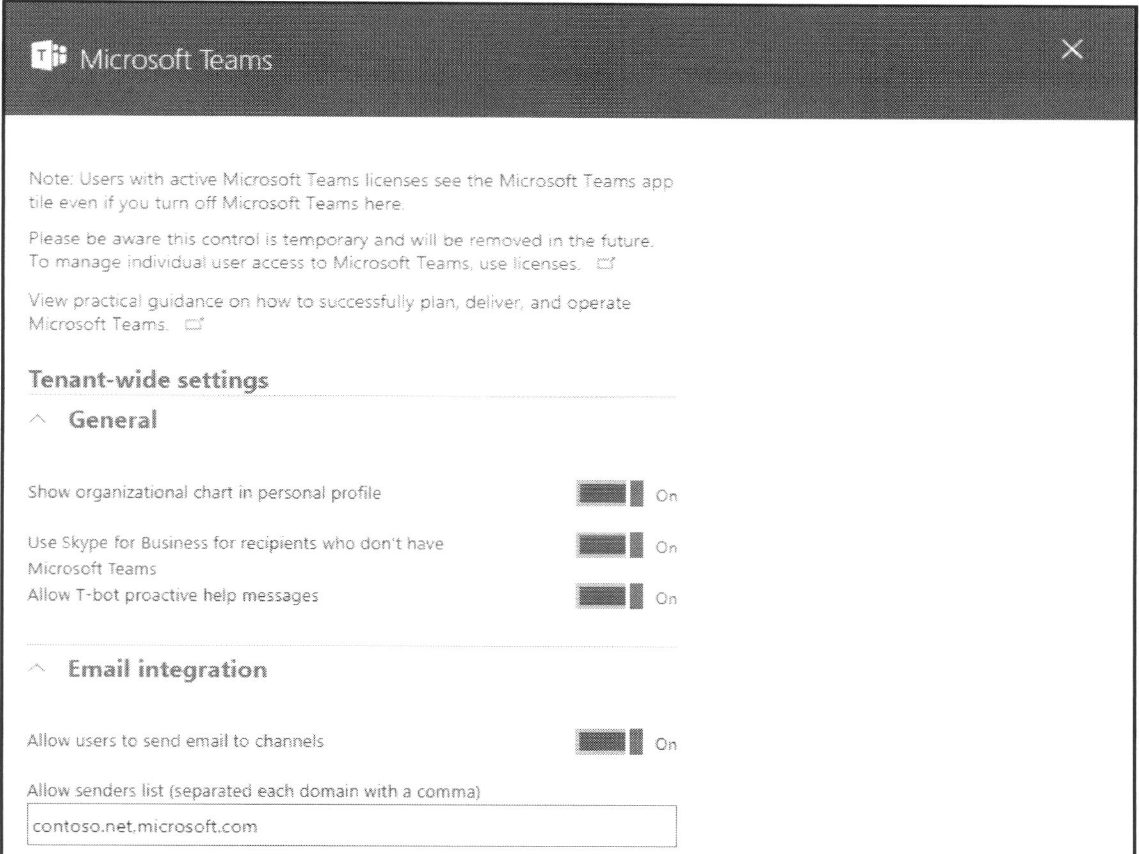

- The **Apps** and **Custom cloud storage** configurations:

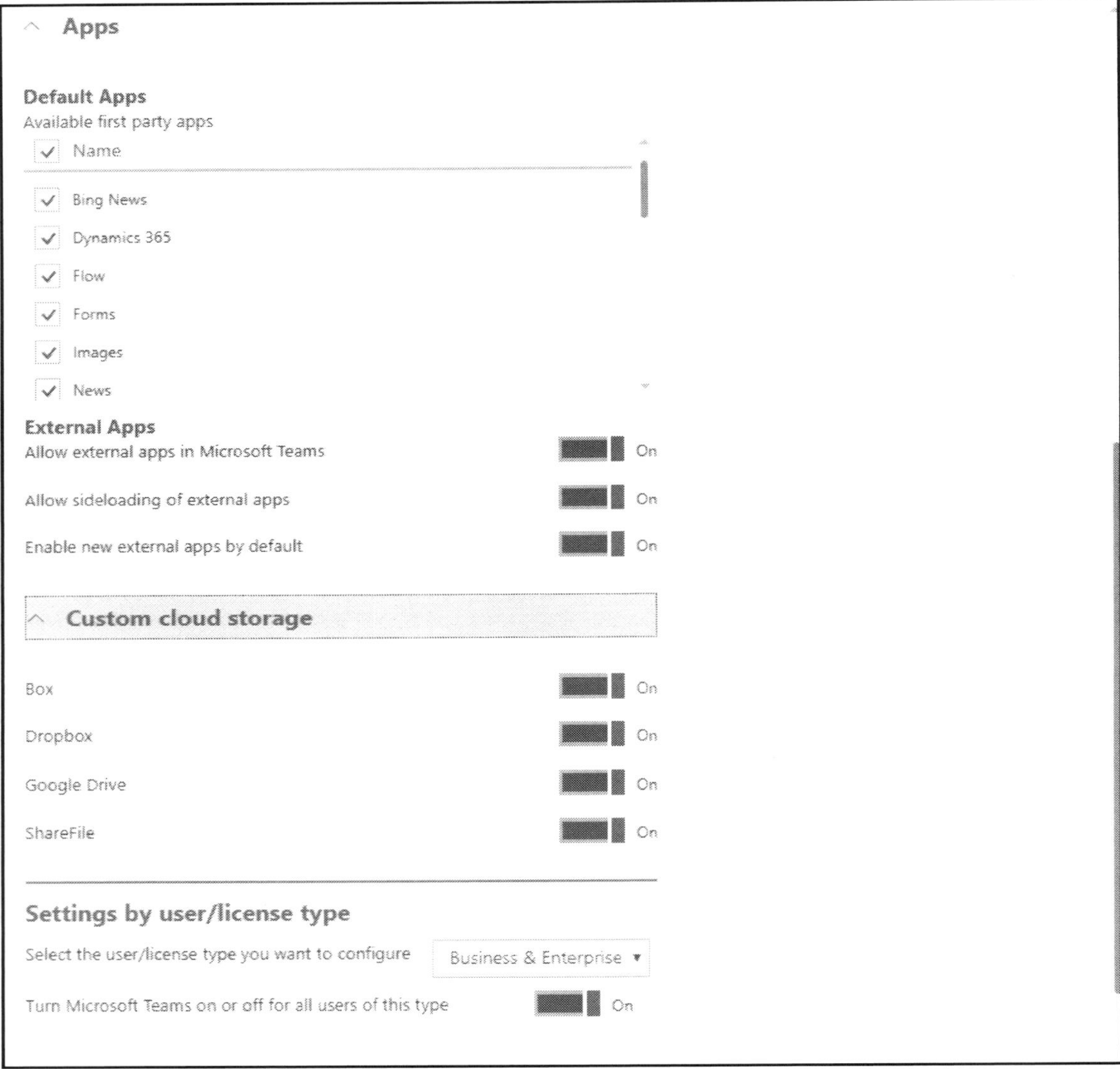

- The **Teams and channels**, **Calls and meetings**, and **Messaging** settings options:

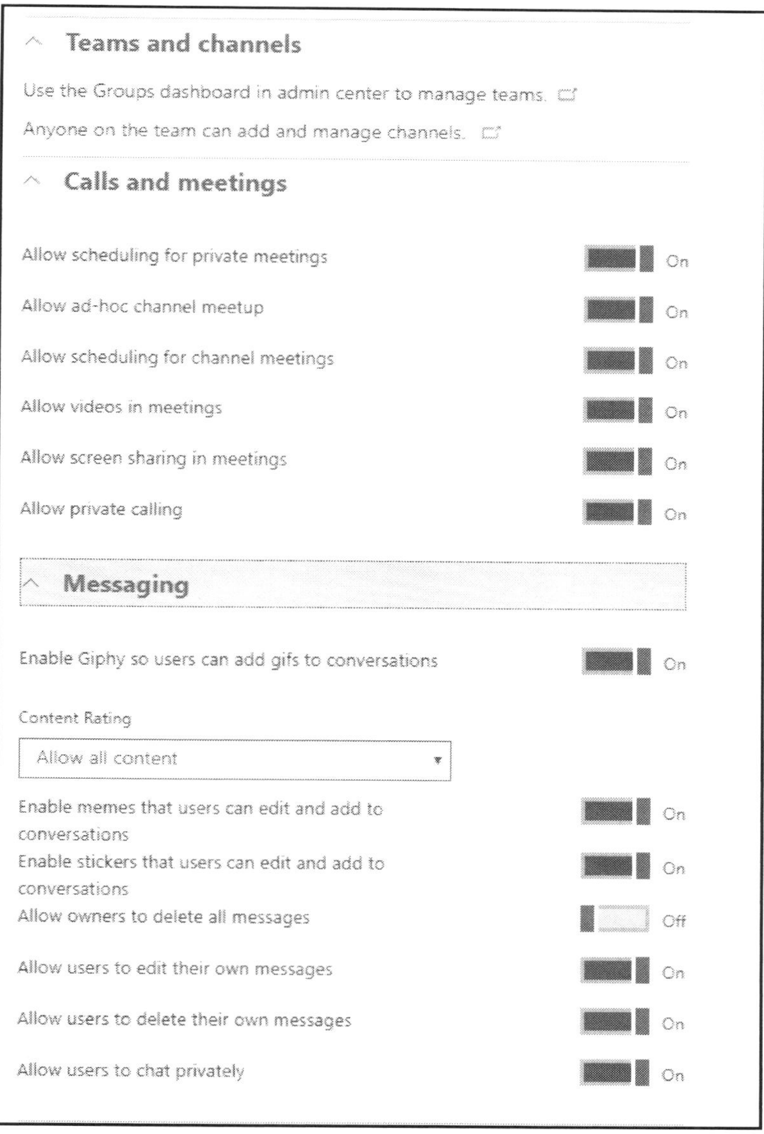

### User-level configuration

Remember that if you need to enable or disable Microsoft Teams for each user, you can enable or disable the product license for each user.

It is always advised that Microsoft Teams is available to all users within your organization for the best experience on collaboration and not to block new technologies and keep the work done for a dynamic organizations that we are facing today across the world. If you need to do a proof of concept, it is also advised to keep Microsoft Teams enabled by default and just communicate the availability to those users who are in scope.

# Extending Microsoft Teams

Microsoft Teams provides a piece that can integrate with other parts of Office 365 and many third-party applications to combine information from different sources to enhance productivity. Microsoft Teams can be extended with **connectors**, **tabs**, and **bots**.

## Connectors

Connectors are a way to let your team get updated data from external services connecting to a channel. A member of your team can use external services using connectors for Microsoft Teams, for example, an external RSS feed to a site that when an updated data is available, such as Office 365 blog or URLs, and IPs addresses of Office 365 or news, to all that updated changes been written directly to a channel of an Microsoft Teams.

You can add connectors from web client or desktop client of Microsoft Teams. Complete the following steps:

1. To use a connector and link to the channel of your choice, just click on the more options (**...**) button on the channel and then click on the Connectors option, as shown in the following screenshot:

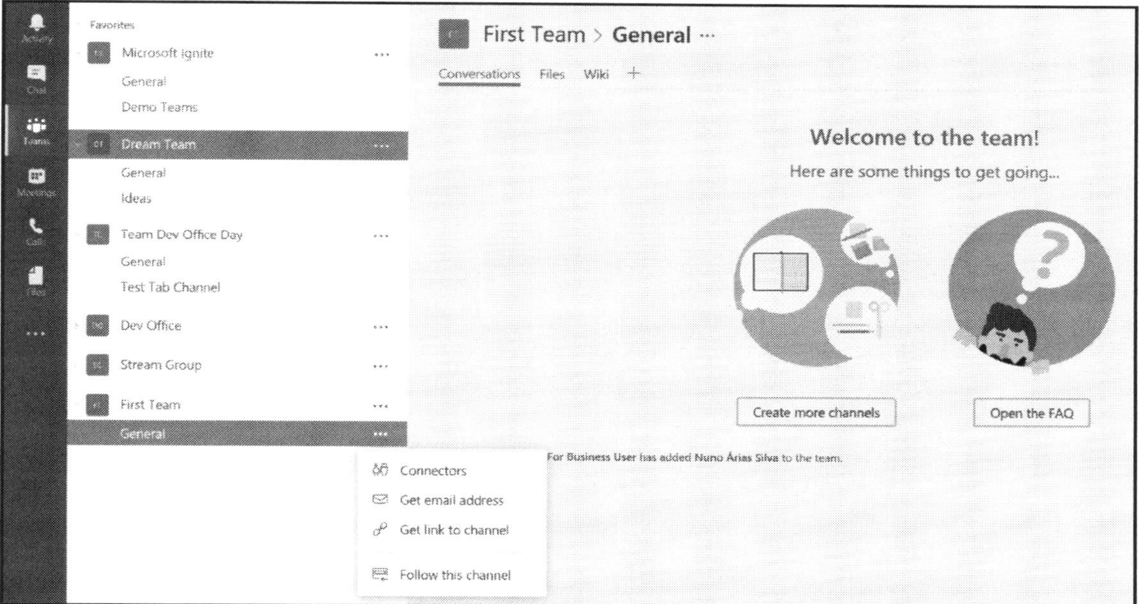

2. You can use several connectors, such as **RSS**, and then click on the **Add** button. The following screenshot shows all the connectors available to add to a channel:

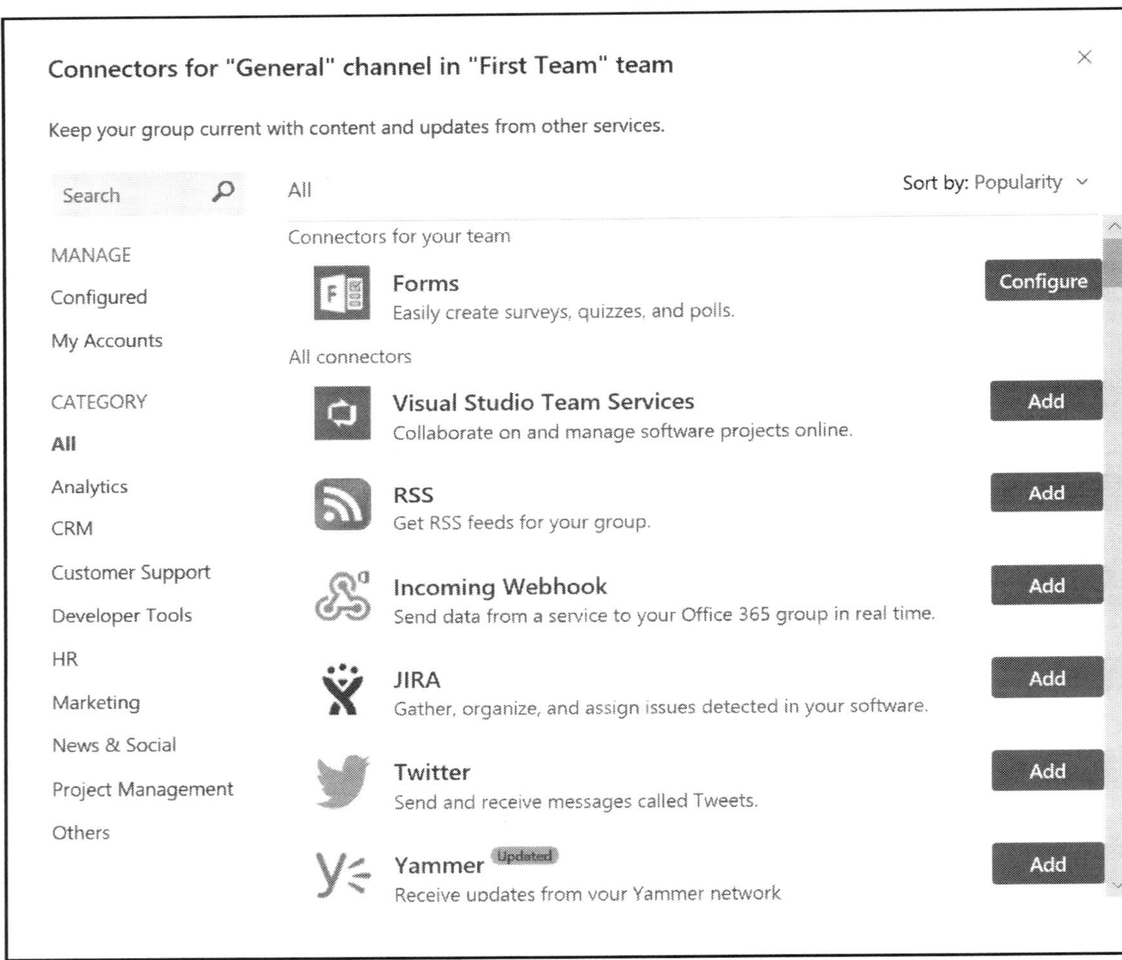

3. Click on the Add button on RSS as an example. The following screenshot shows the installation of the RSS connector:

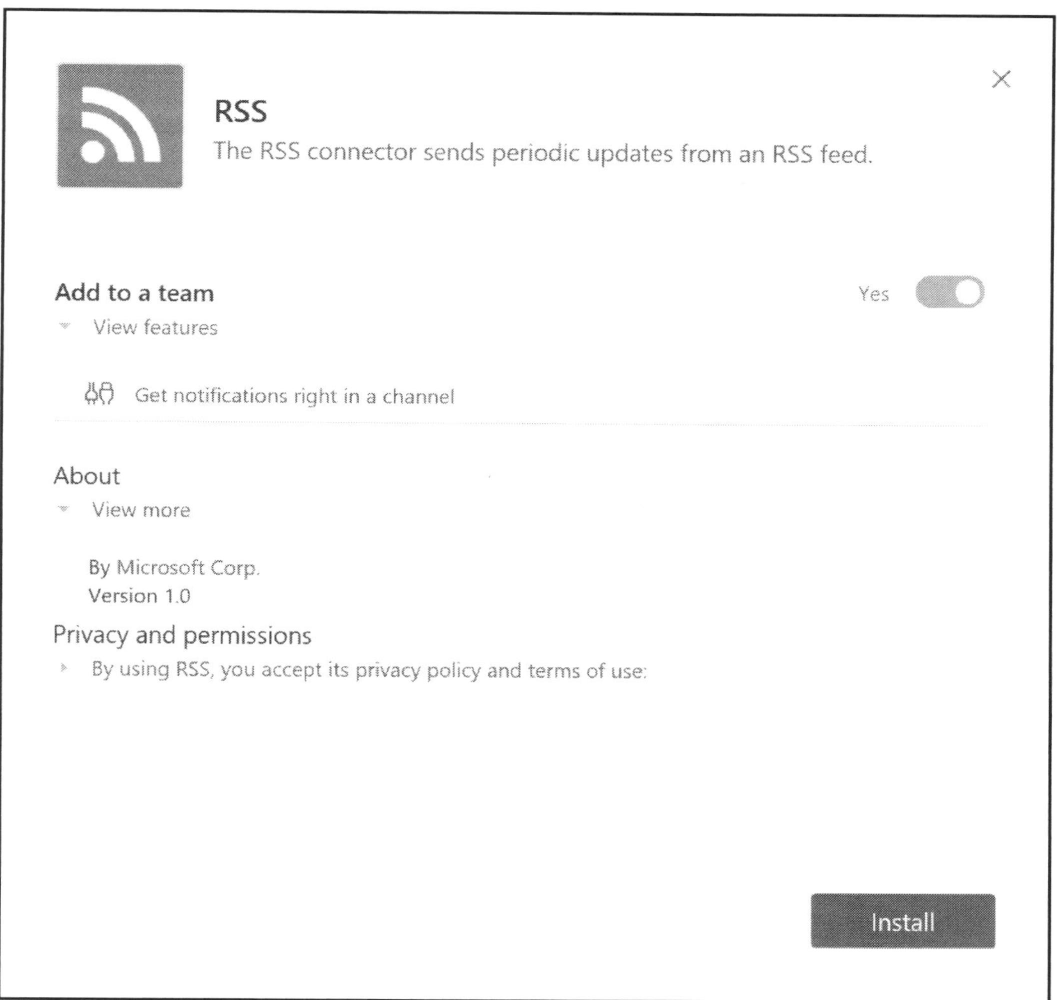

4. Fill in the data of the connector that you are using, for example, a blog. After filling in the details, click on the **Save** button:

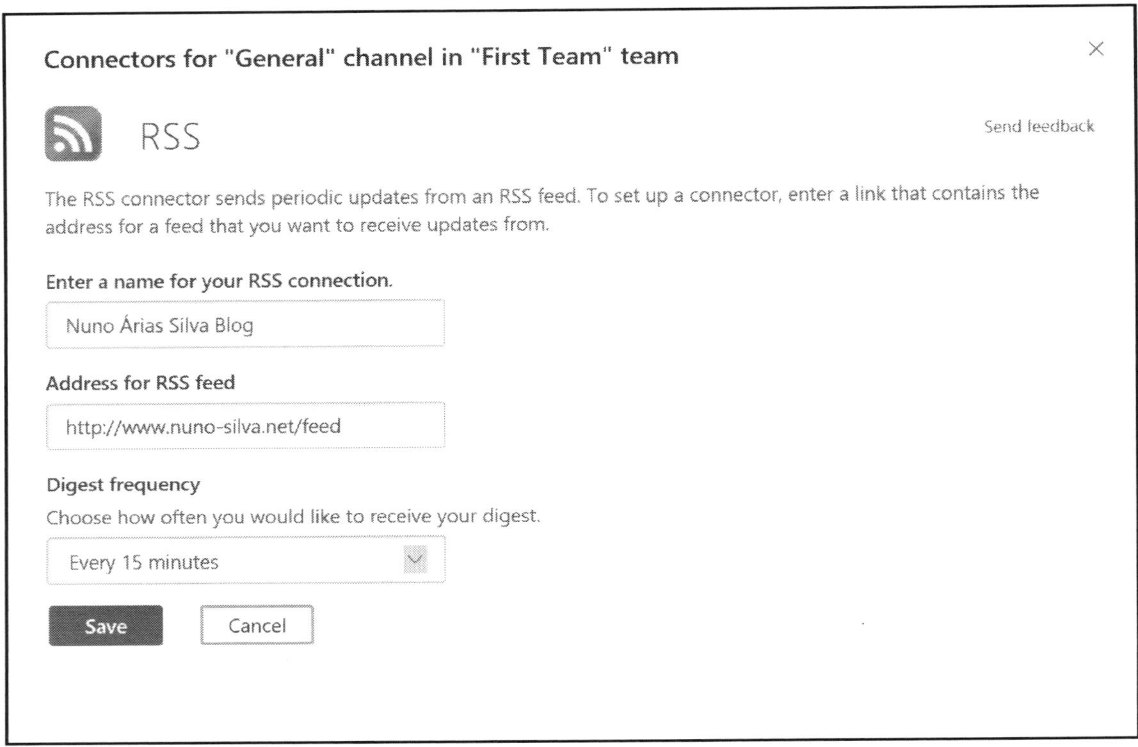

5. After configuring, you can see the properties:

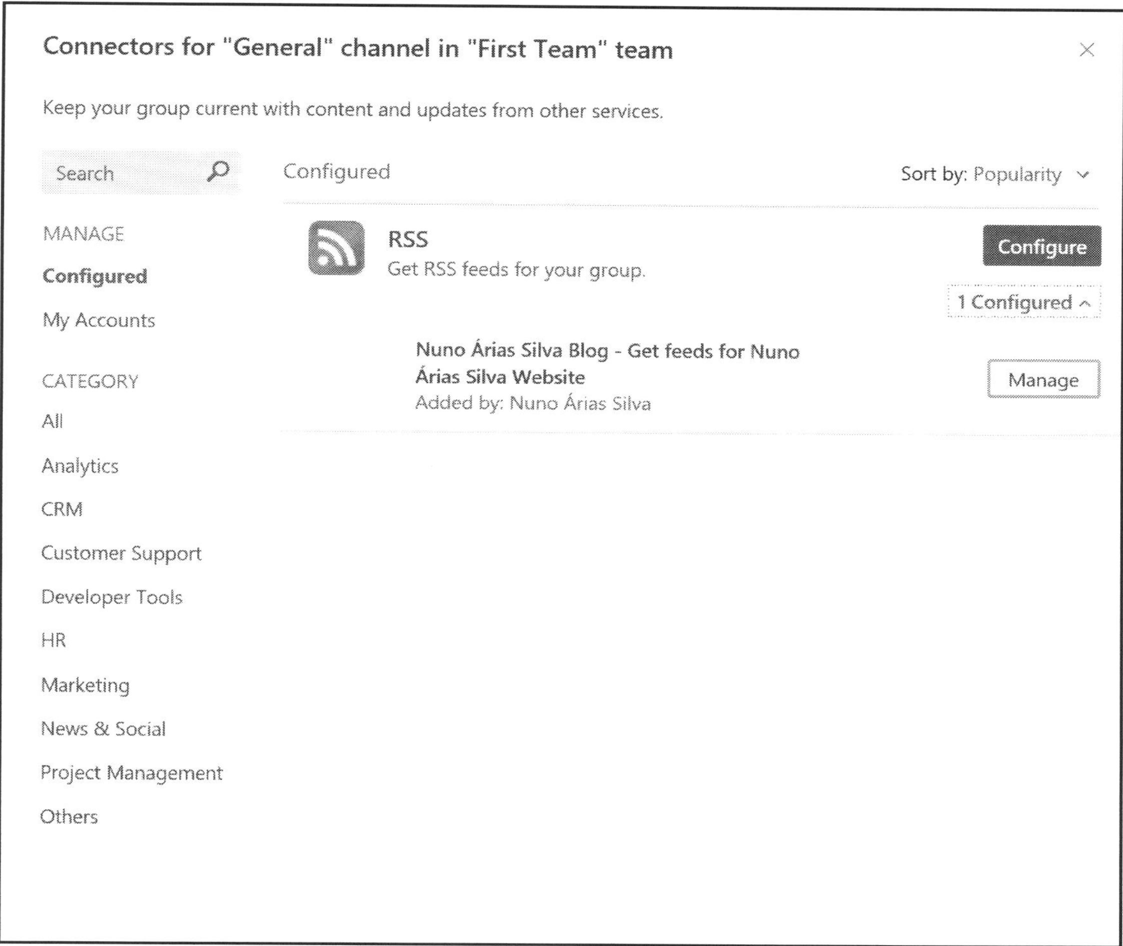

6. You can see the updated information of a site that RSS directly into a channel:

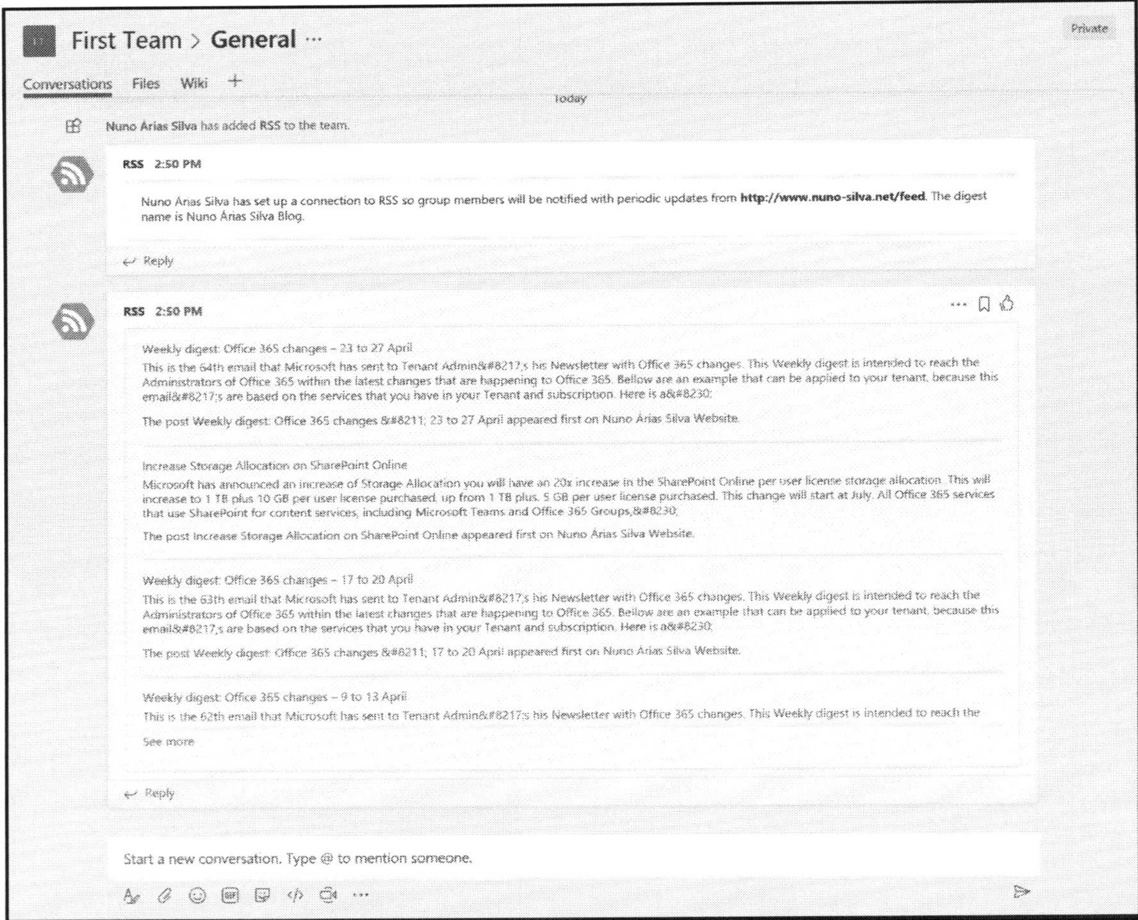

# Developing custom connectors

If you need to develop a connector that has your data from your internal application, or to a third-party service that does not exist yet on the connectors, you can use the internal **Webhook** connector that is built in to Microsoft Teams to create your own connection to a channel using standard protocols, such as HTTP, to pull your data from the source of your application:

1. To use the **Incoming Webhook**, add a connector, select it, and click on the Add button. The following screenshot shows the connector of the incoming Webhook:

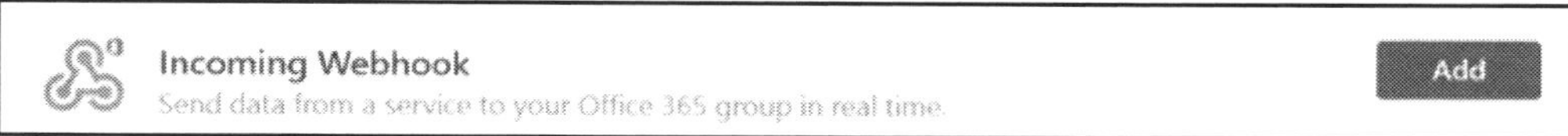


2. To create a Webhook, specify a name, update the image of the Webhook if necessary, and click on the **Create** button. The following screenshot shows the incoming Webhook configuration:

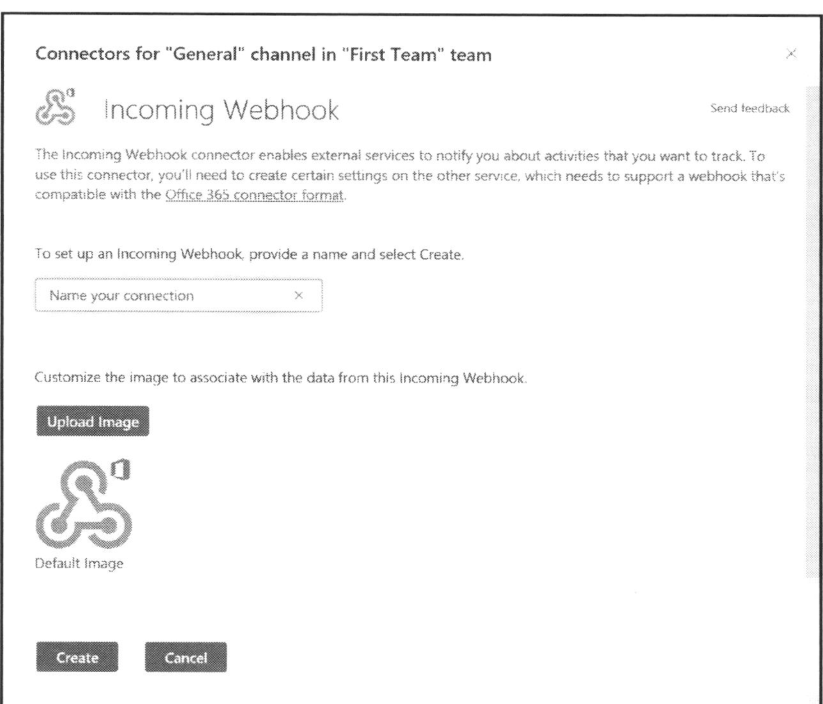

3. To learn more about Office 365 connectors, go to `https://docs.microsoft.com/en-us/outlook/actionable-messages/card-reference`. You can also create cards, using the example at `https://docs.microsoft.com/en-us/outlook/actionable-messages/actionable-messages-via-connectors`.

If your team needs to create custom connectors and a connection to your internal or external applications, follow the guide at `https://msdn.microsoft.com/en-us/microsoft-teams/connectors`.

# Tabs

Tabs is a feature on Microsoft Teams that is tied to a channel. Within this feature, you can have tabs connected to your channel based on your needs. By default, you have a channel that creates two tabs—**Conversation** and **Files**. The following screenshot shows the default tabs:

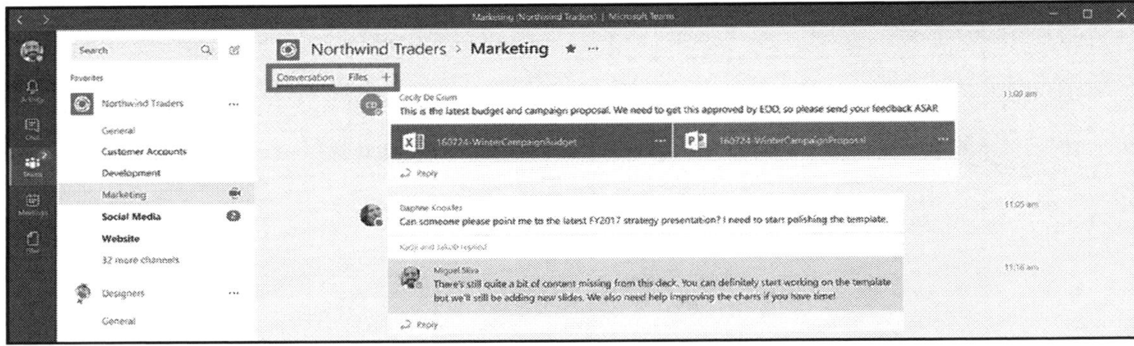

In every channel that you create, you can have a tab with your external services dedicated to a channel. The following screenshot shows adding custom tabs:

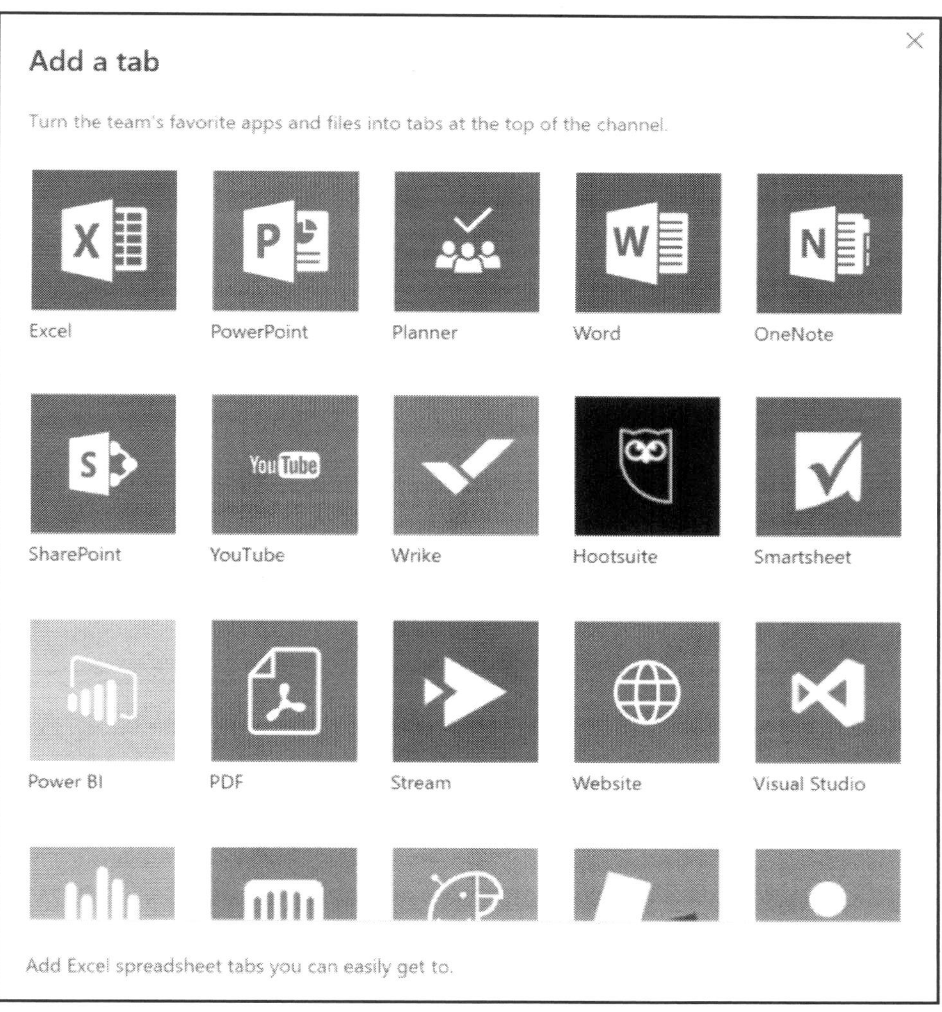

In the **Add a tab** screen, you can have many tabs, such as files, that are needed to be shown on a tab and many other connections to the tab. You can also click on the more options (...) button of a file and select the **Make this a tab** option to create a tab based on a supported file. The following screenshot shows converting files into tabs:

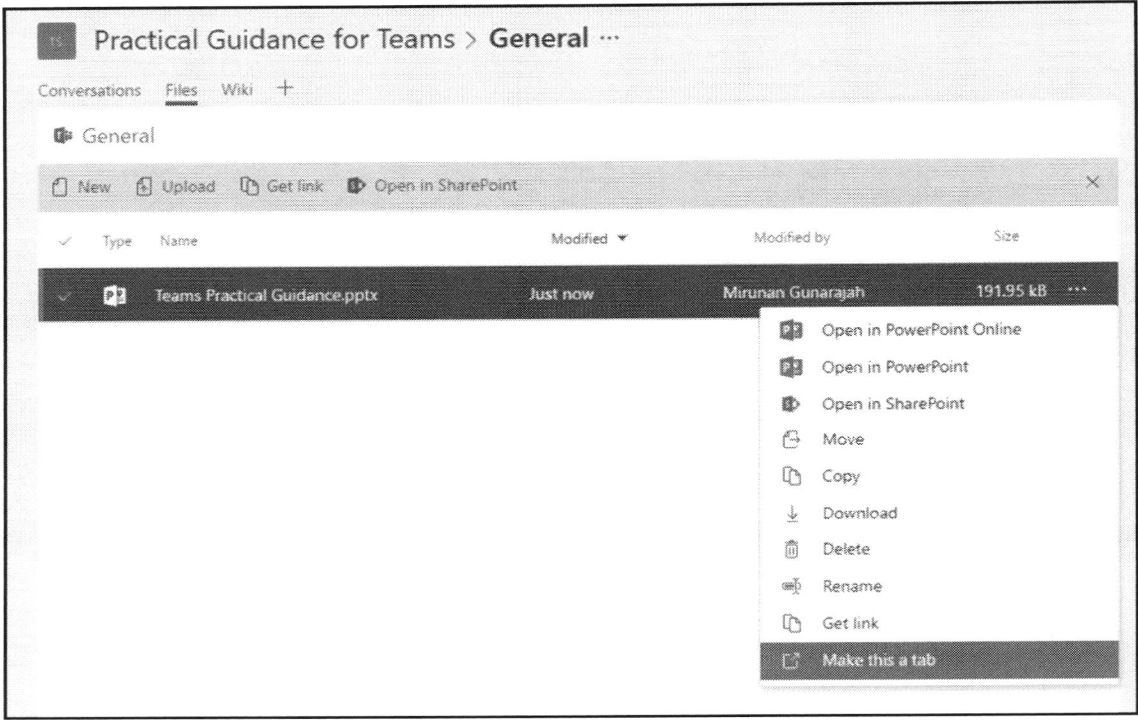


If you need to add a tab to a website, it is necessary for the destination site to have HTTPS (secure site) to add it. The practical way to use a tab is, for example, if you want a file or other content to have more focus to your team, just add a tab pointed to the file that is needed to that channel, and the best way is give access directly to the file that your users need access within directly in an Microsoft Teams tab. The following screenshot shows the tab conversation:

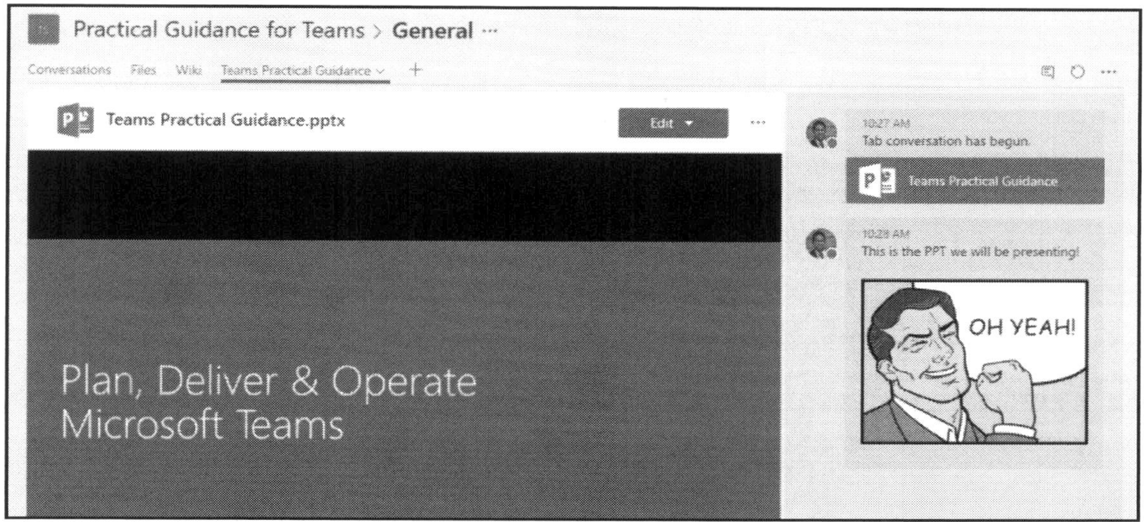


You can also add more tabs to a channel, for example, Microsoft Stream, Power BI, or even your intranet viewed from an tab. The following screenshot shows the Power BI and Microsoft Stream integration with teams:

## Developing custom tabs

If you need to develop a custom tab, it is possible to design your own and you can also share it.

To develop the custom tabs, continue reading at `https://msdn.microsoft.com/en-us/microsoft-teams/design` where you can learn more about how to build your own tab and the best way to accomplish your goal. You can see samples at `https://msdn.microsoft.com/en-us/microsoft-teams/samples`.

The following screenshot shows the sample Bing Map tab integrated into the channel:

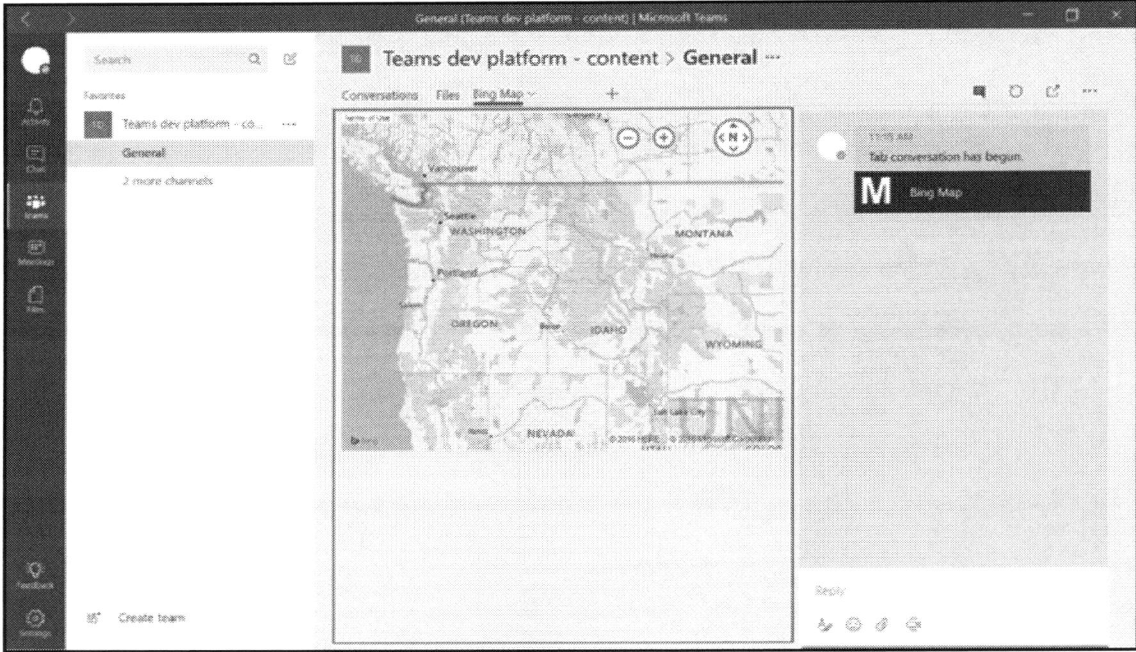


## Bots

You can also use bots. Bots is a way that you can have some artificial intelligence to help the members of each team by responding to their questions and finding information.

You can create your own bot using the *Bot Framework* available at `https://dev.botframework.com/`.

If you are a tenant administrator, you can enable these bots if the user can use them or not.

# T-Bot

By default, each user will have access to **T-Bot**, an embedded assistant that helps users learn how to use Microsoft Teams. Users can interact with T-Bot to ask it questions about how to use Microsoft Teams. The following screenshot shows the T-Bot screen:

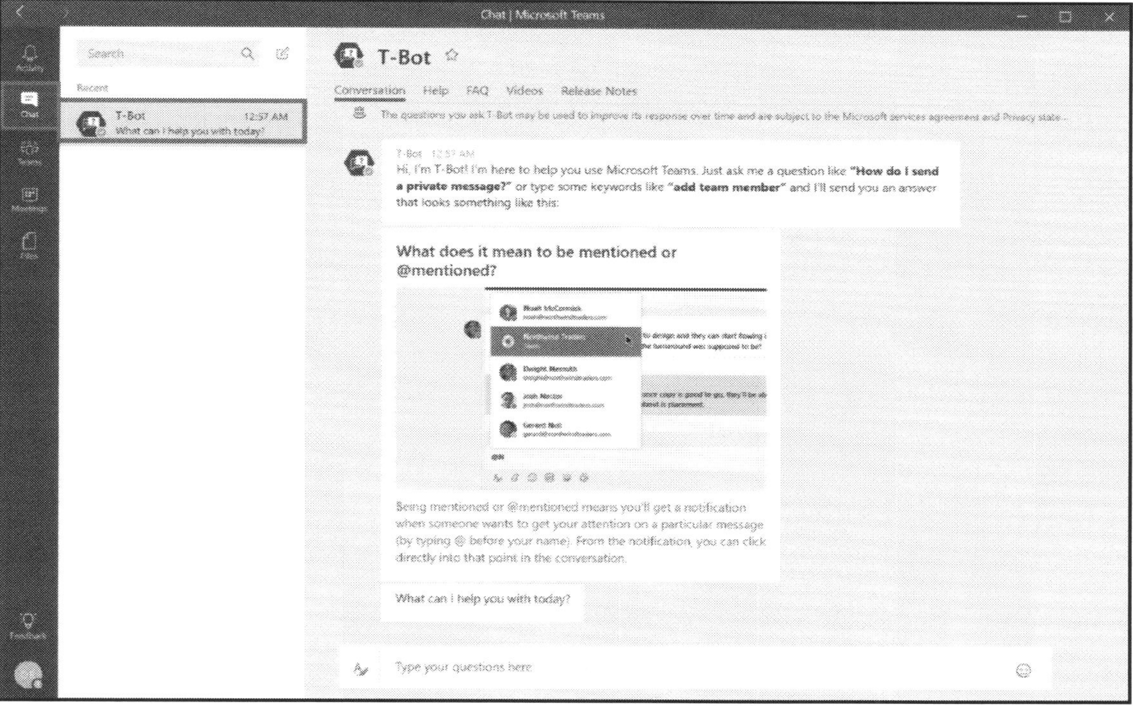

You can ask the bot something and it will help you. The following screenshot shows the T-Bot interaction through chat conversations:

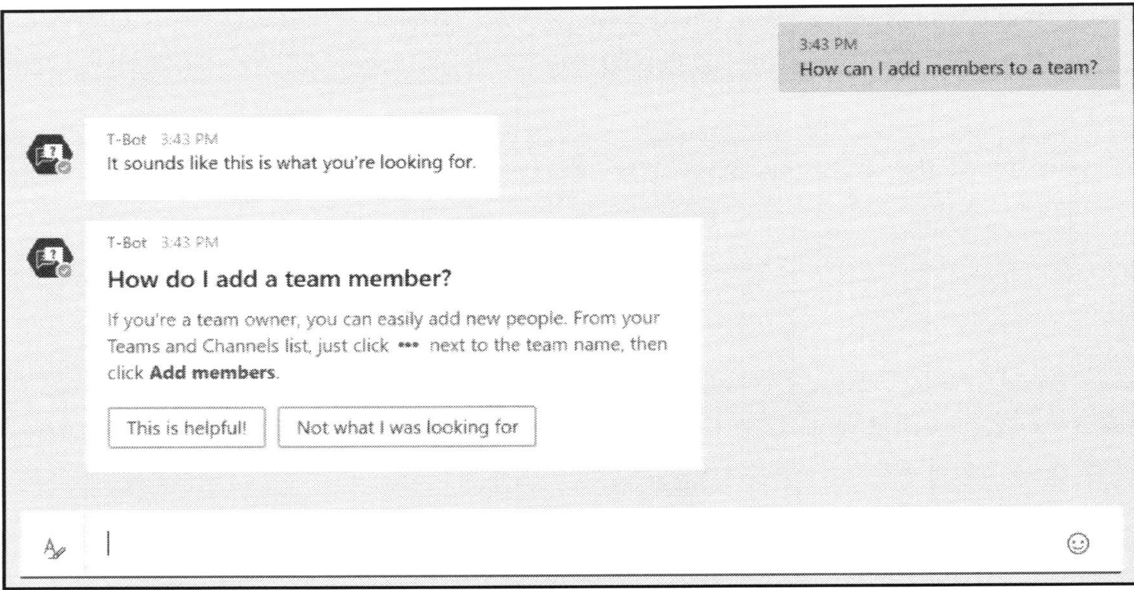


T-Bot also provides alternative assistance methods for users who prefer browsing the content instead of asking a bot questions. The following screenshot shows the T-Bot interaction options:

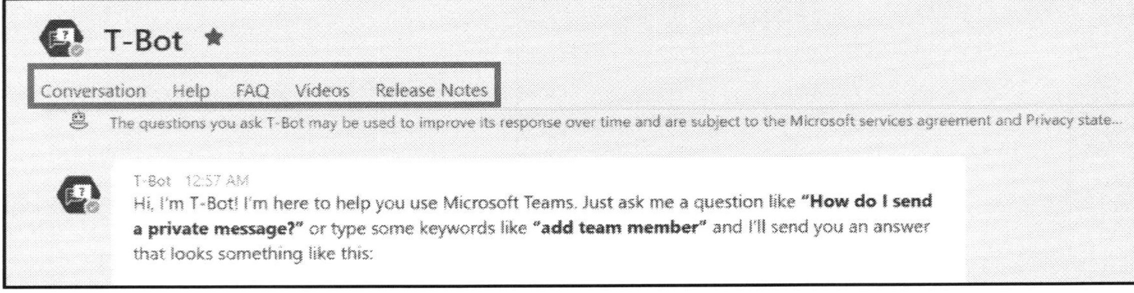

It provides a full slate of **Help, FAQ, Videos**, and **Release Notes** sections through the tabs within the bot chat. The following screenshot shows the browsing content using alternative T-Bot methods (**Help, FAQ, Videos, What's new, About**):

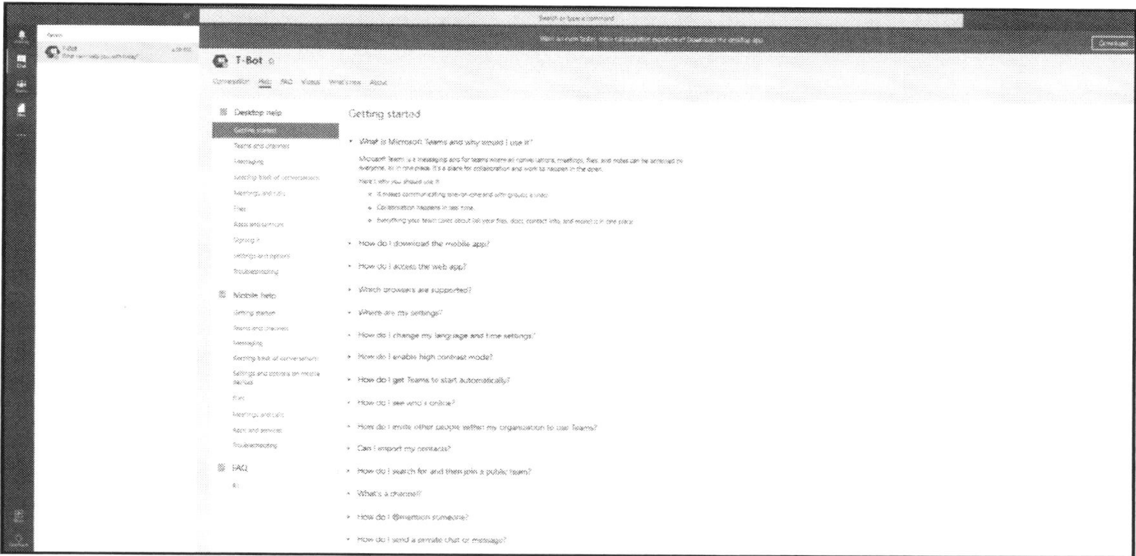


# Additional bots

Bots that have been developed by the community and made available can be leveraged within Microsoft Teams. The bots' functionality and side loading must be enabled on the tenant level for custom bots to be functional.

Bots can be used in private chats or in channels. For channels, bots can be added as team owners or members.

## Adding bots to private chats and channels

There are two ways of integrating a bot in private chats and channels:

1. Install publicly-available bots for private chats or channels.

2. Users can find bots by navigating to the chat, searching for a contact, and instead clicking on the **Discover bots** option. The following screenshot shows adding a bot to Microsoft Teams:

3. Select which bot you would like to have a conversation with. The following screenshot shows selecting a bot you would like to interact with:

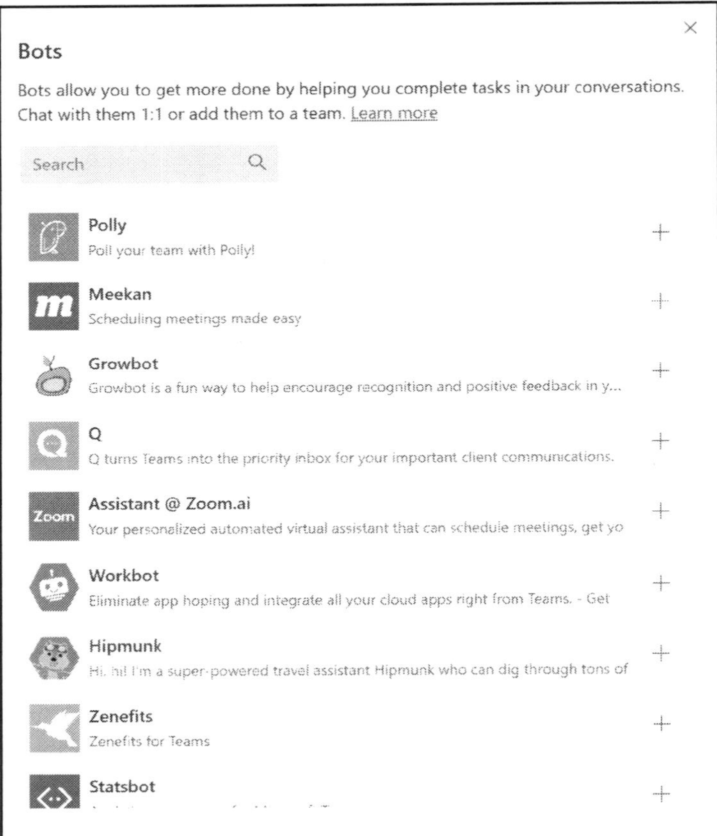

4. Once selected, provide the bot with permissions and select whether you would like to use bots in a private chat or select a team to use it in. The following screenshot shows providing permissions and selecting a private chat or a channel:

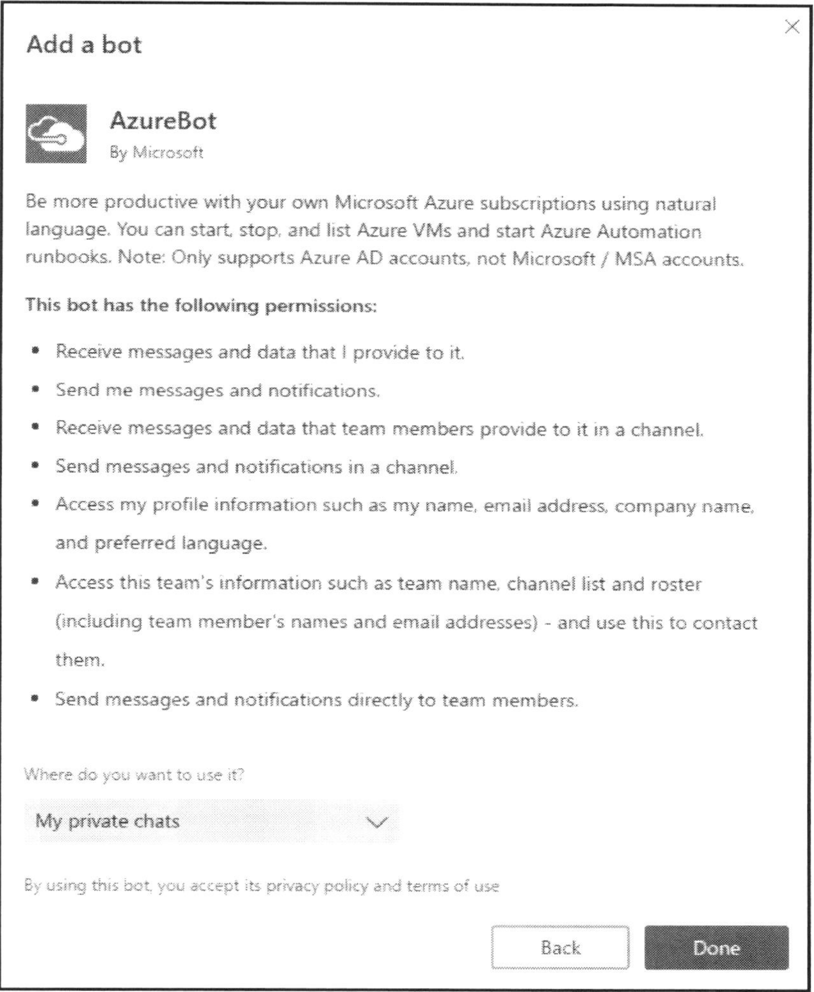


5. Alternatively, to use a bot within a channel of a team, simply click on the **View team** option and **Bots**. Here, you can discover additional bots.

6. Click on more icon (...) near the team, click on the **Manage team** option and select **Apps** to view and remove the bot that you would like to remove. The following screenshot shows removing a bot from a team:

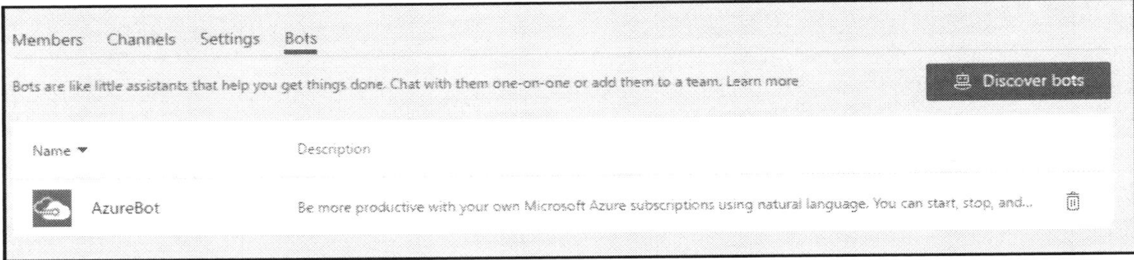


# Developing custom bots

If you need more customized bots, you can create a bot that could integrate with your application or website using Microsoft Bot Framework. To create and to test a bot to teams, go to `https://msdn.microsoft.com/en-us/microsoft-teams/botscreate` for some guides on how to develop your bots as well as a how-to guide.

You can also use the *Bot Framework Emulator* at `https://github.com/Microsoft/BotFramework-Emulator` to test it, and also as advised, you should have a separate Office 365 tenant to test it before going to production tenant.

## Side-load your own bot for private chat

To side-load your own bot, see the website with the instructions on how to give access to your applications at `https://docs.microsoft.com/en-us/microsoftteams/add-bots???history=0pfid=1sample=89ref=1`.

To learn more about Microsoft Teams, go to `https://docs.microsoft.com/en-us/microsoftteams/platform/`.

# Summary

In this chapter, you learned about the basic planning to start implementing Microsoft Teams. You now have more information on how to plan your Microsoft Teams project and implement the basics of Microsoft Teams, including connectors, tabs, and bots.

In the next chapter, you will learn how to use Delve.

# 11
# Delve

In this chapter, you will learn how to use Delve. We will cover the following topics:

- Managing time
- How to be more productive

With this foundation, you will learn more about how to be more productive in your daily tasks using Delve.

## What is Delve?

Delve was created to be a portal to research data from the client organization's website and to be a central point of shared information. It was also created to enable the client to investigate what is happening around them and their peers. Delve is a portal to research, examine, and explore your data. It is available to Enterprise Plans E1, E3, and E5, as well as Business Essentials and Premium.

## Enabling Delve

To start working with Delve, it needs to be activated on your Office 365 tenant. If you haven't activated Delve yet, go through the following steps:

1. Go to your Office 365 portal at `http://portal.office.com`.
2. Select the **Admin Center** option
3. Go to SharePoint admin center

4. Go to the **settings** option and then enable **Office Graph** as shown in the following screenshot:

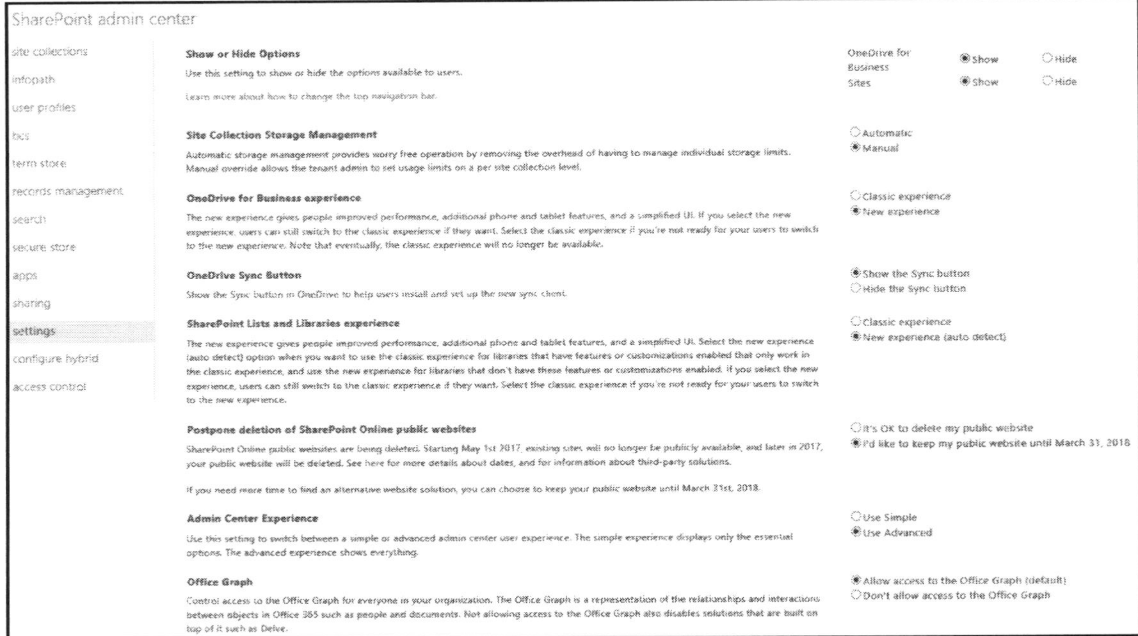


# Using Delve

To fully use Delve, you need to use some workloads in your Office 365 tenant. Some of those workloads are as follows:

- Exchange mailbox
- OneDrive
- Skype for Business

To open Delve, go to `http://portal.office.com` and select the **Delve** option.

When you first open Delve, the home page will look something like the following screenshot:

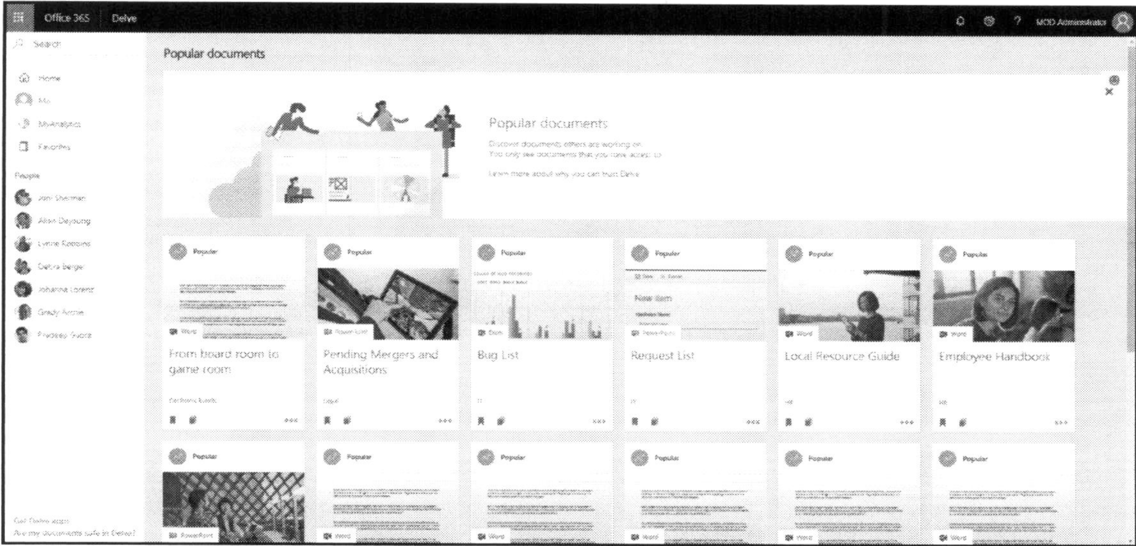


In Delve, you have the following options:

- Open Delve
- Search
- Documents
- My Analytics
- Favorites
- Go to the profile page of a person
- Click on a card to open a document
- Group documents/contents in boards

You can see the location of each option in the following screenshot:

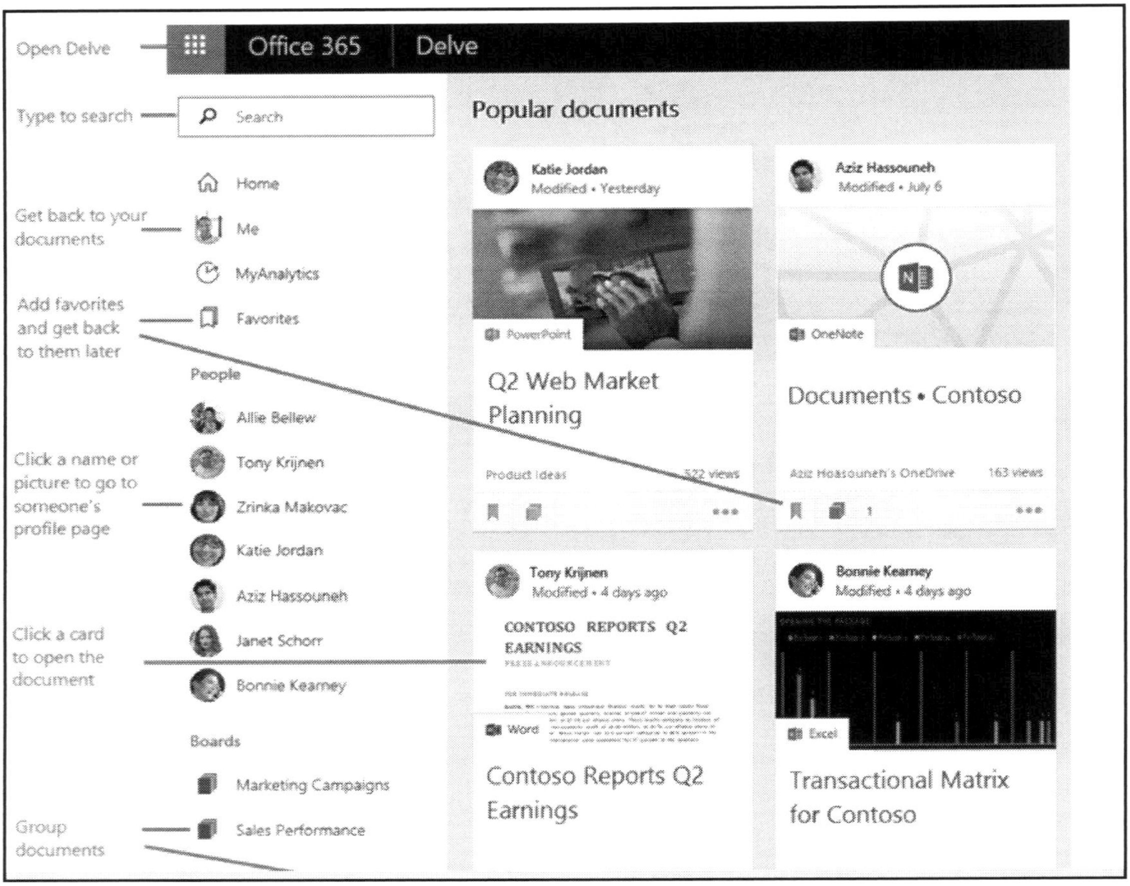

It is advised that you allow your organization's users to update their profiles, namely such details as the following:

- Photo
- Phone
- Projects
- Skills
- Schools and education

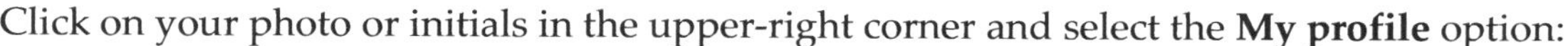

Click on your photo or initials in the upper-right corner and select the **My profile** option:

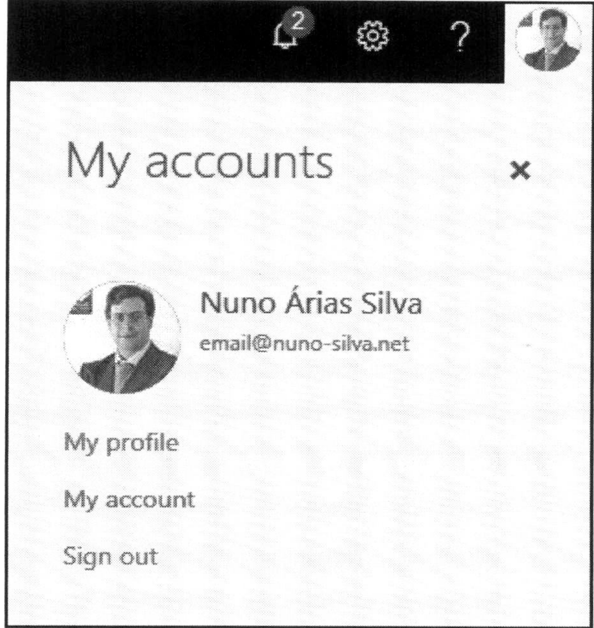


Click on the **Update profile** option to update your details.

Add some of your personal data, such as the following:

- Personal description
- Fill in the projects you are working on, as well as past projects
- Your skills and expertise
- Details about your education and which school you attended
- Your hobbies and interests
- You can also change your photo when you click on the camera icon on the left of your picture

After adjusting your image, you can choose to make the image your profile photo by choosing the **Set as profile photo** option. After adjusting the photo (if you choose), the profile photo will be changed:

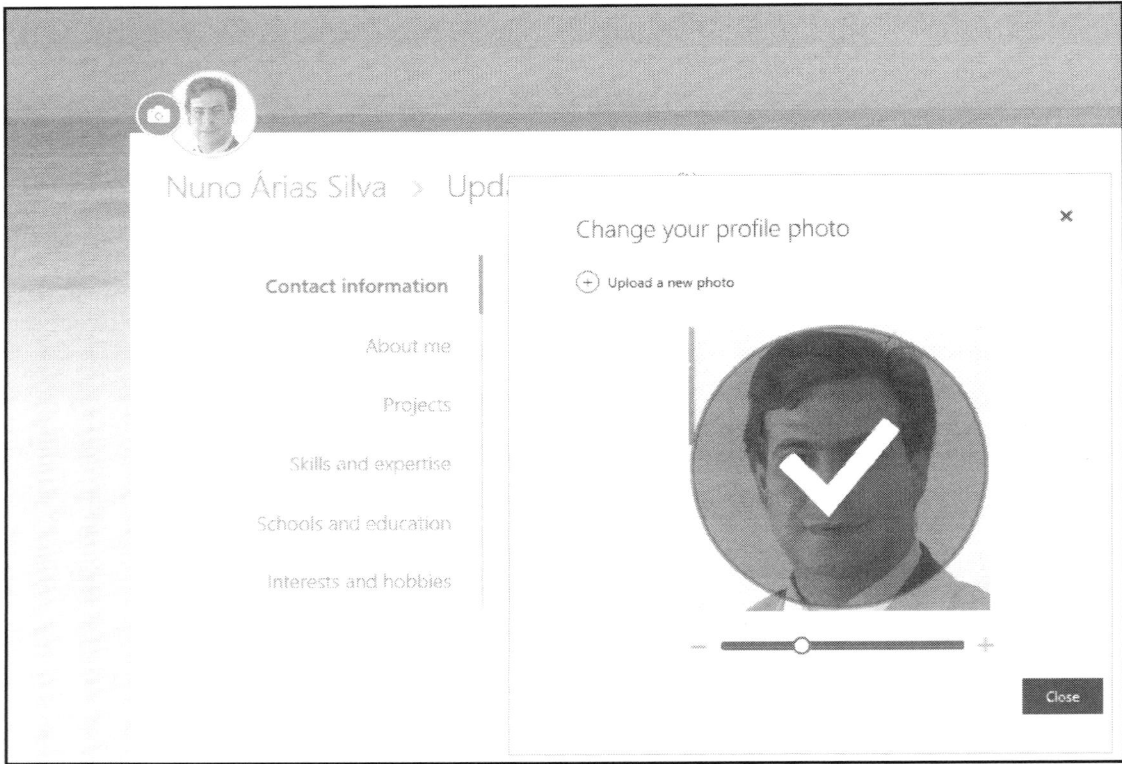

In Delve analytics, you can get insights about your work over the current and past weeks as shown in the following screenshot:

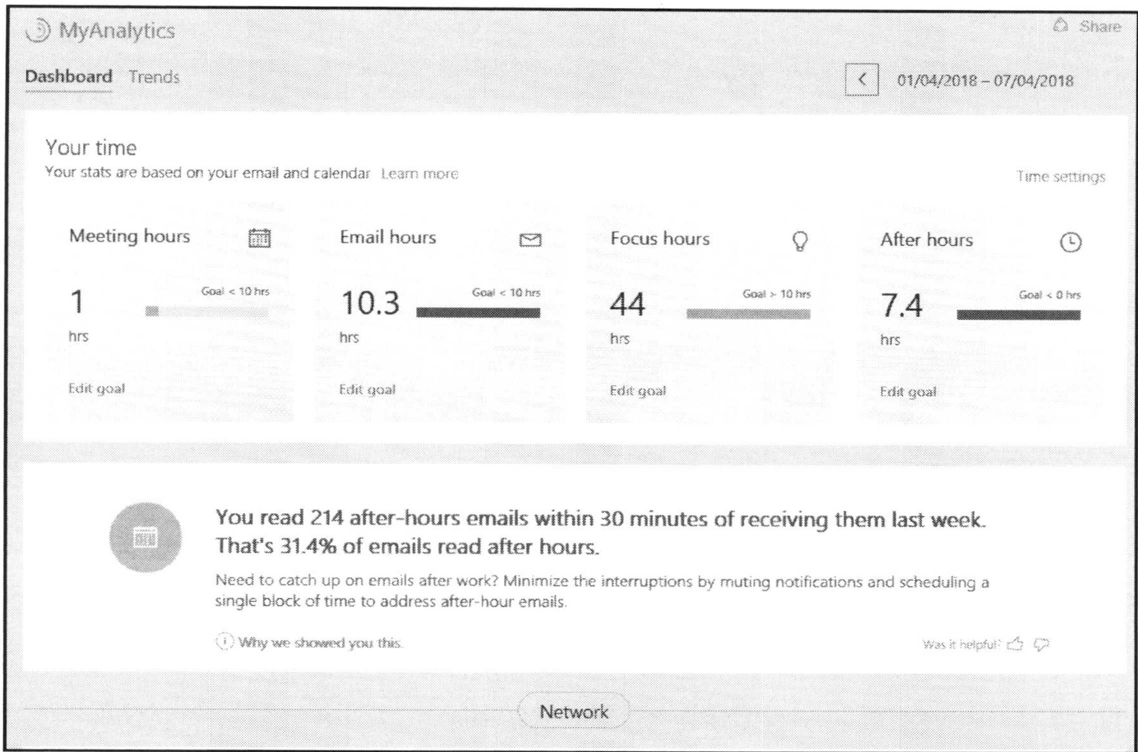


You can also see more details regarding your network, meetings, email hours, focus hours, after hours, trends per week, and trends per month. You can also set up your favorites.

To do this, go to your documents and mark a document as a favorite as shown in the following screenshot:

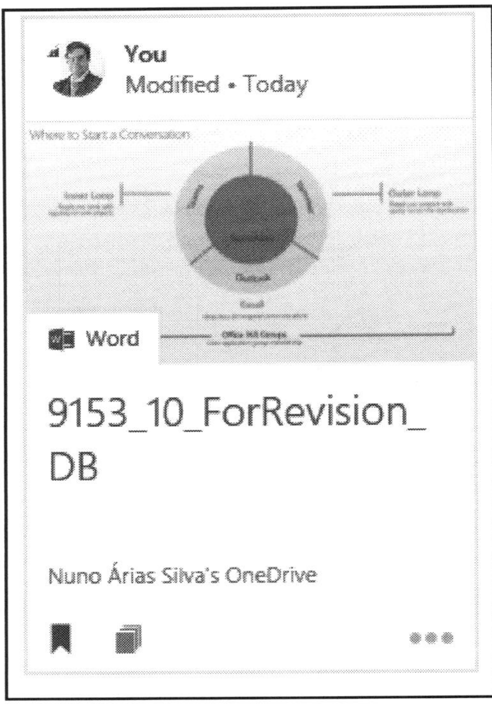


After this change, it will now be shown in the **Favorites** list.

You can continue to read more about Delve at `https://support.office.com/en-us/article/What-is-Office-Delve-1315665a-c6af-4409-a28d-49f8916878ca`. To learn more about the administration of Delve, you can continue reading at `https://support.office.com/en-us/article/office-delve-for-office-365-admins-54f87a42-15a4-44b4-9df0-d36287d9531b?ui=en-USrs=en-USad=US`.

# Summary

In this chapter, you have learned how to be more productive using Delve. You now have more information on how to use Delve and how to be more productive in your daily tasks.

In the next chapter, you will learn how to implement and manage some of the most-used workloads of Office 365.

# 12
# Managing Workloads

In this chapter, you will learn and understand how to manage and maintain Office 365 workloads. We will cover these topics with the help of the following tasks:

- Basic tasks
- Complex tasks

You will learn more about how to manage Office 365 workloads on a daily basis.

## Basic tasks

To start managing Office 365, you need to know what the basic management tasks are. Depending on the workloads that you are using, you need to perform the tasks according to the best practices.

In Office 365, you have several administrator roles that you can use to separate the responsibilities of each person in your organization, depending on the needs of a particular administrative role. Within these roles, it is possible to assign a specific task to each administrator in your organization. Here are the several administrator roles:

- Global administrator
- Billing administrator
- Exchange administrator
- SharePoint administrator
- Password administrator
- Skype for Business administrator
- Service administrator
- User management administrator
- Reports reader

- Security and compliance roles
- Dynamics 365 (online)
- Dynamics 365 service administrator
- Power BI administrator

You can find the updated version of the administrator roles along with what each user assigned to the role can do at `https://support.office.com/en-us/article/about-office-365-admin-roles-da585eea-f576-4f55-a1e0-87090b6aaa9d`.

To manage the workloads and to be informed of the changes, you have the Office 365 Service Management toolkit.

To stay up-to-date, you should visit the *Office 365 Roadmap* at `http://roadmap.office.com` where you have access to all updated information on Office 365 releases, and you can check the upcoming features, as well:

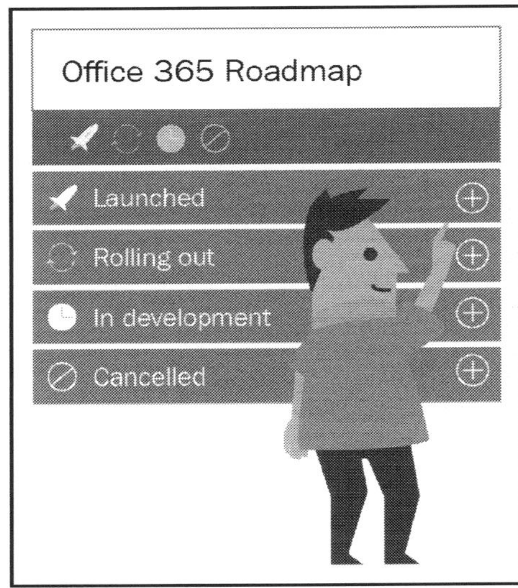


Visit the Office blog to learn more about Office 365 announcements and news at `http://blogs.office.com`:

At the Office blog site, you can filter by Office 365 area to see the latest articles, too. Stay ahead of change with the Office 365 Message Center in the Office 365 admin portal:

To have access to the Message center, go to `http://portal.office.com` and select **Admin center**.

In the Admin center, go to the **Message center** section as shown in the following screenshot:

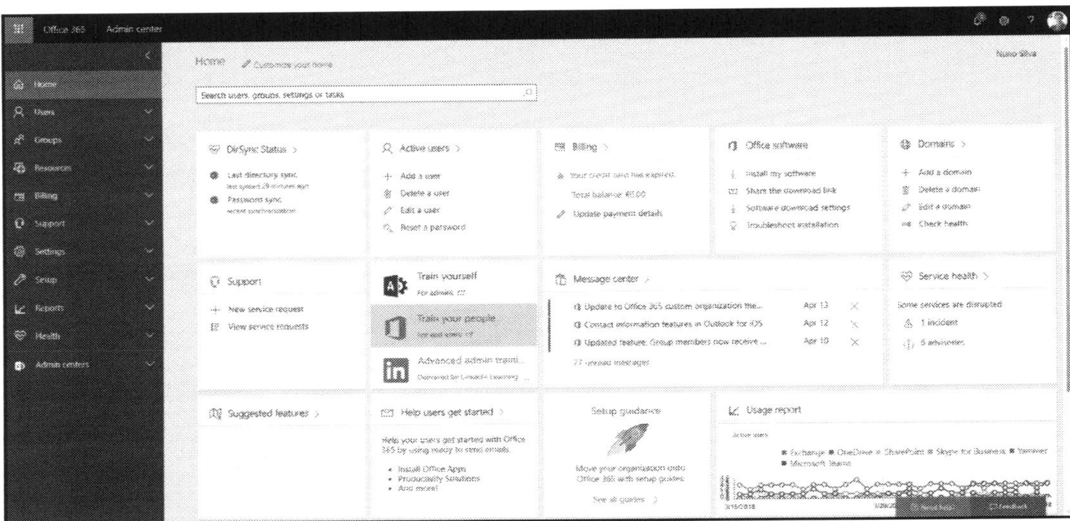

In the **Message center** area, you can view all the updates regarding your Office 365 Tenant, as shown in the screenshot:

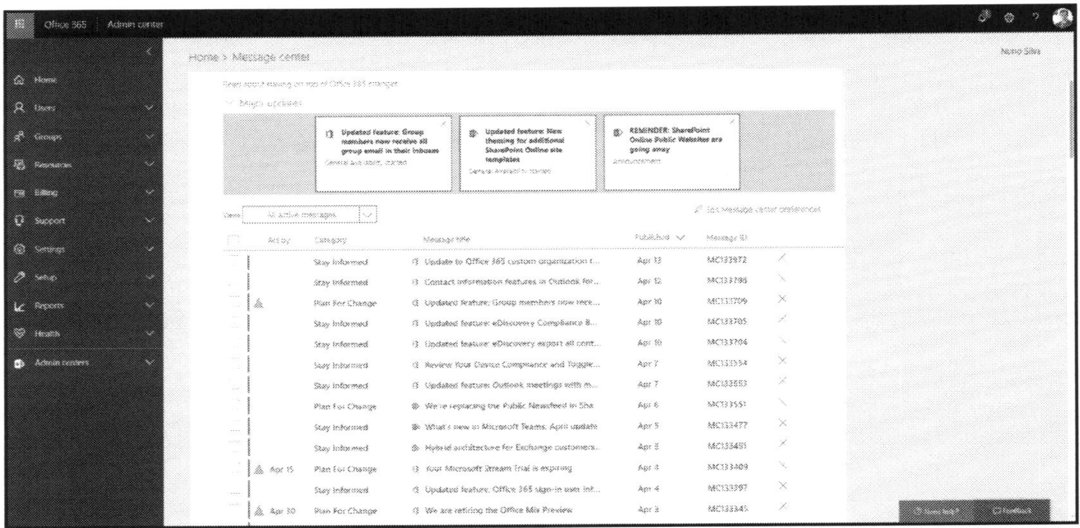

It is advised that you be informed of all changes to Office 365 so that you can plan accordingly before new features are made available or major service changes are deployed.

In the example that follows, you can see an Office 365 message warning you about a new feature. This message is marked with an alert symbol because it requires you to plan for change or to take some action. Make sure you always read these messages:

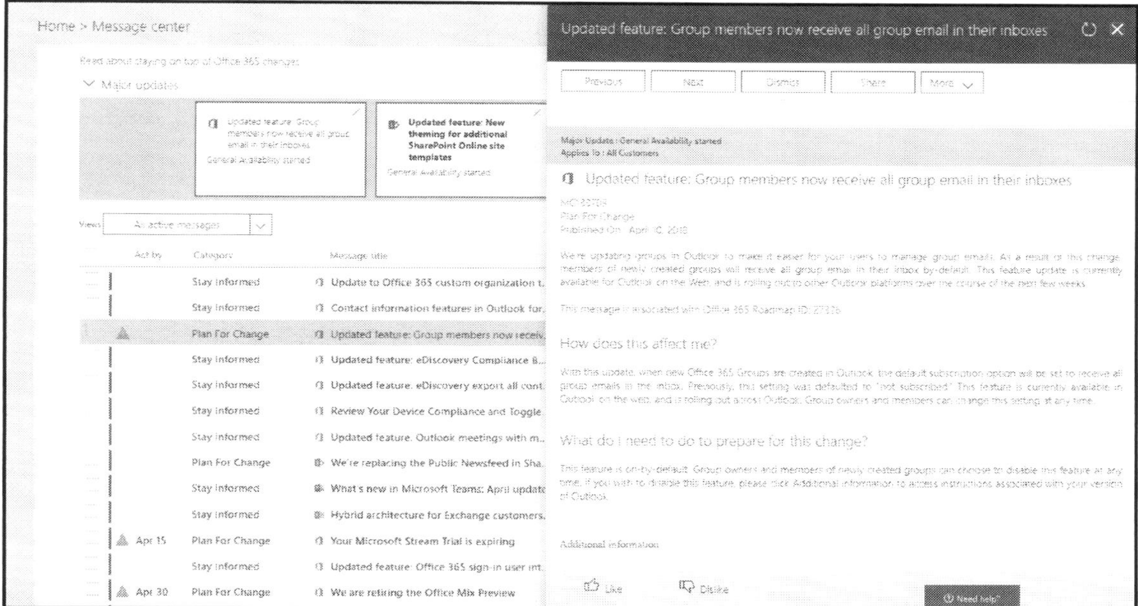


To learn more about this updated feature, click on the **Additional information** link. You can also refer to `https://techcommunity.microsoft.com/t5/Outlook-Blog/Introducing-Follow-in-inbox-and-other-improvements-for-managing/ba-p/102611`.

You can also be informed by the email setting in the **Edit Message center preferences** link:

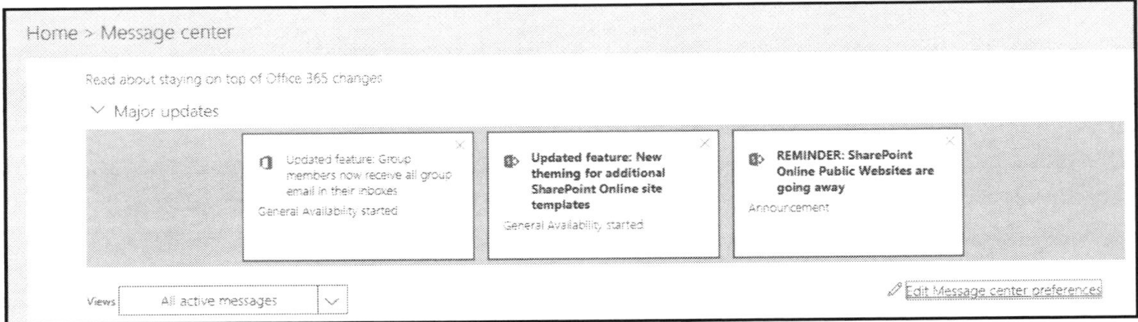


Here, you can set your preferences, such as which products you want to receive messages about, as well as the possibility of receiving these messages in your email inbox:

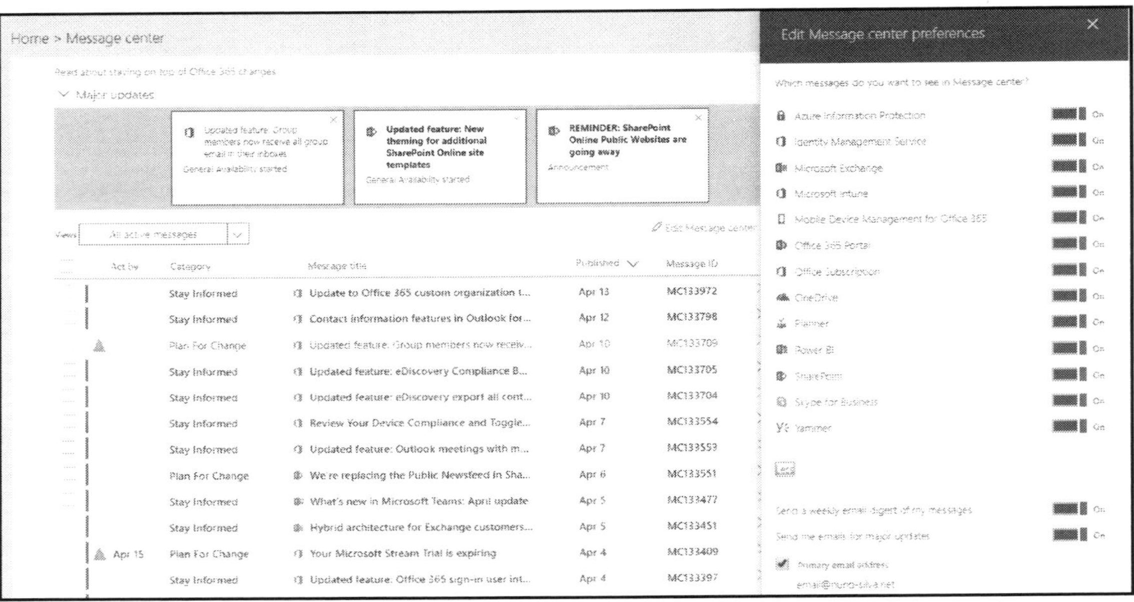


Monitor the **Service Health** dashboard for information about the service health of the Office 365 admin portal. It is where you can find the status of the products that your organization is using:

To view the **Health** dashboard, go to `https://portal.office.com/adminportal/home#/servicehealth` as shown in the following screenshot:

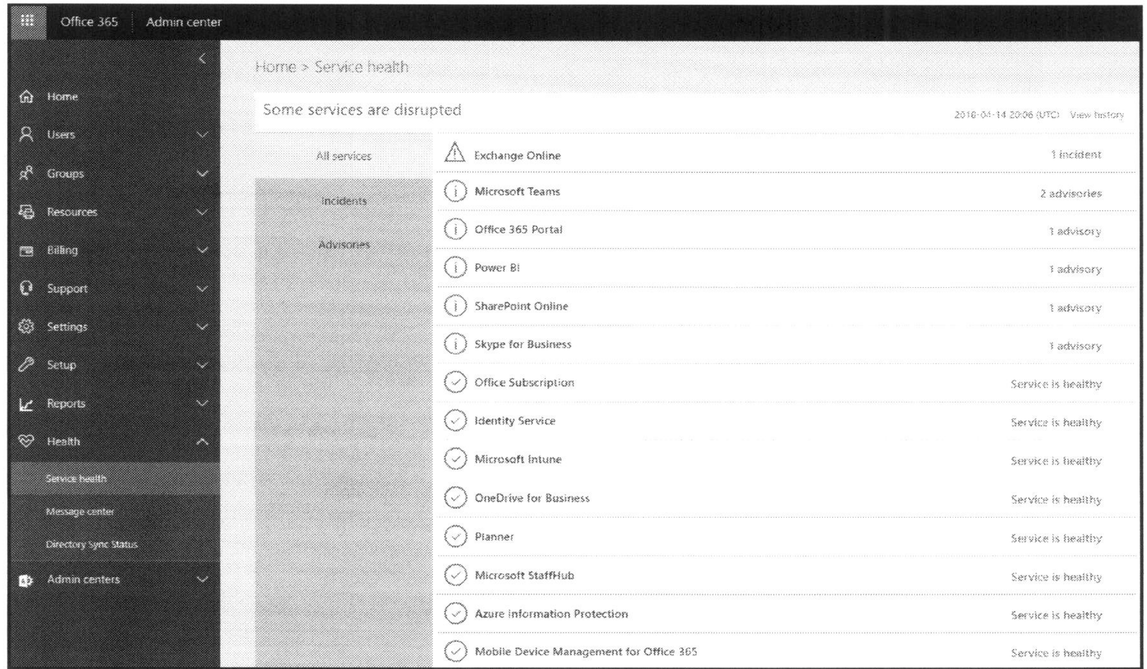

To view an incident, click on it as shown in the following screenshot:

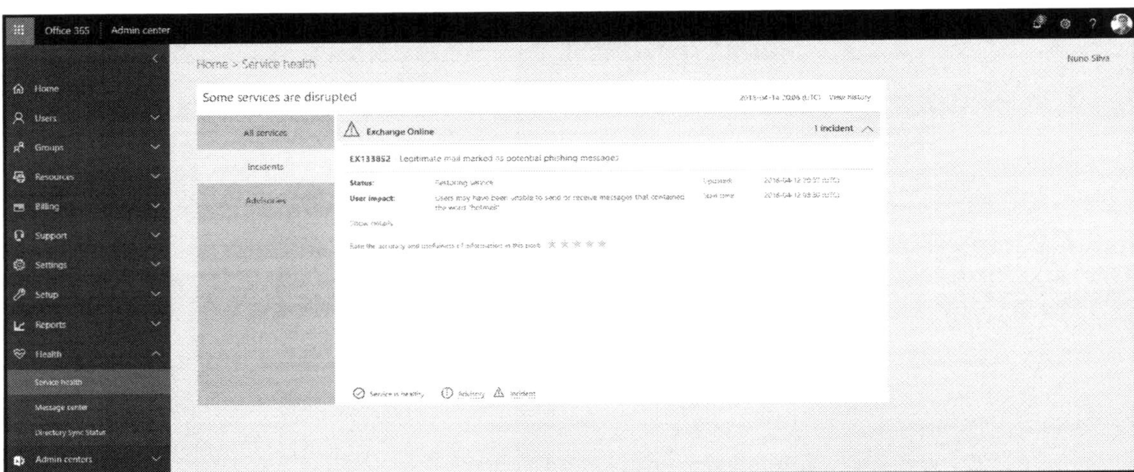


You can click on the **Show details** link to learn more about the incident.

Keep up to date on the go with the Office 365 admin app on your mobile device:

To download the Office 365 admin app, go to `https://products.office.com/en/business/manage-office-365-admin-app` and download the app for your device. You can also stay informed, manage users, and get needed support.

*Have more questions?* Join the Tech Community at `http://techcommunity.microsoft.com`:

# Complex tasks

For complex tasks, you need to have more information and to better organize processes in order to have your organization correctly managed.

It is advised that you use a service management framework like, for example, the **Information Technology Infrastructure Library** (ITIL).

Here is a process that you can use in your organization to best organize your process within the project and gain insight about each phase.

In this process, there are several steps, which are as follows:

- **Deploy**: You deploy your solution based on organizational needs within the Office 365 workload area.
- **Operate**: This is the run state of your project, where you perform tasks to best accomplish your goal; you can separate them into:
    - **Change management**: You register all changes within your organization and have a historical view of what has gone to production and what has changed
    - **Service health**: You see the health of your solution tied to monitoring

        - **Maintenance performance and monitoring**: You monitor your environment based on availability and performance
        - **Support**: You provide support to your project workloads
- **Optimize**: This area is where you optimize the whole process. This can be further divided into the following:
        - **Usage and adoption**: You give the vision of your project to the end users and have the ability, based on your experience, to engage the user to use and to adopt new technologies deployed to your project
        - **Extensibility and development**: You can extend your project to integrate with other workloads or business applications and processes, as well as develop of applications that fit your business needs
- **Ongoing and go live**: This last phase is where you monitor the success plan of your project and use the lessons learned to best fit your organization's needs:
        - **Empowered**: You provide the vision to your departments like: IT, admins, and partners
        - **Engaged**: You provide the users with best practices to be more productive: productive users
        - **Excellent**: You monitor your whole process: service experiences

Here is a diagram of the preceding steps:

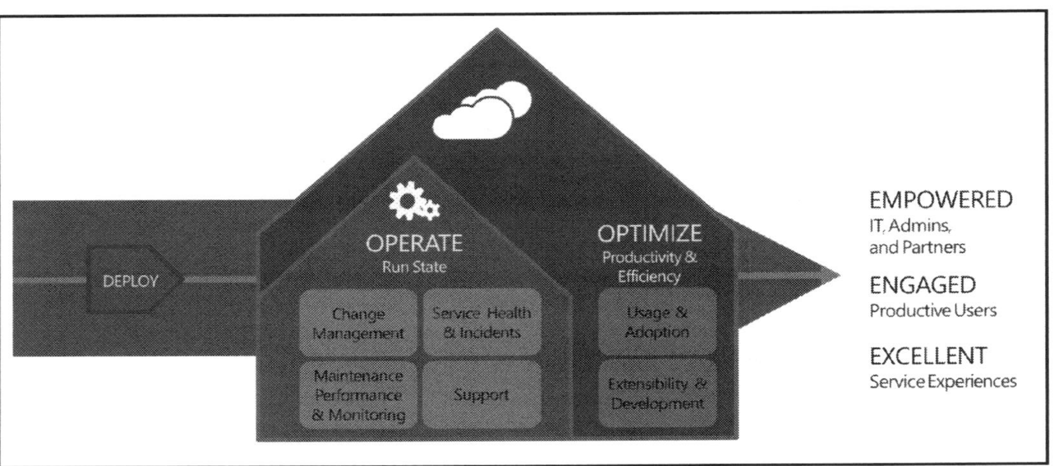


We will now move on to the process that you can use based on best practices.

# Service change management process

In each phase, keep in mind that it is a part of a whole cycle, and you need to stick to the following phases:

- **Plan**: In the plan phase you can have several tasks to do:
  - **Capture**: What information is needed for the phase based on the process, such as requirements, needs, and the people involved.
  - **Classify**: You classify the changes with priorities and risks and measure indicators of your phase.
  - **Discuss**: You discuss things with your peers and sponsors, so that all people that are in the process can be involved and approve the plan to be a success. It is not the most critical, but still a very important part, of the plan.
- **Deploy**: In the deploy phase you can have several tasks to do:
  - **Rings**: Verify the availability of the rings of the phase that you are deploying based on the roadmap. That will allow you to know what is going to happen during your change plan.
  - **Target release**: Deploying on first release is advised to best understand new features and to be prepared for the changes to Office 365.
  - **Telemetry**: Learn about and monitor what the users are doing and monitor the adoption of the new technologies.
- **Communicate**: In the communicate phase you can have several tasks to do:
  - **Policy**: Have a communication policy for the users sponsored by your communication department and management team.
  - **Playbook**: Create a Playbook, where you provide information in a single page or a few pages, on how to work with the new product.
  - **Resources**: Create resources and put them in Office 365, such as Stream, Yammer, and SharePoint. Create some Skype for Business presentations or Skype broadcasts to launch the change management phases.
- **Listen**: In the listen phase you can have several tasks to do:
  - **Signal versus noise**: Stay connected with users and listen to their new experiences and combine them with other departments
  - **Feedback**: Ask for feedback; you can use Forms or Yammer
  - **Measure**: Always measure your success in each phase and present successes to the sponsor team

For the whole process, it is advised that you perform the following phases as a cycle:

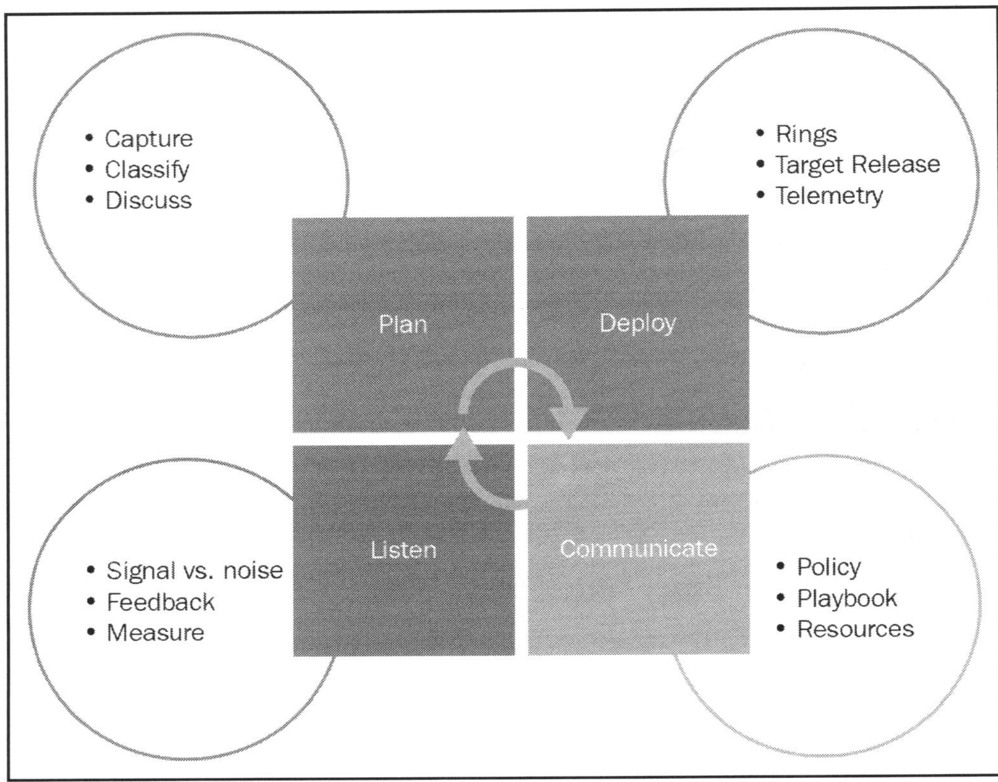

## Understanding the rings in Office 365

Office 365 is composed of different rings. When the development team creates and updates new features, these features are first released to **Ring 0**, which is used by internal feature teams.

Then, when approved, they are promoted to **Ring 1**, which is used by the Office 365 team and so on, until they get to all customers Office 365 tenants in **Ring 4**.

You can always change the configuration of your tenant to target release and you will get the new features first rather than regular Office 365 tenants. By default, each tenant is set to standard release. Targeted release will get you new features first, but also not fully tested features, and you might incur small issues, so the decision of activating targeted release should be carefully taken. The following image shows the different rings in Office 365:

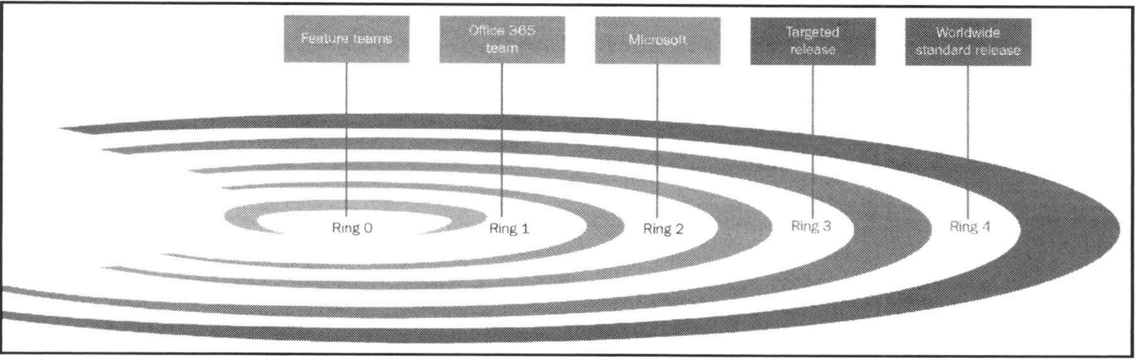


It is a best practice to have a separate tenant of Office 365 to test the targeted release on the whole tenant and then enable it in your production tenant just for a few users.

To configure your tenant, follow these steps:

1. Go to `http://portal.office.com` and then to Admin center
2. Go to the **Organization profile** option in the **Settings** drop-down
3. Click on the **Edit** button in the **Release preferences** section:

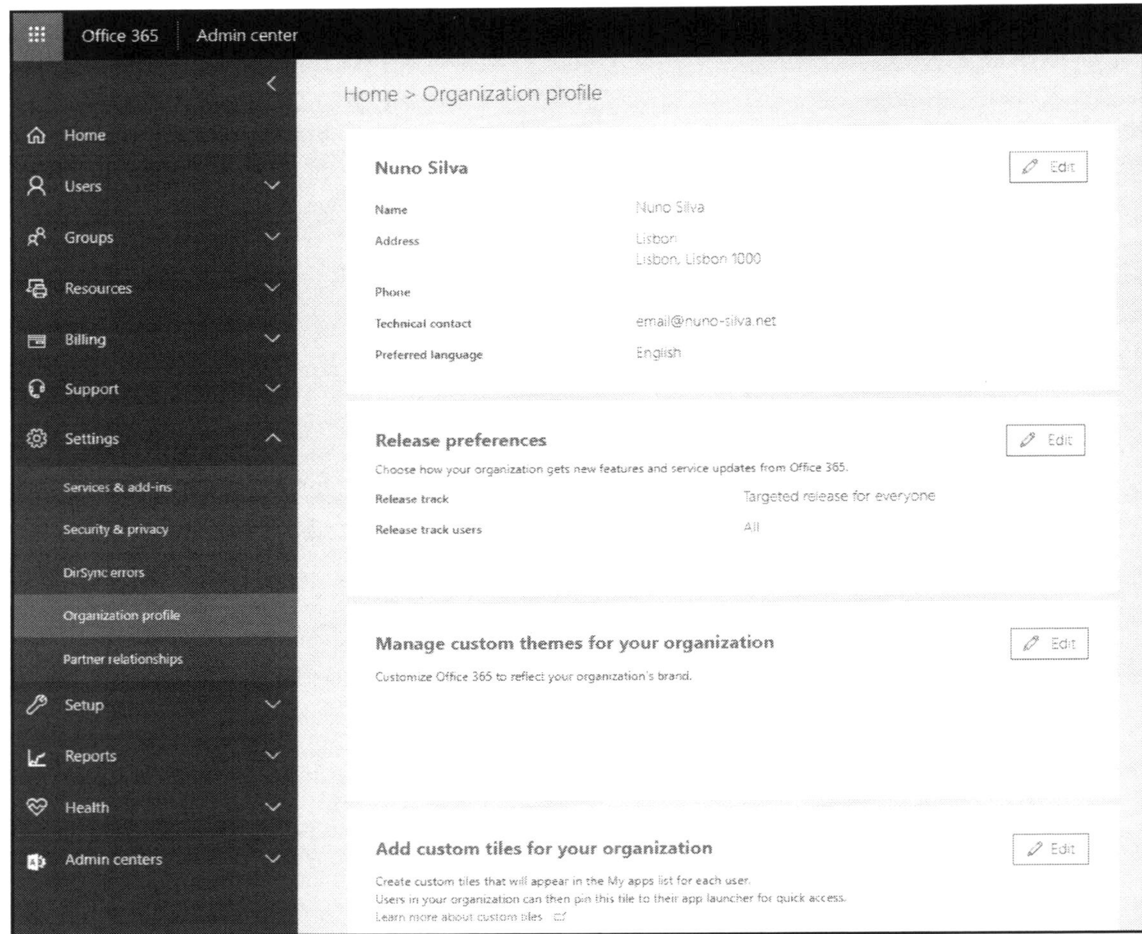

4. Select the best option based on the best practices described previously:

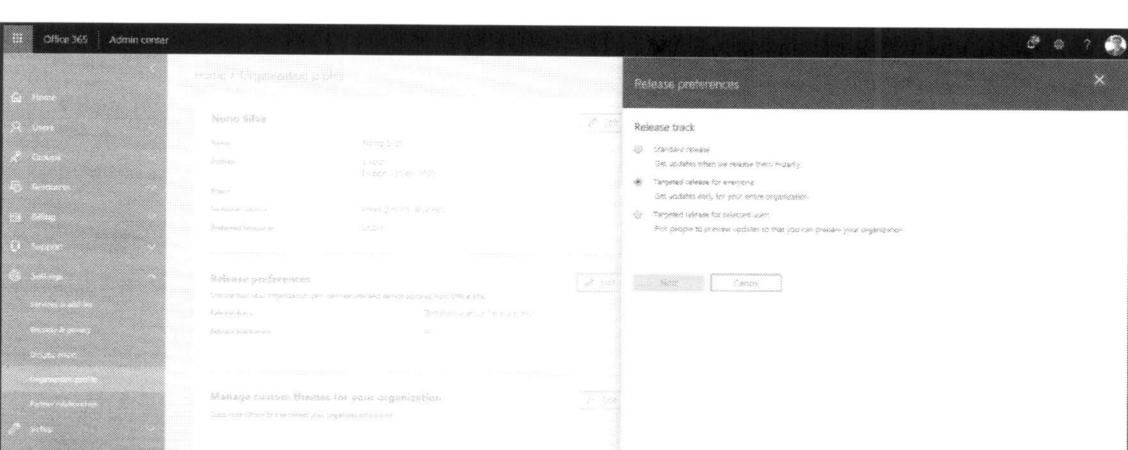


To learn more about *Set up the Standard or Targeted release options in Office 365*, refer to `https://support.office.com/en-us/article/set-up-the-standard-or-targeted-release-options-in-office-365-3b3adfa4-1777-4ff0-b606-fb8732101f47`.

# Summary

In this chapter, you have learned how to manage and how to maintain Office 365 workloads. You now have more information on how to maintain your Office 365 environment using basic and complex tasks.

In the next chapter, you will learn the best practices to adopt Office 365's most commonly used workloads.

# 13
# Adopting Office 365

In this chapter, you will learn and understand how to Adopt Office 365 in your organization. The chapter will cover the following topics:

- Adopting Office 365
- Change management in Office 365

## Adopting Office 365

Following the best practice adoption rules is crucial for a successful Office 365 deployment. To have a successful project, you will need to adopt Office 365 workloads. When adopting Office 365 workload, you will need to have several phases based on best practices; those phases are represented in the following diagram:

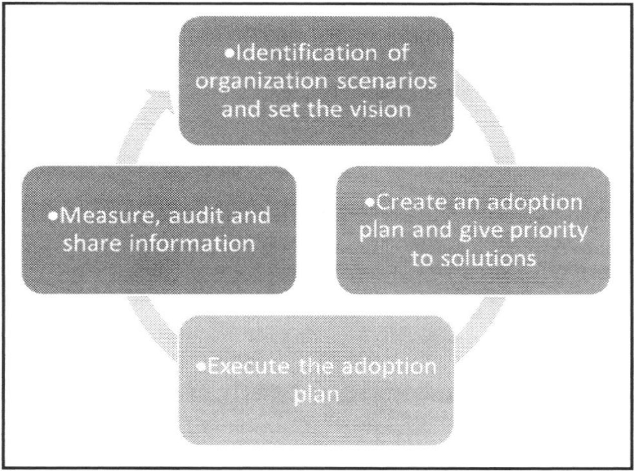

This cycle can be used in the adoption phase at your organization. You can use this process in the full implementation of Office 365 or on a specific workload. Going deeper into the cycle of adoption of Office 365, it is suggested to use the process described as follows:

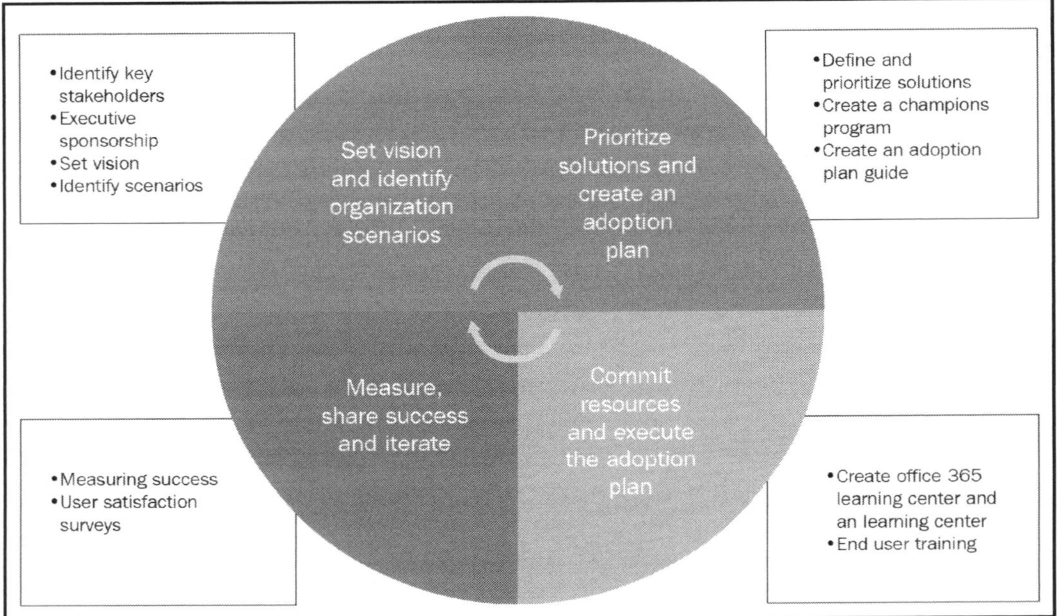


When you are facing an adoption project, it is advised to have a change management strategy:

1. Set your approach and vision for each scenario that is needed
2. Make a logical connection to your scenario and create an adoption plan
3. Put your adoption plan into practice and measure it
4. Make it a cycle of best use and share the successes

It is particularly important to define your success criteria and it is recommended that you choose your criteria based on success and end user satisfaction.

Use the **SMART** mnemonic. This term first appeared in the November 1981 issue of *Management Review* by *George T. Doran*, in a paper titled *There's a S.M.A.R.T. way to write management's goals and objectives,* to understand your success criteria better:

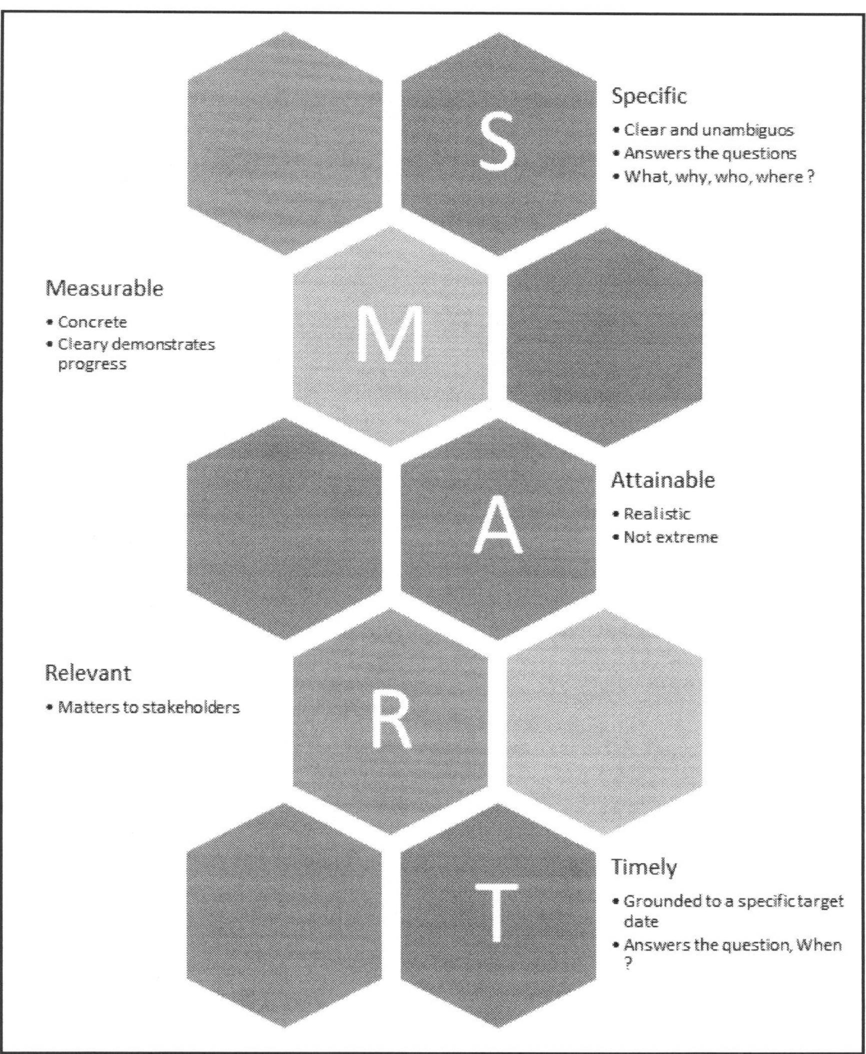

# Changing management in Office 365

To use adoption in Office 365, you will also need to change management to take your service to the next level. You need to use some strategies to maximize your results, such as the following:

- Engagement events
- Communication
- Training

For each of the preceding part, consider the following diagram:

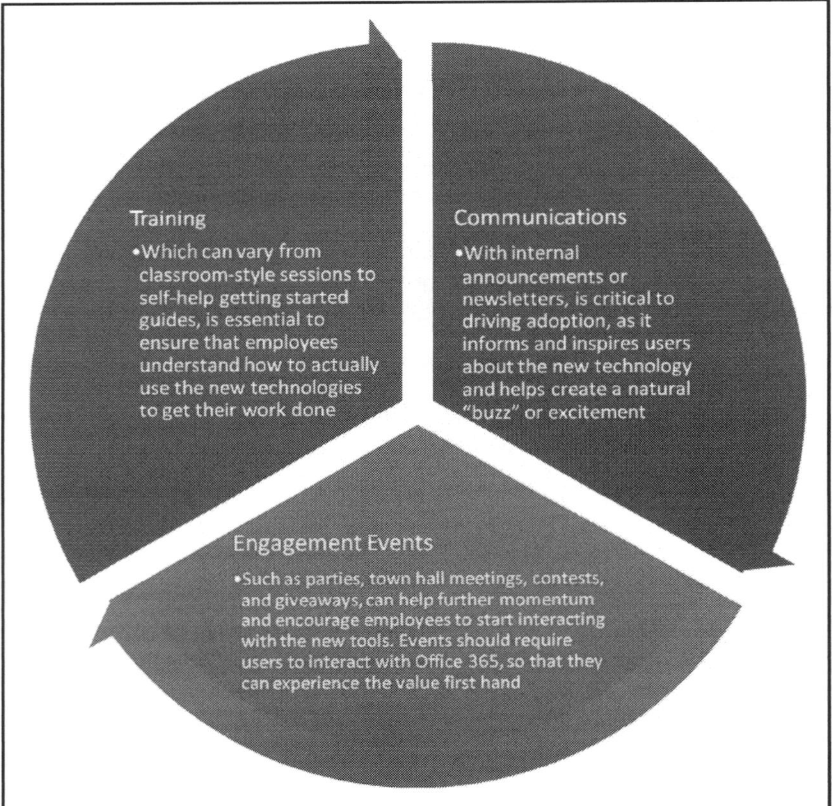

Keep in mind the more communications, events, and training sessions that you organize, the more likely your colleagues will engage with Office 365 during the project launch and afterward.

In order to drive awareness and excitement, do the following:

- Show people what's in it for them
- Clearly communicate goals and milestones
- Tailor your language and target your audience

*"If people understand how it's going to help them they will be more motivated to learn it."*

*—Sharepoint adoption guide, Microsoft*

The preceding quote explains that if we provide the right tools to users to make them more productive they will be more motivated to use and learn new technologies.

Create a campaign wherein all users are involved. It is crucial that all users see the advantages of new services and how to be more productive. It is advised that your campaign should have many types of communication, such as newsletters, training sessions, emails, flyers, and events, both in person as well as online. You can download the various communication templates from the following links:

- **Posters**: To download the posters template, refer to `https://productivitylibrary.blob.core.windows.net/dlc/en-us/Office/Office_EditablePoster_Template.docx`
- **Flyers**: To download the flyers template, refer to `https://productivitylibrary.blob.core.windows.net/dlc/en-us/Office/Office_FlyerTemplate.docx`
- **Countdown email**: To download the Office countdown template, refer to `https://productivitylibrary.blob.core.windows.net/dlc/en-us/Office/Office_CountdownTemplate.docx`
- **Announcement email**: To download the Office announcement template, refer to `https://productivitylibrary.blob.core.windows.net/dlc/en-us/Office/Office_AnnouncementTemplate.docx`

## Launch and engagement events

The key points to launch and engage events are as follows:

- Schedule a meeting event to a wide audience. It is always advised to have sponsorship from top management for the team with the responsibility of the rollout present in Office 365.
- It is advised that you have the key users or champions be active during the event to interact with the public with questions and milestones, and to have the audience engaged with the adoption of Office 365.
- You can also create Microsoft Teams for the champions group to engage with the audience or, if the organization is big, create a Yammer group.
- Make questionnaires using Microsoft Forms and create prizes, contests, and some small events in several locations of the organization with an door open policy.
- Create stickers, flyers, posters, and give T-shirts to the champions.
- You can also make some playbooks to distribute to the audience to provide some daily activities to show them how to be more productive.

## Awareness and communications

To help you create awareness, refer to the following points.

## Creating emails and newsletters

The key points for creating emails and newsletters within a few weeks before the launch are as follows:

- It is advised that you create mono sheets—concise and with a short and clear message.
- Create a page on SharePoint with the adoption program and plan FAQs about Office 365.
- Use Stream to publish videos about the presentations and short videos on how to embed them on the SharePoint page and give the links when you send the newsletters.
- The communications in emails or newsletters must contain a short and concise subject about the objective, such as *Office 365 is coming* or *How to be more productive with Office 365*. Listen to your champions, executives, and marketing and communications departments regarding the best message to keep in mind.

- Keep your communications effective using your communications template; you can also combine the templates offered by Microsoft to keep the message short and direct.
- You must have an email address active to the project and a site dedicated to the project including support, FAQs, videos, how-to guides, and among others relevant to have back-to-back communications within the users of your organization.

# Launching date and first impressions

Within a few weeks before the launch of the Office 365 project to end users, host an event in the main area of the organization to show the advantages of a new technology and how it will help them to be more productive on a daily basis.

# About two weeks before launch

The key points to remember about two weeks before the launch are as follows:

- Create an informal break to give to users the chance to become interested in the project by asking questions. It is an opportunity for the key users to show how they can help with adoption and to show the advantages of Office 365.
- It is advised to continue with these kinds of events through some recurring dates to have all the organization members on board.

In order to drive adoption and increase confidence, do the following:

- Deliver simple, targeted, and engaging training
- Leverage early adopters and champions
- Bring people together

The tips and tricks templates for doing so can be downloaded from the following links:

- `https://productivitylibrary.blob.core.windows.net/dlc/en-us/Office/Office_TipsandTricks_1_Template.docx`
- `https://productivitylibrary.blob.core.windows.net/dlc/en-us/Office/Office_TipsandTricks_2_Template.docx`

# Training for end users

The first step is understanding your users. Do an assessment to learn more about the end users. Conduct interviews with the end users to understand their questions and what are they expecting about the project and at what level they are in the moment of the interview.

It is necessary to learn more and keep in mind the following:

- *Who are you training?*
- *What is their role in the organization? What are some of the everyday jobs they do?*
- *Where do users do these tasks? On a mobile device? In the workplace using a computer unit or a laptop?*
- *When do users do these tasks? When do they need the tools? When should training be finalized?*
- *How combined is the tool set in daily activities?* Does *your organization have policies about the new features and what is the policy about sharing documents, storing files, collaborating with externals, and using email attachments, among others?*

All people learn in a different way. Training should take on multiple methods to accommodate diverse learning styles, geographical barriers, and resource limitations. You'll want to develop a complete training plan that considers the technologies being rolled out, the core tasks your audience will need to learn, and the available training budget. Training is the most important thing in the organizations. Without training, you could have blockers about adoption and it is necessary to end users to be always informed and updated with new technologies. Without proper training, you could have issues with your project because end users could complain that they do not know how to work, and it could be a huge obstacle to daily basic activities that keep your organization running. It is advised that you present the benefits of new technologies in the training, and the new way of working is called **change management**. You can benefit from the training and here are some tips:

- Make sure you understand your users; get to know their challenges.
- An organization storytelling is needed on how to work, not an IT story.
- If you want to get people to do something, allow the entire team to collaborate with each other, train them at the same time, give them time in training to discuss and collaborate together, listen and make notes about some issues that could be a blocker, and give them immediate feedback and answers that best fit your goals and will not be a blocker outside of the training.
- Give examples on how other teams work.

- Provide the opportunity for the managers to reveal best practices using Office 365 technology to work better in new technologies and what is the best way to do their daily basis activities.
- Ask questions to get them involved and to allow them to become comfortable with the project.
- Have a governance model to help keep the organization informed about the whole process.
- Create a SharePoint site with a *Learning Center* to provide how-to videos and FAQs.
- Keep key users updated on changes and any kind of issues or ideas from other groups.
- Communicate every week with tips, statuses, how-to guides, ideas, and new features. Always keep the users informed.
- Give prizes to the champions and end users if they find something that could be better or offer treasure hunts.
- Make some questionnaires with prizes and create an event to give them out.
- Always make the communication personal; keep users updated and send messages with their names and make them feel that they are important in this process.

Any time that Office 365 has a new feature, continue to inform end users.

# Ongoing usage and support

Increase the depth and breadth of usage and manage upcoming changes to the service. You have access to resources to use in your adoption:

- *Office Training Center Bill of Materials* at `https://www.microsoft.com/en-us/download/details.aspx?id=54088`
- *Workplace productivity training* at `https://support.office.com/en-us/article/Workplace-productivity-training-af07cb6b-980d-4f33-8599-322582767408?wt.mc_id=otc_homeui=en-USrs=en-USad=US`
- *Office 365 Training Center* at `https://support.office.com/en-us/office-training-center`

# Driving new behaviors and staying engaged

Rally people around the solution, keep listening, and drive change:

- Establish communication avenues
- Maintain momentum and dialog among users
- Seek feedback and act on it

## Feedback loop tips

The feedback loop tips are as follows:

- With your champions, create a feedback form to address end-user inquiries at the appointed time. The team can create a Yammer group for users to submit questions and provide advices on where to access information.
- You can maintain a FAQ list to address the most predicted questions. Post the FAQ to your intranet, SharePoint, Yammer, and depending on the size of the organization teams.

## Ongoing usage, feedback, and success

As you develop your success criteria and surveys, take advantage of the examples we provide here:

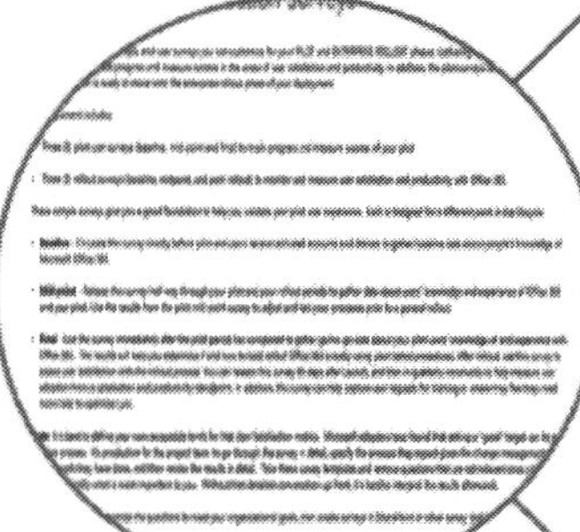


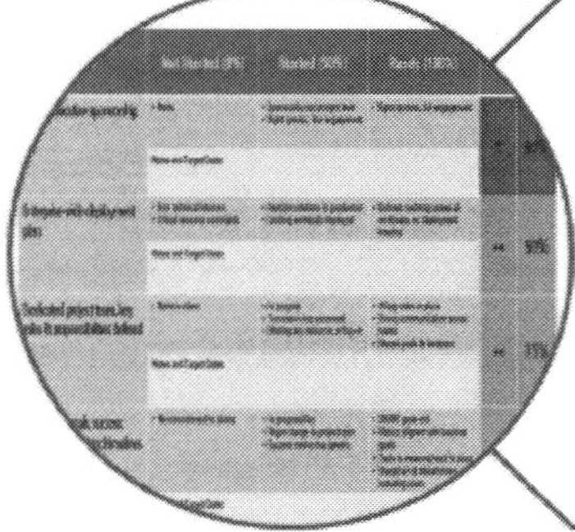


Download the *Measure and share success guide* at `https://productivitylibrary.blob.core.windows.net/dlc/en-us/Measuring_Success_Guide.pptx`.

Download the Office 365 User Satisfaction Surveys at `https://productivitylibrary.blob.core.windows.net/dlc/en-us/Sample_User_Satisfaction_Surveys.xlsx`.

# How to drive Office 365 adoption

A successful Office 365 rollout involves driving adoption and helping everyone recognize the benefits of working in an innovative way. Microsoft has a four-step strategy that can help you create a successful project and perform the adoption of Office 365. A better solution is to create a four-phase plan, as shown in the following diagram:

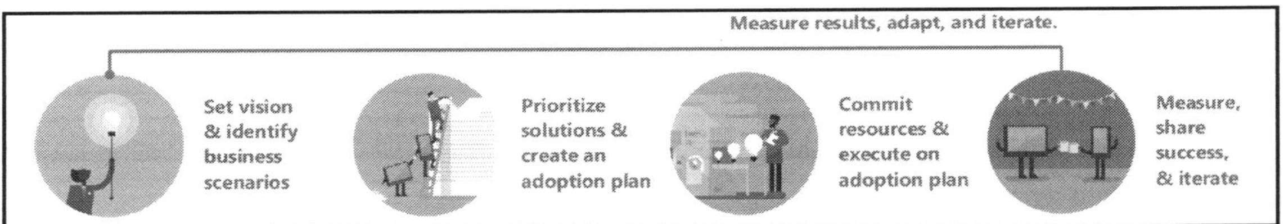


Always measure results, adapt and iterate with your organization:

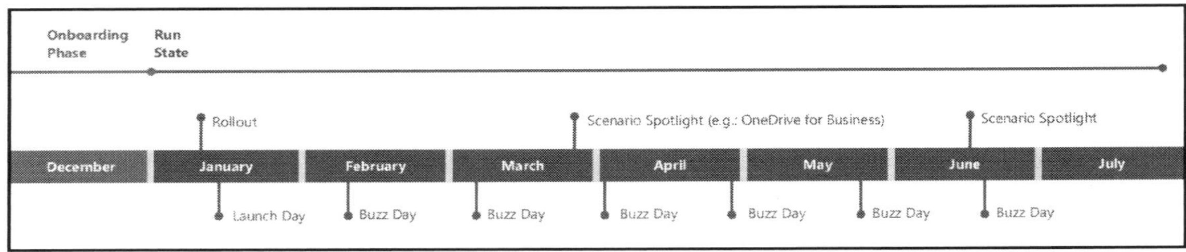


# Useful tips, tricks, and resources to drive adoption

You can see my session, *How to be productive with Microsoft Office 365*, at Microsoft Ignite 2017 regarding adoption at `https://myignite.microsoft.com/sessions/55888`.

It is advised that you hire a partner with experience of the adoption of Office 365 to best leverage your business and to help you adopt the products based on your needs.

# Summary

In this chapter, you have learned about how to drive the adoption of Office 365 in your organization. You now have more information on how to plan your Office 365 implementation and how to use guides to adopt the workloads based on your organization's needs. In the next chapter, you will learn how to monitor and support Office 365.

# 14
# Monitoring and Support

In this chapter, you will learn how to monitor and support Office 365. We will cover the following topics:

- How to monitor Office 365
- How to support Office 365

With this foundation, you will learn more about how to monitor a critical system and how to provide support for your organization's users.

## Monitoring

To monitor a cloud service such as Office 365, you need to know what technologies it's using and what workloads you're using in your solution.

To best accomplish the monitoring of your Office 365 solution, you will need to collect all the information about what workloads you are currently using, the environment technologies, architecture, and so on.

First, you need to make an inventory of your current environment, for example:

- Azure AD Connect
- **Active Directory Federation Services** (AD FS)
- Exchange hybrid
- SharePoint hybrid
- Skype for Business hybrid
- Office 365
- Any other services

In the case that you need to improve your monitoring solution beyond what is available out of the box, you may need to use third-party software to best monitor your Office 365 solution.

Microsoft also has other products that you can use to improve your monitoring solutions, for example, **System Center Operations Manager** (**SCOM**), **Operations Management Suite** (**OMS**), or native tools.

# Operations Manager

Microsoft SCOM is widely used in organizations to monitor their environments. With this product, you can monitor your on-premises components including Office 365. To know more about SCOM, go to `https://docs.microsoft.com/en-us/system-center/scom/welcome?view=sc-om-1801`.

In SCOM, there are **Management packs**, which are packages created by Microsoft as add-ons to SCOM that allow you to monitor several services, such as the following:

- Office 365
- AD
- Exchange
- Skype
- Windows Server
- DNS
- LAN
- ADFS
- IIS
- Any other services depending on your choice of Office 365 package

The link to download the Office 365 Management pack is at `https://www.microsoft.com/en-us/download/details.aspx?id=43708`.

An example of an Office 365 dashboard in SCOM is shown in the following screenshot:

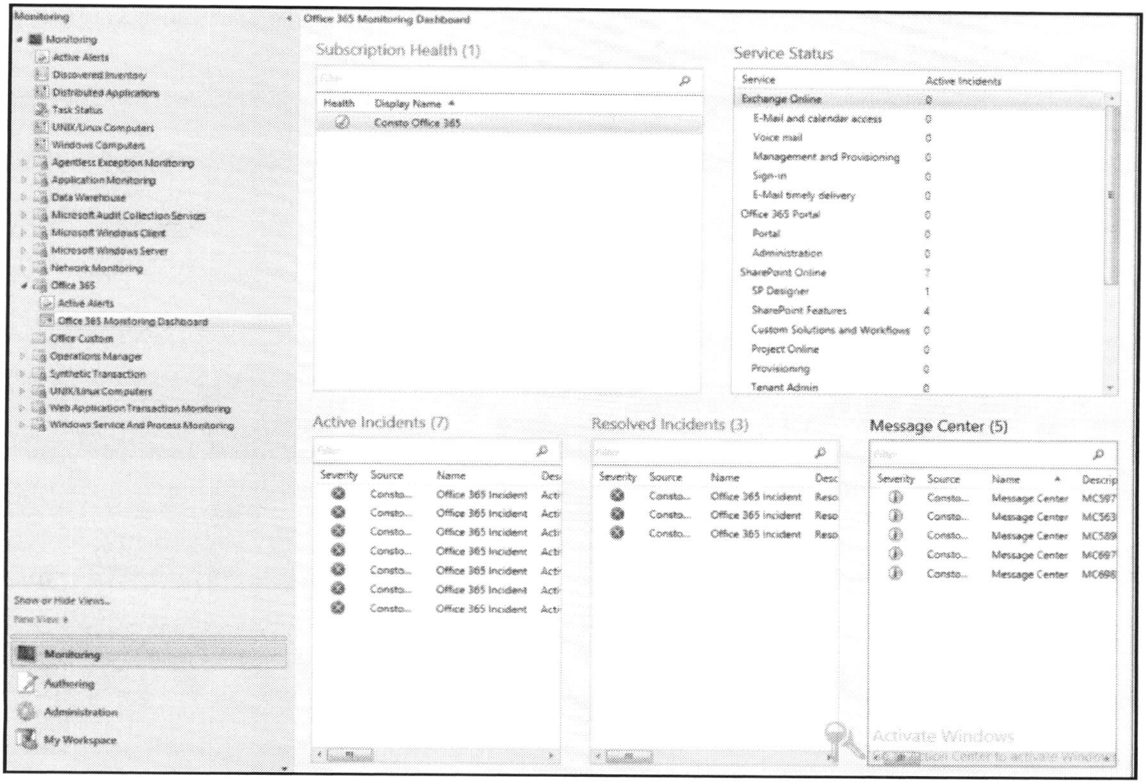

With this dashboard, you can see an overview of the health of your subscription, your incidents, planned maintenance, and other messages from your Office 365 environment.

# OMS

OMS is a part of Microsoft Azure, and can be used to monitor Office 365 and your infrastructure, both on Azure and on-premises. Depending on the services that you use, you can have the right to use SCOM in your on-premises infrastructure.

Some of its features are as follows:

- Monitoring workloads
- Monitoring servers
- Log analytics
- Other services

To access OMS and learn more about it go to `https://www.microsoft.com/en-us/cloud-platform/operations-management-suite`.

In OMS, you can monitor your on-premises environment by installing agents directly on virtual machines or by integrating it with SCOM. There are a plenty of solutions available to use in OMS to monitor your solutions, as shown in the following screenshot:

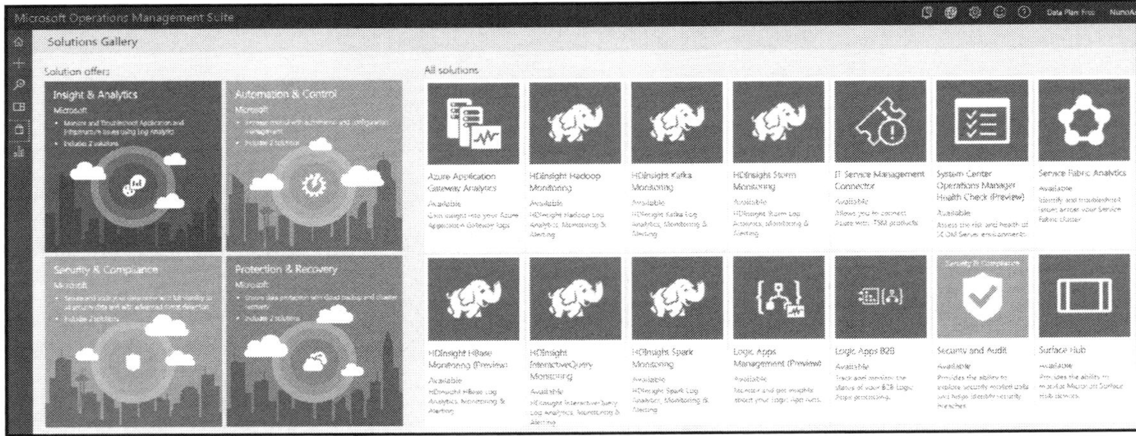

You can also use Office 365 Analytics, which monitors user activities such as SharePoint, Exchange, or Azure AD. You can see an overview of the dashboard in the following screenshot:

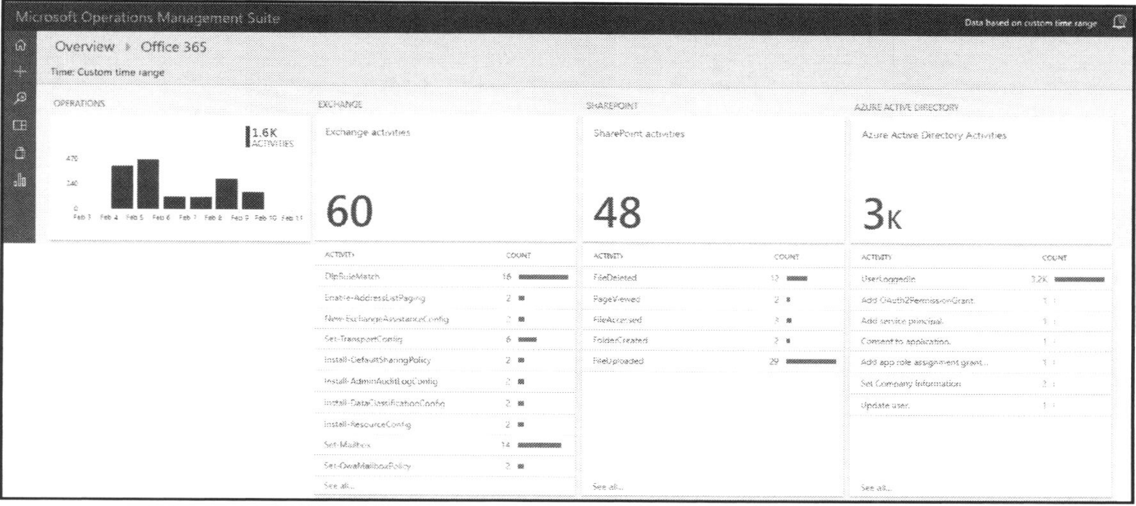


You can read more at *Office 365 management solution in Azure (Preview)*, at `https://docs.microsoft.com/en-us/azure/operations-management-suite/oms-solution-office-365`.

# Monitoring Office 365

To monitor the health of Office 365 using native tools, you have several options, for example:

- Office 365 service health
- Azure AD Connect

As a starting point for monitoring, navigate to `https://status.office365.com/` or follow on Twitter at `https://twitter.com/Office365Status`.

To see all options, please continue reading the documentation by visiting the website at `https://support.office.com/en-us/article/monitor-office-365-connectivity-53cdb60c-a6b2-4848-b3ff-e7b75dc3fd1f`.

You can also monitor health using your Office 365 portal at `http://portal.office.com`.

## Service health

In the **Health** section of the admin portal, you have the **Service health** dashboard, which monitors how the services are doing and the present status of each one, as shown in the following screenshot:

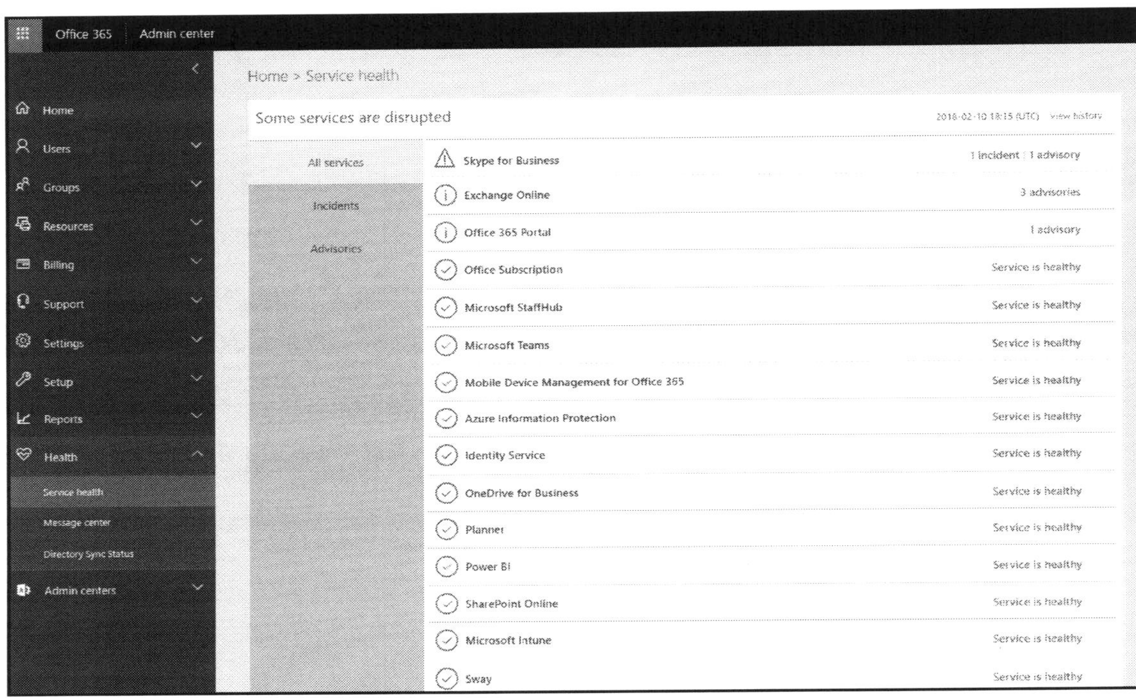

For example, this incident has the following status:

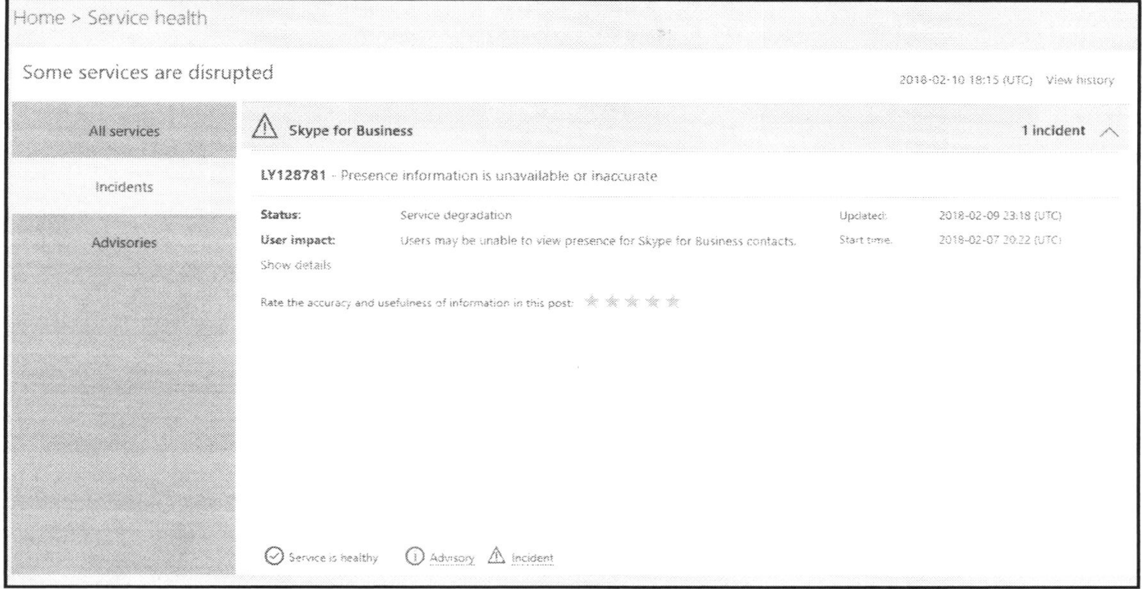

When you click on the **Show details** link, you can see the detailed information for this incident, as shown in the following screenshot:

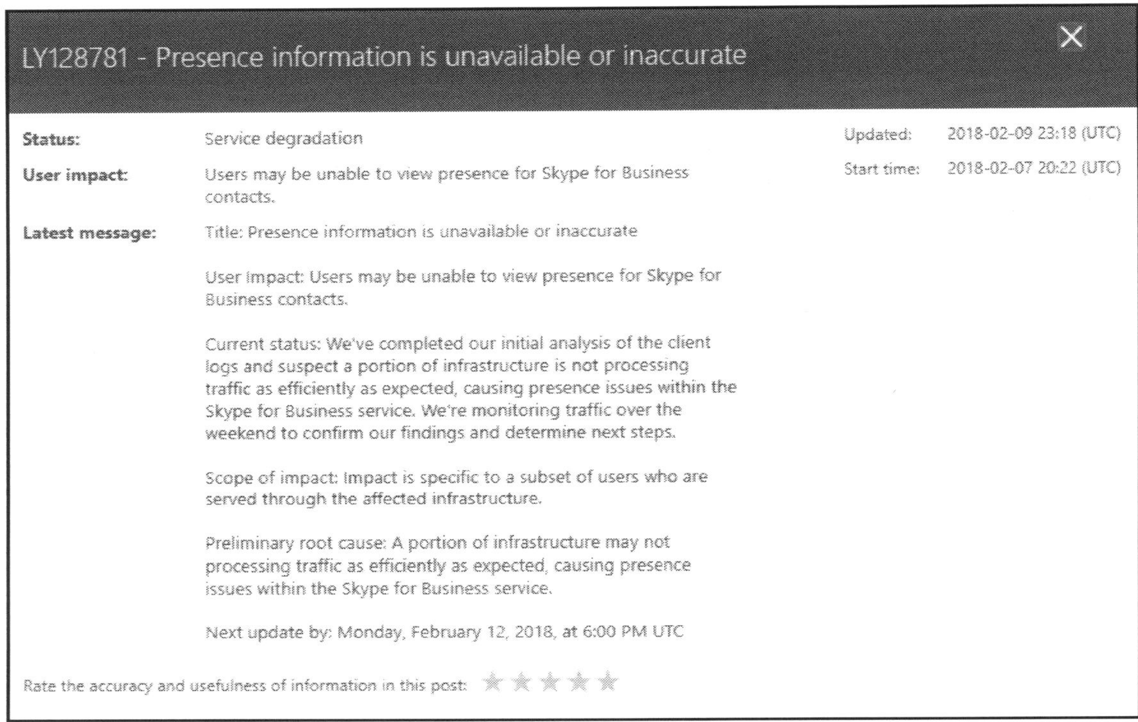

You can see more details under the **Message history** section, as shown in the following screenshot:

**Message history**

Title: Presence information is unavailable or inaccurate — Updated: 2018-02-09 23:18 (UTC)

User Impact: Users may be unable to view presence for Skype for Business contacts.

Current status: We've completed our initial analysis of the client logs and suspect a portion of infrastructure is not processing traffic as efficiently as expected, causing presence issues within the Skype for Business service. We're monitoring traffic over the weekend to confirm our findings and determine next steps.

Scope of impact: Impact is specific to a subset of users who are served through the affected infrastructure.

Preliminary root cause: A portion of infrastructure may not processing traffic as efficiently as expected, causing presence issues within the Skype for Business service.

Next update by: Monday, February 12, 2018, at 6:00 PM UTC

Title: Presence information is unavailable or inaccurate — Updated: 2018-02-09 00:25 (UTC)

User Impact: Users may be unable to view presence for Skype for Business contacts.

Current status: We're continuing our efforts to review the client logs and determine our next steps for remediating the issue.

Scope of impact: Impact is specific to a subset of users who are served through the affected infrastructure.

Next update by: Friday, February 9, 2018, at 11:30 PM UTC

Not all incidents shown in the portal affect your Office 365 environment. This monitoring is a proactive way that Microsoft provides to customers on the region that your Office 365 is based to inform them that an issue is occurring and may affect you.

# Message center

Message center is the central point where Microsoft informs your organization of changes, new features, and planned maintenance actions in Office 365. To be informed about Office 365 changes, you will need to make some decision about product cycles and manage the updates accordingly.

With Office 365, you receive new product updates and features as they become available, instead of scheduled updates that are months or years apart. As a result, you and your users will routinely experience new and improved ways to do your job rather than a costly and time-consuming company-wide upgrade. The challenge with such a model is keeping up with the changes and updates. Here are a few ways that you can stay on top of the Office 365 updates in your organization:

- Message center
- Target release
- Roadmap
- Blogs and community

For more information, refer to the following URL at `https://support.office.com/en-ie/article/Stay-on-top-of-Office-365-changes-719f4904-cbdd-4889-a0cf-fbd7837dfecd`.

# Overview of the Office Message center

In this section you can have an overview of what are the news, messages, and updates. The following screenshot shows the Office Message center:

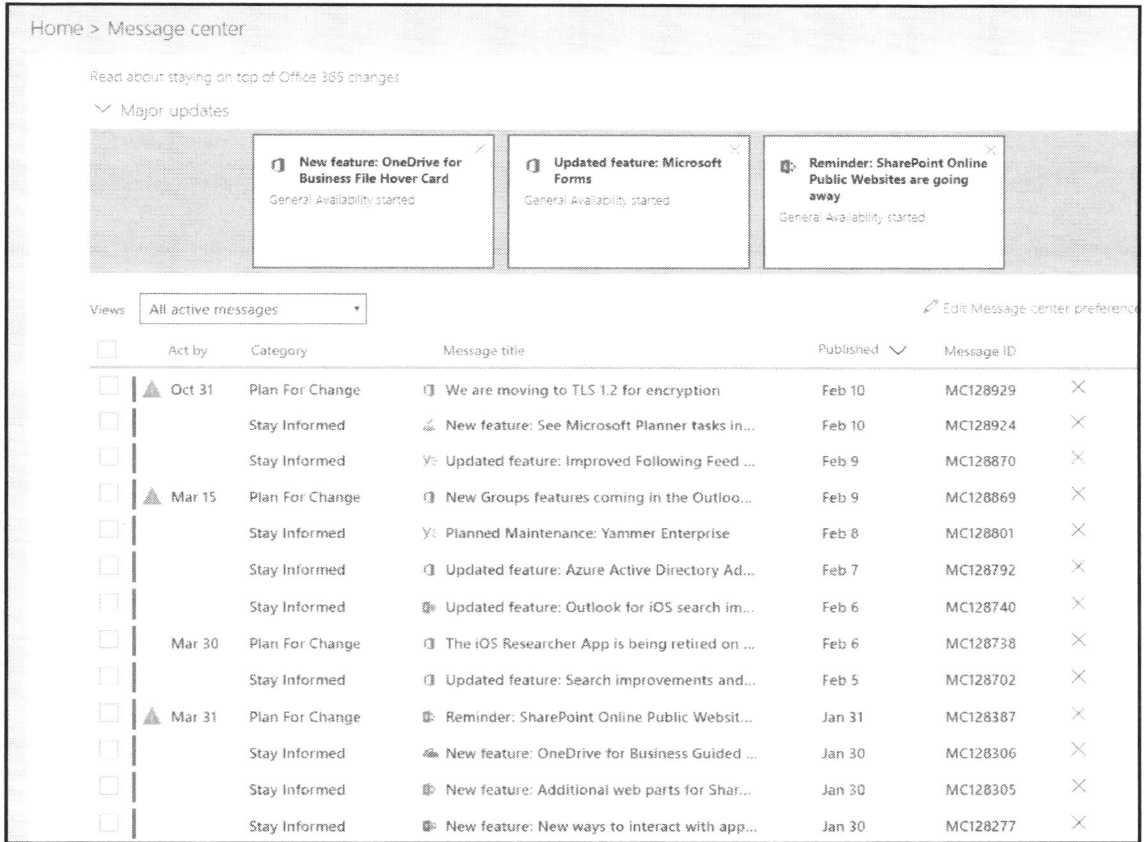

When you click on a message that has **Act by** column information, it is important that you read it and plan your actions, as shown in the following screenshot:

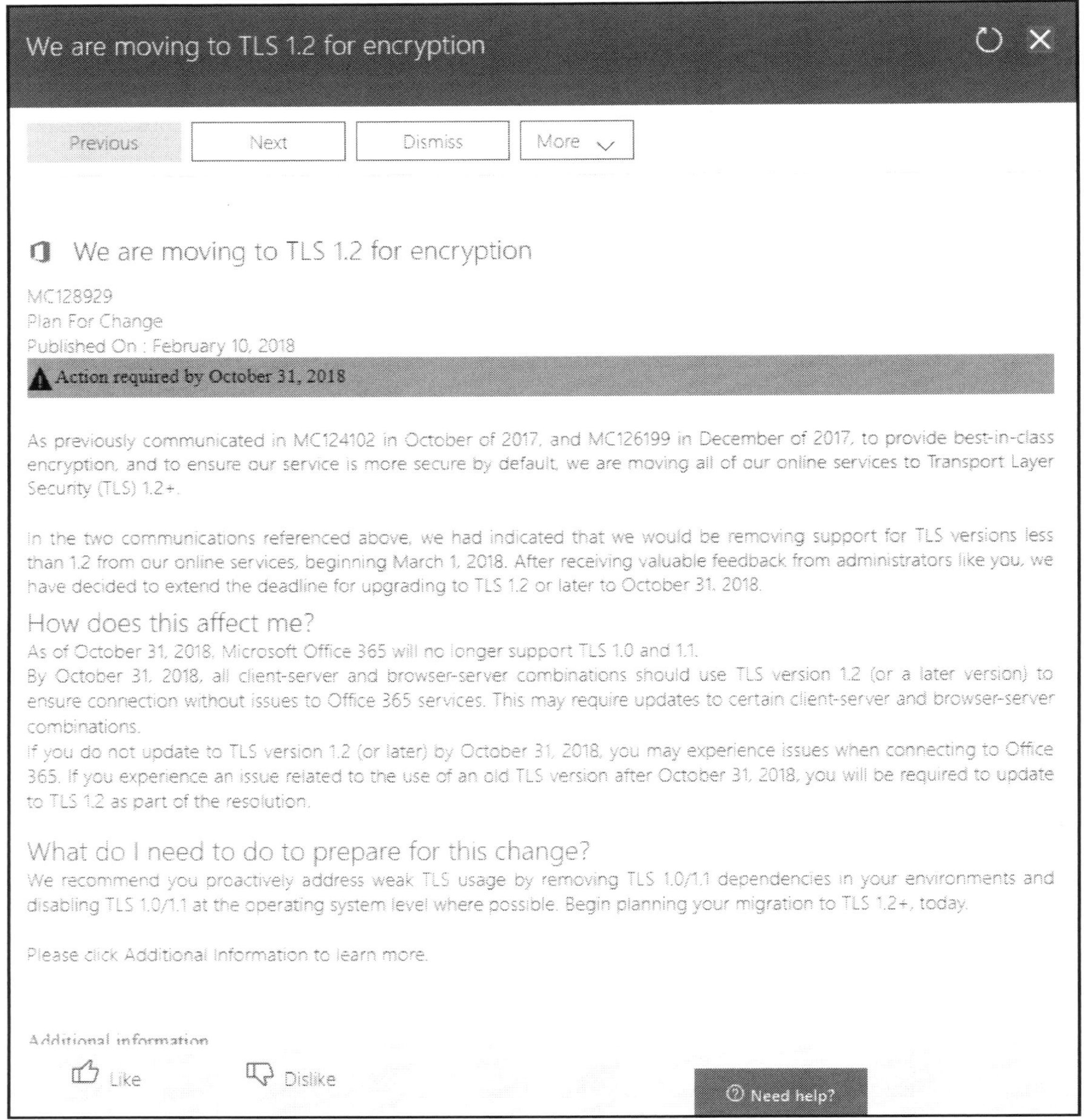

When you click on the **Additional information** link, you will be redirected to a support article that describes the change, at https://support.microsoft.com/en-us/help/4057306/preparing-for-tls-1-2-in-office-365.

You can also edit your preferences in the **Edit Message center preferences** section and receive emails notifying you of the changes.

# Directory sync status

In this section, you can monitor your status about the integration with your Windows Server AD, and monitor the basic status of the sync process, as shown in the following screenshot:

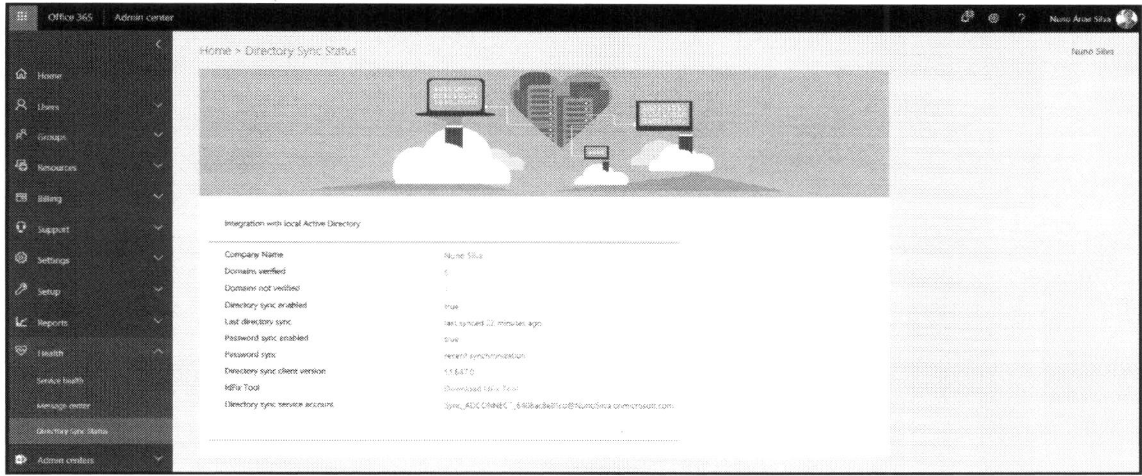


Using Microsoft Azure Portal, you have access to more information by visiting the website at https://portal.azure.com/#blade/Microsoft_AAD_IAM/ActiveDirectoryMenuBlade/AzureADConnect.

Using Health and Analytics service, you have access to AD Connect Health. To learn more, go to https://docs.microsoft.com/en-us/azure/active-directory/connect-health/active-directory-aadconnect-health.

# Support

Given that Office 365 is a SaaS service, it's outside your responsibility to provide certain support tasks. When you run into an issue in Office 365, knowing how to contact support and opening a ticket is important.

To start, you have four main options to get support on Office 365:

- Portal support
- Phone support
- Premium support
- Other help forums such as *Answers* or *Tech Community*

There are other support sites that you can use such as the following:

- *Office support* at `https://support.office.com/`
- *Office 365 Admin help center* at `https://support.office.com/en-us/office365admin`

# Portal support

Using the preferred support option depending on the issue you are facing is the best way to start have Microsoft support. You can go to your portal and create a support ticket. Go to `http://portal.office.com` and in the **Support** section, click on the **New service request** option:

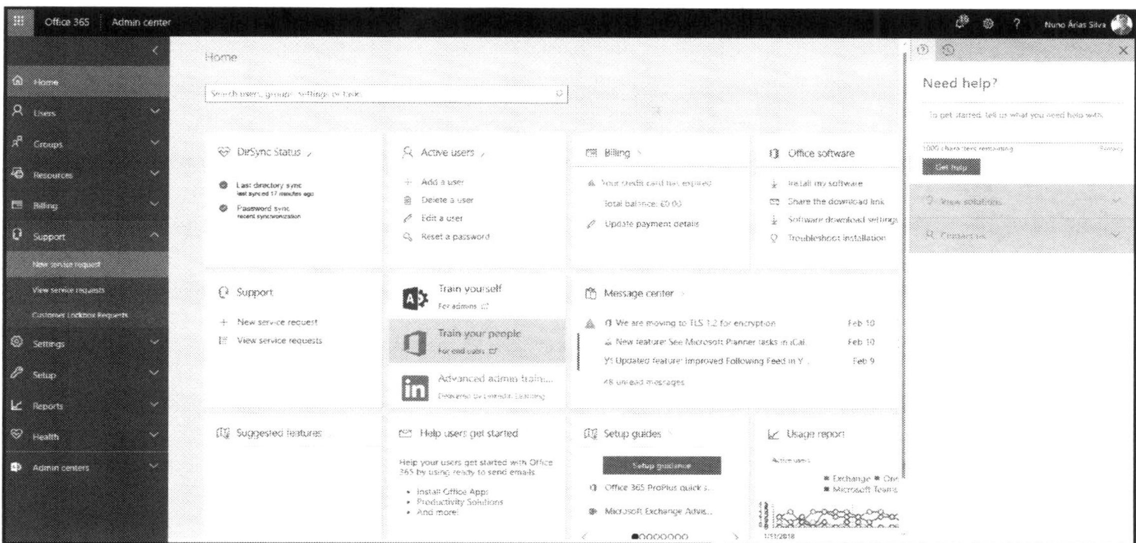

You can read more at `https://support.office.com/en-us/article/contact-support-for-business-products-admin-help-32a17ca7-6fa0-4870-8a8d-e25ba4ccfd4b`.

Let's write something like `Skype for business contacts` as shown in the following screenshot:

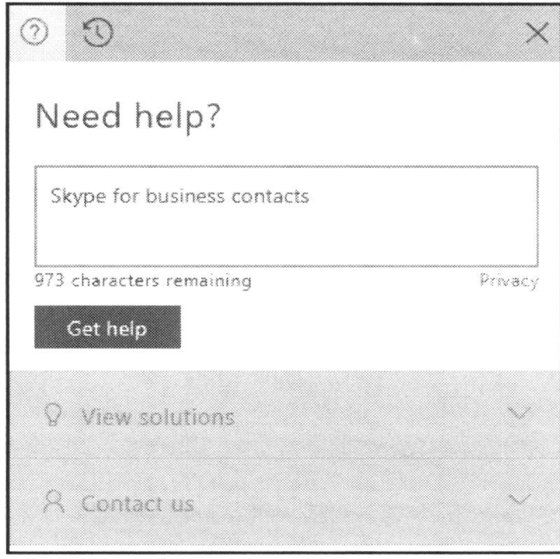

Click on the **Get help** button.

We can see that we have a service incident that is related to the phrase that we have written. You can check the details of the issue by clicking on the **View details** link:

You can click on the **View solutions** section to look at the possible solutions to your problem.

If you click on **Let us call you** section, a **Confirm your contact number** option is shown. You can also attach five files containing up to 5 MB of data on the support case. In order to get the call, you should click on the **Call me** button:

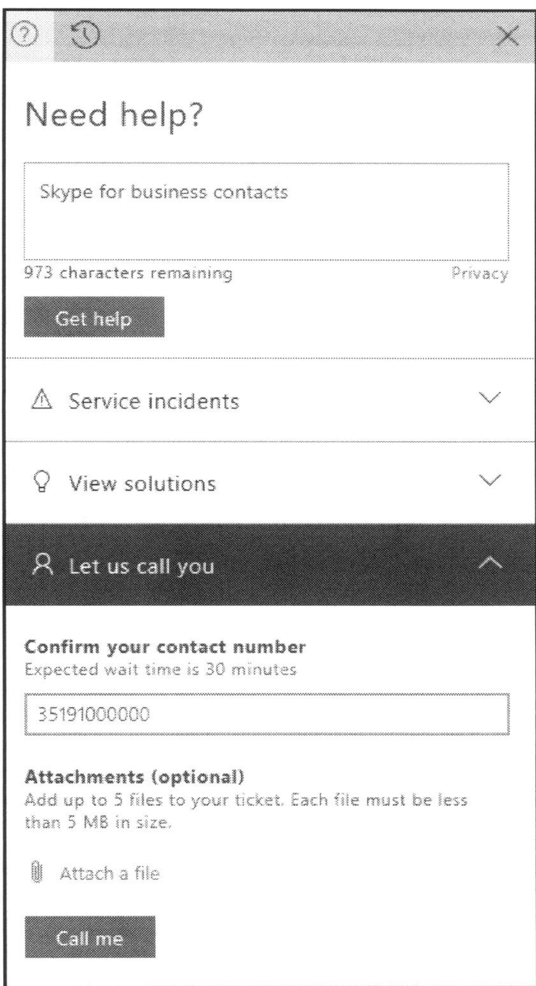

## Phone support

If you do not have access to your admin portal, you have the option to call Microsoft Support using a phone number.

You can have access to the support phone numbers at `https://support.office.com/en-us/article/contact-support-for-business-products-admin-help-32a17ca7-6fa0-4870-8a8d-e25ba4ccfd4b#ID0EAADAAA=Phone_support_`.

If you do not have access to the internet, you can call the following numbers:

- In the United States, call `1 800 865 9408`
- In Australia, call `1 800 197 503`
- In Canada, call `1 800 865 9408`
- In the United Kingdom, call `0800 032 6417`

## Premium support

The premium support service for a cloud service such as Office 365 is Microsoft Premier Service. You can read more at `https://go.microsoft.com/fwlink/?linkid=279816`.

If you have a contract with a Microsoft partner who has the Premier Service, you can use their services to open Office 365 tickets with a Premium Service.

## Answers and Tech Community

If you have some problems and you need help, you can go to Answers or Tech Community to ask for help based on your needs.

### Answers

Answers is a central place to help you with Office 365 topics, with basic support given by Microsoft and the users community. For more information refer to `https://answers.microsoft.com/en-us/msoffice`.

## Tech Community

Microsoft Tech Community was created to have several user communities in one place, and gives you a platform to help with your Office 365 implementation, among many other things. For more information refer to `https://techcommunity.microsoft.com/`.

To get started, visit the website at `https://techcommunity.microsoft.com/t5/Getting-Started/bd-p/Day1Guide`.

At the time of writing this, Tech Community is the fastest-growing central community of IT professionals, developers, decision makers, and so on. Please join. I'm available at the community to help. You can follow me at `https://techcommunity.microsoft.com/t5/user/viewprofilepage/user-id/50`.

# Summary

In this chapter, you have learned about the monitoring and support options in Office 365. You now have more information on how to monitor your Office 365 subscription.

In this book, you have learned about the Office 365 essential workloads. This book is meant as an introductory resource, to help you take the first steps in using a new technology and guide you through the planning, deployment, adoption, and monitoring of Office 365, the world's most powerful and popular productivity suite.

# Other Books You May Enjoy

If you enjoyed this book, you may be interested in these other books by Packt:

**PowerShell for Office 365**
Martin Machado, Prashant G Bhoyar

ISBN: 978-1-78712-799-9

- Understand the benefits of scripting and automation and get started using Powershell with Office 365
- Explore various PowerShell packages and permissions required to manage Offi ce 365 through PowerShell
- Create, manage, and remove Office 365 accounts and licenses using PowerShell and the Azure AD
- Learn about using powershell on other platforms and how to use Office 365 APIs through remoting
- Work with Exchange Online and SharePoint Online using PowerShell
- Automate your tasks and build easy-to-read reports using PowerShell

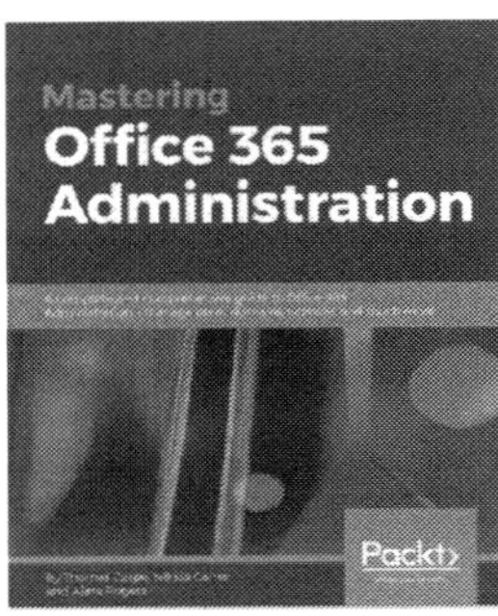


**Mastering Office 365 Administration**
Thomas Carpe, Nikkia Carter, Alara Rogers

ISBN: 978-1-78728-863-8

- Get an understanding of the vast Office 365 feature set
- Learn how workloads and applications interact and integrate with each other
- Connect PowerShell to various Office 365 services and perform tasks.
- Learn to manage Skype for Business Online
- Get support and monitor Office 365 service health
- Manage and administer identities and groups efficiently

# Leave a review - let other readers know what you think

Please share your thoughts on this book with others by leaving a review on the site that you bought it from. If you purchased the book from Amazon, please leave us an honest review on this book's Amazon page. This is vital so that other potential readers can see and use your unbiased opinion to make purchasing decisions, we can understand what our customers think about our products, and our authors can see your feedback on the title that they have worked with Packt to create. It will only take a few minutes of your time, but is valuable to other potential customers, our authors, and Packt. Thank you!

# Index

## A



## B



## C

# H



# I



# L



# M

# N



# O

## T



## U



## V



## W

## Y

18318930R00216

Made in the USA
Lexington, KY
21 November 2018